The British Army, 1783–1815

The Pen and Sword
History of the British Army

The British Army, 1783–1815

Kevin Linch

Foreword by Ian F. W. Beckett

Pen & Sword
MILITARY

First published in Great Britain in 2024 by
Pen & Sword Military
An imprint of Pen & Sword Books Limited
Yorkshire – Philadelphia

ISBN 978 1 52673 799 1

A CIP catalogue record for this book is
available from the British Library

Typeset by Mac Style
Printed in the UK by CPI Group (UK) Ltd, Croydon, CR0 4YY.

Pen & Sword Books Limited incorporates the imprints of After
the Battle, Atlas, Archaeology, Aviation, Discovery, Family History,
Fiction, History, Maritime, Military, Military Classics, Politics,
Select, Transport, True Crime, Air World, Frontline Publishing, Leo
Cooper, Remember When, Seaforth Publishing, The Praetorian Press,
Wharncliffe Local History, Wharncliffe Transport, Wharncliffe True
Crime and White Owl.

For a complete list of Pen & Sword titles please contact

PEN & SWORD BOOKS LIMITED
47 Church Street, Barnsley, South Yorkshire, S70 2AS, England
E-mail: enquiries@pen-and-sword.co.uk
Website: www.pen-and-sword.co.uk
or
PEN AND SWORD BOOKS
1950 Lawrence Rd, Havertown, PA 19083, USA
E-mail: uspen-and-sword@casematepublishers.com
Website: www.penandswordbooks.com

Contents

List of Illustrations

Lists of Tables

List of Charts

Foreword

There has been no multi-volume history of the British army since the completion of Sir John Fortescue's monumental history in 1930 and Fortescue effectively ended his story of the army in 1870. A new series was begun in the 1990s by another publisher but it was never completed. Only three of a projected nine volumes were published: two of these were subsidiary volumes on the auxiliary forces and the British army in India and only one of the seven chronological volumes. As it happens, these two supporting volumes have been republished by Pen & Sword with new introductions as *Britain's Part-time Soldiers* (2011), and *The Military in British India* (2013).

The aim of the revived series remains that of the original concept: to draw on the most recent scholarship to present the Army's story in the context of wider military, political, socio-economic and cultural developments. Whilst each volume will stand alone, they will all deal with such institutional aspects as organization, training, the recruitment of officers and men, conditions of service, and the relationship of the Army with society and state.

Over the last 30 years research has advanced still further with a multiplicity of interdisciplinary approaches being applied to the impact of war on states, societies, institutions and individuals. The series will be an invaluable guide to the new scholarship for undergraduates and postgraduates and will appeal equally to specialists and the wider readership interested in military affairs.

This second volume of the new series covers a period from 1783 to 1815, embracing the French Revolutionary and Napoleonic Wars. Contributed by an acknowledged expert on the period in Kevin Linch, it shows the remarkable range of multinational units that comprised the army, the efforts to maintain them, the experience of those serving in them, and their impact on state and society. In so doing it fully meets the expectations of the series as a whole in transforming our understanding of the evolution of Britain's army.

Professor Ian F.W. Beckett,
General Editor

Acknowledgements

This book has taken much longer than anticipated to produce, and this written thanks does not fully convey my sense of appreciation to all those involved. I am incredibly grateful to Rupert Harding and Harriet Fielding, the editors at Pen & Sword books, for their patience and support as the manuscript developed in spite of challenges that were both global and personal. To all archivists, past and present, without whom a work like this would be impossible. Special thanks needs to go to staff at The National Archives of the United Kingdom, London, for all their work opening their collections as COVID-19 restrictions were eased. These were important moments in maintaining progress with the book; and it affirmed my continuing appreciation for the work of all archive staff. This book is also a reflection and product of a vibrant community of scholars of which is has been my pleasure to have been part for around a quarter of a century, especially PhD candidates and early-career scholars. Many PhD studies are available through the British Library's valuable EThOS service, and several generously gave me early access to these. This book would have been very different without the work of postgraduate students, and it has been my pleasure to meet many of them and to have worked closely with some. In this regard, the endnotes and Bibliography are not just references but also starting points for further reading that I encourage readers to turn to. Thanks must also go to all the undergraduate and postgraduate students I have taught and worked with. Their enthusiasm for the subject, questions, and debates have all, sometimes unconsciously, filtered into this book. Special thanks need to go to Edward Davies, Aurelius Noble, and Olivia Winnard who worked with me on the 'Waterloo Lives' project and helped gather data about Army officers which underpins part of this book's chapter about officers. Finally, I would like to thank colleagues in the School of History at the University of Leeds. A part of this was financial assistance for the research and production of this book; more important were the discussions and support from colleagues.

I am grateful to the following for permission to reproduce the images in this book. The Trustees of the British Museum for illustrations 1 and 5. The Anne S. K. Brown military collection at Brown University for illustrations 2, 6, and 11. Lady Willoughby de Eresby for permission to use an image of the Perthshire Fencibles (illustration 8), which was kindly provided by National

Records Scotland. The S. P. Lohia Collection of rare books for illustration 3; the Council of the National Army Museum, London for illustration 9; and The Met, New York for illustration 10.

Introduction

<blockquote>

The number of convicts going out to Botany Bay, in the fleet now under orders, amounts to 1000; 500 with the *Neptune*, Capt. Gilbert at Plymouth; 250 with the *Scarborough*, Capt. Marshall; and 250 with the *Surprise*, Captain Thrale, at Spithead. The *Gorgon* is the only King's ship that goes at present on the above voyage, as she is to make the best of her way, without any sort of regard to the transports. The *Gorgon* carries out the Botany Bay Rangers, consisting of about 300 men, and her own compliment of officers and seamen exceeds 190. The whole of Captain's Marshall's transports are male convicts, one half of which have been cast for death. To guard against those desperadoes, he has only thirty unexperienced Rangers, with a Lieutenant, and his small ship's company.[1]

</blockquote>

This letter printed in *Saunder's News-letter* of 16 December 1789 documented the early days of the New South Wales Corps (or Botany Bay Rangers as they were then known) in the Second Fleet that sailed to Australia. Given what we know of the events to come, with the deepening revolution in France and then the 22-year conflict between Britain and France from 1793 to 1815 (with a brief respite in 1801–03), focusing on a transport fleet that carried a few hundred soldiers may seem an odd place to start a history of the British Army. There is, however, a heavy dose of hindsight in such a view. Although the international situation in Europe in the late 1780s was not without incidents and conflicts, a pan-European war against France was not a predictable outcome. For Britain, it was tensions with Spain and the consequences of Russian expansion into south-eastern Europe that were on ministerial and military minds. In both cases conflict would have been economic and maritime rather than campaigns on the European continent.

France had proven to be militarily weak through its inability to react to British and Prussian intervention in the Netherlands in 1787, a judgement further confirmed by the inaction and mutinies of the French Army during the events of 1789. Edmund Burke, prophet of the tyrannical undertones of the French Revolution, declared in a 1790 debate in Parliament about the Army that 'France is, at this time, in a political light to be considered expunged out of the system of Europe' and consequently there was no need to increase the

Army's funding.[2] Tim Blanning has made the strongest case for the French Revolutionary Wars originating in international conflicts that started in eastern Europe in 1787. Through a series of miscalculations, mainly on the part of the Habsburg Emperor as well as the Brissotins party in France rationalizing external conflict for internal political reasons, France became snarled in the diplomatic and military moves between Austria, Prussia and Russia. That Britain would be woven into this tangle was not that obvious either. It was only the successes of the French in late 1792 that re-affirmed France's expansionist outlook and prompted a series of declarations of war in early 1793.[3]

The place of the New South Wales Corps in Australian history echoes the tendency of the studies of the British Army to be compartmentalized into distinct places and chronologies. John Fortescue's *History of the British Army* (with twelve books covering the period 1792–1815) and Charles Oman's *History of the Peninsular War* (seven volumes, covering the British Army's campaigns in Spain and Portugal 1808–14) have cast long shadows in the history of the Army. Both reflect the interests and attitudes of the historical profession in the United Kingdom (UK) in the early twentieth century. It is not just about their narrative approach, Eurocentrism (though not exclusively so), judgements (modern readers should be prepared for some shocking comments by Fortescue about Afro-Caribbeans that the British Army fought in the 1790s), but also about what, and who, was the focus of their writing. Their works were 'Great Man' histories focused on individual politicians and generals in command of thousands and studying their decisions, particularly in battles. The recent slew of works on the Battle of Waterloo that emerged in the run-up to and after the bicentenary in 2015 show that this form of history is still popular and continues to provide insights to the reader. This style of history extends further than just campaigns and battles, as the glorification of commanders extended to individuals like the Lieutenant-Governor of the Channel Islands as the bulwark against Revolutionary and Napoleonic France to the exclusion of the contribution of the local population.[4] Against this backdrop, the New South Wales Corps sailed into a different history in 1789, and the same can be said of British Army soldiers serving in North and South America, the Caribbean, and South and South-east Asia.

Alongside these strands in the history of the British Army, wider perspectives have emerged about the Army as an institution and a social organization. They have rooted the Army much more in the social, political, and cultural context of the era. Research that started with a few, but important, doctoral theses in the mid to late twentieth century has been massively expanded upon in recent years and transformed the history of the British Army. These publications, research degrees, and this book are a product of the historical records that have come down to us for study. There are lots of government records, and in fact the increase in their volume is part of the history of the Army. It is, however, important to recognize what we do not have. What was said and then not written was significant. Not all conversations were done through the written word. Some government and military offices were physically very close; discussions between King George III (and later George, Prince Regent) and government ministers were not minuted. Outside of official channels, it is worth remembering the personal relationships that existed. The King's son, the Duke of York, was the Commander-in-Chief of the Army for most of the period covered in this book. So sometimes we get a sense of what was decided, but not why.

With a topic as broad as it is, choices must been made in this book. For one, it cannot be a history of the operations of the British Army. The size of the works by Fortescue and Oman from a century ago indicate just how huge such a task would be, and modern, thorough studies of a campaign should be larger still to include allies and enemies, logistics, the soldiers, and training. This soon adds up as shown, for example, in the 448 pages of a study of the Anglo-Russian invasion of Holland that lasted a little over two months in 1799.[5] Moreover, there are plenty of operational studies of the Army to turn to. Likewise, this book cannot claim to be exhaustive in its use of original historical documentation, and rich material almost certainly remains unused in archives. Indeed, the chapters may read to some a little distant from primary sources, and quotations may feel limited for a history book. This is a conscious choice to stand back from the material and survey it, considering why and who created it, patterns and peculiarities, the under-represented and the common. This book, then, is an institutional, social, and cultural study of the Army. I have endeavoured to maintain a balance across different, but interrelated, areas such as organization and recruitment, lived experience, and the Army's management and training.

It is also important that the book begins in 1783 and more carefully examines the 1780s rather than starting with the French Revolutionary Wars. Taking a different periodisation helps adopt a more holistic framework to the Army. To cope with this large geographic range some terminology has been adopted for consistency and clarity. Modern geographic terms for global regions have been utilized instead of names from the era: so, Caribbean is preferred to the West Indies, and South Asia for India. This should help avoid assumptions about what is being discussed: South Asia, for instance, includes modern-day India, Pakistan, and Sri Lanka, but the eighteenth-century 'East Indies' included South-East Asia. Determining a shorthand term for England, Wales, Scotland, Ireland, the Channel Islands, and the Isle of Man is awkward. Excepting the offshore isles, all were bought together politically as the United Kingdom in 1801, but that did not equate to a uniform identity. All had different political, legal, social, religious and cultural backgrounds and relationships to each other. For simplicity, Britain and Ireland is used, as it is a misnomer to consider all these islands British, though I recognize this marginalizes Scotland, Wales, and the offshore islands.

In common with many works about the Army in this era, for infantry units I use the shorthand of battalion number followed by regiment number (or in a few cases name) to identify units. This means that the 2/1st Foot is the second battalion the 1st Regiment of Foot and the 1/2nd Foot refers to the first battalion of the 2nd Regiment of Foot. Fortunately, both only co-existed for a short time in the late 1790s and other such potentially confusing combinations are uncommon. (If the infantry unit only had one battalion then it is simply referred to by its regiment number or name, e.g. 2nd Foot when it only had one battalion in the 1800s.) Regimental titles have been left out of the text when the unit had a designated number as titles changed and, as we shall see, territorial associations were often aspirational. Where different units had the same designated number then titles or dates of their existence are included; so, the 95th Foot (1794–5) was a different unit from the more famous 95th Rifles that was formed in 1800.

There is more ambiguity and potential confusion when it comes to categorizing units in the British Army. As this book explores, there was a huge range of military forces raised outside the numbered regiments of foot and cavalry and the Guards. These incorporated a wide variety of titles: fencibles, battalions of reserve, garrison battalions, companies of invalids, émigré corps, foreign and colonial troops. Those predominately recruited from outside the Britain and Ireland are grouped together as foreign and colonial units following the terminology of the time. The labels used in the era were not consistent. For example, the units that were raised in Canada for their defence (technically in the crown colonies of Upper and Lower Canada, Nova Scotia and Newfoundland) were termed North American Fencibles, yet the unit raised by Major Smith for the defence of Corsica when it was also a crown colony between 1794 and 1796 was referred to as a regiment of foot. So how do we refer to Major Smith's Regiment of Foot: a foreign or a colonial unit, or a regiment of foot? Wherever possible I have been as specific as I can in classifying units, or avoided generalizations, but I encourage readers to remember that the categorization of units in the Army was loose.

The structure of the book is driven by the approaches and themes discussed above, and has nine chapters organized around themes, approaches, or issues. Chapter 1 – A Composite Army explores what constituted the British Army, which may perhaps seem obvious but was not straightforward. In Chapter 2 – A Global Army and Global Conflicts we look at the scale and range of the Army's services in the period, providing a backdrop that contextualizes the Army's famous campaigns. The complex management of the Army is examined in Chapter 3 – Authority and Control. This is followed by a study of recruitment, a fundamental issue for the Army as it faced the global demands placed on it, in Chapter 4 – Waning and Waxing. In Chapter 5 – Numbers, this book takes a more detailed look at the size, strength, and casualties of the Army, exploring the history of the Army as a population. Following on from this come two chapters – Chapter 6 – Enlisted Men and Chapter 7 – Officers – exploring the people of the British Army. Chapter 8 – Soldiering considers how soldiers were created and trained, the military structure of the Army and its effectiveness. Chapter 9 – Army, Society and Culture then considers the wider relationships between the Army, the communities it recruited from, was stationed in, and fought for, alongside, and against. It then considers the Army's place and participation in British and Irish culture at the time, and the influence this has had on the subsequent history of the Army, circling back to some points made in this introduction. In some ways, the order of these chapters is circular, but we need to start somewhere and so we turn to defining the subject of this book: the British Army.

Chapter 1

A Composite Army

With hearts gratefully elate and all due thanks to Heaven for the event, we have this day the supreme happiness of announcing one of the most splendid and comprehensive victories ever obtained even by British valour, or the illustrious Wellington himself. Its consequences we do not hesitate to pronounce completely decisive of the fate of BONAPARTE, whose army had been completely overthrown.[1]

This triumphant announcement of the Allied victory at the Battle of Waterloo was published by the *Morning Post* on the morning of 22 June 1815, soon after the Duke of Wellington's despatch had reached the Prince Regent on the evening of 21 June.[2] As well as announcing the victory, it is one example of the glorification of Waterloo as a British victory.[3] A good deal of printer's ink has been used analysing and debating the 100 Days campaign of 1815, and the essential contribution that German, Dutch and Belgian soldiers played in those events has been rescued from the condescension of an Anglo-centric world view.[4] The conflation of Britain – and Britons – with the British Army hides the complex structure and organization of Britain's land forces (or to put it more technically the land forces of the British Crown) which grew more diverse in response to multiple military needs in the period 1783–1815. Underneath the umbrella of the term British Army was an array of soldiers from across the globe, serving under different terms and conditions.

The Allied army that faced the French in the battles of 16–18 June 1815 under the Duke of Wellington was a composite force. It was a mixture of units from the British Army, the Kingdom of Holland (a creation of the 1814 peace that joined Holland and Belgium), Hanover, and Brunswick. Such a multinational force was not unique to 1815. Almost 22 years to the day before, a similar patchwork of European military forces under British command had assembled in the Low Countries to fight the French Army. In June 1793, the recently promoted General Prince Frederick, Duke of York and Albany, second son of King George III, took command of an Allied army compromised of units from the British Army, Hanover, Hesse, and Austria. In this 1793 army 6,500 men of just over 35,000 were from the British Army, equating to 19 per cent, whilst in comparison during the Waterloo campaign 40 per cent of the forces under British command were from the British Army. Within these, the British Army itself was a layered and multinational force.

Layers

The complexity of the Army is frequently hidden behind the beguiling exactness of statistics presented about it. The strength of the British Army in 1793 is usually reported to be 38,945, often followed with a comment about its inadequacy for the war that was about to come.[5] This figure comes from a return presented to Parliament in 1806, and included the caveat 'As far as the same can be made up from Documents in the Adjutant General's Office'.[6] This is a crucial point, as it excludes several things that are not immediately obvious. It does not include artillery and engineers as they were administered separately from the Adjutant-General's office. Also, before 1800 Army units paid for by the Irish Parliament (known as the Irish Establishment and explored in more detail below) did not report to this office in London, so they were not included either. Nor do the figures include sergeants and officers. When all these are added in, the total for the Army is closer to 64,000 (around 3,500 officers and enlisted men for the artillery and engineers, 15,000 for the Irish Establishment, plus 6,700 officers and sergeants calculated at an additional eighth). Then if we think about the land forces available to the British Crown it gets more complicated. What about the English and Welsh militia, or all the other land forces that the British government could call upon? Or troops from other states that could be integrated in the British Army as had been done in the American War of Independence? These were potentially significant numbers. The various militia acts passed from 1767 put 30,000 militiamen at the disposal of government for home defence in the 1780s, before more reforms increased militia numbers from 1793. In 1787 the government secured a subsidiary treaty with Hesse-Kassel by which 12,000 men were held ready in case of a war. The treaty was in force for four years,[7] and Hessian troops were hired again at the outbreak of the war with France. In additional to these auxiliaries, George III could also call upon the army of the Electorate of Hanover, which had an establishment of 24,000 men.[8] So in 1793, alongside our revised total for the British Army the government could call upon another 20,000–25,000 more for service in Europe and 30,000 militiamen to defend England and Wales. All together a force of close to 120,000.

Within what was referred to as the British Army there were layers and complexities to its organization. At a basic level, the British Army can be viewed as the units recorded in the annually printed *Army List*.[9] This includes the Royal

Regiment of Artillery and Royal Engineers even though they were administered completely separately from the rest of the Army by the Master General of the Ordnance.[10] Similarly, the Corps of Invalids was managed by Chelsea Hospital.[11] As the wars continued new layers were added. A commissariat department of the Army was formalized in 1809 headed by the new Commissary-in-Chief,[12] and in 1812 commissary officers began appearing in the *Army Lists*.[13] Like the Royal Artillery and Royal Engineers, these officers had a different master from the Guards and line regiments of the British Army, as they were a section of the Treasury. The *Army Lists* also included the Household troops of King George III – two regiments of Life Guards (before 1788 the troops of Horse Guards and Horse Grenadier Guards), and three regiments of Foot Guards – which also had a unique position within the Army. As the monarch's troops their functions and deployment were more restricted than other units in the Army. They never served or expected to serve in the Caribbean for instance.[14] Officers in the Guards held dual rank (so that a lieutenant in the Guards ranked as a major compared to the rest of the army) and before 1793 colonels of the Foot Guard regiments had direct access to the King about promotions in their regiment, bypassing the administrative structures used by everyone else.[15] The two regiments of Life Guards were not included in statistical returns of the Army until December 1812.[16] Financial reforms to the Army implemented in 1783 in the wake of the American War did not apply to the Household troops.[17]

There were other quirks of privilege and tradition that are not easily categorized. The Royal Regiment of Horse Guards was gradually assimilated from a regiment of horse (and the only one in the army after 1788) into the Household Cavalry. This process was not straightforward nor clear. When the regiment's colonel Hugh Percy, 2nd Duke of Northumberland, claimed some privileges about officer promotions in 1812 in response to the creation of a Household Cavalry brigade for service in Spain, the Commander-in-Chief sharply contradicted these assertions stating that the 'common rules of the service' still applied to the unit.[18] To emphasize the point Northumberland was replaced by the Duke of Wellington as colonel. All these layers are represented in Anthony Cardon's print *A View of the British Army* of 1803 (Plate 1). This documents the grouping and distinctions within the Army, and provides a sense of hierarchy too, in which cavalry are positioned above infantry, and Guards before or above the numbered regiments of infantry or cavalry.

As well as these distinctions, the Army contained units that had practical limitation in their use, particularly older soldiers who were fit only for garrison duty. In the 1780s the Army kept thirty-six invalid companies plus a regiment (the 41st Foot) as garrison troops,[19] and the Royal Artillery maintained separate invalid companies too. Although the 41st Foot became a regular unit of infantry from 1787,[20] by 1795 the invalid companies had expanded to fifty companies, with a budget for 3,800 men.[21] In that year the Royal Garrison Battalion was created, which existed until 1802 when seven new garrison battalions were formed. By 1813 there were thirteen royal veteran battalions (as they had become titled) with 9,000 men, stationed across the United Kingdom, Europe, and North America.[22] Efforts to get more soldiers, discussed in more detail in Chapter 4, raised men with different forms of limitation on their service too. In 1799, militiamen who transferred to the British Army enlisted only for service in Europe, and so some units were unavailable for the expedition to Egypt.[23] In 1803, units were created only for service in the United Kingdom. Initially named battalions of reserve, they adopted the title of garrison battalions when the royal veteran battalions were established in 1804. These garrison battalions gradually diminished in strength and number during the war, dropping to 4,200 men by 1808, as after 1805 there was no further legislation to maintain their numbers.[24] The experiment of offering short service of seven years in 1807 to new recruits further complicated matters, and in 1808 66,504 rank and file from a total of 194,007 had some form of limitation on their service.[25]

The Army also maintained and expanded penal units, even though this was not always openly expressed in their conditions of service. The third and fourth battalions of 60th Foot raised in 1787 were partly used as such, as they were never to return to Europe.[26] From 1799 new units were created or designated to receive such men, including the Royal African Corps, Royal West India Rangers, and York Chasseurs. As will be discussed in Chapter 6, we need to be careful about assuming that all the men in these units were hardened criminals. Still, their status necessarily limited deployment options as they were intended as a form of punishment and the Army tended to employ them only in garrison duty in Africa and the Caribbean.[27]

The most numerous category of units with restricted service were full-time home defence forces raised mostly in Britain known as fencible corps. Taking their inspiration from the Scotch term 'defensible', they had geographically-limited terms of service, usually the nation they recruited from. Their origins can be traced back to the Seven Years War when a unit was raised in lieu of a militia in Scotland. Fencible units were re-raised and expanded to nine regiments in the American War of Independence of which three were Scottish, but it was in the 1790s that the idea of this type of force was adopted on a huge scale both in and outside Scotland.[28] Their numbers expanded rapidly in 1793 and 1794 when both fencible cavalry and infantry were created, such that by the end of 1795 around one in five of the soldiers in the British Army was in a fencible unit.[29] One of the distinctions of fencibles was that their officers held temporary rank only for the existence of the unit (and so did not appear in the *Army Lists*) and although they had a variety of terms of service none of them agreed to serve anywhere in the world. All but one of these units were disbanded at the Peace of Amiens in 1802. The surviving unit was the Manx Fencibles and its existence reflected the Isle of Man's status as a Crown Dependency. The idea of these units was resurrected in Canada, but not in Britain and Ireland, when the war resumed in 1803.[30]

Alongside the fencibles there were other home defence forces. The militia had a long existence in Britain and Ireland, and the English and Welsh militia was reformed during the Seven Years War.[31] Through these reforms, central government set a quota of men for each county, which in turn set quotas for parishes to raise through a ballot of men between the ages of 18 and 45. Personal service could be avoided by finding a substitute, and they only served in their respective country. The militiamen were then formed into county units that ranged from Carnarvon's 80-man company to the 1,600 expected from Middlesex.[32] Militia reforms were instituted in Ireland in 1793 and Scotland in 1797, and further changes followed in 1802.[33] These gave the British government the means to raise 51,489 men in England, Wales and Scotland, which could be supplemented by half as many men again with Parliamentary approval.[34] To these forces a further 15,000 militiamen were raised in Ireland, and although militia units were seldom complete, there were 89,800 serving militiamen in 1805 and the total was usually over 70,000 between 1803 and 1815.[35] Often presented as a constitutional counterpoint to the Army, they were placed under the command of British Army generals once mobilized (or embodied to use the contemporary term) but officers within these units held rank in the militia, so there was a separate *Army List* for them (which also included fencible regiments in the 1790s).[36]

Alongside the militia were volunteer part-time soldiers. Bought into being at the same times as fencible regiments in 1794, the government encouraged volunteer infantry or cavalry units.[37] Service in these volunteer units proved to be incredibly popular. Their numbers were significant in the mid-1790s, with 51,000 volunteer infantry and 15,000 yeomanry or volunteer cavalrymen in Britain by 1798. These numbers rapidly expanded during the invasion scare of that year to 146,000 by 1801, peaking with a staggering 450,000 men across Britain and Ireland during the invasion scare of 1803–05.[38] Most of the volunteer infantry transferred into the newly-formed local militia in 1808 (which was distinct from the 'old' militia described above). Before 1803 the volunteers had considerable independence to determine their own terms and conditions, such that some would only serve within their local parish or town. These geographic constraints were gradually reduced so that by 1799 only a few volunteer corps were restricted to their locality, and in 1803 all units were required to serve throughout the UK if an invasion occurred.[39] There were other local defence units outside Britain and Ireland too. The Channel Islands, for example, had a long-standing militia system that dated back to the 1200s,[40] and there were part-time military units across Britain's colonies, with formations in Canada, the Caribbean islands, and in Southern Africa.[41]

The multiple layers of Britain's military forces resulted in some confusing terminology, where the same word or phrase could be used to describe multiple different types of soldier. For example, the term 'volunteer' had several uses. In general terms, as a military dictionary of 1805 put it, a volunteer was someone who 'enters into the service of his own accord' but this covered several types of soldier.[42] There were the part-time volunteer corps just described above, but also there were full-time regiments of foot that included 'volunteer' in their title, like the 81st Regiment of Foot raised in 1794 and styled Loyal Lincoln Volunteers (this title was not confirmed until 1832).[43] In this case, it owed its title to the fact that the government did not issue any money to enlist soldiers, although it did not stop its officers offering financial bounties to recruits.[44] Almost at the same time the 81st Foot was being created, the government suggested adding volunteer companies to the militia.[45] Militia legislation made bewildering references to different volunteers. Men could join the militia as volunteers (by enlisting before any ballot happened), parishes could find volunteers to serve in place of its manpower quota, and members of volunteer corps were exempt from the militia ballot.[46] During the period a series of Acts of Parliament permitted militiamen to transfer to the British Army (discussed in more detail in Chapter 4), who were also known as volunteers.[47] And yet there was another type of volunteer in the British Army. These were men who served in the rank and file of the British Army hoping to become officers.[48] For example, on 1 August 1796 Volunteer M.B. Dwyer was appointed an ensign in the 81st Foot, a regiment with 'volunteer' in its unofficial title.[49]

Outside of Europe, Britain also had other armies it could draw upon. The most numerous of these was the East India Company's (EIC) army. The expansion of the EIC's military developed through a series of conflicts in South Asia, and it was divided into three forces, one for each of the presidencies of Madras, Bengal and Bombay. Between 1763 and 1782 their armies grew from 18,000 to 115,000 men, going on to reach over 190,000 by 1805.[50] Additionally, from 1781 the EIC paid for British Army regiments of foot and cavalry deployed to India, which relieved the Treasury of the costs but meant negotiations with the EIC's Board of Directors about moving troops to or from there or changing the overall size of the force.[51] This emerged as an issue in 1787, when four new regiments were raised for service in South Asia due to the diplomatic tensions with the Dutch Republic. By the time these units were ready, however, the crisis had passed and the EIC did not need them, nor was the government prepared to finance them. The government prevailed, but not without negotiation and further regulation in the 1788 Declaratory Act.[52]

Many of the expeditions involving the British Army, particularly those outside Europe, were amphibious combined-arms operations with the Royal Navy. Where working relations between the commanders of the naval and military forces were good, then the Army could incorporate marines and sailors. The 1794 expedition to the Caribbean commanded by Lieutenant General Sir Charles Grey and Admiral Sir John Jervis was a particularly good example. Sailors often helped with the artillery, both moving and manning guns. Co-operation even went as far as combining the forces together. The initial landing in Guadeloupe at Point-à-Pitre mixed grenadiers of the foot regiments, marines and sailors, with Navy officers place under the command of the Army.[53] Similar was seen in the invasion of the Cape of Good Hope and Buenos Aires in 1806 when Captain Home Riggs Popham, commander of the naval forces in the expedition, created a 'sea battalion' of Royal Marines for use on land as well as a battalion of 'Blues' of 400 sailors in the fleet.[54] Co-operation like this was not ubiquitous, though. In 1795, for instance, general orders from the Duke of York that seemed to exempt soldiers at sea from naval discipline led to the 'Admirals' mutiny', which was only smoothed over by the First Lord, Lord Spencer, and the rescinding of the order itself.[55]

Most significant in the layering of the British Army was Ireland's status as a sibling kingdom. Although there was no separate Irish Army, Ireland had a separate military establishment before 1801 paid for by the Irish government.[56] This relieved Britain's taxpayers of the costs of 15,000 soldiers (who were mostly stationed in Ireland) but involved the Irish Parliament in Dublin in discussions about the Army in Ireland. The Lord Lieutenant of Ireland had broad responsibilities to carry on the King's government and he held a delegated power from the King in terms of administering the Army. And such, he was intimately involved in officer promotions in units on the Irish Establishment, which were used extensively as a patronage system to influence Irish politics.[57] Throughout the period the Lord Lieutenant of Ireland had to be consulted with and kept informed of decisions about the Army.

The Irish Establishment also extended to having its own Ordnance department (with an artillery regiment and engineers) and a complete military administration which duplicated functions, but not always arrangements, in Britain. As we will see in Chapter 3, working with these differences was not always straightforward. Before 1788 there were structural disparities too, as units on the Irish Establishment were organized and financed differently from their counterparts paid in Britain. This made interchanging units between the two isles complicated.[58] Indeed, before 1788 Ireland maintained four regiments of horse, the equivalents of which in Britain had been converted to dragoon guards in 1746, effectively isolating these units to Ireland. The Dutch crisis of 1787 demonstrated the problems caused by the distinctions between units on the British and Irish Establishments. The Pitt government created an expeditionary force of three regiments of foot from Britain (22nd, 43rd, and 55th) and three from Ireland (9th, 48th, and 49th). The process of drafting men from other units into these six was hampered by having different-sized units between the two establishments. And so from December 1787 regiments of foot on the Irish Establishment were raised to ten companies, matching their British counterparts that had been recently augmented.[59] The 41st Foot was converted to a regiment of foot in 1788 so it could be sent across the Irish Sea.[60] Although the Act of Union in 1801 discontinued a distinct Irish military establishment, Ireland continued to have its own Commander-of-the-Forces who had an ill-defined relationship with the Lord Lieutenant of Ireland and the military hierarchy leading up to the Commander-in-Chief based in the Horse Guards building in London.[61]

The layers of Britain's composite land forces were further complicated by legal geographical definitions and jurisdictions. The status of the Channel Islands and the Isle of Man as crown dependencies outside of England, Ireland, or Scotland meant that British and Irish militia units could not be required to serve on these islands, and so the Channel Islands' garrison had to be units of the British Army.[62] On the other hand units recruited outside Britain and Ireland, which as we shall see soon were a significant component of Britain's land forces, were not permitted on the mainland of Britain without express authority of Parliament. As a result the smaller islands around Britain, such as the Isle of Wight and the Channel Islands, became bases for many of these units as well as for soldiers of Britain's allies.[63]

A Multinational Force

Serving alongside allies as part of a larger military force was not new for the British Army, although by 1793 it was some time since it had done this. The last time British Army units had served in an allied army was in western Germany during the Seven Years War. Before that, the British Army had served in continental Europe during the Wars of the Spanish and the Austrian Succession in the early 1700s and 1740s respectively. More recent was the hiring of troops to serve alongside the British Army, and during the American War of Independence several regiments were employed from German states and served in North America and Gibraltar.[64] Units were also recruited in North

America during the Seven Years War and particularly in the American War of Independence. These formed a significant component of the troops available the Britain during these wars, where as many as 21,000 served in provincial, militia and local defence units during the American War of Independence.[65]

Repeatedly throughout the French Wars of 1793 to 1815 the army commanded by British general officers included quite large contingents of allies. In 1799, 17,500 Russian troops were hired to go with 8,000 men from the British Army for the invasion of Holland.[66] The Russian and British armies served together again in 1805 for a campaign in southern Italy.[67] Most significant of all were the Portuguese and Spanish units that fought alongside units of the British Army during the Peninsular War. It was unusual for Britain's soldiers not to be part of a larger allied army (usually when fighting in Europe), or to serve alongside locally-raised troops (especially outside Europe). Where the British Army was the sole military force it was often in short-term and small expeditions of less than 30,000 men.[68] There were over fifty expeditions during the Revolutionary and Napoleonic Wars. Some were extended raids, but no less destructive for it, such as the invasion of Denmark in 1807 that deliberately bombarded Copenhagen to force the capitulation of the neutral Danish fleet.[69] Others hoped to become part of a larger multinational force that never materialized, such as the armies sent to north-west Germany in 1805 and to the Baltic in 1807 in support of the Third and Fourth Coalitions respectively.[70] The strategic aims of both were undone by the rapidity of the French victories between 1805 and 1807. The biggest European expedition solely of the British Army was the attack on Holland in 1809.[71]

The multinational character of the British Army was particularly apparent in 1813. In the Iberian Peninsula the army under Wellington's command included 52,500 from the British Army, of which at least 6,000 were foreign units within it, alongside 28,800 Portuguese, to which were added Spanish units totalling 46,200.[72] A force mixing the British Army with units of the Kingdom of Sicily (the Bourbon half of the former Kingdom of the Two Sicilies) garrisoned Sicily and operated in the Mediterranean and the east coast of Spain;[73] and the British Army served as part of an Allied army in north Germany and Holland in 1813 and 1814.[74] By 1813, just over 50,000 – or one in five – soldiers in the British Army were units classified as in 'Foreign and Provincial Corps'. What connected these forces was that they were paid for by the British government and were under the command of British Army generals, meaning that the British Army was less about nationality and more about who footed the bill and who was in command.

Classifying the variety of multinational units in Britain's army needs some care. Alongside soldiers hired from other states, there were units that were managed directly by the British state but were recruited from beyond Britain and Ireland. For these units to formally become part of the British Army they needed to be included in the annual Army establishment (a financial instrument that detailed the money allocated for the Army, discussed in more detail in Chapter 3). Then the officers of these units would be entered into the *Army Lists* and announced in *The London Gazette*. The 60th (Royal American) Foot was the most long-standing foreign regiment in the British Army. Created in 1756 by an Act of Parliament, it recruited Protestant Germans, Swiss and American colonists, as well as Britons.[75] The regiment survived peacetime reductions in the Army after 1763 and 1783, and it was expanded from two battalions to a peak of eight by 1813, with the 5/60th becoming particularly famous for its service in the Peninsular War.[76] Although reduced to two battalions after 1815 it continued to be part of the British Army, changing its title to The Duke of York's Own Rifle Corps and Light Infantry in 1824 and then the King's Royal Rifle Corps reflecting its shift from a foreign to a British infantry unit.[77] More typical of units in this category was the King's German Legion: an army within an army of infantry, cavalry and artillery that was put on the establishment of the British Army in 1803 and grew from 1,500 men to 16,000 by 1813. Initially, it was a Hanoverian army in exile that had been created after its territories were overrun by France and Prussia in 1803–05, although as the war went on it recruited a wider range of Europeans into its ranks.[78]

Outside these were units that were raised in Britain's colonies or from Europeans and paid for the British state but were not formally placed on the establishment of the Army. Throughout the French Wars, Britain continually recruited soldiers and formed units from outside of Britain and Ireland and added them into the British Army. The Duke of York's army in the Low Countries included new units created from continental European manpower. For example, within the 6,500 soldiers of the British Army at the siege of Dunkirk was the Loyal Emigrant Regiment, a unit raised by *comte* Claude-Louis de La Châtre from French émigrés around London, which were then joined by Flemish recruits when the unit arrived in Flanders.[79] Outside Europe, 'provincial' units were raised and paid for out by the colonial administration. These included units in Saint-Domingue, Nova Scotia, and the Cape of Good Hope in the 1790s, and the practice continued with the Maltese Provincials in 1804.[80]

Such units had a vague status as part of the British Army. They were not included in the *Army Lists* and it was not until 1796 that a budget was presented to Parliament for the European units, even though they numbered around 20,000 in 1794–5.[81] As we shall see in Chapter 5, the strength of all foreign and overseas units were not included in returns of the British Army until after 1803, and it was from that year that these corps began to be more regularly included in the annual *Army List*. The status of some these units was reflected in their uniforms too. Some of the French emigre units wore the white cockade of the French monarchy rather than the black cockade of the Hanoverian dynasty. Nor was this a minor matter, as during the Terror in France anyone wearing the white cockade was automatically deemed a traitor, and captured soldiers from French émigré units in the British Army were executed.[82] After 1795, a few units were formally moved into the establishment of the British Army, such as the York Hussars, giving their officers permanent rank in the Army, but others were still left as temporary units with an uncertain status. Among the latter was the Loyal Emigrant Regiment, mentioned above, despite active service in Flanders, Quiberon, and Portugal between 1794 and 1801.[83]

The need to keep units outside the formal structures of the British Army was partly driven by constitutional legislation. The Bill of Rights and Act of Settlement in the wake of 1689 meant that laws were necessary to enlist foreigners.[84] The size of the 60th Foot had to be specifically approved by legislation. It was necessary to introduce Acts of Parliament in 1794 and 1804 to allow foreigners, and particularly Catholics, to enlist in units in the British Army. The success in recruiting for the King's German Legion by 1807 meant another amendment to these laws was necessary, as the maximum number permitted in the UK specified in the Acts was in danger of being exceeded.[85] Most of these units had specific terms about where they could be used. Those raised under the 1794 Act could only serve in Europe or the former domains of the French King. A further set of units were raised through contracts (known as capitulations) with individual commanding officers that were set for a fixed time and so had to be periodically renegotiated. The British government's first agreement for the De Meuron regiment was in 1796, and a new agreement was signed in 1798 for ten years, and another in 1809.[86]

The second aspect of Britain's multinational army was the forces raised outside Europe, usually for defence of colonies. Sustaining Britain's military presence in the Caribbean was a significant challenge in the 1790s and early 1800s in the face of a deadly combination of an epidemiological environment that proved lethal to recently-arrived European soldiers and insurgencies by both enslaved and free people across the Caribbean stimulated by the French Revolution. The solution to these twin problems was the creation of West India regiments. Manned by black and coloured people from the Caribbean and Africa, but with white officers, they were an entirely different type of unit, so much so that it was not clear where they fitted in the Army at first. Initially, they were considered temporary units for limited service in particular islands in a kind of colonial defence establishment, yet General Sir John Vaughan (appointed Commander-in-Chief in the Windward Islands in 1794) wanted them to be permanent and for general service albeit composed of Africans and intended for service in the Caribbean. It was not until 1798 that the West India regiments became the sole and official name for these units.[87]

Units composed of enslaved and freed black and mixed-race Caribbeans were not a completely new feature of military forces available to British government in the 1790s. Their use dated back to the 1730s and the Maroon Wars in Jamaica, and they became increasingly involved in offensive operations across the Caribbean during the mid and late eighteenth century through the creation of ranger units as well as providing military labour as pioneers.[88] These traditions of black military service were extended to North America during the War of Independence.[89] The West India regiments therefore stood in a line of black soldiers serving Britain, but what made them regiments distinctive from their predecessors was both their size – by 1798 there were twelve regiments with a total establishment of 12,000 men compared to the hundreds raised in previous wars – but also their position as established units in the British Army.[90] Moreover, the idea of incorporating people from outside Europe into the Army was extended with a regiment raised at the Cape of Good Hope, the four Ceylon regiments raised in Sri Lanka, and units raised in Mauritius.

One thing that was common to all these units, however, was segregation. As indicated by the titles of units discussed earlier, the British Army tended to form its foreign soldiers into discrete units, at least outwardly, that had some notional national or ethnic basis in the eyes of the British government rather than into units that mixed races and ethnic groups. So there were French émigré corps, units of Germans (particularly Hanoverians), Maltese and Sicilian corps, and battalions of enslaved Africans. There were a few exceptions, such as the Royal African Corps, which included British, Irish, European, and African men, but even here the principle emerged as the unit sorted its manpower into separate companies of black and European soldiers.[91] The reality beyond these official arrangement was frequently more complicated, as Army recruited wherever it went and so units were more multi-ethnic than they might seem.[92] It was white, usually English-speaking Europeans officers that commanded, though, pointing to the way that the Army managed and combined its multinational force.

Combinations

These layers of Britain's military forces were gradually assimilated through the 1790s and early 1800s. It has the appearance of a straightforward progression, but changes were prompted by events, opportunities, and in a few cases emergencies. This transformation often required amending or new legislation, bringing the structure of the Army and the armed forces into wider political debates. 1798 and 1799 were significant turning points in the integration of Britain's military forces and by the end of this process in 1815, the British Army had a command structure and the necessary legal authority to mix different units and forces in a way that was not possible in the 1780s and early 1790s. Moreover, they were utilized in operations across the globe. Combining the multiple layers of Britain's armies and the units in the British Army was essential to the ultimate success of Britain as a global military power.

The militia regiments of Britain and Ireland provided large numbers of men for the defence of Britain and Ireland. Despite being a distinct force from the units of the British Army, once the militia was mobilized and formed into units it was subject to the same rules and regulations as the Army that were laid out in the annual Mutiny Acts and Articles of War (for more on these see below in Chapter 3).[93] Crucially, militia units were placed under the command of British Army general officers. In 1792 military districts were instituted in Britain, mixing together British Army units and the militia, and the system was gradually expanded and refined with the appointment of staff officers and brigadiers through 1793 to 1795.[94] This arrangement was strengthened in 1797 when militia units in Britain were brigaded, again with a general officer commanding them.[95] Likewise, the new units of the British Army (fencibles and foreign corps) were integrated into the command structure of the Army.

Initially, volunteer units in Britain and Ireland remained a separate force. The 1794 legislation that governed these units stated that they could only voluntarily place themselves under the command of general officers and even then only in case of emergency or invasion, a situation that meant their position within any larger plans or command arrangements was conditional.[96] In Ireland, the growing danger of an insurgency by the republican United Irishmen combining with a French invasion through 1796 and 1797 began changing this arrangement. These threats posed an operational problem for the military staff in Ireland as there were insufficient full-time soldiers to both police Ireland, undertake any counter-insurgency operations, and unite enough of a force to meet a French invasion. The appearance of a French fleet in Bantry Bay in December 1796 with an invasion force of 15,000 men shocked the military and political leadership into making changes. The military forces in Ireland more than doubled between January 1797 and 1798, and by 1800 had reached 116,600, but more important was the flexibility in its use.[97]

A key response to Bantry Bay was the creation of the Irish Yeomanry, Ireland's equivalent of volunteer corps, and soon they became an integrated part of the military forces in Ireland. In 1797, Major-General John Knox, commander at Dungannon in the Northern Military District, began using Irish yeomanry units to seize arms from suspected United Irishmen. By April 1798, the Irish

Yeomanry had been integrated into wider military plans. Units were combined into brigades with fixed assembly points and standing orders. These brigades were divided into stationary and moveable, depending on whether the local general needed a brigade to stay in its district or decided to make it available to serve across Ireland.[98] The transformation of the Irish Yeomanry, plus the existing arrangements for fencibles and militia units, meant that when the British Army faced a civil war in Ireland from May 1798 and then a French invasion in August it was able to draw upon the full range of Britain's military forces to respond to this crisis.[99]

1798 was also significant for the rest of the forces in Britain and Ireland. At the same time as the growing threats posed to and within Ireland, the end of the First Coalition when Austria signed the Treaty of Campo Formio in October 1797 left Britain and France as the only protagonists in the war, with France dominating Italy and the Netherlands. The threat of an invasion of Britain prompted new legalisation to bolster military forces in Britain, specifically focusing on part-time soldiers. In a tortuously constructed clause of the 1798 Defence of the Realm Act, volunteer corps would be placed under the command of general officers but only in the event of an invasion or the imminent threat of one.[100] This phrasing masked a change from the 1794 Volunteer Act, as the volunteers lost the ability to decide if they were to be commanded by British Army generals should an invasion happen. Nor was this just a nominal development in the Army's jurisdiction, as general officers commanding military districts were involved in meetings of county authorities required by the Defence of the Realm Act, so starting the integration.[101] As such, the military district commands combined British Army units, militia and volunteers. The threat of invasion pushed this development further, so in 1804 volunteer units were arranged into brigades and inspecting field officers (almost always Army officers on half pay) were appointed to oversee and to command them if an invasion occurred.[102] Plans were also made for the distribution and movement of volunteer corps to the outskirts of London from across Britain should the French land, in what would have been the greatest feat of British military planning of the nineteenth century if it had occurred.[103]

The idea of organizing the different tiers of Britain's military forces into a single command structure was adopted across the globe. In South Asia units of the British Army had fought alongside the EIC's army in a series of campaigns in the 1790s and 1800s.[104] The organization of the Army that fought against Mysore combined brigades of the British Army (referred to as the King's troops), brigades of EIC units, and also brigades that intermixed the two.[105] In the Channel Isles, local militia units were integrated into counter-invasion plans,[106] and brigaded like their counterparts in Britain and Ireland.[107] Likewise, during the British occupation of Madeira between 1809 and 1814 the island's militia was built up to three regiments and formed part of the garrison, supplemented by a further 15,000 men in part-time forces.[108] In Canada during the War of 1812 with the United States of America, this system was instrumental to the way the conflict was fought. In the operations along the Niagara border in 1814, Lieutenant Colonel Thomas Pearson commanded a brigade composed of a detachment from the 19th Light Dragoons, the Glengarry Light Infantry (a Canadian provincial regiment), Merritt's Troop of Provincial Dragoons, and the Incorporated Militia of Upper Canada, plus the 1st Militia Brigade itself made up of detachments from the 1st, 2nd, 4th and 5th Lincoln Militia and 2nd York Militia. The 2nd Brigade mixed the 1/8th Foot, the 103rd Foot and some companies from the 104th Foot and the 2nd Militia Brigade (again formed from detachments of Canadian Militia).[109]

1799 was another turning point in the British Army's development of combining its multifarious land forces, but this time focused on offensive operations. As the Second Coalition began to form in 1799, the government sought ways to strengthen British units in the Army as the usual forms of recruitment had almost dried up (explored in more detail in Chapter 4). With a much stronger defensive base for operations, the government and Army high command began looking at ways of boosting the strength of the Army. Key to this was deploying existing military forces in new theatres. Firstly, many fencible corps agreed to extend the geographical limits of their service in 1790s, including to Europe and further afield, and in 1799 those that had not were threatened with disbandment.[110] Secondly, offers from militia regiments in the same year to serve outside their kingdom suggested that militiamen, who had been mobilized for over six years by that stage, might be willing to serve as soldiers in the Army.[111] To permit this, however, required legislation as the militia laws specifically forbade militiamen from enlisting in the British Army. The debates about these 'transfers' from the militia were not without political controversy in Parliament. Once the legislation was passed, militiamen provided a boost in the British Army's strength that enabled the Dutch expedition in 1799 and the invasion of Egypt in 1801.[112] From then on until 1811, the land forces oscillated between large-scale recruitment of home defence forces (particularly in 1803 and 1806) followed by drafts from the militia into the Army as it sought to shift to offensive operations in 1805, 1807 and 1809. In 1811, the transfer of men from the militia became a recruitment system rather than a one-off event.[113]

The extension of the geographic terms of service of militia regiments was a recurrent theme through the Napoleonic Wars. Sometimes these came from the units themselves, particularly in 1808 during the enthusiastic response to Spanish popular resistance to the French invasion. The government and the Commander-in-Chief, although warmly welcoming their patriotism, wanted to retain control of any changes in the militia and avoid adding yet further complexity of what units could serve where (and when).[114] Changes were brought in for the militia so that in 1811 the militia's three-kingdoms structure – England (and Wales), Scotland, and Ireland – was reformed to create a single militia of the United Kingdom, allowing militia units to circulate throughout Britain and Ireland (the Channel Islands still remained outside the militia's remit, though).[115] The closer integration of the home defence forces in the British Isles culminated in 1813 and 1814. It was clear to the government that the war was entering its final phase, and to strengthen Britain's hand in the expected peace negotiations there were plans to deploy more forces to the Netherlands and north Italy as well as continuing to support the Army's campaign in the south of France. In November 1813, legislation was introduced to create a 'New Military System' allowing militiamen to volunteer for service in Europe within militia units under their own officers and retaining the privileges of being a militiamen: keeping the allowance that was given to their family whilst militiamen served that was lost if they joined regiments of the Army. These militia units were either formed into provisional militia battalions or, if three-quarters of the men from one unit agreed to these new terms the unit would be a separate unit.[116] Alongside this, the government amended the local militia laws (which had largely replaced the volunteer corps in 1808) to allow these units to do duty for forty-two days and take on garrison duty across the United Kingdom in lieu of the militia.[117] A militia brigade of three provisional militia battalions was formed in early 1814 and sent to Europe, but arrived too late to be involved in action.[118]

It was not just soldiers in British units that were encouraged to extend the geographic range of their service. One of the greatest shifts from a local to a regional force was the use of the EIC's troops outside the Indian subcontinent. Sepoy units were used in this way in the Egyptian campaign, where they formed a large part of the force under Major-General David Baird that was sent across the Indian Ocean and marched up the Nile, arriving just after the Battle of Alexandria (21 March 1801).[119] During 1806, plans were discussed between William Grenville, 1st Baron Grenville, and William Windham about using sepoy units to garrison the Cape of Good Hope and as reinforcements for further invasions of South America, but these were undone by the defeat at Buenos Aires in 1807.[120] Sepoys were increasingly used in campaigns against the French colonies in the Indian Ocean, concluding in the invasion and capture of Java in 1811 (which became a French colony when the Kingdom of Holland was incorporated in the French Empire in 1810).[121] The 11,000 men sent to Java were equally split between European troops of the British Army and sepoys from the EIC's forces.[122]

What fused Britain's land forces was the organization of these units under the command of officers of the British Army. Although the British government had multiple armies at its disposal – units of the British Army, hired auxiliaries, militias, locally-recruited units across the globe, and part-time home defence forces – these did not have their own command structure outside of the unit. Almost invariably, the highest rank in all the units outside of the British Army was colonel, with the EIC being the exception with a few appointments at higher rank.[123] The primacy of the British Army as a command structure allowed the composite army to form and function. This was particularly emphasized in Anthony Cardon's print of Philippe Jacques de Loutherbourg's *The British Army in Egypt* (Plate 2) where images of the British Army generals of the 1801 campaign in Egypt are arranged in a pyramid and surrounded by soldiers representing the variety of forces used in the campaign, including a guardsman, artilleryman, light dragoons, sepoys, Anthony Lutz of the Minorca Regiment and Royal Marines.

This mixing of forces reached its apogee under Arthur Wellesley in Spain and Portugal, and finally in the Waterloo campaign. He already had experience of working in and with a composite army from his time in South Asia during the campaigns against Mysore and the Marathas. From February 1810, the British Army in Portugal was integrated into an Anglo-Portuguese force, in which divisions were created as formal structures in the army that combined two brigades of the British Army with a brigade of Portuguese troops, with attached artillery, under the command of a general with a staff to support him. This arrangement was expanded to eventually reach eight divisions by the end of the Peninsular War, plus cavalry brigades arranged into a nominal division, and was fundamental to operations, command, and control during the campaigns in Portugal and Spain.[124] The system was replicated and extended in 1815, when the Allied army combined into divisions brigades of the British Army with Hanoverians, Brunswickers, and Dutch troops.[125] Much of the credit for introducing these operational-level military organizations goes to Wellesley, and certainly he refined the practice (in particular he kept brigades of national armies and then mixed together brigades, rather than a complete amalgamation of units within brigades). Yet there was a longer history of mixing forces before the Peninsular War, in that the Portuguese or German or Dutch troops had replaced fencibles, militia or volunteers corps. Outside of Ireland in 1798, these earlier arrangements were never tested, so their historical profile is much lower, but they played an important part of how the British Army learned to make a workable composite army.

* * *

The profusion of new units and the total size that they attained during the period 1793–1815 makes the Army of these years distinctive. The size of the documents presented to Parliament to finance the Army provides indicates the growing complexity of the Army. In 1785, when the Army was entering a peace-time establishment, it only needed nine pages. In 1813 it required fifty-four pages to detail the projected expenditure. Some of this expansion occurred through new units of the existing types of dragoons, light dragoons, and infantry of the line (as the numbered regiments of infantry were known). Between 1803 and 1813 the number of cavalry units was relatively stable, changing from 30 to 32, and the infantry of the line expanded to 104 regiments from 78.[126] The most significant changes occurred outside of units of line infantry and cavalry. Most of these different elements were combined into a single establishment for the Army from 1803. The 1813 Army Estimates specified funds for thirty-eight corps, including garrison battalions, veteran battalions, eight West India regiments, five regiments of Canadian fencible infantry and six other units. The foreign corps included the five regiments of cavalry and ten battalions in the King's German Legion, plus a further regiment of cavalry and twelve infantry units. Some of these new units had precedents from before 1793, but not to the scale that they were recruited between 1793 and 1815. Most did not survive the post-1815 retrenchment, when all the European foreign corps were disbanded (except the 60th Foot), and by 1818 the 'Miscellaneous Corps' had been reduced to four West India regiments, four penal units mostly comprising deserters (the Royal African Corps, the Royal York Rangers, Royal West India Rangers and York Chasseurs) and two Ceylon regiments.[127]

The nature of Britain's land forces was partly a response to the need for so many troops overseas, but this came at the expense of operational flexibility as not all troops could be used everywhere nor did the Army and government have absolute control of all military forces. The British Army was not wholly British, and the British Army was not Britain's sole land force. It was a composite and multi-layered force with a range of units that included some raised for specific purposes or service. The impact of overseas service on the deployment and use of the Army also influenced the Army's structure. This makes defining the British Army complicated. As one definition we have the unit recruited in Britain and Ireland on the establishment of the British Army; another is that it was an organizational structure into which slotted various units of the land forces available to the British government. This was made possible by Britain's other armed forces changing from local to regional forces. Care is needed, then, not to conflate the British Army with only British and Irish units, and not to repeat the simplistic contemporary reporting of the actions of the British Army, of which the *Morning Post*'s reporting of Waterloo was just one example.

Chapter 2

Global Army and Global Conflicts

O'er the hills and o'er the main
Through Flanders, Portugal and Spain
King George commands and we obey
Over the hills and far away.[1]

These words will be familiar to any viewer of the *Sharpe* TV series from the late 1990s, where the tough, outsider officer in the form of Richard Sharpe, promoted from the ranks, serves in the British Army's campaigns across Europe. This song is based on a traditional folk tune that dates back to the 1600s and appeared with similar words in George Farquhar's 1706 play *The Recruiting Officer* at a time when Britain was engaged in another long and wide-ranging conflict with France.[2] The geographical range of the service of the British Army in the 1790s and 1800s was far wider than given in this song, and further even than the service of Richard Sharpe in Bernard Cornwell's novels. As well as fighting in Flanders, Portugal and Spain, the British Army was deployed to Scandinavia, France, Italy, Greece, Egypt, Canada, the United States of America, the Caribbean, South America, Africa, South Asia, and across the Indian Ocean from the Persian coast to Java. A small detachment of fifty soldiers even served as an escort to Lord George Macartney's embassy to China in 1792–4.[3] Through these deployments and conflicts the British Army became a global, multi-theatre military force. The concurrent deployment of major forces across the globe was a shift in the role and reach of the British Army from a European force that sometimes engaged in transoceanic expeditions, to what Bruce Collins has coined a global enclave-based power, where troops were maintained at strategic ports and garrisons over the world to provide bases for the projection of power as and when required.[4] Although the Peninsular War and the Waterloo campaign may have had the lion's share of historical attention, both only accounted for around a quarter of Britain's military force.

Deployments

What marks out the wars between 1792 and 1815 was not just new theatres into which the British Army was deployed, though the eastern Mediterranean, southern Africa, Egypt and South America were that, but the sheer numbers sent overseas. As the land force of an island state, the Army necessarily served overseas, and through the eighteenth century the scale of the forces sent to fight across oceans increased as the reach of British military power expanded. Not for nothing was the Seven Years War known as the first global war, with the Army campaigning in North America, Africa and South Asia, alongside fighting in Germany.[5] The descent on Havana in the Seven Years War, one of that war's largest expeditions, combined 17,000 men from North America, troops already in the Caribbean, and units sent directly from Britain. The American War of Independence was almost entirely fought beyond Europe, except for the long siege of Gibraltar and the invasion of Jersey in 1781. At its peak, 50,000 soldiers of the British Army were in Northern America, with a few thousand at other stations outside Britain and Ireland.[6] Between 1793 and 1815, however, the Army often had multiple theatres with large numbers of soldiers. Military records about deployments provide us with a much more detailed picture about where the Army served, figures that are summarized in Appendix A. At its peak overseas deployment in the summer of 1813 to early 1814, 184,000 soldiers in the British Army were serving beyond Britain and Ireland, around 70 per cent of its total strength (what these figures cover, and what they do not, is explored in more detail in Chapter 5). In June 1813, the British Army had 65,000 in the Iberian Peninsula (excluding garrisons in Lisbon and Gibraltar) alongside 37,600 across Southern Europe, 17,100 in North America, 22,800 in the Caribbean, 10,900 in Africa, 23,300 in South Asia, and 3,600 in South-eastern Asia and Australasia.

Within these deployment figures is a more important point: that Britain was not fighting a single war, but multiple conflicts. Although France was the persistent enemy throughout the years 1793 to 1815 (besides the brief peace of Amiens between 1801 and 1803) Britain was also at war with: Mysore (December 1789–March 1792, and February–May 1799); Spain (October 1796–March 1802, and October 1804–May 1808); the Batavian Republic and its successor the Kingdom of Holland (May 1795–March 1802, and June 1803 until the state was annexed to France in July 1810); faced the Second League of Armed Neutrality combining Denmark, Sweden, Prussia and Russia (December 1800–April 1801); the Marathas (1803–December 1806); Denmark (August 1807–January 1814); Prussia (June–September 1806); the Ottoman Empire (January 1807–January 1809); Sweden (November 1810–July 1812); Russia (October 1807–July 1812); and the USA (June 1812–February 1815).[7] Most of these were linked to the war between Britain and France, as some were allies of France whilst other sought to preserve their interests, but they further broadened the scope of the conflict. War with Spain bought into military consideration not only Spain's Caribbean possessions but also South America. Likewise, war with the Batavian Republic transformed the Cape of Good Hope, Sri Lanka, and Java into potentially hostile bases. The global perspective of Britain's rivalry with France encompassed states outside Europe too. Richard Wellesley, Baron Mornington and Governor-General of India between 1798 and 1805, justified the conflicts with powers in the Indian subcontinent by highlighting French influence there and the threat this posed to British possessions and trade, a rationale shared by others in the British government.[8] Potential French influence in Persia and the rapprochement between France and Russia turned the attention of Gilbert Elliot, 1st Earl Minto (Baron Mornington's successor), to the North-West frontier, Sindh and French possessions in the Indian Ocean, as well as pre-empting French influence in Dutch colonies.[9]

The British Army's role as a global armed force was confirmed after the Napoleonic Wars. The strength of the post-war British Army was twice to three times as large as it was during peacetime in the 1780s. In 1816 the Army Establishment was set at 135,505 rank and file (plus 12,219 for the Ordnance), with its lowest total of 79,000 in 1822 and usually 80,000–90,000 men through the 1820s and 1830s.[10] That such a large military force was maintained after 1815 was a symptom of an increasing demand for the deployment of the Army across the globe. The idea of the Army holding key strategic posts and waiting for relief from elsewhere was conceived in 1783 during the transition to peacetime establishment. Yet as General Henry Seymour Conway, the Commander-in-Chief at the time, pointed out, the forces and positions needed to be strong enough in the first place to hold out.[11] His foresight was proved accurate during the 1790s and 1800s as the number of troops stationed overseas escalated. The size of the British Army stationed outside Europe generally grew throughout the Napoleonic Wars and was always higher than the commitment to the Iberian Peninsula. A combination of resorting to military power for colonial gain when opportunities arose and seeking security for existing colonies drove and maintained the deployment of the Army outside of Europe.

Trade revenue was crucial to Britain's financial and so military power, but protecting this required the commitment of huge naval and military forces. The primary defence of trade rested with the Royal Navy, but bases were required to supply and maintain ships that were blockading European ports to prevent French and Allied fleets interdicting convoys and for escorts for trade convoys.[12] The principal reason for the large forces maintained in the Mediterranean was to supply the naval blockade of southern France and Italy. Sicily provided supplies for the fleet and for Malta.[13] Capturing the Cape of Good Hope in 1795 and again in 1806 neutralized the possible threat to convoys to and from South and South-eastern Asia, as well as providing a stop-over point for these fleets. Moreover, it offered somewhere for troops to acclimatize before going on to South Asia and an operational reserve that could be drawn upon in an emergency by commanders across the Indian Ocean.[14] These operational and strategic needs mixed with the anxiety of an attack from French and later Dutch and Spanish colonies. And so, to ensure the security of British colonies, more and more enemy colonies were invaded and occupied.[15]

Often the Army is presented as separate from trade networks,[16] yet it was itself an agent in global trade and woven into international finance systems. Paying soldiers and providing subsistence for them utilized and entrenched the trade networks the Army was there to defend. The Army was a huge market, both in its demands for essential items and its combined purchasing power for goods and services. Financing the Army overseas relied largely on international trade. Shipping the cash (coins in precious metal) to pay soldiers and for commissaries to buy food and forage was risky. A ship carrying precious metals was exactly the sort of prize that sailors and privateers dreamt about. Additionally, in 1797 it became illegal to export bullion from Britain after the Bank of England suspended cash payments in response to a panic-induced monetary crisis that followed a small French force landing in Pembrokeshire. Indeed, the acquisition and circulation of specie (silver and gold coins) was an important aspect of Britain's global wars. Demand for precious metals increased because of the wars in Europe whilst supply was affected by the Spanish American empire beginning to disintegrate, itself a result of European conflicts.[17]

Bills of exchange were used mainly to finance the Army overseas, a well-established financial arrangement for trade, the movement of large sums of money, and to raise specie locally.[18] These bills were sent out from Britain which local merchants would then buy in cash or other bills. The local merchants used the bills of exchange to pay directly for goods from Britain or in transactions with other merchants who could use them. Soldiers and commissaries then used the locally-obtained cash to pay for things, so the coins would end up back in the hands of local merchants. This financial circuit was not completely self-sustaining, and regular supplies of specie were needed to keep the system moving.[19] In 1809, £465,667 was sent to Portugal in specie, whilst £2,174,097 was paid out in paper money. The value of government-issued bills reflected market conditions when and where they were offered, and so they were often sold at a discount. It was also open to abuse and corruption, both of which were particularly uncovered in the 9th Report of Commissioners of Military Enquiry that examined Army expenditure in the Caribbean. This revealed that £160,000 had disappeared into the private purses of those involved in disbursing Army money.[20]

Yet the defence of trade only drew Britain into more territorial disputes, fuelled new concerns of raids and invasion, and so further military action. Plus, newly-occupied territories needed garrisons themselves. As a result, the broad trend shown in Appendix A is that the British Army overseas increased practically everywhere it was stationed. Deployments in South Asia went from 3,000–5,000 in the 1780s to figures in the 20,000s after 1806; southern Europe (which for the Army meant units stationed across the Mediterranean) from 3,000 to the Army's biggest deployments outside of Britain and Ireland in January 1807, 1808–09 and continued to grow through most of the 1810s. The trend was particularly noticeable in the Caribbean, where the garrison of around 3,000–4,000 men in the 1780s more than tripled in the 1790s. Although peak numbers in the Caribbean came in 1797, through the Peninsula War era it was never less than 20,000, six to seven times what it was in the 1780s.

The Caribbean islands, which combined were a relatively small land area, had a dense concentration of British military manpower compared to elsewhere in the globe. Perpetual and multiple concerns about security resulted in large numbers of troops being stationed there. Alongside threats of French, American and sometimes Spanish armed forces to British colonies, there were recurrent operations against internal threats. Resistance to slavery and racial discrimination often led to rebellions, revolts, and insurgencies mostly by enslaved blacks but also combining free blacks, mixed-race people, and white revolutionaries. The result was, as Michael Craton has put it in *Testing the Chains*, like 'damming water with sand'.[21] The Army faced insurgencies on islands it invaded, such as Guadeloupe and especially on Saint-Domingue, but also in existing territories, including the Second Maroon War in Jamaica (July 1795–March 1796) and the Second Carib War on Saint Vincent, whilst the war on Grenada led by Julien Fédon involved half the island's enslaved population and paralyzed British forces there for two years. Although resistance to slavery and British occupation lessened from 1797 (and particularly from 1802 when France reintroduced slavery), the abolition of the slave trade in 1807 focused planters' attention on restraining Maroons and the enslaved, for which they needed soldiers. For example, rumours circulated in Tobago that emancipation would follow the abolition of the slave trade,[22] and in Dominica there was a *de facto* Maroon war between 1809 and 1814.[23] There was also the persistent challenge of the independent Haitian black republic in the midst of the slave plantation economy.[24] Major-General George Nugent, Governor of Jamaica, was told not to interfere with the French efforts to retake Haiti in 1801.[25] Formal diplomatic recognition and political acceptance of the Haitian Republic took some time after it declared independence from France in 1804, though trade and economic links came sooner.[26] It is not surprising, then, that by the end of the 1811 the Duke of York recommended reinforcing the Caribbean because of the growing tension with the USA.[27] With American privateers active in the Caribbean,[28] in 1813 the Duke of York highlighted how the Leeward Islands were barely in 'a state of safety'.[29]

War begetting war, or more specifically economic expansion, security, and war operating in a cycle, particularly characterized British expansion in South Asia. The British Army was fundamental to this process, not just as a military force but also because the EIC had to pay for units of the British Army, further adding to the EIC's need for revenues. In the 1790s, Britain's and the EIC's conflicts with Mysore aimed to stabilize the complex inter-state political environment across the region to the EIC's outlook, but it was based on a diplomatic and political view that did not align with the social, economic, and political realities in India. The ambition of Charles Cornwallis, Marquess Cornwallis, to create a stable state system with Mysore during his time as Governor-General broke down by 1798. The subsequent war to remedy the situation – at least from the perspective of the EIC and Baron Mornington – only served to lengthen the borders that British Army and EIC soldiers now had to police and defend. It also brought it into a closer contact with the Marathas. Attempting to construct and support the Marathas as a confederacy failed, again fuelling further intervention and conquest.[30] Although there were no major inter-state wars involving the EIC between 1805 and 1815, military power was continually used. Sashi Bhusan Chaudhuri's *Civil Disturbances During the British Rule in India* shows the persistent resistance to British rule across in the Indian subcontinent, particularly in Malabar with the Kottayathu War between 1793 and 1806, a lengthy guerrilla conflict in Kerala, and later the Travancore rising between 1808 and 1809.[31] The scale and intensity of these conflicts may have been unusual but the perpetual recourse to military force to uphold rule was not. The military was routinely used to enforce payments of taxes and tributes. The numerous (and not all have been studied) incidents include suppressing the Vellore Mutiny of 1806 and the Travancore rebellion of 1809, to the capture of forts held by 'marauders' that typified the 56th Foot's activities in 1809.[32] V.C.P. Hodson's *List of the Officers of the Bengal Army 1758-1834* shows that almost every year there was military activity. Not all these operations involved regiments of British Army but most at least involved British Army officers.[33] Expansion through conquest resumed in 1814–19, and so the EIC and the British Army continued chasing rainbows of absolute security across the Indian sub-continent.

Contact with societies on the borders of and within existing and newly acquired territory also sparked conflicts. At the Cape of Good Hope the Army was called on to suppress the Graaf Reineters rising in 1799 against British control of the eastern Cape region (which had declared itself independent of the Cape of Good Hope in 1795). The Army expelled the Xhosa from Zuueveld and across the Fish River in 1811–12, and another expedition was sent out in 1813.[34] The abolition of the slave trade sparked a rising in 1808 at the Cape.[35] The occupation of former Dutch colonies on Sri Lanka led to two wars with the Kingdom of Kandy.[36] Troops were still needed in Britain's existing colonies too. In Australia, the small force there was involved in almost constant operations including territorial conflicts with Aboriginal peoples, suppressing convict revolts, and expeditions against bush-rangers.[37] Tensions continued with the USA between 1783 and 1795 along the ill-defined boundary with Canada and in the Caribbean in 1794.[38] Despite the 1795 Jay Treaty settling some issues, relations deteriorated after its ten-year term expired: in 1807 Robert Stewart, Viscount Castlereagh, the Secretary of State for War and the Colonies, feared an US invasion of Canada.[39] The compound effect of all these deployments was significant, and in January 1811, when Britain was almost the sole European colonial power, the Duke of York presented startling figures in his review of defence to the government, showing that 55,000 infantry and six regiments of cavalry were required for colonial garrisons.[40]

Movement

Distances, and the logistical and communication difficulties they caused, also accounted for the large force overseas. Robert Sutclife's *British Expeditionary Warfare* has fully revealed the immense shipping demands of the British Army, both in terms of the number of ships and cost. There was no distinct naval transport service and so merchant ships were used, which from 1794 was organized by the Transport Board, a department of the Treasury. The usual allocation was two tons of shipping per man and eight to ten tons per horse.[41] These quotas placed an upper limit on the force that could be transported at any one time. In 1799, an expedition was planned to attack the French naval base at Brest, planned at 60,000 rank and file. When officers, sergeants, cavalry, artillery, medical and commissariat staff were added the total was 83,600 people. Ammunition, supplies, fuel and stores would also be needed, such that was calculated that 350,125 tons of shipping would be needed, equating to around 1,400 ships. It was impossible to assemble that many ships and so the expedition, and any other ideas of the direct invasion of France, was abandoned as it was beyond Britain's logistical capacity.[42] The expeditions that were undertaken placed a significant strain on Britain's merchant fleet. Ships over 220 tons were preferred by the Transport Board, but most merchant ships were not that big. At times of peak demand, like 1795, 1805 and 1808, over 30 per cent of the entire fleet of large merchant ships was hired by the government to transport the Army.[43] All these ships needed sailors, and the ships' owners paying. Between

1794 and 1815, £42 million was spent chartering merchant ships to transport soldiers, horses, equipment, and supplies.[44]

Transporting horses overseas was a massive problem. Colliers were the most suitable ship for this role but at eight to ten tons per horse the numbers required were enormous even for a small force of cavalry and artillery, let alone the requirements for all the other tractive power needs of the Army.[45] Only twelve cavalry units ever served outside of the Europe, and of these four (the 8th, 22nd, 24th and 25th Light Dragoons) spent the entire Napoleonic Wars in South Asia. These four were joined by the 21st Light Dragoons that was sent to the Cape of Good Hope, part of which then participated in the Rio de la Plata campaign in 1806, and then went on to Bengal. The experience of the 20th Light Dragoons was untypical of the British cavalry in the period because of the range of places it served. Raised in 1792 as the Jamaican Light Dragoons, it was only mounted once it arrived in Jamaica. In the Napoleonic Wars it was split into two, with part going to the Mediterranean where it was stationed in Malta, involved in the attack on Italy in 1806, and then the Peninsular War. The other part was sent to the Cape of Good Hope and then, like the 21st Light Dragoons, was involved in the Rio de la Plata campaign.[46] The trans-oceanic transport of horses was either impossible or if attempted rendered them unfit for service. A detachment of 298 rank and file of the 6th Dragoon Guards, for example, arrived in South America in June 1807 after a six-month voyage. They served dismounted, brigaded with the also dismounted 9th Light Dragoons and the 40th and 45th Foot.[47]

Scale was the issue. Shipping troops and supplies was usually much faster than marching overland, and so small shipments of troops were much more efficient. Large expeditions, however, took time to assemble the required number of ships, load them and arrange them into a convoy with Royal Naval protection. As Robert Sutcliffe has shown, the management of military transportation by sea was sometimes spectacular given the technology of the day to organize and co-ordinate these operations. It took between ten and fifteen weeks to prepare a major expedition, and the Walcheren Expedition in 1809 was noteworthy in that it was the largest and ready within ten weeks.[48] But to put ten weeks in context, in 1805 the French Army left its camps on the Channel coast on 26 August, marched to Germany and surrounded an Austrian army at Ulm on 20 October, and fought the Battle of Austerlitz on 1 December – a total of fourteen weeks; in 1806, the *Grande Armée* destroyed Prussian military power within a month.[49] There was a paradox, then, that shipping troops and supplies by sea was much quicker than marching or transporting materials in wagons, but because large expeditions took time to assemble the Army could not respond rapidly to events overseas. This further reinforced the need to maintain large number of troops overseas in garrisons.

Co-ordinating redeployments across multiple theatres around the globe added further impediments to rapid movements. At the end of the American War of Independence the government faced enormous difficulties moving units from where they were to where they needed to be at the same time as reducing and disbanding units. Hanoverian units were retained in Gibraltar until June 1784 and some units scheduled to be disbanded in South Asia were kept on into 1785 as a result.[50] In response to the escalating tensions with Spain around Nootka Sound in the Pacific North-West during 1790–1, reinforcements were sent to the Caribbean and Gibraltar, some regiments of foot were used as marines on Royal Navy ships as the fleet was mobilized, and a force was concentrated in Britain for a planned attack on Central and South America. It took over a year, however, for the Army to redistribute units from these deployments and it affected what was available in 1793.[51] From 1802 the perambulations of British Army units were conveniently compiled into a series of regimental abstracts by the military administration, and they reveal the time spent travelling. Six months or more was typical for a passage to South Asia. The 1/24th Foot left Cork on 29 July 1805 and arrived at the Cape of Good Hope on 8 January 1806, leaving there in June 1810 and arriving at Madras a month later. The records of this unit reveal the hazards of overseas troops shipments too, as the convoy was attacked by a French squadron in the Mozambique Channel on 3 July 1810 and the *Windham* and *Ceylon* transports were taken with 381 men on board. The *Windham* was recaptured, but those from the *Ceylon* had to wait until Mauritius was conquered in February 1811 to be reunited with their comrades.

The biggest hazard to expeditions, reinforcements, and redeployments was the weather. A catalogue of problems delayed the sailing of the expedition to the Caribbean planned for October 1794 so that it eventually sailed four months late. The impact of this was compounded, as it meant these soldiers arrived in the Caribbean in the worst season for their health.[52] Most famously, gales in the winter of 1795/6 repeated disrupted the massive reinforcements planned for the Caribbean. Not only were troops delayed, but some got through the storms and sailed on whilst others returned to ports in Britain and Ireland.[53] Such problems added further levels of uncertainty about the supplies needed for an expedition. As an army could not forage at sea, any sea movement of soldiers needed to have a good surplus of supplies to cover an unpredictable voyage. This meant holding a reserve in case of evacuation and the voyage back, as well as enough for supplies once the landing had taken place. This massively multiplied the volume of food needed even for expeditions over short distances. For instance, six weeks' supplies, as well as reserve of fifteen days' supply of meat and thirty of bread for 40,000 men, were allocated to the transport ships for Walcheren Expedition.[54]

Movement across the North Atlantic between the Britain and Ireland, Iberia, Gibraltar, North America, and the Caribbean could take between one and two months, with the 1/23rd Foot experiencing most of these routes as it moved from England to Nova Scotia (4 February to 16 April 1808), from there to the Caribbean (29 November 1808 to 16 January 1809), and back again (6 to 17 April 1809). Its movements indicate that Nova Scotia was being used as an operational base for the Caribbean and western Atlantic. The 1/23rd then joined the army in Iberia, arriving at Lisbon on 11 November 1810 after a journey of one month and one day from Nova Scotia.[55] In total, the 1/23rd spent almost half a year at sea between 1808 and 1810, and added to which was the time spent waiting at ports to be embarked, load, and unload. When such movements are aggregated across the Army a significant proportion of Britain's manpower was at sea or preparing to embark. The figures in Appendix A indicate some of the number of troops on passage. Indeed, large numbers could temporarily disappear from official figures whilst they were at sea. In October 1807, for example, there was no report for the 25,000 troops that were returning from Denmark after having participated in the expedition to Copenhagen, compounded by a further 4,000 that were returning from Egypt for which exact figures were missing.[56]

All these points need to be framed in the context of changing military situations, shifting politics in the UK, and distances and the time communications took. This meant that the deployment of the Army could spiral out of control. In 1807 the collapse of the Fourth Coalition and Spain and Portugal increasingly being viewed as soon-to-be enemies coincided with the Portland ministry replacing the Ministry of All the Talents. The incoming government initially decided to withdraw troops from the Mediterranean, where the Talents had sent them to put pressure on the Ottoman Empire and counter French expansion. In October 1807, the Portland Cabinet changed its mind and wanted to keep the force there. However, Lieutenant-General Sir John Moore, commanding at Sicily since July 1807, had evacuated Egypt (as per instructions of June),[57] withdrawn 7,200 troops from Sicily and was heading back to Britain. Uncertain of where Moore's force was, the government despatched a reinforcement to Sicily, and another force to secure Madeira. It was only the weather that restored the situation, as in December 1807 Moore's force made it back to the Britain and a gale stopped the outgoing reinforcement for Sicily.[58] The Army's wanderings were not over though, as Moore then commanded a force sent first to Sweden and then back again to Iberia. Perhaps the only upside to this was that it kept the British Army out of the immediate offensive reach of the French Army when it was probably at the peak of its military effectiveness between 1805 and 1809.

Yet sea power and the movement of troops by ships could also facilitate the projection of military power. One of the most ambitious and successful conjunct operations was the invasion of L'Ile de France in the Indian Ocean in 1810 (which eventually liberated the captured soldiers of the 24th Foot discussed above). It combined 8,000 soldiers from the Cape of Good Hope and all three Presidencies of the EIC that mixed British Army units, sepoys and other locally-raised troops in a co-ordinated assembly and assault of the northern part of the island.[59] Plate 3, an illustration by Richard Temple of the 65th Foot, who produced a series of drawings, watercolours and prints during his military career,[60] gives some idea of what was involved in disembarking troops for a beach-head assault, which in this case was through a narrow passage between coral reefs that had been identified by Royal Naval officers and was unknown to the French. As a result, this landing was unopposed, but this calm conveyance of troops from ship to shore was not a typical experience and the British Army's amphibious operations included fighting on the beaches of Caribbean islands, Holland, southern Africa, and Egypt.

As well as spending time being transported at sea, soldiers were used as marines. During the 1790 crisis with Spain and between 1793 and 1795, the Marine Corps (it became the Royal Marines in 1802) was not strong enough to meet the needs of a fully mobilized Royal Navy and so regiments of foot filled this gap. Decisions about how many soldiers and were from were usually taken by the Admiralty and Home Secretary without much consultation with the Army command, which had significant impacts on the units and the Army as a whole. Between May and July 1790 detachments from eight battalions (3rd, 12th, 17th, 29th, 34th, 37th, 53rd Foot and the New South Wales Corps) were drafted onto Royal Navy ships, practically leaving Britain without any infantry for its own defence.[61] As they were often sent in small detachments of less than a hundred men these units were broken up and so took time to be reconstituted into useable infantry units after marine service. The need for marines was just as acute during the war with Revolutionary France, and ten units served as marines at some time between 1793 and 1795 (2nd, 25th, 29th, 30th, 86th, 91st, 97th, 108th and 118th Foot). Again, they were deployed in small detachments and sometimes with frequent changes of ships. Soldiers from seven different units, for example, served on HMS *Boyne* between February 1793 and January 1795.[62]

The time and effort required to transport troops meant that when units were sent overseas to distant garrisons they often stayed there for many years, with their strength gradually being worn down by service and disease. Often when units were ordered back to Britain and Ireland they drafted any private soldiers into remaining units, so cutting down on the demands on the transports but leaving these units ineffective for some time.[63] When the 33rd Foot left Fort

St. George (Chennai) in February 1812, for example, 531 rank and file were spread across other units in South Asia and only 135 sailed for England.[64] During some of the few peacetime years in the eighteenth century, a system of shifting regiments around different postings was implemented, although not encompassing all garrisons and units. In the 1780s, an ambitious annual rotation system was implemented, linking Britain, Ireland, Gibraltar and Canada in a transatlantic regimental merry-go-round,[65] but it took time for units to be rotated back to Britain or Ireland. The 14th Foot was stationed in Jamaica from 1782 until it arrived back in Britain on 10 June 1791.[66] Units in South Asia served there for even longer. The 73rd Foot embarked for India on 21 January 1781, and did not return to Britain until June 1806, spending 25½ years overseas.[67] The experience of the 73rd was not peculiar to the 1780s, as the 12th Regiment of Foot was sent to India on 8 June 1796 and only came back 21 years later.[68]

For the artillery, the system was slightly different, but no less affected by the challenges of distance and transportation. As it was relatively easy to ship men in small batches to stations across the globe, artillery companies tended not to move once deployed. Between 1793 and 1815 one in seven of the marching companies were stationary, and three troops of the Royal Horse Artillery were based in Britain and Ireland throughout too. Of those that did move, changes were few, infrequent, and tended to be exchanges of manpower rather than moving the company and all its equipment. Typical of this experience was Captain Abraham's company of the 2nd Battalion Royal Artillery, which spent the entire French Wars period in Gibraltar, except for when a small detachment was sent to Toulon in 1793. Those that were redeployed were not always immediately effective, as companies sent out with expeditions were usually sent without horses to move their guns and equipment. Where the campaign was relatively close to shore, the artillery could rely on sailors and soldiers to provide the muscle to move guns, but generally the difficulties transporting horses overseas immobilized artillery and severely limited what could be sent overseas. Although the Royal Artillery expanded from a force of around 3,000 men in the 1780s to over 25,000 by 1813, the expansion was largely contained within Britain and Ireland. At its peak in 1814, 6,500 men of the Royal Artillery of all its branches (so including drivers) were in Iberia, yet there were twice that number in Britain and Ireland. Between 1794 and 1814 most of the corps was stationed in Britain and Ireland, with on average 15,000 artillerymen – and as much as 80 per cent of its manpower in 1804 – stationed there during the Napoleonic Wars.[69] The high numbers reflect the important role that the artillery had in defending against an invasion, just one of the various demands on the Army's numbers.

Demands

Soldiers were needed in Britain, Ireland, and the Channel Islands as they faced major and sustained threats of invasion, which were particularly acute in 1798, 1801 and 1803 to 1805. During these years, the French plans for invasion were largely based on an armada of small craft designed for a descent across the English Channel, but invasions though fleet landings were also a possibility outside of these years.[70] Indeed, a French fleet with 16,000 men made it to Bantry Bay in December 1796, only to be dispersed by a storm.[71] It might be supposed that the Battle of Trafalgar removed the threat of invasion, but it persisted through the Napoleonic Wars and it was not until late 1813 that the potential for a French invasion completely receded. By 1810, with the annexation of the Kingdom of Holland and north-west German states into the French Empire the entire continental North Sea coast from Calais to Denmark was under French rule or influence. This ensured French control of the river systems of northern Europe, enabling them to transport men and material from central Europe to the coast. More worryingly, it facilitated Napoleon's plans to undertake a massive shipbuilding programme, coupled with developing ports, building new harbours and improving fortifications at them. This effort aimed at having 150 ships of the line by the mid-1810s, not only outnumbering the Royal Navy almost 50 per cent (and with larger battleships) but crucially all concentrated in European waters. This build-up was serious enough that the Commander-in-Chief's staff produced a memorandum on how to counter an expected invasion by a 160,000-strong French army in 1811.[72] As can be seen in Appendix A, for the years 1793 to 1810 five or six out of ten of the soldiers of the British Army were in Britain, Ireland, or the Channel Islands. French invasion plans were finally undermined by Napoleon's decision to invade Russia in 1812, and the subsequent drafting of workers and sailors to rebuild the army in 1813. Yet at the end of the war in Europe, France had rebuilt a fleet of eighty battleships.[73]

The Army was not well prepared to counter an invasion of Britain and Ireland. In the 1780s the rotation of units to fulfil global demands and rebuilding after the American War of Independence meant that many infantry units were weak and composed of young soldiers, and in no real state to face an invasion.[74] In January 1784, the Army in Britain and the Channel Islands was 3,800 men below its establishment of 16,300, and in 1791 the fourteen battalions there averaged 411 rank and file, each about 100 men short of their set total.[75] In early 1794 Charles Lennox, 3rd Duke of Richmond, reviewed the defence needs for the British Isles and reckoned that 10,000 more infantry and 3,000 more cavalry were needed. As he held the roles of Master-General of the Ordnance, general commanding the Eastern Military District and Lord Lieutenant of Sussex his views were be taken seriously.[76] Yet in December 1794 infantry units in Britain were 6,334 men short of their establishment of 25,401, and by June 1795 the deficit had grown to 18,060 from 65,686.[77]

More significantly, all of Britain and Ireland came under direct threat. In previous conflicts potential invasions had been orientated around French and Spanish bases on their Atlantic coasts, and British naval and military defences and plans had focused accordingly, particularly with the establishment of the Western Squadron and the Channel Fleet. The French conquest of the Dutch Republic in early 1795 and the subsequent creation of the Batavian Republic changed the strategic situation significantly, and the entire east coast of Britain was now exposed to a potential invasion.[78] Not long after taking office as Commander-in-Chief, the Duke of York queried generals commanding military districts in England about their need for troops, and calculated that at least 98,000 infantry and cavalry were needed for its defence, with additional 30 troops of cavalry and 10,400 infantry required for Scotland.[79] Soon after the resumption of the war in 1803, the Duke of York considered that 143,000 men would be needed to remain at 'home', both to provide drafts for troops overseas, depots to train recruits, and to provide an anti-invasion force.[80]

There were also other reasons for more troops within the Britain and Ireland. The extent of insurrectionary movements in Britain is still debated but there was plenty of cause for the government to be worried.[81] The French Revolution had reinvigorated radicalism in Britain and Ireland, and the rapid overturning of the *ancien regime* in France from 1789 suggested that the existing social order was not as secure as once thought. Concerns about law and order led the government to mobilize the militia in December 1792 – the first time it had been done in peacetime.[82] In the absence of a police force outside of London, the full range of internal security tasks increasingly fell to soldiers, from providing garrisons near places that were considered 'disturbed', or large towns where nervous magistrates increasingly wanted soldiers to support their authority and respond to riots.[83] Although these roles could be taken on by militia units, and occasionally part-time forces too, the government recognized that units from the Army were needed as it could never be completely sure of the obedience of militia and volunteer corps. As organizations that had closer ties to the locality as they were territorially-raised units, these home-defence forces sometimes took the side of those agitating.[84] The demands of war also exacerbated economic, social, and political tensions, with food riots in the mid-1790s, massive economic and social distress in 1800 and 1801, an attempted coup by Colonel Edward Despard in 1802, riots in London in 1810 as a result of Francis Burdett's trial, and machine-breaking by the Luddites in the north of England in 1811–12 and again in 1814.[85]

Ireland featured significantly in fears of insurrection, which were realized in a full-blown civil war in 1798. Shortly before this, Lieutenant-Colonel Alexander Hope, then a young staff officer, thought that 50,000 men were needed in Ireland,[86] and it was not just in the Revolutionary Wars that Ireland worried military minds in London and Dublin, as martial law was repeatedly imposed in Ireland.[87] Counter-insurgency operations (not that contemporaries used the term) continued well into 1803 in County Wicklow.[88] In July 1803, a coup was attempted in Dublin led by Robert Emmet, and in 1804 the Duke of York cautioned that 30,000 of the troops in Ireland should not be Irish as he was concerned about their loyalty and effectiveness if an insurrection broke out.[89] Later in 1807, Sir Arthur Wellesley, then Chief Secretary in Ireland, explored how the French might accomplish the conquest of Ireland by landing a relatively small force but one that came prepared to ferment an insurrection.[90] More generally, civil power was frequently buttressed by visible military support.

The Army should not be viewed as wholly underwriting law and order, as there were disturbances, and more often apprehension of them, within the Army and other land forces. As will be discussed more fully in Chapter 6, soldiers had a strong sense of their rights and frequently viewed their service as a contract. Soldiers were prepared to resort to withdrawing their service and occasionally mutiny when they thought that terms regarding pay and conditions were not being met or were threatened. Anxiety over the military turning their bayonets to other purposes were not limited to disputes about working conditions. In the early 1790s, there were concerns about radical ideology taking hold in the rank and file across Britain and Ireland.[91] As early as 1794 radical or anti-war handbills were being thrown into barracks in Ireland.[92] Billeting, once seen as a mechanism to maintain a close relationship between soldiers and society and so avoid military despotism, became feared as a source of infiltration for popular radicalism. The result was a massive barrack-building programme intended to separate soldiers from society.[93] The Foot Guards were viewed with suspicion as they were dispersed throughout London and so close to the artisan communities that were receptive to the ideas of the French Revolution and especially Tom Paine's *Rights of Man*.[94] On 11 May 1797, William Windham recorded that the Cabinet met to discuss the reports of an intended mutiny by the Guards the next day, and although he thought it unlikely the risks were incredibly high as they could easily take control of the Tower of London, the Mint, the Palace, and the Cabinet.[95] Unsurprisingly, in June 1797 inciting mutiny or attempting to seduce a soldier from his duty was made a specific offence punishable by death.[96] As radicalism in Ireland turned into the insurrectionary organization of the United Irishmen, so Irish soldiers came under suspicion. Papers taken when the United Irishman leader Lord Edward Fitzgerald was captured in 1798 indicated that soldiers had been sworn in as United Irishmen members in the Inverness Fencibles, Suffolk Fencibles, 'Green Horse', 6th Dragoon Guards, Louth Militia, 9th Dragoons, and Tyrone Milita.[97] Such was the worry about this that when reports circulated that radicals had enlisted in the 5th Dragoons as part of a plot to join insurgents in Wicklow it led to the court martial of three soldiers. When one man of the 5th Dragoons, James M'Nassar, was found to be involved, the whole regiment was disbanded in 1799 and a gap existed in the Army List until 1858.[98]

With the variety and complexity of the demands for troops overseas and within the Britain and Ireland, the rotation system for colonial garrisons was not sustainable, nor appropriate as it risked not having sufficient nor well enough trained troops to face an invasion. Rotation was gradually replaced by units having depots that periodically sent drafts to their parent unit overseas. At first, this was done through a system of recruiting companies that were established for units in South Asia and extended to other units in the 1790s, and this idea was more fully embraced with the creation of second battalions for many of the infantry regiments. Legislation in 1803 to 1805 that raised recruits only for service in the United Kingdom provided a boon for the Army to recreate and expand the numbers of second battalions, and further units were added during the Napoleonic Wars. In total seventy-three additional battalions were added to existing regiments.[99] This arrangement worked reasonably well, although the ideal of a first battalion serving overseas and the second battalion serving in the Britain and Ireland was not always the reality. It still resulted in units that were understrength or full of new recruits, just as they had been in the 1780s. This was particularly the case during and after major expeditions. In June 1795, for instance, the Army in Britain and Channels Islands was 26,900 men short of its establishment of 109,300, with an additional 10,500 sick.[100] In 1810 there were thirty-nine battalions of regiments of foot in England totalling 24,800 men, an average of 635 men. Worse, 7,700 of them were on the sick list, many recovering from fevers they had contracted in the Walcheren Expedition.[101] Not every regiment of foot received a second battalion, and without mechanisms to supply them they dwindled. Such was the situation of the 65th Foot, where the inspecting general noted in 1810 that it was well acclimatised to service in South Asia but so small to be off little use.[102]

Shuffling units around the globe (and they often moved as units) meant that it was not always possible to keep second battalions in Britain or Ireland, especially when there were demands for troops in Europe. So, second battalions ended up serving in European expeditions and then in Iberia, and the Duke of York agreed that if a regiment of two battalions totalled over 1,600 men then both battalions could serve overseas.[103] As the European war wore on, a tussle erupted between the Duke of York who wanted second battalions in Iberia returned to the UK and Wellesley who wanted to keep experienced units serving with him. Provisional battalions formed by combining weak units emerged after the Battle of Albuera, and although the Duke of York wanted them broken up and sent back to rebuild, the correspondence about it bounced between the two individuals for years until January 1814 when they were finally ordered home.[104] The shifting needs for troops across the globe posed conundrums for the Commander-in-Chief's office. In 1810, the French conquest of Andalusia and the consequent need to reinforce the Mediterranean coincided with calls from the commanding officer in Malta that two units there needed to be relieved and with a reorganization of troops in South Asia and the Cape of Good Hope. So, the 2/30th and 2/47th Foot were moved from Gibraltar to South Asia (their first battalions were already there) to replace the corps coming home. To get them to India, they were to move to Madeira where they would be picked up by the annual Indian convoy.[105] Later that year, the 2/4th and 1/28th Foot were moved from England to Gibraltar to reinforce the garrison, and also in the hope that a change of climate would improve their sickness rates.[106] Malta did not receive the requested relief, and all the succour that could be offered was to wait to see if the occupation of Corfu would release some troops from elsewhere in the Mediterranean.[107]

The cavalry proved to be trickier to adapt to the growing demands and deployment of the Army. As we saw earlier, because of transport and logistical constraints, a large cavalry force was not deployed until the later stages of the Napoleonic Wars, and, even then, few were sent beyond Europe. There were multiple reasons for keeping cavalry in Britain and Ireland too. Cavalry were preferred for policing duties, and ten regiments were kept in Britain in the 1780s with three units of light dragoons deployed to patrol coasts.[108] It was this need for cavalry the prompted the creation of so many fencible cavalry regiments in 1794 (as well as the Yeomanry regiments). They also continued in the peacetime role aiding the Revenue Service in the prevention of smuggling, particularly along the south coast of England.[109] Furthermore, the government and the Army's high command recognized the advantage that a large cavalry force in Britain and Ireland would provide in an invasion. As a result, some cavalry units spent most of the period stationed there. The 1st Dragoon Guards were sent to Birmingham in 1791 to assist magistrates in the wake of riots, and then fought in Flanders and Holland between 1793 and 1795. After this, however, it did not serve overseas again until the Waterloo campaign. The 7th Dragoon Guards never served outside Britain or Ireland.[110] The twin demands of policing and an anti-invasion force were not compatible either. Whilst acting to support law and order, cavalry were spread out into small detachments, inhibiting the training and co-ordination of the force in larger organizations that was necessary for it to be an effective military force to face a French invasion. Dispersion was particularly acute when units were billeted. In 1809, a troop of seventy-four men with eighty horses was spread across twelve different public houses and inns in Guildford, and some men even had their arms and horses billeted in different locations.[111] Units could oscillate between these two demands in a cycle that could last for years within Britain and Ireland without ever seeing military service overseas.

* * *

With all the competing demands on the British Army, gathering a force together for offensive operations was not easy. Something of the problems about this can be detected by the terminology used to describe these troops: the 'disposable force'. This proved to be a quite small proportion of the total man (and horse) power of the Army. At the end of 1807, for example, the Duke of York informed Lord Castlereagh, the incoming Secretary of War, that Britain's disposable force amounted to 10,100 men, of which 3,900 were Foot Guards.[112] This was not much of an improvement after nearly fifteen years of war from the brigade of Foot Guards that the Army pulled together to send to Flanders in 1793, yet in 1807 the Army was three and a half times larger than it had been in 1793. Although the size of the Army increased significantly, as we shall see in Chapters 4 and 5, outside of the periodic boosts to the Army's strength it usually only had a few thousand troops spare. One of the key differences about the commitment to Iberia from 1808 onwards was that numbers could be built up over time, and between January 1810 and 1812 the army in the Peninsula increased by around 12,000 men a year, after which it expanded at a slower rate through 1813 and 1814. This rate of growth reflected the logistical constraints of and diverse demands on a global army.

The web of conflicts, threats, and military demands across the globe through the 1790s and 1800s, both actual and in the minds of decision-makers in London and headquarters across the Caribbean, Africa and South Asia, set a framework combining the demands of security, available military resources, and the logistics to move it, which in itself was determined by the distances involved. Throughout the wars, the government and military high command proved unwilling to risk breaking out of the requirements for defence that they set themselves. Although there was a low chance of any sudden new threat overseas that required a significant deployment of military power outside Europe, the impact that a captured colony or damage to trade would have had was such that the government and the Army were cautious in their deployment of troops, choosing to keep them dispersed across the globe. Yet sustaining this commitment meant using Britain and Ireland as a depot, which deepened problems when they were threatened directly by invasion and more of the Army was needed for policing and security roles (including policing itself). The potential impact of any invasion of Britain and Ireland was magnified because it was not easy to rapidly return units from overseas. New theatres of operations were added through the war with France and its allies and satellite states, extending into Africa, South America, and South-east Asia. As a result, the growing global Army only just kept pace with the global conflicts and security needs it was set.

Chapter 3

Authority and Control

For, at a crisis of peculiar peril, when the great, if not the only means of our safety, may depend upon the judicious organization and able direction of our military force, every man in the community must feel a lively interest in the object which my motion has in view.

These words come from a speech in the House of Commons by Gwyllym Lloyd Wardle, MP for Okehampton in Devon, on 27 January 1809.[1] They opened an inquiry into perceived abuses in the commissioning of Army officers. The proceedings that followed, although not convicting the Commander-in-Chief the Duke of York of corruption, raised suspicions amongst MPs that all was not right. Votes on motions against the Duke were too close for the government and on 18 March the Duke of York resigned. Sir David Dundas, famous for standardizing the drill of the British Army in his 1792 *Rules and Regulations for the formations, field-exercise, and movements of His Majesty's forces*, became the new Commander-in-Chief on the same day until the Duke was reinstated on 26 May 1811.[2] This striking intervention by Parliament – the dismissal of the Commander-in-Chief in wartime – could be attributed to the weakening of the government headed by William Cavendish-Bentinck, 3rd Duke of Portland, in the wake of two failures to make the most of the potential of the Spanish uprising against the French. By January 1809, the government was under pressure and had bowed to demands for an inquiry into the Convention of Cintra that had allowed the evacuation of the French army in Portugal, and London already knew of the retreat of the British army through Galicia.[3] Yet we also need to be careful about reading too much into Wardle's words. His views were on the radical end of the Opposition, and he had personal reasons to dislike the Duke of York, as the private contracting system for clothing of the Army had excluded Wardle's cloth-manufacturing interests. Nevertheless, this inquiry was just one incident that reflected the Army's close relationship with politics and politicians of the era. The regulation and administration of Britain's land forces was driven by the often-competing demands of efficiency and economy, and it was the product of long-standing political and cultural bureaucratic norms, almost all stemming from the late 1600s and the development of the machinery of government. This does mean that judged against modern standards (as it often has been) the administration of the Army in this period seems elaborate, diffuse and, at times, bewildering.[4] Richard Glover went as far in *Peninsular Preparation* to declare it 'utterly irrational'.[5] This does make it even more important to understand why it was seemingly so.

Regulation

Parliament had an essential role regulating the land forces that was formalized in two ways: the Mutiny Act and financing the Army. Without these, the Army's existence was constitutionally precarious, and the requirement that Parliament sanctioned both annually ensured that there was a regular opportunity for politicians to discuss the military. In the debates on the 1812 Mutiny Bill, for example, Robert Grosvenor, 2nd Earl Grosvenor, took the opportunity to bring up the enlistment of foreigners, reports that Irish recruits were being excluded from some regiments, enrolling criminals in large numbers into some regiments, and regimental schools.[6] The range of issues that Earl Grosvenor raised may have been unusual, but it was not just opposition MPs and Lords that viewed the Mutiny Act as politically important. As the Prime Minister Robert Jenkinson, 2nd Earl Liverpool, put it in December 1813 'the annual passing of that Bill [Mutiny Bill], and the attention which the legislature was by that means enabled to pay it – the army being by this means, as it were, kept constantly under the controul [*sic*] of parliament – as one of the best securities of the constitution'.[7]

The Mutiny Act, or to give it its full title *An Act for Punishing Mutiny and Desertion, and for the better payment of the army and their Quarters*, was fundamental to military law and governance, without which the Army was unable to enforce military discipline. Originating in the events of 1688, when some soldiers mutinied against orders to be sent overseas by the new monarch William III, the Mutiny Act became a cornerstone of the constitution of the eighteenth century.[8] It both enforced military law and protected soldiers' rights as citizens, so ensuring legal limits in the use of arbitrary military force against British society.[9] (Ireland had a duplicate Mutiny Act until the Act of Union in 1801). The Act's preamble, repeated in every instance, made clear its importance: 'Whereas the raising or keeping a standing army within this kingdom in time of peace, unless it be with the consent of parliament is against the law.'[10] The importance of the Act is affirmed in the forty-eight pages devoted to it in Charles M. Clode's two-volume *The Military Forces of the Crown* of 1869,[11] the constitutional history of the Army that provides the basic stock for any analysis of the management of the Army in this period. Clode's discussion of the Mutiny Act is second only in length to the chapter on the complex history of reserve forces.

Parliamentary debates about proposed changes to whom the Mutiny Act applied demonstrated its continuing relevance. In 1787, the Opposition, led by Charles James Fox, attacked the application of the Act to officers with brevet rank (explained in more detail in Chapter 7) who were without a commission in the British Army. In 1788, there was resistance to a new clause extending the Mutiny Act to the Military Artificers, a unit of 600 tradesmen that had been recently created to help maintain fortifications. This clause particularly raised the ire of some MPs, as it applied martial law to civilians. Richard Brinsley Sheridan was the most strident, as he 'conceived the object of it to be so important that he was determined to oppose such an innovation in every stage, and to take the sense of the House at its alarming tendency'. In both debates, the issues raised were sufficiently important that the Opposition put them to a vote knowing that they would probably lose (which they did by around fifty votes).[12]

Parliamentary time spent on the Mutiny Act mirrored the broader political situation. With the accession of the Portland Whigs into Pitt's government in 1794, Parliamentary debate over the Mutiny Act all but disappeared in the mid to late 1790s, reflecting the commanding position of Pitt's government. The break-up of this coalition and the emergence of new political factions and alliances from 1801 onwards resulted in the Mutiny Act again becoming an important feature of the Parliamentary diary. Every year from 1805 there were discussions on the Mutiny Act that were of sufficient political interest that they were included in the published *Parliamentary Debates* (excepting 1809 when the passage of the Act coincided with the inquiry in the conduct of the Duke of York). Repeatedly throughout the period, clauses were proposed to enable complete freedom of conscience in religious worship, attempts to limit or abolish corporal punishments in the Army, and moves to ensure that officers could only be dismissed by a court martial.[13] Nor were these just sniping attacks from Opposition and radical MPs. A clause passed in the 1807 Mutiny Act confirmed that all former enslaved Africans in His Majesty's service were free men.[14] Later that same year, the Ministry of All the Talents resigned from office after the King refused to allow Catholics to serve in any capacity in the Army, a proposal that started as an amendment to the Mutiny Bill of that year.[15]

The Mutiny Act also had political significance as a vote of confidence in the government. Because it only lasted a year, the Mutiny Act was essential business for any government, and so it became bound up with any wider political instability.[16] There were three Mutiny Acts in the tense political situation of 1783 as the Shelburne government collapsed and was replaced by the Fox-North coalition; the first lasted one month, the next two months, and only in

June 1783 was the Mutiny Act secured for the rest of the year.[17] As Fox put it in 1784, 'Of all the acts by which confidence of a minister could be expressed, perhaps the passing of a Mutiny Bill was the most striking: it was entrusting to the direction of a minister a standing army, of which this constitution was so justly jealous.'[18] Indeed, Fox's speech was part of political manoeuvres to forestall the dissolution of Parliament in that year. The short-lived Fox-North coalition government had fallen in December 1783 over the King's opposition to Fox's bill to regulate the East India Company, and the King had replaced it with a minority government led by William Pitt. Whilst Pitt's ministry was unable to pass the Mutiny Bill elections could not be held. Pitt managed to gradually wear down the Parliamentary opposition to his administration, with motions to delay the next stage of the Mutiny Bill gaining ever smaller majorities, until it passed in the Commons on 11 March 1784. With the bill secure, supplies for the Army were also voted through, and Parliament was dissolved on 24 March, the day the 1784 Mutiny Bill received royal assent.[19]

The Mutiny Act was at the heart of the overlapping relationship between Parliament and the royal prerogative to direct, command and organize the Army. This tension was evident in the twinning of the Mutiny Acts with the Articles of War. The Mutiny Acts were the government's and Parliament's business, but the Articles of War were issued by the Crown (and by the delegated authority of the Commander-in-Chief from 1793). The Articles of War covered much the same thing: military duties, roles and responsibilities, military crimes, and punishments. The King, and his powers, mattered in the era, especially when the war in Europe was frequently portrayed as a conflict to preserve the existing social order in the face of Revolutionary France and then Napoleonic military tyranny. So the nascent Tory party of the followers of William Pitt focused their objections to William Windham's short-service scheme in 1806 as it was done through new clauses in the Mutiny Act and so changing the Crown's powers to determine soldiers' terms of enlistment.[20] John Fane, 10th Earl of Westmoreland, declared that such a move was changing the constitution of the Army because 'His Majesty called upon to sacrifice a material portion of his power and prerogative'.[21] Part of the defence that the Perceval and Liverpool ministries developed against demands to legislate for soldiers' religious freedom in the 1810s was that the Commander-in-Chief already permitted it through a general order. And so, to introduce a clause on the issue within the Mutiny Act would bring into doubt the sincerity and legitimacy of orders issued by the Commander-in-Chief, and by implication the King.[22] There was a degree of politicking in these debates, and Tory governments after 1807 extended the remit of the Mutiny Act, and so limited royal governance of the Army, when it suited them. In 1811, Charles Manners Sutton, the Judge Advocate General, secured a clause to make imprisonment an option for punishments given by courts martial.[23] The work of Henry John Temple, 3rd Viscount Palmerston, the Secretary at War from 1809 to 1828, saw the Mutiny Act expand to 147 clauses by 1813, from the 83 of the 1786 Mutiny Act.[24] These tended to be detailed clauses for particular situations. For example, as the Waterloo campaign was beginning in 1815, Palmerston introduced a new clause to deny pay, and arrears in pay, to captured soldiers if it was determined in a court martial that the soldier had not used 'due exertion and energy to save himself from being taken prisoner'.[25]

Outside of the Mutiny Act there was an impetus to examine government administration that stretched back to the American War of Independence. Generally bought together under the heading of economical reform, this was both a response to political unease about government expenditure, the influence of the Crown, and a desire to improve efficiency in the face of mounting war costs. The result was a series of reports and recommendations to reform government practices.[26] There was a further round of inquiries with a Commission on Fees that examined the payment of staff in government departments, although their recommendations were largely ignored. It took a Select Committee on Finance that reported between 1797 and 1798 to expose the rocketing fees that were being collected by officials for change to occur. In the War Office, fees to officials due on bureaucratic processes increased eightfold to £43,000 in 1796. Under such attention, reform of the system quickly followed, and clerks and office holders moved from receiving payment through fees, commissions, and contracts, to salaries that placed their roles on a much more professional standing with pay scales for service.[27] Further attention was paid to the Army through a Commission of Military Enquiry, which between 1806 and 1812 conducted investigations across the Army administration. In its nineteen reports it covered the departments of the Barrack Master General, the Army Medical Department, the War Office, Army Expenditure in the West Indies, the Royal Military College, Adjutant General's office, Quarter-Master General, Ordnance, Royal Hospital Chelsea, Royal Military Asylum, Royal Military Academy Woolwich, Commissariat and Commissary-General of Musters.[28]

Generally, the Army was subject to increasing number of enquiries from Parliament. MPs could request information about the Army to inform debate, score political points, or support their standpoints on issues. The volume of this material was substantial, and between the 1783–4 and 1814–15 Parliamentary sessions nearly 1,600 requests were made for papers to be presented about the Army. In a relatively quiet year, the basic requirements for Parliament's military business accounted for about twenty-five papers, mostly relating to Estimates for the Army. When the Army was under scrutiny this figure could double, treble, or in the case of 1810 quadruple. Peak Parliamentary sessions for interest in the Army were 1787–8, 1794–5, 1795–6, 1801–02, 1805, and then each session between 1807 and 1810.[29] These papers became more specific as the period went on. In the 1794 and 1794–5 sessions, Parliament required the Army to provide an account of the casualties the Army had suffered in the opening campaigns of 1793. The number and arrangements for foreign corps were a repeated request. In debates about the Army between 1803 and 1808 papers included information on yearly, quarterly, monthly, and even weekly, figures for the recruitment of the Army. Underlying this was an increasingly statistical approach to the Army's activities (explored more in Chapter 5), especially enlistments and casualties whereby different viewpoints about Army recruiting measures were discussed and tested in relation to their productivity and the number of desertions. This was exemplified in the papers presented in 1810 from the Adjutant-General's office on the number of desertions from the Army at home between 1807 and 1809. This gave monthly figures for desertions, and then compared a quarterly total of desertions to average effective strength in the same period, allowing MPs to explore the impact of the different military policies of the Talents and Portland ministries.[30] Corruption and profit-making were also targeted, even to the point of a request in 1806 for information about the sale of manure and 'sweepings' from barracks.[31] From 1810 onwards, each February Parliament received regular annual reports on the strength of the army and the casualties for the previous year, adding to the raft of papers Palmerston presented to Parliament.[32]

Finance

The second strand to Parliamentary oversight of the Army was the annual Army Estimates. Much like the Mutiny Act, there was an element of ritual and performance to it as the process dated back (again) to 1688 and they were usually presented at the same time as the Mutiny Bill. Fundamentally, the presentation and approval of the Army Estimates sought a balance between the Crown and Parliament. The latter voted for and agreed to the amounts that were proposed on behalf of the monarch, through the Secretary at War who bought the Estimates before the House of Commons. It was the Crown, through the administrative machinery of the Army, that made any payments from these sums. Nominally, the Army Estimates set a budget for the Army for the forthcoming year, preserving the principle that no troops would be paid for except those approved by Parliament.[33] The financing of the Army was divided into two parts, which were not always that distinct. The ordinary account listed the pay and allowances for units of the British Army up to their established strength for the future (in effect, their maximum strength), whilst the extraordinary account retrospectively detailed other monies issued for the Army through warrants that had not been budgeted for in the ordinary account.[34]

This system was open to misappropriation, corruption and delay. In the American War of Independence more and more was provided through the extraordinary accounts, such that the two forms of financing the Army were almost equal in the early 1780s.[35] Moreover, the Paymaster-General, the principal recipients of the funds, accumulated huge sums that were not overseen by any government department.[36] Political unease about this, as it gave so much control to the Crown and government ministers, led to reforms in the 1780s. Legislation of 1782 and 1783 made the Paymaster-Generals of the Army responsible to the Treasury, shifting financial arrangements from an official's personal banking arrangements to clearly managed accounts held by the Bank of England.[37] Predictability, the Ordnance Office was left out of these arrangements, and this was not rectified until 1806.[38] The Paymaster Act of 1783 meant that the Secretary at War had to present a more itemised Army Estimate, as many funds and services that previously came out of deductions from soldiers' pay were replaced with new Army-wide accounts for separate items, such as recruiting.[39] This gave the government much closer involvement in enlisting men in the Army, which we will turn to in Chapter 4.

The ordinary and extraordinary accounts continued, though. The office of the Commander-In-Chief was paid through the Army extraordinaries, as was the office of Barrack-Master General and the building a barracks across Britain in the 1790s. Gradually, the financial arrangements of the Army shifted to the ordinary account. From 1812 the Commander-in-Chief's office was paid for by the Treasury after a Parliamentary vote, though Army extraordinaries were not abolished until 1836.[40] The Army extraordinary account was smaller than the ordinary account between 1793 and 1815, with a peak of £3.8 million running alongside the ordinary account of £6.9 million for 1797, and during 1804 to 1811 the extraordinary account was never above £1 million. Between 1812 and 1815, however, huge sums were issued through the Army extraordinaries, totalling £25.3 million, but these included subsidies of money, military equipment, and supplies to European allies fighting France.[41] In 1815, the Army extraordinaries included £4.24 million in subsidies and £1.72 million for the subsistence of the Hanoverian, Dutch, Belgian, and Brunswick units in the Duke of Wellington's army.[42] In the detail, though, there were revealing figures, such as the escalating costs of supplying the Army where £4.6 million more was issued than planned for by the Commissary-General in 1814.[43]

Financing the Army was usually a focus of Parliamentary attention, though in tune to the general political situation at the time. In the 1787 the King forwent funds for the Household Cavalry to cover the extra £60,000 cost of mobilization for the Dutch crisis and so reduce the expected Parliamentary opposition. The reforms to the Household Cavalry in that year were framed as a cost-saving opportunity, with the expectation that £9,000 would be initially saved per year, followed by up to £18,000 in the future once compensation payments ended.[44] Likewise, forcing the EIC to pay for the four new regiments raised in 1787 through the Declaratory Act demonstrated the sensitivity of military finance as a political issue. In 1809–10 there was significant pressure from both within government and from Parliament to reduce military finances. William Huskisson, the Portland government's Secretary to the Treasury and one of the sharpest financial and economic minds in Britain at the time, warned in autumn 1809 that cuts were essential to continue the war and suggested reductions of £2 million from the Army, plus £1.5 million from Navy, £2 million from transports, and £1 million from the Ordnance. George Rose, Treasurer of the Navy, went further, and suggested that without cuts Britain would be doomed.[45] In Chapter 2 we saw that a shortage of specie was a particular problem, which had only been made worse in 1809 by the £2.5 million sent to the army in Portugal and the £884,275 spent on the Walcheren Expedition.[46] The expected retrenchment in the Army meant that Palmerston had to work hard to justify the Army Estimates to Parliament in February and March 1810, going through key features of savings that were made (such as dismounting twenty men per troop of cavalry) at the same time as arguing that the Army was improving and would be made more effective. Even with his efforts, the costs for military staff in Britain were not approved initially.[47]

Having voted for the funds, Parliament expected to see the ranks filled and excessive shortfalls below the Army's establishment potentially exposed a ministry to criticism. In the particularly politically charged years between 1803 and 1809 the see-sawing between the ministries of Addington, Pitt, the Talents, Portland, and then Perceval demonstrated this. During Pitt's ministry, Colonel Robert Craufurd (later famous as the commander of the Light Division) required several returns to Parliament about the strength and establishment of the Army, and then initiated a lengthy debate of the military administration.[48] William Windham, having been a consistent critic of Pitt's military policies, could point with some pride to reducing the number of men 'wanting to complete' the Army from 54,288 that the Ministry of All the Talents inherited from the last Pitt administration to 35,656 on 1 January 1807.[49] The recruitment and size of the Army was a politicised issue, and one on which ministerial competence was judged.

Financial control and scrutiny only went so far. The whole system of financing the Army was complicated by the system of army agents. These pseudo-functionaries of government were private bankers acting under the power of attorney from colonels of regiments, and through them money for clothing, expenses, and pay and food when in Britain or Ireland, were channelled.[50] (When a unit was overseas pay was issued directly from a deputy paymaster that accompanied the force.) They also handled the private banking concerns of individual officers. Army agents were not public bodies so there was no way of tracking the money issued to them until final accounts were sent to the War Office and settled.[51] £6 to £7 million a year was advanced to army agents, but the War Office could not know their cash balances; indeed, the army agents were not sure either.[52] Agents made money through an charge of 2d for every £1 for soldiers' pay that passed through them (equivalent to a fee of 1.6 per cent),[53] as well as an allowance of 1s 2d per day for each troop of cavalry and 6d per day company of infantry that they acted as agents for.[54] Additionally, although they were not banks they could accumulate large sums from advances for the regiments they administered and from officers' pay. This capital could then be offered as loans and used in other financial activities. This meant, however, that army agents were exposed to the risks of the financial markets and to errors in their own accounting or legal situation. In March 1804, the army agents Ross and Ogilvie collapsed and declared bankruptcy, caused (at least in Alexander Ross' view) by the War Office not settling accounts and their partnership having advanced money that was due to them.[55] Although wilder speculation thought that £800,000 was lost,[56] it certainly ran into the £10,000s. Their collapse forced the War Office to implement direct payments for the seventeen affected units and, typifying the complexity of the accounting and legal arrangements of army agents, government lawyers were still chasing £90,000 through the courts in the 1850s.[57]

Army agents were also a deeply entrenched arrangement within the culture of the Army and became increasingly concentrated in a few firms. In 1780 there were fifty-one army agents but by 1807 this had been reduced to twenty-four. The largest, Greenwood, Cox, and Co., acted for 194 regiments and they also handled the Duke of York's personal financial affairs.[58] Something of the dominance of Greenwood, Cox, and Co. can be judged by the £2.3 million that it received in 1811 from the Paymaster General, just shy of half the total issued to all army agents.[59] Politicians were aware of the ambiguous status of army agents and the potential waste of public funds, if not corrupt practices, and the army agent system received regular attention, but war inhibited reform. William Windham, when Secretary at War, ignored Parliamentary recommendations for changes in 1798, claiming that if they were implemented the public service would be endangered. When army agents were reviewed again in 1808, proposals were limited to clearer roles for the different parties involved and faster processing of accounts.[60] Army agents continued long after the Napoleonic Wars, and

Greenwood, Cox, and Co. continued to dominate this sector of the financial arrangements of the Army, eventually becoming part of the Lloyds Banking Group.[61] As a result, a large part of the administrative records on the Army are now held outside of The National Archive's government collections in a business archive, reflecting the status of the army agents themselves.

Management

Though Parliament had some control over the Army, it did not manage it. The management of the Army was meshed between a suite of government minsters, offices and departments, all of whom had some delegated power from the monarch. Between 1783 and January 1793 the formal management of the Army was detailed to four men: the King, the Secretary of State for the Home Department, the Secretary at War, and the Lord Lieutenant of Ireland (if it concerned a unit or military role in Ireland). Alongside these four posts sat the Board of Ordnance, to which we can add further boards and departments described below. In terms the actual management, the Home Office had nominal oversight of the Army; the Secretary at War usually got on with the business of the running the Army and only reported to the Home Secretary when he needed to.[62]

These arrangements were changed by the war with France from 1793. By 1795 two new roles had been added to the administration of the Army: the Commander-in-Chief and a Secretary of State for War, and generally more of the government related to Britain's military machine. The Commander-in-Chief was the monarch's lieutenant for the internal administration in the Army. The overlap between this role and the Secretary at War in part stemmed from the 1780s, when George III took on the function of Commander-in-Chief and worked with the Secretary at War to run the Army, and the two fixed staff roles in the Army (the Adjutant-General and Quarter-Master General) reported to the Secretary at War. In 1789, it was suggested that the Army should have a commander-in-chief to avoid the Army being too subjected to political interference.[63] General Jeffrey, Baron Amherst, was appointed to the role in 1793, with the Adjutant-General's and Quarter-Master-General's departments shifting to this new office, which became known as Horse Guards as it was housed in the Horse Guards building in Whitehall.[64] As a military appointment, the commander-in-chief's office became the executive of the Army. The re-creation of the office was particularly seen as beneficial for officer appointments and promotions, as in theory the Commander-in-Chief could deliberate on these decisions upon professional rather than political considerations.[65] It was for this reason too, that the Commander-in-Chief from 1795 was not a Cabinet member. Nevertheless, the extent of the Commander-in-Chief's jurisdiction was imprecise. At first, the Duke of York, who replaced Amherst in 1795, thought that every part of the military service was vested in his office, but the role became increasingly focused on the internal administration of the Army.[66]

The management of the Army started with the monarch, and George III was deeply interested in the Army and could intervene in all military matters.[67] Although he was unable to take personal command of operations, he did exercise the royal prerogative to direct it through the Royal Closet: the small, and often one-to-one, private meetings between the King and a select group of ministers and government personnel.[68] George III knew many of the Army's officers, certainly the senior ones, and kept an eye on military appointments.[69] He was hostile to the government's recruitment policies between 1793–5 (explained in more detail in Chapter 4), partly as he viewed them as subverting his right to appoint regimental colonels.[70] In 1806 Lord Grenville, the Prime Minister for the incoming Talents administration, intimated that they would consider new defence measures to which the King reaffirmed his right of deciding on military measures.[71] George III particularly sought to uphold the authority of his son the Duke of York as Commander-in-Chief, for example opposing the idea of a military council advocated by opposition MPs between 1803 and 1805 and by the Talents government.[72] Nor was interest in the Army confined to George III. Prince George, as Prince Regent, intervened in the long-running questions of jurisdiction between the Commander-in-Chief and the Secretary at War in 1811, coming down firmly on the side of his brother, an awkward situation for the government that was sidestepped by suggesting that the Prince had been ill advised.[73] Alongside direct intervention in the running of the Army, the King also had considerable patronage in it. The King chose regimental colonels, royal aides-de-camp, reviewing generals, and local commanders and their staff.[74] The King could convene boards of general officers to provide advice on any aspect that was thought relevant for discussion, though in most cases it dealt with matters relating to clothing.[75] Significantly, much of the business of the military was undertaken through royal warrants, royal orders, or required a signature from the monarch. For example, the Board of Ordnance could not itself issue any arms or stores but required a royal order,[76] and all officers' commissions were approved by the monarch. Such was the importance of the monarch that during George III's incapacitation in 1788 and 1789 military business was brought to a halt.[77] Nor was this as one-off incident, as there were repeated episodes of illness in 1801, 1804 and then from 1811 onwards. Lastly, the King approved all military honours and rewards.[78] This role was maintained in the 1811 Regency Act, despite restrictions that prohibited the Prince Regent from creating other peers.[79]

As was explored in Chapter 1, before 1801 the Army had a separate Irish military establishment, and the relationship between the monarch and the Irish Lord Lieutenant was fundamental to its working arrangements. In 1788 George III refused to approve the recommendations of the Lord Lieutenant George Nugent-Temple-Grenville, 1st Marquess of Buckingham, as their relations soured. Buckingham's inability to secure this patronage led him to resign the next year.[80] Within Ireland before 1801, the military establishment outwardly mirrored that of Britain, with a commander-in-chief and a staff consisting of an adjutant-general, quarter-master-general, and general officers. The commander-in-chief was subservient to the Lord Lieutenant and was more of a principal general officer amongst a board of general officers. Usually, army officers wrote directly to the authorities in Dublin Castle than through the Irish commander-in-chief, much to the annoyance of some who held the post.[81] As well as administering the army in Ireland, the staff there also served as alternative source of military advice to the monarch and minsters. Pitt, for instance, sought information directly from David Dundas about using troops on the Irish Establishment as an expeditionary force.[82] To blur lines of authority further, much of the correspondence to and from the government in Dublin went through the Home Office.

The Board of Ordnance was the oldest of the departments involved in the running of the Army, dating back to the Tudor period. As was seen in Chapter 1, the Master-General of the Ordnance had direct responsibility for the Royal Artillery and the Royal Engineers, but the Ordnance office's remit was much wider than this. It was, in effect, a munitions ministry dealing with all aspects of the design, testing, contracting, supply, and delivery of arms and munitions to both the Army and the Navy, from bayonets, millions of muskets, to the largest cannons, and the gunpowder needed to fire them. It also managed and maintained fortifications. The Board's Master-General was usually a general of some experience or political standing and had a seat in the Cabinet.[83] Under the Master-General there was a board consisting of the lieutenant-general, and four principal officers: clerk of the ordnance, clerk of the deliveries, surveyor-general and principal storekeeper. Each had clear lines of responsibilities and met collectively, and so could act as a check on each other's activities.[84]

The Ordnance is need of more modern scholarly research. Much of its historical perception stems from the Crimea era and the political campaigns that sought its abolition. The scathing opinion of it offered in Glover's *Peninsular Preparation* focuses too much on complaints without the wider context of what went well. There were, to be fair, high-profile incidents where the Ordnance was blamed for failures, such as the lack of equipment to besiege Dunkirk in 1793. During the Peninsular War the Duke of Wellington was a critic of its maladministration, but then he was critical of most government departments, and there was certainly some hostility between the Board and the Commander-in-Chief's office.[85] Nevertheless, Gareth Cole's work on the Royal Navy and the Ordnance has shown how effective it was, and although a closer study of the Army and the Ordnance is still needed, its basic performance in arming the British Army – as well as European allies and the Navy – was credible. Difficulties were caused by poor inter-departmental communication rather than outright administrative failings;[86] indeed, the Ordnance's basic rationale was sound enough that the idea of a body overseeing munitions was resurrected in the twentieth century. The Ordnance was subject to Parliamentary enquiry, but though the Commissioners of Military Enquiry (the most detailed examination of its workings) recommended changes they did not suggest that it should be abolished.

The Secretary at War, and the War Office that he ran, was admitted at the time to be an ill-defined position.[87] This was made clear during parliamentary debates about the Army estimates in March 1789, when Sir George Yonge, the incumbent Secretary at War, 'conceived it was the notion of our government that he was some sort officially responsible for every measure taken in the military department'.[88] During the years 1783 and 1793 he had wide-ranging powers as was the King's military secretary. The Secretary at War was also accountable to the Cabinet and Parliament. Moreover, the role was the primary point of contact for complaints from British society about the Army.[89] The sheer range and scale of this correspondence is conveyed in the 118 volumes of 'General' and 'Miscellaneous' in-letters now in WO 1 at The National Archives.[90] The ambiguity of the role was echoed in several aspects: it was established through a military commission, but it was a political appointment and one that was always held by a MP who reported to Parliament. They were not automatically in the Cabinet, but Sir George Yonge and William Windham (who between them were in office from 1783 and 1801), and Lord Granville Leveson Gower who held the role for a few months in 1809, were;[91] yet like ministers of state they had direct access to the King. Generally, their role related to law and finance, plus they authorized any movement of troops within Britain.[92] As Secretary at War in 1809, Lord Palmerston stated that:

> The Secretary at War seems, indeed, to be the officer who stands peculiarly between the people and the Army, to protect the former from the latter, to prevent the public revenue from being drained by any unauthorised increase of military establishments, and their persons and property from being injured by any misconduct of the soldiery; and upon him would Parliament and the country justly fix the responsibility for any neglect of this part of his duty.[93]

Palmerston's statement was the result of increasing tensions between him and the Commander-in-Chief about their respective roles, particularly on the regulation of the Army. Both offices published general orders and regulations, which the Commander-in-Chief thought was solely his responsibility.[94]

In the 1780s the Secretary of State for the Home Department, a post created in 1782, had oversight of the War Office and the Army because of this minister's colonial responsibilities (until 1801) as well as the use of the Army within Britain and Ireland.[95] The actual extent of this depended on the situation and personalities of those involved. For most of the 1780s the War Office conducted its business and reported what had been done to the Home Secretary, so requests for military aid within Britain against smuggling or riots went direct to the War Office rather than to the Home Secretary. The Home Office's tasks expanded rapidly in the 1790s. It included all aspects of 'internal defence' of Britain and Ireland, encompassing the management of the militia, volunteers and other paramilitary forces, as well as preparations for potential invasion, and in Ireland's case actual invasion. It also included responses to radical activity and insurrectionary threats plus specific new departments like the Alien Office. All of these provided part of the justification for a new secretary of state. Just as significant was Pitt's desire to keep Henry Dundas, the Home Secretary, in the Cabinet whilst incorporating the Whigs headed by the Duke of Portland in 1794 (Portland became the new Home Secretary). The role of Secretary for War was vague.[96] They received communications from general officers appointed to command overseas expeditions,[97] and as the war continued, Dundas became increasingly involved in measures to expand the armed forces in the face of invasion threats, almost all of which were outside of the Army. Partly, this change was the result of Dundas and Pitt filling in the Secretary for War's portfolio in the absence of major overseas expeditions, but Dundas also recognized that home and overseas military policy were inseparable.[98] During the Napoleonic Wars, the role became much clearer as they were key in the development of policies to increase the size of the Army, as well as the decisions about deployments overseas. Additionally, from 1802 the role gained responsibility for colonies.

There were other authorities that related to the management of the Army; for example there was a distinct Army Medical Department, a Clothing Board (essentially an inspectorate and auditing function of a board of general officers) that maintained patterns for uniforms and equipment, and an Army Chaplaincy Department was formed in 1795.[99] As was discussed in Chapter 2, the Transport Board had a fundamental role in the movement of the Army. At the head of all these departments was the Treasury, with the First Lord of the Treasury being the Prime Minister. The military was the principal expense of the state and the Army's ordinary budget grew enormously from £2.4 million in 1786 to £42.5 million in 1815.[100] The Treasury also supervised the commissariat that provisioned the Army.[101] This bought in not only broad considerations of expense, but also practical issues about financial responsibilities and audit. All of these needed to be co-ordinated too. The creation of a new regiment, for example, involved the War Office corresponding with at least five different offices: the Treasury to fund recruiting and subsistence; the Paymaster-General for pay to the army agents; the Ordnance for arms and equipment; the Clothing Board for contractors to arrange a meeting to view clothing patterns; and the Medical Board to issue medicines.[102]

More broadly, the Cabinet could discuss military deployments, plans and operations, but it seldom took on this role before 1793.[103] It only discussed military movements three times, and then in response to international crises of 1787 and 1790 and the movement of the 49th Foot from Barbados to Jamaica in 1791 as the situation in Saint-Domingue presented new threats to the island.[104] The lack of Cabinet attention to the military reflected Pitt's approach to government, where he was more likely to seek advice from military officers directly. This tendency was reinforced as Pitt was not on good terms with Thomas Townshend, 1st Viscount Sydney, the Home Secretary between 1783 and 1789, and whilst Pitt was close to the Master-General of the Ordnance, Charles Lennox, 3rd Duke of Richmond, the latter did not attend Cabinet meetings.[105] The situation improved with the successive appointments as Home Secretary of Lord Grenville and then Henry Dundas in 1789 and 1791 respectively, whom Pitt worked better with.[106] Almost all the other major departments of state related in some way to the Army too. The Foreign Office was intimately concerned with the deployment of the Army overseas as it related to Britain's diplomatic relations, particularly in Europe but also across the globe. Likewise, the First Lord of the Admiralty's concerns extended to the Army, from the grand strategic issues of protecting the infrastructure of the Royal Navy down to practical issues such as the need for regiments of foot to serve on board the Navy's ships as marines. The India Board of Control encompassed the security needs of the EIC and so the units of the Army employed across the Indian Ocean. All these offices meant that there was a wide range of people involved in running the Army.

Personnel

These administrative roles just discussed were not static. They changed and adapted in response to external factors, the individuals who held these positions, and the dynamics of their interaction with other offices. Pitt had been relatively un-engaged in military business in the early 1780s, but he increasingly intervened in the management and decisions about the Army in the 1790s. For example, in 1792 Pitt and Dundas set up a new Barrack Master General's department under Oliver de Lancey, which oversaw the biggest barrack-building programme in Britain up to that date and bypassed the responsibilities of the Master-General and Board of Ordnance for military accommodation.[107] This further contributed to the Duke of Richmond's political isolation, although his abrasive character did not help. He fell out with both Dundas and the Duke of York and was effectively ejected from office by Pitt in January 1795 because he could not work with others.[108] Additional responsibilities were grafted onto existing roles too. When William Windham joined the government in July 1794 as Secretary at War (and with a seat in Cabinet) he also became a minster responsible for foreign corps in the Army and supporting French royalists more generally. Yet Windham only heard that Pitt was going to reduce the foreign corps in 1797 through the Duke of Gloucester, indicative of some of the blurred responsibilities and inadequate communication between ministers.[109]

The political situation also bought new challenges. Bringing the Portland Whigs into government involved shuffling office-holders, the creation of new posts, and changing roles of existing ones to accommodate new personnel. They also bought different ideas about the war and the nature of the conflict against France. Portland and Windham were politically inspired by Burke and so overturning the French revolutionary government was the only way they could foresee any future security for Britain and Europe. Hence Windham's enthusiastic support for French royalists.[110] Yet it was not immediately obvious how different the conflict with France would be to others less enthused with Burke's prophesies. Initially Pitt, Grenville, and Dundas thought about war within the standards and practices of the eighteenth century, and so capturing colonies whilst defending Flanders made sense if Britain was going to treat with France at some point.

Such a diverse range of interests, and personnel, meant that the Prime Minister's role involved arbitrating between different, if not outright rival, demands.[111] Although the Cabinet bought together all the secretaries of state, the Master-General of the Ordnance, and the First Lord of the Admiralty, and was formally the decision-making forum, it was not mandatory to discuss strategy there. During the French Revolutionary Wars, Pitt generally tried to avoid Cabinet meetings, and he formed a triumvirate with Dundas and Grenville (then Foreign Secretary) to discuss policy and then presented decisions to Cabinet.[112] Yet this did not necessarily avoid clashes, as Grenville favoured direct intervention in Europe whilst Dundas favoured colonial expeditions. In effect, Pitt became the chief minister of defence, but this was largely down to his political and administrative influence and abilities.[113] During the Tory ministries of Portland, Perceval, and Liverpool, the Cabinet became better established as a policy discussion forum, where papers and memorandum were presented by ministers for discussion and decision.[114] The gradual improvement of the management and decision making relating to the Army was not linear, though. A lot of progress was made in the late 1790s, exemplified by the competence at all levels shown in the expedition to Egypt, but it was undone by the second period of political turmoil between 1802 to 1809. In the opening six years of the Napoleonic Wars there was a succession of ministers and ministries who bought their own ideas and agenda to the direction of the Army. As is detailed Appendix B, in this phase of the war with France there was five ministries, six secretaries of war and seven secretaries-at-war; the Board of Ordnance was relatively stable in the circumstances, with three changes but two officeholders (John Pitt, 2nd Earl Chatham, served twice between 1801 and 1806 and then 1807 and 1810).

The insurmountable logistical demands of any direct invasion of France and Britain's relative military weakness as an independent force meant that the Cabinet was left to debate alternatives: some championed intervention across Europe (and then there were further decisions between western or southern Europe), others looked for ways to encourage alliances and allies through deploying troops, whilst others promoted colonial gains. This meant that any minister could shape and contribute to the direction of the Army. This was most acutely shown in 1808–09, when it was George Canning, the Foreign Secretary, who was the keenest advocate of committing to defend Portugal and convinced the Cabinet to send further reinforcements to Portugal under Arthur Wellesley in 1809.[115] These debates were shaped by the diplomatic and military situation across Europe, which was more complex that it might appear at first glance. At the start of the Napoleonic Wars, the Secretary for War Robert, Baron Hobart, created an expeditionary force for service alongside any potential allies to break the strategic deadlock of solely fighting against France and its partners. Based on early discussions with Russia as a potential ally, Naples emerged an area for co-operation that had some strategic alignment between both powers. Pitt, when he became prime minister in 1804, continued this policy, but Castlereagh (who replaced John Pratt, 2nd Earl Camden, the Secretary for War in Pitt's government) wanted a British Army presence in northern Germany, where an expedition was sent in 1805.[116] All these plans were undone both by Napoleon's victory over the Austrians and Russians and then Pitt's death, which led to the new Ministry of All the Talents. Grenville (as Prime Minister) and Windham (Secretary for War) were the principal ministers directing the war, and they were particularly pessimistic about involvement in Europe and looked to expansion outside Europe, particularly South America.[117] The Ministry of All the Talents had barely time to turn their ideas into operations before they were out of office and replaced by the Second Portland Ministry, which contained many ministers who had served with Pitt in 1804–06. Generally, they were proponents of supporting allies and potential allies in Europe, but the difficulty was where to send them and who to support. A force was sent to Stralsund in the Baltic in the final stages of the Fourth Coalition. As this coalition collapsed, Canning, the Foreign Secretary, was instrumental in making the case for the pre-emptive assault on Copenhagen in 1807.[118] In June 1808 British troops were deployed to Portugal, but it is indicative of the fluid state of international relations at this moment that this force could have been sent to Spanish America as an expedition against Spain, but within weeks shifted to become a force supporting Spain and Portugal in their fight against Napoleonic France. This was not the main arena of Britain's military effort, though. The huge expedition against Holland in 1809 demonstrated the continued importance of the area in the minds of ministers, particularly Castlereagh. It was not until after this failure, the collapse of the Fifth Coalition and the Portland ministry that by 1810 the Iberian Peninsula became the focus of Britain's military effort against the Napoleonic Empire.[119]

The remit of government also expanded. It was not just the strategic direction of war but also military policy more broadly, especially recruitment as we shall see in Chapter 4, that became part of ministerial portfolios. Whilst Windham was Secretary for War and the Colonies, he was principally focused on addressing home defence forces by reforming the volunteer corps system and the recruitment of the militia.[120] Additionally, government discussions and decisions were also subject to personalities and domestic politics of the day. In some cases, ministers were circumvented, or appointed for patronage or for reasons of political management. Earl Camden, Pitt's Secretary for War between 1804 and 1805, was practically a nonentity and the business of the office was largely done by Pitt.[121] Richard Fitzpatrick, the Talents' Secretary at War, was in poor health in 1806 and had opposed the war in 1793 and 1803. Yet arrangements for replacing him (indeed anyone in government) required delicacy and time, and the plan to replace Fitzpatrick with Samuel Whitbread could not be implemented before the Talents government resigned.[122] Probably the most damaging incident of political and personal clashes spilling into different areas occurred in 1809. As the Portland ministry began to look weak, tied to the health of the Duke of Portland himself but also the difficult political and military situation, Canning's manoeuvring for power within the government not only led to a duel with Castlereagh but also distracted the government.[123] The decision to withdraw the army from Walcheren in Holland was delayed, and the soldiers stationed there paid the price, exposed to disease and dying unnecessarily.[124]

The collapse of the Portland ministry was not an isolated incident of political turmoil. Throughout 1809 to 1811 the Perceval ministry was threatened with being replaced as George III's illness became more acute and persistent, and the expectation that the Prince of Wales as regent would bring in a Whig government. Massive changes in government still loomed into 1812. The fact that the Prince of Wales would eventually settle on the existing set of ministers under Perceval when restrictions ended on the regency in February 1812 and, even more remarkably, that they would continue in office after the murder of Perceval in May 1812 were unexpected outcomes. It was not until after an election in September 1812, Wellington's victories of that year, and the news of the destruction of the French army in Russia that the government looked secure from turmoil for the first time since at least 1809 and arguably from 1803.[125] For military commanders, and the ministers in Whitehall themselves, establishing and maintaining control over operations was hard enough without unstable political situations, like the shenanigans that led to Canning and Castlereagh's duel.

Lack on information sharing between departments caused problems too. In the early 1790s, with the massive expansion of the Army and number of regiments that are discussed more in Chapter 4 it is understandable that new Secretary for War Henry Dundas lost track of what units were going where and when. For example, in April 1794 Sir Charles Grey received a letter from Henry Dundas declaring that eight regiments of foot that had been scheduled to be returned to Britain and Ireland should be retained in the Caribbean, yet five of them had already drafted their men into other regiments and were on the way back across the Atlantic. The reinforcements Dundas planned for Grey (1st and 18th Foot at Gibraltar) were already allocated to Corsica.[126] Dundas learnt to micromanage the Army less as the war went on,[127] but his problems were a symptom of lack of processed and accessible information about the Army. Better working relationships between departments were important to this too. For example, in July 1805 Castlereagh set broad figures for the disposable force that he wanted to assemble (30,000–35,000 infantry and 8,000–10,000 cavalry), and left it up to Horse Guards to work out what regiments to allocate to this force.[128] Equally important was access to information about the 'effective strength' of the Army, and its use by government ministers in abstracted totals and memoranda.[129] The response for better information can be seen in the documents that the adjutant-general began to create and keep, with the first 'Statistical Returns' starting in 1802, which in 1805 shifted to a page for each station listing effective strength each month and any casualties, alongside the regimental records series that detailed the establishment of each regiment and its movements.

Nevertheless, we should be careful about emphasizing the problems and potential disunity within the governance of the Army. The buildings that these offices and personnel were working within were quite physically close to each. Most of them were in Whitehall in London. The War Office and Horse Guards were next to each other, and Nash's 1814 print (Plate 4) shows how close they were to the Admiralty too. Many other offices were all within a short distance of each other. The Board of Ordnance was an outlier at Grosvenor Square, but it was only about 2km away. Sometimes, though, individuals would work away from the office. A lot was done by Pitt and Dundas at the latter's home in Wimbledon. Later in the French wars Pitt sometimes worked from Walmer Castle, the official residence of the Lord Warden of the Cinque Ports (an office that Pitt held from 1792). The King was perhaps the most physically distanced at Kew and when he was in Dorset.

Most of the records we have from these offices are letters, rather than minutes of meetings, which on reading imposes a sense of physical separation between these different sites. But these letters would have passed to and from each other quite quickly, and we find snippets about this such as the Commander-in-Chief Amherst returning three letters about raising new regiments to Henry Dundas after Evan Nepean (Dundas' undersecretary) had taken them to Amherst the day before.[130] The silences in the archival records relating to the administration of the Army are tantalizing gaps where it can be tempting to imagine quick discussions that could have taken place between officials in an office or corridor in the government buildings, in private houses or inns over a drink or meal, or in the streets and squares around Whitehall. Again, we get occasional oblique references to these, such as Amherst enclosing a paper that he wrote after a meeting with Pitt and Dundas in December 1794, although it says something about these types of meetings that Amherst added the caveat that it was what he understood had been agreed.[131] Certainly, social, political, and professional networks were closely entwined in the period, with Canning's diary (just for example) detailing the round of entertainments and social events of London where issues could be discussed.[132]

A crucial development in the effectiveness of the administration of the Army was the rise of the 'men of business' who increasingly staffed permanent roles within the government. As Roger Knight has shown in *Britain against Napoleon*, a group of professional administrators developed in this period. Their appointment to positions such as undersecretaries was much less political than secretaries of state, and they did not always change as governments came and went. One of these positions was the military undersecretary which became formalized from 1807 as a military officer who advised the Secretary for War. Some in these role-holders had long service and personified the institutional memory for their organization. Robert H. Crew was a long-serving Secretary of the Board of Ordnance; Matthew Lewis was Deputy Secretary at War from December 1775 to August 1803; and William Merry, appointed Deputy Secretary at War in December 1809, had been all his working life in the War Office, including roles as a clerk and Examiner of Army Accompts.[133] An important aspect of the importance of these deputies and secretaries was the co-operation and communication between these men, so sharing information and expertise. In 1809, several key appointments were made: Colonel Henry Bunbury as Military Undersecretary for War and the Colonies, Sir Henry Torrens as the Commander-in-Chief's Military Secretary, and John Willougby Gordon as Quarter-Master General then Commissary-General. They routinely consulted each other. Torrens and Bunbury worked together on periodic reviews of military capability, determining which units were available – crucially considering both numbers and their state of discipline – to reinforce the army in Iberia.[134] When Willougby Gordon moved to become the new Commissary-General, he again worked with Bunbury alongside George Harrison, assistant secretary at the Treasury, forming an inter-department committee that provided advice on supplying the army in Iberia.[135]

Just as important as providing clear information for ministers about the Army were their roles in military intelligence. Bunbury took on the role of military analyst, providing secretaries for war and foreign secretaries with intelligence summaries across the spectrum of military operations from strategic to tactical.[136] This was just one aspect of a sophisticated, but diffuse, military intelligence system that developed and help address the inadequacies of the 1790s. During the French Revolutionary Wars, gathering intelligence was not a significant problem,[137] but ministers tended to see what they wanted to in this information. This was most evident when it came to the hoped-for insurrections against the French spearheaded by an intervention of the British Army, firstly in Quiberon in 1795 and especially in the Netherlands in 1799.[138] In Iberia, the sifting of information from multiple sources undertaken by personnel immediately outside of decision making gave the Army a clearer picture of the strategic situation there from 1809 onwards.[139]

Working for the ministers and undersecretaries was a burgeoning group of professional administrators, who were working increasingly longer days. It is through their hands, literally, that we know as much about the Army as we do, as they were the ones who copied, kept, and indexed the records. The number of clerks and secretaries in the offices that ran the Army increased from 590 in 1797 to 1,669 by 1815. The War Office increased from 58 clerks to 208, and the Ordnance Office from 353 to 886, though the latter was also involved in supplying the Royal Navy.[140] These figures does not include clerks that were employed on the staff of the Army outside London. New, generally young, men were recruited into the running of government, with a class of professional administrators emerging in, and formed by, this expansion of the state. Attention was also paid to how things were done. The War Office is a case in point. This office audited and cleared regimental finances, and it had a backlog of 2,197 accounts in 1797. After recommendations for reforms were implemented from 1798 this was reduced to 354 by the end of 1806,[141] but it was still receiving and processing accounts from the 1780s and 1790s in the 1810s. The expansion of the War Office staff meant that it was generally keeping up with recent regimental accounts that were sent in.[142] Sadly, we know little about these people who undertook the huge volumes of paperwork that the running of the Army generated, as often the total for salaries are given but not names.

*   *   *

The Army's governance was a large, and very human, organization and criticisms of it presume that it could have started over with a blank page and recast entire structures at will. Organizational change is difficult in many circumstances, but it was especially so in the 1790s and early 1800s regarding the Army. The very flat and diffuse military administration reflected the longer political history of the Army where the formal structure and regulation reflected two, sometimes competing, sources of authority: the monarch and Parliament. Britain's military governance also suited the politics of the time. When the British government was fighting the military tyranny of the French Revolution and Napoleonic Empire so long-standing cultures of Parliamentary and political regulation of the Army were heightened. It is telling that the reviews by the Commission of Military Enquiry were thorough and detailed but did not make recommendations for fundamental changes. The administrative structure that managed the Army in the 1780s is often declared to have been ill-equipped for the forthcoming struggle with Revolutionary and Napoleonic France. The difficulty with the management of the Army was that it was so closely tied to the political situation of the day. Not just the personnel holding the offices (and their ideas and agenda) but also shifting roles. During the period 1793 to 1795 the management of the Army changed significantly, and the effects of these changes were reflected in strategic decision making and the performance of the military administration.

The management of the Army was subject to all the inflections and dynamics of British politics. Ministers changed with governments, and those that occupied roles were not always there because of their competence or interest, as appointments were also made for patronage and political reasons. Arguing that the administration of the Army was unprepared for war in 1793 is too simplistic, as the political re-alignment of 1793–5 upset existing structures and so created problems. This instability occurred again in the years 1803–12, when although the roles were better defined there was a rapid turnover in personnel. The range of different roles and departments tasked with running the Army was pliable, and deliberately so. This was both an asset and a problem. It meant that individuals could be bypassed if another minster with more nous was available to take on the roles, but this also meant boundaries were fuzzy and multiplied the effort, seen in the correspondence required to do things. Rather than thinking of the administration of the Army as a structure that should have had clear responsibilities, it is better conceived as a network that was multi-valent. It could adapt to underperformance in one area but was liable to be overwrought by a powerful individual, particularly so if the roles and personnel were in a state of flux. Pitt in the early stages of the war was the primary case of this. The Army was also subject to political scrutiny, both from a wider, long-standing wariness of the land forces and any concentration of political power in its governance, and specific politics of the moment where those outside government sought to challenge it, score political points, and hold it to account. Again, this was a strength and a weakness. It led to inquiries and debates about the Army that were partisan and could be damaging, but the military administration also became more effective in response to requests for information. This meant that the Army got to know itself much better than it ever had done.

Chapter 4
Waning and Waxing

In the reducing of the army, he remarked, that there were two methods. The one was, by reducing the number of regiments very low, but then to keep up a larger compliment [*sic*] of them, than was usual, in those regiments, that stand. The other was, by keeping a larger number of regiments with all their officers, but with few of them.

This last mode was one which Government had adopted, because it enabled them, without infringing that economy so essentially necessary to relieve us from our present embarrassed circumstances, to reward many worthy and deserving officers, by retaining them in the service and to keep up a skeleton of a large army; which, in case of a future war, might be readily filled and recruited with men.[1]

With this statement Richard Fitzpatrick, the Secretary at War in the Fox-North ministry in 1783, cut the Army by over 90,000 men down to 30,000. The necessity of a reduction given Britain's massive debt following the American War of Independence was not queried and the government was able to reduce the expense of the Army by £100,000 compared to the peacetime establishment of 1763. The Army also needed to discharge thousands of soldiers who had enlisted for the duration of the war only and were becoming understandably unruly (and in a few cases mutinous) at being kept on.[2] Fitzpatrick's statement shows there was a question about the structure of the Army in the peace. Alongside the financial benefits of a skeleton army, he further justified the policy by looking to any future increases. Expanding existing regiments would allow new recruits to learn military habits from old soldiers, and Fitzpatrick highlighted the evidence from the American War of Independence which showed that completely new regiments lost larger numbers through sickness and poor management of their personnel.

Fitzpatrick had set a blueprint for the expansion of the Army. His policy was abandoned before the war started with France in 1793 and although nothing was brought in to replace it, the Army and military administration could draw upon a back catalogue of recruiting initiatives and policies from the Seven Years War and American War of Independence.[3] The financial and administrative reforms of the 1780s also meant that from 1783 the recruitment of the Army had become more explicitly a government function,[4] and the new position of Secretary for War increasingly took Army recruitment into its portfolio from 1794. Enlistment into the Army was broadly divided into two forms: routine recruitment undertaken directly by the Army, which became known as ordinary recruiting; and interventions to boost the Army's strength by government, often in the form of legislation. As Fitzpatrick outlined, one fundamental choice was between enlarging existing units or creating new ones, and within the latter whether they were to be regiments of the line that could serve anywhere in the world (so more militarily useful) or restricted in some way (which tended to produce more recruits). The policies adopted oscillated between different options throughout the period, often a result of the political situation as much as military need.

Frenzy of Recruiting

When appreciated in the context of the era, the decision to keep a larger number of over-officered but small regiments was a sensible choice. Had William Pitt's ministry wanted to alter this arrangement in the 1780s it would have involved valuable political capital, as the size of the Army was a broadly supported financial settlement and upsetting this was risky. Although Pitt had secured a Parliamentary majority in the 1784 election, there was still a large group of independent MPs whose support was necessary,[5] and who gave Pitt's government a series of Parliamentary rebukes about the military in the mid-1780s. The Duke of Richmond's plans, and their associated costs, to improve the fortifications across the south coast of England were defeated in 1785 and 1786 despite being intimately linked to Britain's maritime power. The Duke of Richmond's heavy-handed approach to managing the process did not help, but this itself was evidence of the conditional support for Pitt's government.[6]

The Army's structure in the 1780s ostensibly left some officers spare for recruiting and capacity for expansion but the Army's global commitments thwarted the plan. Available officers and NCOs did not mean that they would be good at recruiting, especially when most regiments were outside Britain and Ireland. The Dutch crisis of 1787 highlighted these issues. Many units had not been recruiting between 1783 and 1787, as their officers were needed with the units and so they lacked territorial influence or connections to draw recruits from. When they did go on recruiting duty, they proved to be inexperienced in the work (especially newly-commissioned officers).[7] As a result, the Army proved unable to recruit men up to its increased establishment.[8] In response four new units were raised (74th to 77th Foot) to reinforce the British Army in India,[9] and two battalions were added to the 60th Foot for the Caribbean. The

Nootka Sound crisis of 1790 provided a second opportunity at mobilization, and then expansion came through creating independent companies that were then transferred into existing units. Usually raised by officers from the half-pay lists, the independent companies recruited 5,700 men in six weeks.[10] This highlighted the potential of those who could make a business of recruiting men to boost the numbers in the Army.

The experience was not lost on William Pitt and the War Office, and in the early years of the French Revolutionary War they instigated a bewildering expansion in the number of units in the Army. In early 1793 infantry units were given the chance to expand up to 1,050 men with a deadline of three months to achieve it. Not one unit managed this,[11] and so the government turned to creating independent companies and then whole new units. There were three waves of independent companies: in early 1793, March and then October 1794. Keeping track of exactly how many of these companies were created is not easy, as they had no other designation than the officers in them, which in some cases changed frequently, nor is it clear if all of those which were planned were created. Still, there were 124 in the 1794 *Army List*. Essentially, adverts were placed in *The London Gazette* calling for officers, both those serving and on half pay, to put themselves forward to raise the men through these companies with the offer of promotion as an incentive.[12]

Alongside the independent companies, the government received offers to raise entire new units, as well as sometimes suggesting to individuals that they might like to try and raise a unit. This resulted in a massive expansion of the number of units at the outbreak of war, and some with different terms of service. As Appendix C shows, forty-two new units were added in 1793, mostly regiments of foot and fencibles. This was a big enough change, but nothing compared to 1794 when 152 new units were raised, mixing new line regiments of cavalry and infantry, units recruited in north-west Europe, and yet more fencibles. The motivations for offering a unit were varied. For many, it was an opportunity for promotion within the Army. More generally, it was a chance for reward or recognition from government ministers, an opportunity to flex and expand their own patronage network, cement ties or increase influence.[13] In a few cases, it was a new theatre in which to play out existing political tensions. In the north-east of Scotland for example, the rivalry between the Gordon and the Hay families in Aberdeenshire led to the creation of separate units.[14]

Recruiting with Britain and Ireland was divided broadly into two forms: territorial and commercial. The former meant that new units were built from a patchwork of connections and influence. On some occasions this patchwork was quite a tight geographical range of men recruited from the same region serving under officers from that area. This was certainly the case for the many fencible cavalry units raised in early 1794, where, with the support of county meetings, local subscriptions and locally well-known gentlemen becoming officers, men joined their respective county unit.[15] Fencibles also had the attraction of geographically-limited service, and they accounted for a large part of the increase in the size of the Army in early years of the war with France. The second basis for recruitment was to turn to individuals who could find men, resulting in some officers contracting out their quota of recruits. These crimps, as they were known, were notorious.[16] Furthermore, under time pressure to meet quotas and so secure their commissions, officers of even overtly territorial units could turn to the soldier trade. Francis Humberstone MacKenzie used London crimps to find men whilst raising the 78th Foot as a 'highland' regiment,[17] as did Sir James Grant of Grant when he raised the 97th (Inverness-shire) Foot. All this meant that regional titles were often meaningless; indeed, recruiting in London for the 97th Foot brought in Italians and Portuguese.[18] In 1794 'town' regiments were authorized whereby 'magistrates and principal persons' could take on the patronage of these corps. This offered officers a promotion for raising a certain number of recruits, in a pseudo-pyramid scheme where the unit would be made up to 710 mostly by new captains finding fifty men each and lieutenants twenty.[19] New units were raised in Manchester, Aberdeen, Norwich, Bristol, Glasgow, Coventry, Wakefield, Liverpool, Lincoln, Exeter, Leeds, Sheffield, and Birmingham.[20] Raising a unit was an opportunity for boroughs and corporations to show their loyalty. The 104th (Royal Manchester Volunteers), for example, were supported by Manchester's Church and King club.[21] Despite their titles, we should be wary about assuming that they were full of their name's townsfolk.

In its worst excesses the desperate scramble for men to secure rank in the Army in 1793–5 became human trafficking. Bounties offered to recruits shot up to as much as £33 in London, ten times what they had been in the 1780s, and money was to be made through recruiting through 'finders' fees'.[22] As just one example, Charles Reilly a sergeant in the Earl of Granard's regiment (which later became the 108th Foot) was convicted of kidnapping John Walsh in Dublin. As the newspaper report of the trial recounts, John Walsh was:

Proceeding between the hours of ten and eleven at night on the 21st ult. To his lodging in High Street from his master's in Skinner-row, and was met by a woman, who endeavoured to allure him to go drink, and put a shilling into his hand. He refused the invitation to drink, and rejected the money. During the altercation with the female, the prisoner [sergeant Charles Reilly] came up, and, insisting he was enlisted, collared him, the woman at the same time going for the Police, by whom he was taken to Werburgh's watch house, and there held in close durance till next morning.

The jury saw through the scam and sentenced the sergeant to six months' imprisonment.[23] Female involvement in recruiting was not limited to colluding with sergeants in late-night scams. Perhaps there is not so much difference, except one of social class, between this incident and Lady Madelina Sinclair (daughter of the Alexander Gordon, 4th Duke of Gordon) reputedly offering kisses to every man who enlisted for the regiment her husband Sir Robert Sinclair, 7th Baronet of Stevenson, was helping her father to raise. This incident was later corrupted into the legend that recruits for the 100th Foot (later renumbered the 92nd Foot) took the King's shilling from Jane, Duchess of Gordon's own lips.[24]

Crimp houses were established in major towns across Britain and Ireland, and men were lured into enlisting through various combination of drink, sex, induced debt, false promises and kidnapping.[25] The social tension this caused erupted into anti-crimp riots in London in August 1794. Fuelled by agitation against the government, the war, and new militia legislation in the City of London, the flashpoint came with the death of George Howe who was kidnapped, bound and then later found dead in Johnson's Court, Charing Cross. Londoners attacked a crimp house and released those held inside.[26] As the print *Kidnapping, or a disgrace to old England* made clear (Plate 5) they had every right to be angry. Although we need to be cautious about the circulation and intended audience of prints like this, the incident was widely reported in newspapers across Britain.[27] Nor was this the last incident of recruitment for the Army leading to disturbances. Finding crimp houses, releasing those inside and then sometimes destroying the property continued into 1795.[28]

A further source of manpower that was extensively utilized at the start of war with France was recruiting soldiers from western Europe. In the 1793–5 campaign in Flanders, the Army had access to the well-established soldier trade in the *Reich*, which was supported by Britain's, and the British monarchy's, long-standing relationships with states in northern and western Germany.[29] This involved both raising new units or agreeing contracts with existing units. For example, Captain George William Ramsay (30th Foot) raised a unit of riflemen, which became the York Rangers (also known as Ramsay's or the York Chasseurs); Moritz Gustav Aldoph, Prince of Salm-Kyrburg, offered a unit of hussars and light infantry that were added to the Army in 1794.[30] The British Army bought, literally, other units into its service, like the Legion of Béon that saw a lot of fighting as part of the Dutch Army in 1793 and 1794 and was taken into British pay when the Netherlands were evacuated in 1795.[31]

People fleeing the French Revolution presented new manpower opportunities for the Army too. Émigré officers of the former French Royal Army who had dispersed through western Europe offered to raise units and fight against the Revolutionaries. Care is needed when categorizing such units; they were often distinguished as either white (for émigré) or black cockade regiments, but the boundaries were blurred. Some clearly started out as émigré units, at least in terms of their officers, such as the Loyal Emigrant Regiment we met in Chapter 1 or Charles Jean d'Hector, comte d'Hector's *La Marine Royale* regiment. Yet the *Royal Louis* regiment and Maclean's Chasseurs, both raised in Toulon and so ostensibly also French counter-revolutionaries, were not counted as white cockade units. The greatest extent of émigré recruitment came in May 1795, when small cadre units were created composed of a skeleton establishment of officers, with 'gentleman volunteers' serving in the ranks, that were intended to provide leadership and a military framework to incorporate soldiers recruited in France after a landing. The disaster at Quiberon in 1795 undid all these plans. Sometimes these offers were from 'foreign' officers within other European armies. Such sources of manpower were particularly welcomed by William Windham for both ideological and military reasons.[32]

The results of the recruitment efforts at the start of the French Revolutionary War were spectacular and terrible. More than 77,000 men from Britain and Ireland were added to the Army between April 1793 and December 1795, but it came at an awfully high social and military cost. The Army now had numerous units composed of new recruits and NCOs, commanded by a mixture of officers returning to the service and recently-commissioned officers, most of whom owed their rank to their ability to get recruits rather than any sense of seniority, let alone military ability. Furthermore, in the case of the fencibles they were limited to where they could serve. As the Duke of York put it, the new corps 'were generally composed of very bad Materials, and from the ignorance and inexperience of the Officers were very slow in obtaining a degree of Discipline'. In contrast, most of the pre-1793 regiments were only up to a third of their establishment strength and had practically been prevented from recruiting because of the competition with the new corps.[33] The outrage at the methods used to enlist men when coupled with the deaths and sickness so evident from service in the Army between 1793 and 1795 did huge injury to the Army's relationship with British and Irish society. In 1796 and on through 1797 and 1798 the size of the Army declined and its means of sustaining it, let alone increasing it, were nearly destroyed.

Regaining Control

The need to tackle the social damage caused by Army recruitment was voiced in the debates about the Army Estimates for 1795,[34] and the new Commander-in-Chief, the Duke of York, understood the need to address it too. In March 1795, the War Office rescinded all existing beating orders (the legal document permitting a person to enlist men for the Army), resetting the entire recruitment system. Moreover, on the decision of George III and the Duke of York, any officer who offered a bounty higher than fifteen guineas for general service or ten for fencibles would lose their commission.[35] Nor was this an internal Army matter, as the letters sent out to commanding officers were printed in newspapers.[36] Further reforms followed. Forty-three numbered and ten unnumbered regiments of foot were disbanded and the men transferred to other units.[37] The remaining regiments were given the mechanism to recruit through the addition of dedicated recruiting companies (or troops for cavalry), so providing the necessary manpower for the job and, just as importantly, ensuring that they were within the regimental command chain.[38] Alongside this, recruiting districts were established, each under an inspecting field officer who in turn were overseen by the inspector-general of recruiting, providing an additional level of control over the activities of recruiting parties. Crucially, the recruiting districts included a medical staff to inspect recruits, so addressing the lengthy arrangements where recruits were not reviewed until the unit was complete or they reached their regiment. With relaxed, and probably fraudulent, attitudes towards standards, this often led to men being discharged the first time they were seen by someone who did not have a financial interest in their enlistment. All the new arrangements were codified in 1796 with a published set of regulations.[39]

It is easy to add these actions to the list of reforms instigated by the Duke of York to modernize the Army and eradicate corrupt practices from the 1700s, but they stand in a longer line of efforts to better administer recruitment that had been undertaken since the 1780s. The two mobilizations of 1787 and 1790 highlighted problems in tracking and controlling recruiting parties, particularly between units in Britain recruiting in Ireland and vice versa. In response Colonel Henry Edward Fox was made superintendent of all recruiting parties in Britain of regiments overseas, and alongside him were two inspector generals – one each for Britain and Ireland – who oversaw recruiting by units stationed within each country.[40] The arrangements for regiments overseas to recruit were set down in published regulations of 1792.[41]

The 1790s reforms were not the end, either. The commander-in-chief, adjutant-general, and inspector-general of recruiting continued to improve regulations and control of recruiting. Inspecting field officers gained more authority over recruiting parties and recruiting officers, so that by 1812 they assumed command of recruiting parties with the manpower seconded from regiments. The legal and financial processes of recruiting were broken down and scrutinized, resulting in a two-stage process whereby a recruit received 'intermediate approval' and was paid half the bounty after approval by a recruiting district surgeon, before going on to his regiment to receive the rest of the money due to him. Streamlining and codifying recruiting eventually rendered the inspector-general of recruiting redundant, and the overall control of it moved to the adjutant-general's office. Harry Calvert bough his characteristic detection of irregularities to the role, and routinely made inquiries into poorly-performing officers in recruiting parties, and the inspecting field officers themselves.[42]

Despite the Duke of York's aversion to contract recruiting, either by officers for an increase in rank or by officers outside regimental structures, he was unable to resist further instances of this by the government. Between 1793 and 1806 there were a number of 'levies' or 'draftable' corps – essentially contracts with individual officers to raise men. This involved issuing an officer a letter of service stipulating the number of men to be raised and a date they were all due by. They were never constituted as regiments, often just having an adjutant, a few officers and some NCOs. Although the number of individuals involved in these arrangements were not huge, they were allocated large cash advances and generally perpetuated sharp – if not corrupt – practices in Army recruitment. Captain Thomas Steele was advanced the considerable sum of £12,000 in 1795 for recruiting.[43] This looks miserly compared to the £102,500 Lieutenant-Colonel John Henry Loft was advanced in 1795 and 1796, and there is evidence that he used some of the funds to bribe voters in his efforts to become a MP.[44] Lieutenant-Colonel John Ogle's actions and lack of accountability for the sums issued to him led to his suspension from the Army in 1800, an investigation, and his case was bought up in the 1809 session of Parliament.[45]

Such arrangements continued into the Napoleonic Wars. In the last moments of the Addington ministry new levies were raised particularly focused on western Ireland and northern Scotland. Battalions were added to the 78th and 79th Foot, whilst Irish levies went on to be the 98th-100th Foot, and some augmenting the 87th.[46] Alongside these, 5,700 men were raised, mostly for the cavalry, between September 1803 and January 1805 by individual officers.[47] The contract with Colonel French to raise 5,000 men was an utter failure. William Windham was already alert to the fiasco in 1805,[48] and it later attracted the ire of Parliament in 1809 when an MP calculated that it had cost £150 per man. Although William Huskisson was able to show that did not cost that much, and presented the Commons with a full account of the levy, it still showed that it had cost £41 5s per recruit.[49] Worse, it was a central part of the corruption accusations against the Duke of York and his involvement with Mrs Clarke, which was all the more ironic given the Duke's aversion to this means of recruitment.[50] One final attempt was made in 1805–06 by the Hon. Henry Augustus Dillon, the former colonel of the Irish Brigade raised in the Revolutionary Wars. Recruiting in Connaught he was able to form the 101st Foot. The poor results from these levies finally resulted in the demise of this system of recruitment, despite offers continuing to be sent to the government and Army.[51]

Recognizing the difficulties of regiments recruiting using their own manpower, efforts were made to find other ways to enrol soldiers. Firstly, men could enlist at the headquarters of regiments, something that became more practical when units developed a fixed presence within communities as the wars went on: 2,000–3,000 men joined the Army this way every year from 1805.[52] Secondly, who could recruit could be diversified, but to avoid the mass crimping of 1793–5 the Army attempted to use existing military personnel. In 1806–07, extra recruiting officers were created from half-pay officers and instructions were issued to the sergeants of volunteer corps about enlisting men. None of them proved that successful and the schemes were abandoned within a year.[53] The government and the Army returned to the idea when the local militia replaced volunteer corps from 1808, hoping that sergeants and adjutants in the new units would also be recruiting agents. The Army even went as far as allocating specific regiments of the foot to local militia regiments. Like the militia transfers (which are covered in more detail below), commissions in the regulars were on offer to local militia officers if fifty local militiamen enlisted. Local militiamen, however, had to pay back any bounty they received for joining the local militia, with a predictably negative impact on the results. Indeed, canny potential recruits would have realized they were better off joining the militia and then transferring to the regiments of the line.[54]

A further way that the Army sought to rationalize the recruitment of the Army was to address and reduce the different terms of service offered to potential recruits. The recruiting surge of 1793 and 1794 resulted in Scottish fencible units that could only serve in Scotland (unless an invasion occurred, in which case they could serve in Britain), a mixture of other terms for fencible cavalry and infantry regiments raised in 1794, plus the standard term of service for the regiments of cavalry and infantry. In these circumstances, it was not always straightforward to determine under what conditions soldiers were enlisted. This caused problems, including mutinies, in some of the regiments of foot raised in 1794 when they were drafted in 1795 (which is covered in more detail in Chapter 6).[55] Horse Guards first focused on the Scottish fencible regiments to begin reducing complexity in terms of service, though these efforts were not initially successful. Horse Guards decided to abruptly cease expanding these regiments, having only a short time before canvassed the opinion of commanding officers about enlarging them.[56] In March 1794, Henry Dundas sought to encourage these men to extend their terms of service to Britain, but this was met with resistance as the rumour circulated that they were going to be sold to the East India Company and sent to South Asia. Some regiments openly mutinied about this.[57] Dundas and Horse Guards changed tack and made an approach to individuals rather than whole units by raising new fencible regiments that could serve in Britain and Ireland and offering a bounty of five guineas to fenciblemen to transfer to these new units. Through this arrangement the Inverness Fencibles were created and recruited some men from the 3rd Fencible Regiment, and a third battalion of the Breadalbane Fencibles was raised with different terms of service from the other two. Sir James Grant went further and recruited some fencibles into the 97th Foot (1794–5) that he was raising.[58] This was followed by more systematic attempts to encourage soldiers in the fencibles to join the regiments of the line in August 1795, again for a five-guinea bounty. The scheme, however, ran into difficulties as some commanding officers asserted their right to refuse discharges, effectively giving them a veto over fenciblemen joining another regiment.[59]

To facilitate the recruitment of fencibles into other units and circumvent the problems caused by some commanding officers, Horse Guards sent details to regiment of foot and cavalry of when fencible units would be reduced so they could recruit the newly-discharged men. 1798 provided a turning point, as many units offered to serve in Ireland in response to the military emergency there and the threat of disbandment if they were not deemed militarily useful. Following on from this, some units offered to serve in Europe too. This became an official approach to fencibles from 1799, as units were faced with agreeing to serve across Europe or disbandment. It went even further in 1800, when all the fencible cavalry was disbanded with the hope that they would join the line cavalry regiments.[60]

Taking advantage of opportunities to enlist displaced European soldiers was not confined to the 1793–5; indeed, it became established practice through the 1790s and 1800s. Intervention in Switzerland in the war of the Second Coalition between 1799 and 1801 led the remnants of Swiss troops in British pay becoming Watteville's regiment after the Peace of Lunéville.[61] Although the expected counter-revolution did not occur during the invasion of Holland in 1799, nevertheless 5,000 men were recruited into the Dutch Emigrant Brigade.[62] More famous of these armies in exile were the Hanoverian troops who formed the basis of the King's German Legion, and the Brunswick regiment that was raised in Germany in 1809 during the Fifth Coalition and escaped to the coast to continue the fight against Napoleonic France.[63] Perhaps most extraordinary was the transfer of the De Meuron regiment, stationed in Sri Lanka, from Dutch to British service in 1795–6. The episode revolved around a few individuals. Hugh Cleghorn, who worked for the Alien Office (itself part of the Home Office), heard through private contacts that Colonel le comte Charles-Daniel de Meuron was unhappy with the Dutch government because it was not fulfilling the contract he had with them for his regiment. Its timely transfer to the British Army under a new contract made the occupation of the Dutch colony on Sri Lanka easier.[64]

More generally, the British Army recruited soldiers wherever it went. Commanders of expeditions and established overseas stations were frequently given the authority to raise units.[65] On occupying an enemy place it became practice to raise a unit from the local population or simply reconstitute the existing military force there. In the 1790s, the *Royal Louis* regiment and MacLean's Chasseurs were raised in Toulon by Lord Mulgrave during the town's occupation by the First Coalition armies in 1793;[66] four units were raised in Corsica during its occupation in 1793–5; conflict with the French in the Ionian Sea during the later parts of the Napoleonic War led to the establishment of two units of Greek light infantry (one in 1810 and the other in 1813).[67] This was a global phenomenon too. Almost as soon as war started with France, British military and political leaders in the Caribbean and London sought allies in Saint-Domingue.[68] The military units formed and taken into pay there included the former second battalion of the French Irish Brigade (re-designated the *87ème Ligne* in 1791).[69] In both occupations of the Cape of Good Hope between 1795 and 1801 and from 1806 onwards a Cape regiment was raised from the Khoekhoe,[70] and the occupation of Sri Lanka led to the creation of four Ceylon regiments. When Surinam was occupied in 1804, the unit of free blacks raised there by the Dutch was incorporated into the new Surinam Chasseurs.[71] Indeed, the only places where the British Army did not establish or incorporate local military forces were Rio de la Plata and Australia.

The redrawing of the European political map during the French Revolutionary and Napoleonic Wars meant that it was practically impossible for Army's continental European units to maintain any kind of territorial links for recruitment. As a result, units were amalgamated, transferred, or simply disbanded. Many of the men from the foreign units recruited in the early 1790s ended up in the 60th Foot, itself largely unable to recruit because Germany was closed to Britain from 1795 onwards. French émigré units were gradually merged, although mostly this was a transfer of officers when they wanted to continue to serve. These units increasingly turned to recruiting from the displaced at wherever they were stationed, deserters from enemy units, and enlisting prisoners of war in the UK, of which there was a growing number.[72] These units were microcosms of the dislocation of people due to war. The Queen's German Regiment (later 97th Foot) was raised in Menorca in 1797 from German speaking prisoners of war of Swiss regiments in Spanish service.[73] The practice was turned on its head in the 1810s, and Italian prisoners of war in Britain were offered the chance to serve in a new Italian levy that, it was hoped, would be reconnected with its territorial base when a British army invaded Italy in late 1813.[74]

Much like the reforms to the recruiting service in Britain and Ireland, foreign units were increasing regulated and controlled as the war with France went on. Initially, their status meant that they fell outside the established process and management of the Army. Colonel Nesbitt was appointed a separate inspector-general of foreign corps in 1795, but distinct posts were also created for the Swiss corps in British pay between 1799 and 1800, and when Lieutenant-Colonel Henry Clinton became inspector-general of foreign corps in 1800 his remit did not include Dutch corps. There were also distinct positions appointed by the War Office to oversee pay and their regulation, such as Emperor John Alexander Woodford who was the Inspector and Commissary-General of French Corps. One simple change was the gradual disbandment and amalgamation of corps, so that there were fewer to administer (summarized in Appendix C). Secondly, they were more regularly integrated into the system of audit and control explored in Chapter 5, by placing them on the establishment of the Army. Nevertheless, this took some time to achieve. The York Hussars were added to the Army establishment in 1795, the same time as the West India regiments, but De Roll's regiment did not appear in the Army List until 1803, over eight years after it had been raised. It was not until 1804 that all the foreign and colonial corps were similarly recognized, when the Chasseurs Britannique were finally added to the establishment.[75] As a result, records about foreign units are patchy. The standard returns and inspections for them in the 1790s, which were due for all regiments, do not appear in relevant archival collections (WO17 and WO27 respectively at the National Archives) but are scattered in volumes of correspondence to the War Office, if they were done at all.[76] The disbanding of many units recruited in continental Europe at the Peace of Amiens in 1802 provided the opportunity to rationalize their administration, and all the staff positions relating to them were abolished. From then they came more closely under the purview of Horse Guards. During the Napoleonic Wars new foreign and colonial corps were placed on the establishment of the Army as standard.

Bridging the Gap

Both ordinary recruitment and enlisting soldiers from outside Britain and Ireland were either episodic or unpredictable in their yield and, as will be explored in more depth in Chapter 5, these sources were often not sufficient to cover the casualties the Army suffered, particularly once it had been committed in the Peninsular War. Ordinary recruitment could be increased substantially but the detrimental effects it had on the Army witnessed in 1793–5 meant that it was not an option again in the period. There was, then, a need for different measures, but this meant working at multiple levels. Firstly, any initiative usually required legislation and Parliamentary approval. Secondly, as there was no centrally-run bureaucracy, any initiative needed to be implemented by local government authorities, usually at county level. Thirdly, the measures needed to engage with the potential recruits itself. At each stage there was the potential for confusion, delay, and deliberate obstruction. This all occurred against the backdrop of legislative efforts to improve and enlarge home defence forces (outlined in Chapter 1). In the period 1793–8 the militia was reformed in Ireland and Scotland, a Supplementary Militia was introduced in England in 1797, and defence legislation in 1798 gave enormous powers to the state to requisition land, property and resources and call out men to fight in case of invasion.[77]

During the 1790s there were a series of one-off laws to increase the Army. The first measure was the 1796 Quota Act, the lesser-known successor of the Navy Quota Act of 1795. It included provisions to obtain 6,525 men from England and Wales for the Army through mechanisms like the militia, with an unspecified demand for men from Scotland. Each English and Welsh county was set quotas to fill, a framework was set find the men, and regiments returning from the Caribbean were appointed to receive these recruits.[78] The system worked relatively well for counties with a large urban population, as authorities in them could levy the money from the population to then offer their own enlistment bounties. Middlesex, for example, found 420 men out of its quota of 428, mostly paying £21 to those who joined. All Saints parish in Hertford had posters printed advertising the twenty guineas they offered for recruits.[79] Overall, however, the results across Britain were poor. No summary was collated about the Act but based on the regiments that were allocated to receive men and for which we have returns, around 2,000–2,500 men were raised.[80]

The failure of 1796 Quota Act resulted in Henry Dundas turning his attention to recruiting from the militia, but any amendments to the constitutional force (as its protectors dubbed it) faced potentially stiff opposition within Parliament that was both ideological and practical. The reform of the English and Welsh militia in the 1750s and 1760s centred around concerns about the martial character of the nation and desires for a military force that was independent of the Crown, as well as the strategic need for a force to defend Britain. Additionally, there was a high degree of crossover between those involved in administering the militia and members of Parliament. Principal among these were the lords lieutenant of each county in Britain, and many of the colonels of militia regiments were also MPs (if they were different from the lords lieutenant). Additionally, the costs of the militia, both financial and administrative, were shouldered by counties, and ministries – particularly weak ones – risked the ire of backbench MPs and the wider community of country gentlemen who formed the stock of magistrates and local government officials by tampering with the arrangements for the militia.[81] Furthermore, militia officers were also conscious that their authority could be undermined by public discussion about the future of the force. The ministerial proposal to form combined battalions from militia grenadier and light companies was settled outside Parliament for these reasons.[82] At a strategic level too, the government needed to be mindful of the potential disruption to what was frequently a large part, if not the majority, of the military force it had to defend Britain and Ireland.

Despite regimental traditions suggesting that the 80th and 81st Foot were created from militiamen in 1793, direct recruitment from the militia into the Army was expressly declared illegal in 1767, and the 1786 Militia Act detailed penalties for infringing these stipulations.[83] William Robert, Viscount Feilding, attempted to bring in a bill to allow men to transfer from the militia in April 1793, but it was dropped before the process even formally began in the face of opposition from militia colonels and lords lieutenant.[84] The first ministerial attempt at asking for men from the militia had a very specific focus. Through a June 1795 Act sailors in the militia were allowed to transfer to the Royal Navy to help its manpower shortages, as well as requiring militiamen trained as artillerymen to move to the Royal Artillery.[85] Only 463 were gained by the Royal Artillery, in part because of its requirements for men to be at least 5ft 7in. Nevertheless, this Act breached the idea of militiamen transferring to other services, and further legislation in early 1798, which originated from Colonel Anstruther, focused on those who had been enrolled in the Supplementary Militia but not yet called up and sent to their units (or embodied as it was termed). A maximum quota of 10,000 men was set, bounties were offered, and in a response to the recruiting problems on the early 1790s service was limited to Europe and the duration of the war. Eleven regiments were set to receive men,[86] but like the 1796 Quota Act the outcome was poor. Most lords lieutenant were against the scheme and little direction was given by the government about how to implement it. Sending in recruiting parties from the Army to the assembly points for supplementary militia irritated militia officers too, as the parties and the bounties on offer encouraged drunkenness. Details from twenty-five counties indicate that 1,200 men enlisted, and it is unlikely than more than 2,500 men overall joined through this measure.[87]

Dundas and Pitt took a different approach in the wake of these experiences when it became essential to increase the size of the Army from late 1798. The government was negotiating the formation of the Second Coalition and a significant contribution from the British Army in Europe was an essential part of diplomatic and strategic discussions.[88] Two bills were passed in 1799 allowing militiamen to join the Army, and they were a spectacular success, adding 26,000 men so providing the manpower for the expeditions to Holland and then Egypt. The Acts addressed and negotiated the three different levels – political, implementation, and the potential recruits themselves. At a political level, Pitt and Dundas engaged with the militia interest of lords lieutenant and militia officers to develop the scheme, although there was some sleight of hand. Dundas called a meeting in late May inviting lords lieutenant and militia colonels to discuss the government's plans, but the bill was introduced to Parliament as the periodic meeting of the Parliamentary militia interest was held.[89] The Act itself was framed as amending legislation to the militia, which reduced its size (and so costs) from 90,000 to 66,000 men. The excess militiamen above the new establishment could enlist so counties did not have to make up for those who had joined the Army. The second act was quite specific about the process of advertising and implementing the scheme, things that were entirely lacking from the 1796 Quota Act and 1798 scheme to recruit men from the Supplementary Militia. Detailed instructions were sent from government to militia commanding officers, and the least successful militia regiments were sent further directions about enlisting men for the Army.[90] More importantly the legislation included several provisions to encourage the success of the scheme at all levels. Militia units were permitted to keep supernumerary officers, musicians and NCOs above their reduced establishment. Dundas' allowed militia colonels to nominate militia officers for commissions in the Army if more than sixty militiamen enlisted from the regiment, although the manpower requirement was later increased to eighty men.[91] For the militiamen themselves, there was a bounty of ten guineas, and a legal guarantee that they would not be drafted, were enlisted for five years or until the peace, and crucially only serve in Europe.[92] The success of this scheme led to a similar act for the Irish militia in 1800.[93]

Drafts from the militia proved to be the responsive boost to Army numbers that the government needed, as it was usually able to pass the necessary legislation in preparation for expeditions without much fuss. Militia transfers were implemented in 1805 (Britain only), 1807 and 1809, and each of these could point to specific military operations: northern Germany in 1805, Stralsund and Denmark in 1807, and Walcheren in 1809.[94] Their rhythm echoed the diplomatic situation, as each was synchronized with a new coalition (the Third, Fourth, and Fifth respectively). The Acts became progressively more refined and attuned to the militia interest's concerns. The 1805 Act included a provision that if four-fifths of a militia unit's quota for the regulars was met immediately then no more men were due, and similar was done in the following Acts so reducing disruption in militia units.[95] The Acts included changes to the size of the militia reducing its costs (in 1805) or boosting local patronage through expansion and removing the need for future militia ballots (in 1807 and 1809), as well as continuing the practice of allowing officers from the militia to be nominated for commissions in the Army. In the drive to secure men from the militia, some preferred aspects had to be abandoned. For instance, the Army and government wanted to allocate certain Army regiments to receive transfers from militia regiments, thereby hoping to provide targeted increases in manpower but this was abandoned in 1807 as the lack of choice was unpopular with the militiamen. And so, although the Army got an influx of reasonably well-trained soldiers, it was not always into the units it wanted. All the Army could do to manage the direction militiamen went was to prohibit certain units from receiving militiamen and once a regular unit was full declare that it would not receive any more transfers. Even then, the Army accepted the popularity of the 95th Foot with militiamen and added a third battalion in 1809.[96]

Obtaining much-needed manpower from the militia was not the only solution explored in the era. During the opening half of the Napoleonic Wars there were efforts to provide a direct and permanent solution to the Army's manpower needs. The Army of Reserve enacted by the Addington ministry in 1803 has been lambasted by historians (notably Fortescue) as a failure.[97] It deserves a better reputation as a policy as it was the first serious attempt at directly recruiting for the Army, with each county allocated a quota of men to find. It required 50,000 men to be raised by ballots in parishes but with provisions to find men before resorting to compulsion. The men raised were enlisted in the Army but would only serve within the United Kingdom and Channel Islands. Unlike the militia, these Army of Reserve men could transfer to general service in the Army at any time. Casualties, transfers, and deficiencies were reported to county quarter sessions, where £20 fines could be imposed on parishes, with the money being used as a county recruiting fund.[98] Over the ten months the Act was in operation it raised 45,500, of which 37,300 became 'effective men' after the deduction of those rejected, died, or deserted; in other words, 76 per cent of the intended quota was added to the Army. The scheme fell hard on the population, though, as it came after successive ballots for militia, led to a massive increase in the price for substitutes, and encouraged desertion from all forces, with some 10 per cent alone deserting from the Army of Reserve.[99] Nevertheless, it was not as bad as the excesses of 1793–5. What dammed the act was its association with Addington and his ministry, as the opposition focused on attacking its military policies. In the final moments of the Addington ministry, the suspension of the Army of Reserve Acts was seized by Pitt and turned into a debate about their repeal and its replacement by new legislation.[100] Looking back in 1807 Henry Dundas (by then Viscount Melville) noted to Castlereagh that he could not understand why the Army of Reserve was abandoned 'unless because it was necessary to run down the administration which first introduced it',[101] which was exactly why. Its demise, then, was political.

Having assailed the Addington ministry, Pitt presented his solution to raising soldiers in a new Permanent Additional Force Act.[102] Like the Army of Reserve it was intended to provide a systematic means of supporting the strength of the Army, but unlike its predecessor it focused on parish officials recruiting men rather than balloting for them, further stipulating that the men enlisted had to be from within twenty miles of the parish.[103] An overall quota of 78,951 men were due in 1804, but with men raised for the Army of Reserve and the supplementary militia counting towards this total, 19,782 men were left to find by 10 November 1804. Each year thereafter, 11,000 men were due under the Acts.[104] This proved to be too much for local authorities, who were already worn down from militia ballots in 1803, the Army of Reserve, creating lists of every conceivable military material for the Defence of the Realm Acts, and dealing with the 350,000-strong army of volunteer corps. Many parishes and counties reacted with passive non-compliance, waiting on the government to revisit the scheme.[105] By June 1806 it had yielded 15,778 men out of the 30,782 that were due by October of that year.

As the Acts' supporters pointed out, it took time to be understood and implement by local authorities and in late 1805 and early 1806 they sought out the evidence that it was beginning to work as it was intended. Changes in the political scene intervened yet again, and Pitt's death led to the new Ministry of All the Talents who repealed the legislation.[106] Moreover, they undermined any similar future legislation by cancelling all the penalties due under both the Army of Reserve and Permanent Additional Force Acts. This was a significant factor in Lord Castlereagh turning again to militia transfers in 1807.[107] The weaker governments that followed from 1807 would have very little chance of convincing counties and local authorities that they meant what they said when it came to balloting for the Army, as it seemed that all they had to do was wait for a change of ministry.

The repeal of the previous military recruitment legislation by Windham was part of his wider plan to completely recast army recruitment through mandatory short service of seven years in the infantry, ten in the cavalry, and twelve in the artillery. This was supported by increased pay for each subsequent period or re-enlistment (each of seven years for infantry and cavalry, and five years for the artillery), and the right to a pension after twenty-one years' service. These changes were deemed so significant that there were written in as amendments to the Mutiny Act.[108] Again, like the two measures that had proceeded them, it has largely been written off.[109] Certainly, it was undermined by the extraordinary efforts to recruit men under the new terms, which rendered the statistics about its success in 1806–07 questionable. A fierce debate took place in Parliament during the debates about the Mutiny Act in 1807,[110] and with the return of many former Pittite ministers to government in the Portland ministry, Lord Castlereagh, the new Secretary for War, went straight for a militia transfer and in a tactical political victory secured a clause that allowed militiamen to enlist for unlimited service (i.e. for life), and so started to unravel Windham's system of short service. Indeed, Windham thought the entire scheme was undone, and 'no more to be restored than lost virginity'.[111] Nevertheless, the numbers that continued to enlist for short service were significant, and 65,500 chose short service between 1808 and 1815, of which 48,000 were militiamen.[112] It is difficult to assess how many of these men would not have joined the Army otherwise, but then it would not have taken much to tip the fragile balance between the Army's intake and casualties into the negative after 1807.

That balance was undone by the commitment to fighting in Iberia. Rather than needing men for an expedition in support of a wider effort by a new coalition, the Army needed a sustained source of manpower to meet the persistently increased casualties that the Army was suffering because of fighting in Portugal and Spain. This became apparent in 1810, but many options had already suffered a political knockout and could not resurrected; all that was left was returning to the militia or some form of conscription. The latter was discussed, but the most viable solution was a systematic draft from the militia, and in 1811 annual transfers from the militia were introduced.[113] These had been a feature of service in the Irish militia since 1806, along with allowing the militia to find the necessary manpower to keep up its strength through recruiting parties, just as the Army did. This, although effectively turning the militia into a training and recruiting service for the Army, proved enough as the militia was able to expand the recruitment of full-time soldiers. Through ballots and recruiting, the militia was able to enlist 108,200 men between 1807 and 1815, enough to cover the 94,100 men who transferred from the militia in the same period.[114] Indirectly, the militia sustained the Army and found the numbers it needed whilst avoiding the problems of 1793–5.

* * *

The waning and waxing of the numbers in the Army, and the means to sustain and increase it, was intertwined with British politics. It was shaped by the immediate circumstances of individual ministries, broader attitudes towards the Army represented in Parliament, and the international situation. Each successive ministry, however, was restricted by previous attempts to boost the size of the Army. Every measure by government ministers to strengthen the Army were episodic and contingent, and a mixture of political, social, financial, and military considerations. The effects of the massive expansion of the Army in 1793–5, principally through the creation of new regiments, cast a very long shadow, leading to the stagnation of the Army in the late 1790s and the tighter management of recruiting by the Army, itself restricting how many men were enlisted. The experience of those year also emphasized the need to avoid antagonizing the population of Britain and Ireland, which made recruitment from outside Britain and Ireland into the Army attractive too. The period witnessed a transition from recruitment being series of private political and military arrangements to a legislative programme. Ministries moved away from arrangements between the state and individuals or corporate interests to raise men, replacing these with policies and laws to support the strength of the Army. This was not a sharp transition, though. The first legislation started very tentatively in 1795 and the last recruiting contract was in 1805. The government and the Army tried to find permanent solutions to manpower issues from 1803 onwards, but as they involved Parliament in these efforts, the broader political situation played a significant part in their outcome. Nevertheless, they did provide recruits, and when combined with ordinary recruitment by the Army, and the expansion of units recruited from outside the UK, it proved to be just enough to sustain the Army.

Chapter 5

Numbers

The present magnitude of the Army, the various descriptions of Force whereof it is composed, the numerous stations on which it is employed, occasion a multiplicity of Returns which it requires no small time to examine, and much care and labour to arrange, methodize and combine; and this observation in most peculiarly applicable to the orders which are so frequently received by this Office, through the Secretary at War, from both Houses of Parliament.[1]

This statement by the commissioners of military inquiry in their eleventh report highlighted the information-gathering power of the adjutant-general's office in Horse Guards. This transformed the Army's – and so our – understanding of its composition enabled a closer management of its resources. Echoing the political drivers for change in the administration of the Army discussed in Chapter 3, the quote is also testament to the work of the people in the military administration and the legacy they have provided to us. Through their calculations and abstracts produced from the information flowing in from across the globe we can explore the Army in a way that is practically impossible before the 1790s. Andrew Bamford's *Sickness, Suffering, and the Sword* has demonstrated just how revealing these sources are and what can be done with them.[2] What follows uses these sources for a global view of the Army. The precision of the numbers recorded, and of which some were then publicly presented, should not be taken to guarantee their accuracy. As we shall see, the figures raise questions about what was and was not being counted. The information was created for specific purposes that excluded some people or situations. As such it is not possible to be exact about the size of the British Army. By going beyond what was recorded and thinking about military labour as a much broader category than just soldiers, we can better understand the scale of the human and animal resources needed to sustain the Army in its commitments across the globe.

Strength

Even allowing for some problems with the figures, the Army underwent an enormous expansion in response to the challenge of fighting the war against

Revolutionary and then Napoleonic France between 1793 to 1815 as well as undertaking the multiple global roles discussed in Chapter 2. As Appendix A shows, from a force of around 40,000 rank and file in 1792 it almost trebled in size within three years, and by 1813 the Army was six times its 1780s' size. This expansion was not a story of sustained growth across the period. The period of sharpest growth occurred in the years 1793 and 1795, with an increase of over 100,000 at a rate of 4,000 men per month between April 1793 and June 1795. The size of the Army then declined until 1798, after which it gained 68,000 men to reach a new peak size of 190,000 in 1801.[3] The Peace of Amiens is detectable in the drop from late 1802 to June 1803. Across the early years of the Napoleonic Wars there were regular dips between the winter and summer, but with a trend of growing each year after which the Army plateaued in 1810 at 230,000. There was a further, but much more limited, growth in 1812 and 1813. Much of these trends can be attributed to the Army's recruitment policies discussed in Chapter 4, but not all.

These figures about the strength of the Army differ from those presented to Parliament, and which were subsequently reprinted by Fortescue in *The History of the British Army* and *The County Lieutenancies and the Army* and which have then been re-used. For example, the usual figures give a peak of just shy of 150,000 in 1801 whilst the total given in this book is 188,000; for 1813 the respective figures are 256,000 and 262,000.[4] These differences require explanation relating to the original sources, how they were abstracted at the time, and how they have been compiled into Appendix A. Each month units were required to send back a standardized return of information about their strength, changes in numbers (due to recruitment or drafts arriving, and deaths, desertion and discharges on the debit side) and account for absent officers.[5] These documents were then signed by the commander of the unit or detachment. Alongside these forms, returns were compiled at each command and sent back too, so there are series of returns for Cape of Good Hope for example. The accuracy of these returns was improved by reforms in military finance during the 1780s that removed 'paper' men that were not actual soldiers but used to finance specific funds. Moreover, the new financial framework generally set the tone for accurate details about soldiers.[6]

These returns were then aggregated into statistical summaries held at The National Archives as two series of documents in WO 17. The first series is 'General Returns' and covers 1783–1802 and the second series provides monthly statistical summaries from 1803 onwards.[7] They are quite different in form and function. The 1783–1802 series were compiled about every three months into small books intended as reference works for the War Office and probably the King and government ministers too. They are often inscribed with ML or Lewis on the front, the Deputy Secretary at War. These books list units by their location, giving their strength according to the information that the War Office had at the time they were compiled. In 1803 these books were stopped and replaced by volumes maintained by the Adjutant-General that list monthly strength at casualties at each by military command or region, but without details of what units were where.

The returns from units that underpin these summaries were subject to all the transport and logistical issues that affected the movement of the Army discussed in Chapter 2. This inevitably meant some lag in the figures, so, for example, the summary made in April 1793 was based on the 1 June 1792 returns for units in South Asia and for April 1792 for Australia.[8] The practice from 1803 onwards seems to have been to back-fill information when it arrived, rather than take snapshots as was done before. Without details of what was entered when, however, it is tricky to work out what information was to hand when published summaries were created. When the Adjutant-General Harry Calvert was required to present casualty figures for 1814 to Parliament in March 1815, sixty-six monthly returns had not been received from nineteen different locations. They included the Leeward Islands and Bombay where the latest returns available only went up to May 1814.[9] There were gaps too, reflecting the hazards communications faced in the period, from the information not being collected in the first place, not forwarded on, or the ships carrying the documents being lost at sea. So, some of required documentation never made it to the War Office or Horse Guards in London. The figures for the Madras Presidency were missing for October and November 1808, for example, whilst in 1812 and 1813 no returns were available in London for Java, and so the figures were reconstructed from the unit returns.[10] Such problems with the data fed into aggregated totals and abstracts that the adjutant-general's department produced for the Commander-in-Chief, King, ministers, and Parliament, though these are not transparent.[11]

As was discussed in Chapter 1, the Army was an amalgam of components, not all of which were counted in the summaries made at the time. Before 1802, the reported strength of the Army in contemporary summaries did not include the Irish Establishment. Fortunately, we have compiled figures for 1793–1801 that have been added in,[12] evidence that the Irish government once had similar information to hand as their colleagues in London, but which was either not retained at the time or has been buried in other state papers. The absence of figures about the strength of the Army on the Irish Establishment between 1783 and 1793 means that we can only estimate the force in Ireland for these dates, which was certainly at least 10,000, and may have been as much as 15,000.[13] Additionally, the Irish Establishment figures before 1802 do not include the

Royal Irish Regiment of Artillery, which was administered by a separate Irish Ordnance Office. This regiment grew from an establishment of 386 to a strength of 1,269 in August 1794 and 2,085 by October 1800, the last return before the regiment was incorporated into the Royal Artillery as a new battalion.[14]

Like their counterparts in Ireland, the units of the Board of Ordnance were not included in the summaries compiled by the War Office or Horse Guards. Unlike the information about Ireland, though, we have a wonderful and extensive series of returns about the Royal Artillery for the era, which had been added into our figures. Created by the Adjutant-General of the Royal Artillery (or his deputy), they were not stored within the War Office or Horse Guards offices (they were probably available at Woolwich) nor routinely included in figures they collated. These records show that the artillery grew enormously in the period. Even in the years 1783–93 they contributed around 3,000 more soldiers that are usually missing from accounts of the Army. Ignoring the 27,000 more soldiers they contributed at their peak in late 1813 is a serious omission in strength of the Army.[15] One of the few Parliamentary papers that includes the artillery in statistics about the Army came from that year, but for all the other years we have to specifically go back to unpublished records and add these into our calculations.[16]

The other significant gap in the figures that needs addressing are the units recruited outside British and Ireland between 1793 and 1802. For the few foreign and colonial units that were placed on the British Establishment we have better information as they were more regularly subject to the rules and regulations for regiments of foot. The rest were not covered in a systematic way in summaries collated by the War Office or Horse Guards. The surviving regimental returns for these units are rare, if they were ever sent back to London in the first place. Only four units have a series of information, so we have to turn to the regional returns that sometimes included foreign and colonial units.[17] A lot depended on the attitude of the officer who created these returns, so those from Portugal between 1797 and 1802 include all the European corps there, whilst the returns from Jersey in the early part of the French Revolutionary War do not mention anything about the French émigré corps stationed there.[18] In Haiti, the British Army's provincial units expanded from 1,676 rank and file in July 1795 to 7,303 in April 1796, where there were many militia and paramilitary units that were increasingly viewed as part of the full-time military force there.[19] What figures are available from these general returns have been added into the total strength of the Army. So they, for example, add 19,269 soldiers into the total for June 1795 and 11,564 for February 1802.

Even with these adjustments, the statistical summary in this book is still limited as the Army only counted 'rank and file' in its returns. They leave out sergeants, other senior NCOs, musicians, and officers (the Royal Artillery, though, included all their men – officers, NCOs, and gunners of all ranks). For officers we have information but no regular and systematic totals. Thanks to work by John Houlding, we know that in 1792 there were 4,500 officers, with the totals for peacetime in the 1780s a few hundred less.[20] By December 1795 there were 7,000 officers (not including officers on the Irish Establishment nor foreign units not on the British Establishment), and by 1814 there were 12,500 officers on full pay.[21] Judging by the size of the indexes in the annually-printed *Army Lists* (and so including the Royal Marines, Board of Ordnance troops and half-pay officers) there were around 13,000 officers in the early 1800s and close to 20,000 in the early 1810s. NCOs disappear from our aggregated sources after 1802, but their numbers went from 4,400 in August 1793 to 12,000 by December 1795, and topped 12,700 by February 1801.[22] Based on the ratios for the 1780s and 1790s, which averaged an NCO for every eleven rank and file, there would have been around 21,000 in 1813. Equipped with these estimates, we can better model the strength of the Army, which is portrayed in the chart below. These revised figures show that the total strength of the Army only dipped below 50,000 in mid-1787, and the first peak of mid-1795 was closer to 175,000, that of mid-1801 nearer 210,000. The Army reached its largest size in June 1813 when it topped 310,000 – similar to its strength on the eve of the First World War.[23]

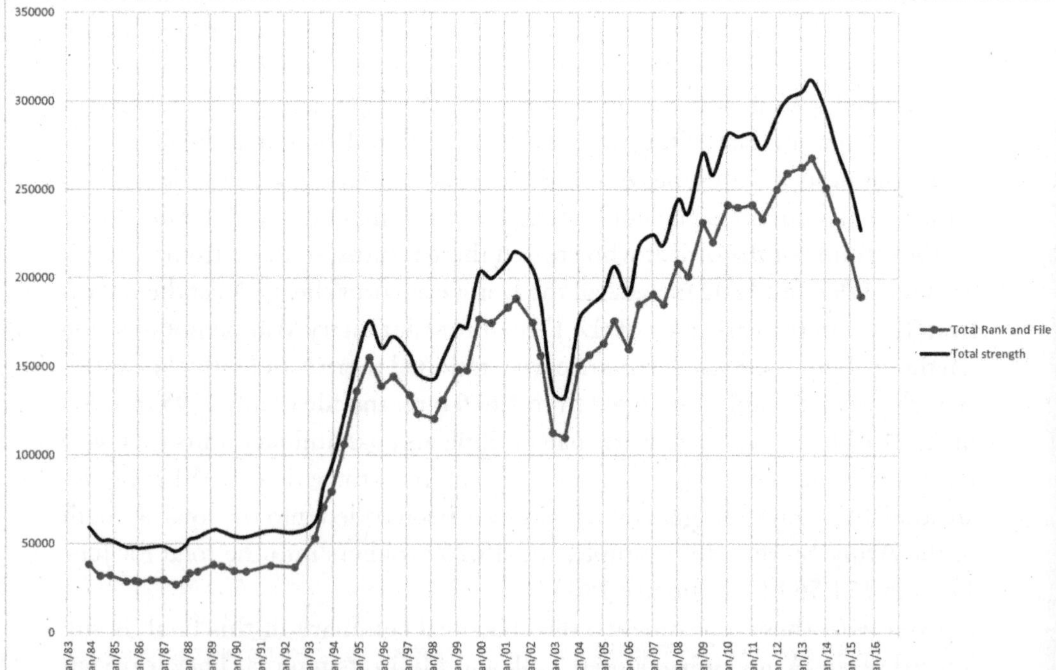

Strength of the British Army, 1783–1815.

Military Labour

The strength of the Army explored above is just a snapshot of it at given moments. The adjutant-general's office got more information from the returns they received that allow us to start to explore manpower by considering how many joined the Army. As saw in Chapter 3, Parliament was increasingly interested in this information, but care is needed when using published information. Like the figures about strength, Parliamentary returns are often reprinted as authoritative statements about the number of recruits into the Army. Their precision, which go down to single figures, obscures some of the problems in collating the information, and who counts and who does not – another reflection of the composite nature of the Army. In 1806 the Adjutant-General Harry Calvert highlighted that up until 1800 the Army only ascertained movement in and out of units, and made no separate account of the number that were transferred between units and those that were new recruits to the Army.[24] This partly explains the large numbers of men – over 40,000 – that were listed as joined in 1795 as many units were drafted into others that year.[25] There were hidden issues too, such as soldiers who were discharged or deserted but then later joined another unit. They would show up in the figures as two (or more) enlistments but only be one person. Outside the years where we know of large-scale disbandment of units to encourage soldiers into others such as 1795 and the reduction of fencible units in 1799 and 1800,[26] the impact of the soldiers who did this on recruitment figures are difficult to ascertain.

In the immediate aftermath of the Crimean War, William Barwick Hodge (future president of the Institute of Actuaries) explored the issue. His work modelled the flow of individuals by looking at casualty rates from 1793 to 1815. His analysis concluded that a total of 519,000 men joined the Army from Britain and Ireland, added to which were 198,000 foreign and colonial recruits and 30,000 temporarily employed foreign corps (presumably meaning soldiers that were hired). Combined with the starting strength of the army of 45,440 in 1793 this gave a total of 793,110 men that passed through the Army.[27] This total has been criticised by John Cookson for making insufficient deductions for transfers.[28]

There is enough information, though, to make a calculation of the number of men that joined the Army between 1793 and 1815 on a different basis than Hodge's 'out-flow' method. For many years details about recruitment are now in public records of the Army and for others we can extrapolate from the strength of the Army. We can be as certain as we can be about the 365,000 individuals enlisted from Britain and Ireland between 1803 and 1815 and for the 26,000 in 1801 and 1802, figures which are detailed in Appendix D. The recruiting returns for the infantry and cavalry in these years form a complete series, and although there is not the same extent of information about the artillery and other ordnance troops these gaps can be filled using the information about strength compiled for this book. Of those recruited for the infantry and cavalry the numbers are split broadly evenly between recruiting directly for these regiments by the Army and various mechanisms introduced by governments to provide manpower discussed in the previous chapter.

Alongside recruitment in Britain and Ireland 83,500 were recruited for foreign and colonial corps. Although no official figures were presented about recruitment into these units, Parliamentary returns and the Army's internal summaries give both actual strengths at the start of each year and the number of casualties suffered annually. Combined, these provide indicative figures for these enlistments. Hidden within the Royal Artillery's recruitment figures, however, were the companies that were composed of men from outside Britain and Ireland, most notably the artillery of the King's German Legion. As a result, although the total recruited between 1801 and 1815 will be the same, at 474,700, the actual composition may have been a couple of thousand more recruited outside Britain and Ireland and a couple of thousand less from within them.

Far more difficult to assess are the figures before 1800. Provided under the vague heading of 'Added to the British Army', 209,000 were recorded as joining the Army between 1793 and 1800, including 28,500 coming from the militia in 1798 and 1799.[29] Alongside the difficulties about discharged and transferred soldiers, as was explored in Chapter 1, what the 'British Army' meant in these years is not straightforward. A different mechanism, then, is needed to overcome these problems. Working from the periodic totals in Chart 1 allows us to calculate net gains in the strength of the Army, so avoiding problems of double counting discharges that were transfers because in the overall strength of the Army they would be neutral. These increases equate to at least 153,000 recruits for the years 1793 to 1800 for units on the British and Irish Establishments (including artillery). Before 1803, Army statistics did not distinguish foreign and colonial corps on the British Establishment, so some of these gains will have been transfers of manpower from one establishment to another, most notably the increase in the 60th Foot in 1797 and 1798, and the creation of the West India regiments from ranger units in the Caribbean.

This figure, however, does not include enlistments needed to replace any casualties in the Army. We can be certain about the infantrymen and cavalrymen who died and were replaced, adding an further 49,000 men and meaning at least 202,000 men joined the Army.[30] Some of 75,100 men recorded as discharged would not have returned to the Army and their replacements need to be factored in as new recruits.[31] It would be unlikely that more than 50 per cent of these discharged men went on to re-enlist. For desertions that were replaced with new recruits we must rely on rates seen between 1803 and 1815. Even at a conservative desertion rate of 3.4 per cent per year of the strength of the army this results in an additional 23,000 casualties. Some allowance needs to be made for artillery casualties that were replaced too (but not reported on); these would have been around 4,000 men. All told, then 266,000 individuals.

As was discussed earlier, the casualty figures and reported strength of the Army did not include most of the foreign and colonial corps. Using the periodic strength data in Chart 1 indicates a gain of 38,000 men in these units between 1793 and 1802, but this is only for the units for which we have returns. Also, it does not include replacements for deaths, discharged, and desertions. It is probable, based on casualty rates elsewhere in the Army, that 60,000 individuals passed through these units. A proportion of these men will have moved onto the British Establishment in the second half of the 1790s, so we need to reduce the 266,000 total accordingly. These transfers were concentrated into fourteen units: the York Hussars; twelve West India regiments; and the 5/60th plus other transfers into the 60th Foot. Conceivably, this may have been as high as 14,000 men, meaning that 252,000 men recruited from Britain and Ireland between 1793 and 1800. These then give totals of 626,000 men recruited from Britain and Ireland between 1793 and 1815, and 145,000 into foreign and colonial corps; altogether 771,000 men.

Finally, all the returns and compiled data exclude officers (except for the Royal Artillery and Engineers). The officer corps, although included in the returns sent into the adjutant-general's office, were not aggregated in any way, and so, like the figures for the rank and file before 1800, a calculation based on what information we have is required. The data underpinning chart 1 provides the strength of the officer corps based on *Army Lists*. Alongside this a model of officer casualties is needed. Fortunately, from 1811 the *Army List* began recording casualties (resignations, retirements, supersessions, dismissals and deaths) from which a casualty rate can be calculated. Casualties will have fluctuated across the period but the average for 1810 (recorded in the 1811 *Army List*) was 5 per cent. Applying this rate to the size of the annual size of officer corps and adding to net gains shows that around 37,000 officers served in the Army. The grand total arrived at by the above calculation is that 808,000 men served in the Army between 1793 and 1815, aligning with Hodge's figures and calculated from different material and with a different method.

These figures, though, are not the full story about the human resources that were involved in the Army. They only count individuals on the official strength of regiments, so exclude any other labour involved in running in the Army outside of these arrangements. Some of these were quite small, it is fair to say, such as the clerks and office staff that were employed by generals, particularly in garrisons and the headquarters of military commands, like Daniel Sutherland and Alexander Purves, the first and second clerk employed by the Adjutant-General in Nova Scotia. Alongside these were employees of the barrack department, commissariat, medical department, storekeepers, accountants (in the comptroller general's department), carpenters, blacksmiths, draughtsmen, labourers in the engineer's departments and chaplains. In total at this station there were 110 people.[32] The composition of these employees would be different for armies that were campaigning, rather than garrisons like Nova Scotia. In May 1815, the British army in Flanders had 281 civilians on the staff, with the majority in the commissariat or medical department.[33]

Far more numerous were the people of other supporting services. Civilians were hired with their carts and mules in Portugal, Spain, Flanders, and France to provide the transport for the Army's supplies. In South Asia, the Army regularly included pioneers, servants, and water carriers as part of its force when on campaign. For the 1798–9 campaign against Mysore, 15,000 banjaras were hired to provides supplies and logistical support to the Army.[34] In the Caribbean, large numbers of enslaved Afro-Caribbean men and women were labourers for the Army. They included artificers and tradesmen – masons, carpenters, sawyers, coopers, and the like – maintained at each fortification and used as field pioneers during military operations. Alongside these, plantation owners hired slaves out as labourers for hard and monotonous jobs: carrying water, gathering and hauling firewood, and moving supplies; cleaning barracks, fortifications and latrines. Some were servants to officers paid through the commissariat department, as majors or above were provided with three enslaved servants, captains two, and ensigns or lieutenants one. These individuals would be in addition to any that the officer bought personally. Military regulations prohibited white soldiers undertaking fatigue tasks, so the Army was dependent on thousands of black people, often levied as a human tax on the estates of plantations. Henry Dundas called for 4,500 'fatigue slaves' in August 1795, and Roger Norman Buckley has calculated that the figure was much higher, with the Army dependent on around 7,000 skilled and unskilled civilian enslaved blacks.[35] The lack of information means that we can only guess at the total numbers involved across the period, but it is feasible that it would be over 10,000 and 20,000 may not be unrealistic for the twenty-two years of war.

Everywhere the Army went it depended on the unremitting, and usually un-remarked, labour of women. They were the consistent and essential support service to soldiers of all ranks. They were cooks, laundresses and cleaners; they were servants, labourers and seamstresses; they were nurses, companions, wives, daughters and sex workers. A very few were the wives of officers who travelled with their husbands. Many were women related in some way to enlisted men. Jennine Hurl-Eamon's *Marriage and the British Army in the Long Eighteenth Century* has recovered their lives, but, as she highlights, to do this we have to get past the institutional misogyny of the Army. In its own image, the Army was a masculine world of enforced bachelorhood, and official attitudes towards women were reflected in the pejorative language used like 'baggage' and 'camp followers': they were not of the Army but living from it. Added to this was a one-sided view of sexual relations that blamed women for all the problems of venereal disease within the Army.[36] Women were exposed to just as much, if not more, risk of deprivation and disease whilst following their soldiers. The appearance of women (and children) in official documents often revolves around tragedies. For example, the wrecking of the *Harponer* transport in St. Mary's Bay, Newfoundland in 1816 showed that the 4th Royal Veteran Battalion had forty women and sixty-eight children present for seven officers and 265 men, meaning that there was one woman for every six soldiers.[37] They were active agents in the Army too. Perhaps one of the most vivid stories is about the wife of a soldier of the 42nd Foot during the assault on the Vigie, Saint Vincent, in June 1796.[38] On pushing on to the fourth and last redoubt in the fortifications, General Stewart turned round:

> … and saw my Amazonian friend standing with her clothes tucked up to her knees; and seizing my hand 'Well done, my Highland lads!' she exclaimed. 'See how the brigands scamper like so many deer! Come,' added she, 'let us drive them from yonder hill.' On inquiry I found that she had been in the hottest fire cheering and animating the men, and when the action was over she was as active as any of the surgeons in assisting the wounded.[39]

Like many women of the army, she was unnamed in the account of her actions.

There are no official aggregated figures for women with the Army, but their presence is unequivocal, and they emerge from their documentary shadows in snippets and stories. The Army officially sanctioned some women on the strength of its regiments as wives of soldiers with the permission of the unit's commanding officer. These 'legally' married wives of soldiers (in the eyes of the military administration) were entitled to half rations. Long-standing military practice, periodically enforced through general orders, was to limit the numbered allowed to go overseas to six women per 100 men.[40] The fact that lots were almost always drawn to see who would stay and who would go is evidence that this ratio was usually exceeded. Around 1809, figures about soldiers' official wives and children started to appear in biannual inspection returns, and these show that the numbers of women varied enormously from regiment to regiment. A sample shown in table 1 from 1813 indicates that units stationed within Britain and Ireland had far more wives than the official allowance, especially in the Foot Guards stationed in London, and there was a great difference for units in active operations overseas like the 22nd Light Dragoons, the 1/36th and 1/92nd Foot. The ratio for the 2nd Line Battalion, KGL, was lower than the figures below indicate as eighteen wives listed were in England not Spain at the time. Still, this sample indicates that the Army's 'official' wives could easily have been double the six per 100 ratio – equating to 36,000 women in 1813. The actual figure was higher still, as there were thousands of wives and women beyond those officially approved who were hidden from the Army (and so its documents) to avoid the censure of military authorities.

Table 1: Women and Children with units, 1813.

Unit	Location	Enlisted Men	Legally married wives	Children under 10	Children above 10	Wives per 100 enlisted men
2nd Dragoons	Birmingham, UK	855	173	177	17	23
22nd Light Dragoons	Arcot, India	663	26	19	2	5
2/1st Foot Guards	London, England	1351	539	485	197	45
1/36th Foot	France	647	15	1	1	3
1/63rd Foot	Martinique	903	52	35	5	7
2/78th Foot	Aberdeen, Scotland	539	73	85	4	16
2/88th Foot	Berryhead Barracks, England	234	51	49	5	31
1/92nd Foot	France	919	21	10		3
5th West India	Fort Augusta, Jamaica	733	32	3	13	5
2nd Line Battalion, KGL	Spain	938	46	15	8	6

Sources: TNA, WO 27/118, /121, /122, /123.

Alongside all the human resources needed to maintain the Army, the equine and animal demands of the Army were just as important. Nor was it just horses for the cavalry and officers that were required. Draught and pack animals – horses, mules, bullocks, and in South Asia elephants and camels – were the principal motive power for the Army's transport needs. Almost everything the Army required had to be moved at some stage by a cart or on an animal's back, from food, clothing, arms and ammunition, and medicines, to the books and records of units that accounted for all these things and those that they were intended for. The sheer scale of the animals involved in the Army has been calculated by Andrew Bamford, who has shown that in 1812 in the Peninsula there were 34,000 animals for the Anglo-Portuguese army that numbered 61,500 men. Even then, this figure does not include oxen nor officers' privately-owned horses.[41] In India, the numbers of animals that were utilized by the Army were enormous. In 1798 as tensions rose with Mysore, the British and EIC Army already had 12,000 bullocks, and Arthur Wellesley thought that 40,000 in total would be needed. As it turned out this was an underestimate, and whilst campaigning in 1799 the Army had 60,000 bullocks.[42]

As with all the forms of military labour beyond soldiers, any kind of accuracy about how many and of what is hard to achieve. Even accounting for all the horses that were integral to cavalry units is awkward, as it all remained in regimental hands, unlike other European states that maintained national studs and centralized recruitment of horses.[43] Details at a unit level can be traced, though, through the monthly returns in WO 17. The demands of maintaining the cavalry can be seen in the example of the 3rd Dragoons Guards: 730 horses in the unit died in the sixty-two months it served in Portugal and Spain between 1809 and 1814. It arrived in Portugal with 604 horses in May 1809, and by February 1813 it had been reduced to 274 horses. Similar difficulties faced the Royal Artillery: 648 horses of the Royal Horse Artillery died during the Peninsular War, whilst the Royal Artillery lost 4,697, with some terrible loses at the start of the campaign when between June and August 1809 its batteries dropped from 703 to 415 horses present and 513 died.[44] Andrew Bamford has again done us a great service in calculating that 24,631 horses died in the Peninsular War, at a rate of around 22 deaths per 1,000 horses per month. This includes harrowing moments of animal suffering, particularly during retreats.[45] One of worst was the withdrawal to Coruña through the winter of 1808/9. The gruesome finale of this provided a terrible reminder of the difficulties of transporting horses, as they simply could not be evacuated in time and so they were shot to prevent them being captured and used by the French: 5,000 horses were lost between December 1808 and the evacuation of the British army.[46]

The study of horse power in the Army for the era waits on further research, so for now an estimate will have to do. Firstly, some calculation of horses is needed in the Army at given moments. For example, in 1806 there were 24,000 cavalry;[47] 4,500 men in the Royal Horse Artillery and Corps of Artillery Drivers (each man likely to have one if not two horses);[48] and some 16,000 officers not all of whom were on active duty, and so with a horse, but those that were sometimes had more than one, especially in the higher ranks. Our estimate comes to 40,000 horses at least in 1806. Over the course of conflicts between 1793 and 1815 it is conceivable that over 100,000 horses were used by the Army, and it could be as much as 150,000. The scale of the equine demands of the Army led to changes in the care of military horses. Farriers had traditionally acted as vets,[49] but in 1796 veterinary surgeons were added to every cavalry regiment. This followed a successful lobbying campaign by the Veterinary College in London (forebear of the Royal Veterinary College) that convinced both Parliament and the Army of their utility in treating horses and saving money. The head of the college, Edward Coleman, was also placed in charge of a new veterinary department in the Army and recommended the appointment of all veterinary surgeons in the Army. All these new veterinary surgeons had to have attended the Veterinary College for at least three months and passed an examination there. To speed up the appointments in the 1790s, surgeons were allowed to be appointed and sent to the college for training.[50]

Casualties and Health

Comparing the strength of the Army with number of men who joined shows the persistent and high level of churn in its ranks, equivalent to its peak strength being replaced three times over. The human costs of the British Army's global commitments are outlined in Appendix D. Casualties totalled 593,000 in the twenty-two years, of which at least 207,000 died and many of those who were discharged will have had their life cut short by military service. The high total casualties in 1802, 1814, and 1815 are mostly accounted for by the discharge of large numbers of soldiers on the advent of peace. Outside of these years, 1795 and 1796 were terrible for the Army and as we saw in Chapter 4 it took years for the recruitment of the Army to recover from this disaster. Not that 25,000 to 32,000 casualties annually in the 1810s were in any way good considering the size of the Army overall.

Most of the deaths and discharges outside 1802, 1813 and 1814 were the result of disease. Although the figures echo the oscillations in the Army's military commitments, with more deaths from 1808 reflecting the commitment in the Iberian Peninsula, proportionally few were the result of battle. It was the constant assault from an invisible army of microbes that drained the Army's strength year in, year out. Diseases that affected land forces (and any large concentration of people) were well documented if not well diagnosed. Typhus and dysentery could strike anywhere, a significant number of men contracted sexually transmitted diseases like syphilis, added to which some places harboured even more lethal contagions, such as yellow fever and malaria. The expanding range of the Army's campaigns also exposed it to diseases that were new to it, including trachoma (known as Egyptian Ophthalmia) and the plague in Egypt. To this list we should add a broader range of environmental factors that could render soldiers ill and potentially lead to death; the British Army's commitments meant that soldiers could be suffering hypothermia in Canada whilst others could be succumbing to hyperthermia and dehydration in western Africa, the Caribbean and South Asia.

The figures hide wide variations in mortality rates, and distinctions between different regions were recognized by the Army in the casualty statistics it collated from 1805. The war in Spain and Portugal led to the most deaths at 43,500, with particularly high mortality rates in 1812 and 1813. The battles and sieges of those years account for some of these figures, with notably higher death rates per 1,000 soldiers after the storming of Ciudad Rodrigo and Badajoz, the battles of Salamanca and Vittoria, and the siege of San Sebastian. The worst monthly death rate in Iberia during the years 1812 and 1813, however, was in January 1813 in the wake of the retreat from Burgos and when a virulent fever devastated a brigade of Foot Guards.[51] Over 2,000 soldiers died that month.[52] In *Sickness, Suffering, and the Sword* Andrew Bamford discovered that the most lethal months for the British Army in Iberia were caused by an epidemic in 1809 when the army under Wellington was stationed in the Guadiana valley in Portugal.[53]

Outside Iberia there were three other regions with notably high deaths: Britain and Ireland (23,600); the Caribbean (22,900); and South Asia (17,500). In part, they represent the distribution of the Army, but the figures for Britain and Ireland and the Caribbean are testament to the impact of disease on the Army. Besides casualties from the 1798 conflict in Ireland, the figures reveal the effect of contagious diseases especially on new recruits and ill soldiers returning home. Alongside background levels of disease, the Army in the UK suffered from epidemics. One virulent outbreak resulted from the Walcheren Expedition, which infected the Army (and transport ships) with a lethal combination of malaria, typhus, typhoid and dysentery that caused 4,000 deaths. By October 1809 the death rate per 1,000 soldiers per month in British corps had increased to 12.4 from a low of 1.7 in July. Some regiments even became 'Walcheren' units and suffered recurrent outbreaks in the following years.[54] Less well known were epidemics in the units that returned from the Netherlands and north Germany in 1795, which when combined with fevers and dysentery that raged in new recruits from early 1794 overwhelmed hospital capacity in Britain: in June 1795 8,843 of 40,654 infantrymen in England were sick.[55] Similar happened in the wake of the Coruña retreat in 1809.[56]

During 1805 the largest number of soldiers died in South Asia: a predictable reflection of the scale of military operations against the Marathas that year. In 1807, a much quieter year in terms of major military operations in South Asia, the death rate averaged 5.2 per 1,000 men per month, but troops in the Madras Presidency suffered worse, with peaks close to or higher than the 1805 average rate of 9.2 deaths per 1,000 soldiers between March and July and again in October. Generally, these figures reflected the prevalence of environmental causes of diseases, coupled with all the familiar problems of soldiering in the eighteenth century, including crowded unsanitary accommodation, poor diet, and alcohol, not helped by aggressive treatment through violent purging, and then the extensive use of mercury in the early 1800s.[57]

The forces in the Caribbean suffered persistently high rates of death from amongst their ranks, particularly the European soldiers stationed there. Michael Duffy's meticulous research about the Caribbean campaigns during the 1790s, given in *Soldiers, Sugar, and Seapower*, calculated that 62,250 men were casualties, of which the horrendous number of 45,250 died.[58] Roger Norman Buckley's research raised this figure to 46,515 by adding in deaths from the soldiers of the West India regiments.[59] To these figures for 1793 to 1801 we can now include 22,900 for 1805 to 1815 and an estimated 4,000 for 1802 to 1804 (based on some incomplete returns), meaning 73,415 soldiers died in the Caribbean – one in three of all deaths in the British Army.[60] This awful count reflects Britain's deadly commitment to the slave-based economy in the Caribbean, and it had more profound consequences.

It took the casualties suffered by European troops in the Caribbean for Henry Dundas to reluctantly agree to establish the West India regiments. The black soldiers serving in these regiments had an impact out of proportion to their numbers. These units increased the strength of the Army by 8,000–12,000 soldiers; without them the 'disposable force' would have been correspondingly smaller. Crucially, most of the west Africans who filled the ranks of these units had acquired immunity to yellow fever when they were very young.[61] As we saw in Chapter 2, the allocation of troops to the Caribbean did not drop significantly between 1793 and 1815, yet the number of deaths in the ten years after 1805 were half the total of the eight years from 1793. Of course, men in the West India regiments still died of diseases but not at a rate that challenged the racial thinking that underpinned their role in the British Army.[62] Without a Caribbean garrison of around 10,000 Africans, the Army would have suffered at least an extra 1,400 deaths a year, without accounting for the number of men who survived illness to then be discharged as unfit for service. This may not seem much, but the cumulative impact of this would have resulted in the Army being sapped even more, as the evidence from the mid-1790s indicates that sending more un-acclimatised soldiers lacking immunity to yellow fever to the Caribbean resulted in them dying faster, which then required even more soldiers.

More significant was the institutionalisation of racialised medical thinking in the Army that asserted that certain races were better adapted to certain climates.[63] James McGrigor used the Egyptian expedition as a giant medical experiment to prove that sepoys were more resilient to the climate and disease, with the future medical director noting their health despite long marches and undertaking additional duties such as clearing roads and digging wells.[64] Based on theories of racial difference and climatic-based disease, the West India regiments became templates for the recruitment of other race-based units. It led to enslaved east Africans in the Bourbon Regiment in Mauritius and the Ceylon regiments in Sri Lanka.[65] It also led to the little-known York Rangers that existed between 1803 to 1805. This unit was established to recruit black and mixed-race men in Britain, Ireland, and North America (probably the Black loyalist community in Canada) for general service.[66] That these men were destined for tropical service based on their skin colour was evidenced by what happened to the few that were recruited when it was disbanded in 1805. The Army ordered the fit 'coloured' men then stationed on the Isle of Wight to the Royal African Corps serving on the West African coast.[67]

Even with recruitment across the globe there was a constant flow of people at the behest of the British Army. This is largely a hidden story after 1801, and especially from 1809, as the deployment of the Army shifted from episodic expeditions, reinforcements or withdrawals to slotting men into existing units or stations. This was always the intention behind the second battalions of the British infantry regiments, where a battalion stationed in Britain and Ireland served as a reception and initial training centre from which men would be then selected for service overseas. Although the system was far from perfect, as not every regiment had a second battalion and the need for troops when first battalions were full of sick soldiers from Coruña and Walcheren led to second battalions serving overseas particularly in 1809 and 1810, the broad principle did much to improve the survival rate of soldiers. The Army of the later 1810s avoided the widespread debilitation of units of young soldiers unconditioned to their environment that it suffered in 1794 and 1795 in the Caribbean and western Europe. Andrew Bamford's work demonstrates that individual units still collapsed in numbers during the Peninsular War, and Wellington understandably did everything he could to retain 'seasoned' soldiers,[68] yet the steady influx of people into existing units stationed overseas reduced casualties and were the implementation of the ideas of Sir Richard Fitzpatrick that opened Chapter 4.[69]

Put against this onslaught of diseases in the Army were its medical staff. The history of these men and their efforts to understand and address the issues the

Army faced have been explored and redressed some extremes of either dismissive criticisms of the Army's physicians and surgeons and excessive focus on and praise of a few individuals.[70] The varying effectiveness of the Army's medics stemmed from deep divisions in medical philosophy and practice of the period. The organization of the Army's medical staff reflected the division of contemporary medical practitioners into physicians (who considered health in the broadest sense) and surgeons. There were separate physician- and surgeon-generals who oversaw the medical arrangements of the Army, which was replicated in military commands and then through hospital staff. Military units, however, only had surgeons. Alongside these pre-existing divisions, the emergence of different approaches to medicine in the late eighteenth century added further realms for disagreements. Most medical training and practice, especially for physicians, was based on humoral philosophies of health that stemmed back to ancient Greece and were taught and examined by Oxford, Cambridge, and Dublin universities.[71] During the eighteenth century a different approach emerged, often referred to as hospital medicine, that based its practice on observation, dissection and an empirical approach to treatment that undertook trials and assessed effectiveness, even if it was not fully understood why something worked. In Britain, Edinburgh University was the centre of this approach, where many army surgeons studied.

Catherine Kelly's *War and the Militarisation of British Army Medicine* has explored the impact of these schisms, which were especially acute in the 1790s and early 1800s. Before 1793 the Army Medical Department was run by Surgeon General John Hunter, as the physician-generals he served alongside were largely incapacitated. He created a career pathway for Army military surgeon from regimental posts through to hospital and staff appointments. On Hunter's death, however, the appointments of Sir Lucas Pepys and John Gunning (who combined formed a new Army Medical Board) undid all Hunter's arrangements and appointed civilian doctors directly to staff medical roles, requiring them to hold a degree in medicine, which debarred many military surgeons from further promotion.[72] The civilian physicians often baulked at military discipline or querying of their practice, and most were simply unprepared for the scale of medical issues they had to deal with. The immediate and tragic result was an increasingly dysfunctional organization and consequent poor care.

The longer-term consequences were a series of bitter disputes played out both within the Army Medical Department (which also drew in other parts of the military administration) and in public through publications. Attempts to reform the army medical board in 1798 only made things worse, and it became notorious for infighting. Exasperated with the strife and ineffectiveness, military commanders made their own medical arrangements directly. The Duke of York appointed Dr Hugh Kennedy Inspector General of Hospitals for the forces on the continent and Sir Ralph Abercromby refused the army medical board's appointment for his expedition.[73] Amongst these tribulations, there emerged a new medical military practitioner that was distinct from civilian medics and particularly attuned to the Army's culture and approach. The medical department was subject to a thorough and scathing review by the commissioners of military enquiry in 1808, and the medical disaster of Walcheren was the final catalyst to recast the entire arrangements into a new board with a single director-general – the old division between physician- and surgeon-general having been done away with.[74]

The impact of these problems with military medicine are difficult to measure, but it certainly made things worse. Indeed, Catherine Kelly has argued that medical staff choosing a side or seeking favour for their career influenced therapeutic choices.[75] Nevertheless, important progress was made, particularly in the approach to disease and hygiene. It was the latter where medical staff could make the most difference, as all medical practitioners still subscribed to miasmic theories of disease and microbiological sources of these diseases lay well into the nineteenth century. Like their contemporaries in the adjutant-general's department, military medical staff turned to statistics to understand medical problems and evaluate treatments.[76] Some of these, such as profuse bleeding, were essentially false positives that made the lot of the soldier harder, particularly when some tropical diseases themselves led to anaemia.[77] But much did improve outcomes: close attention to cleanliness, both of soldiers but crucially also transports and accommodation; diet, where this could be done; and perhaps most significantly arranging hospitals into wards to segregate those suffering from a particular disease or at a certain stage of recovery. The Army even went further and established dedicated hospitals employing specialists, such as the eye hospital at Selsey in Sussex.[78] In this regard, vaccination against smallpox was an important part of wider efforts to tackle disease.

*   *   *

The information flowing into Horse Guards and transformed by the adjutant-general's department into statistics provide us with greater insights into the history of the British Army in this era. This statistical thinking reflected the broader changes in the desire to gather, mobilize, and utilize information that were discussed in Chapter 3. These figures, however, only went so far and focused exclusively on soldiers. The limitations of this viewpoint become clearer when the numbers are reduced in scale but retain the same ratios. So, for example, in 1813 for every fifteen British and Irish infantrymen in the Army there were a further three cavalrymen; three artillerymen; at least one black soldier; four white European or North American soldiers; three officers; and about two NCOs. Alongside them were two to three women, an enslaved African, and probably two to three locally-recruited labourers. In most years two to three of these soldiers would become casualties. The casualty figures, when adjusted to account for the Army's composite nature, reveal the extent of the catastrophe the Army suffered in 1794–5, caused by a combination of massive expansion and disease. There was no great collapse of the Army after these years, but it still had to deal with persistent levels of casualties. There was a complex interplay between casualties and the global commitments of the Army and refocusing on the whole Army shows that the significance of the African and Afro-Caribbean soldiers was massively out of proportion to their numbers. Without them the Army would have faced even greater challenges to find the soldiers to fight in Portugal and Spain under Wellington. That there is a link between having the manpower available for the Peninsular War and using – indeed encouraging – slavery, the slave trade and the forced migration of Africans after 1807 is an uncomfortable and unacknowledged aspect of the wars. As most of casualties were caused by disease, the medical history of the Army is fundamental to understand its strength, and this was not just about surgeons and physicians but a new approach to investigate and treat disease. As a result, military medicine emerged that made soldiers distinct from civilians, and was inflected with racial theories about resistance to disease and suitability for different climates. The overall numbers that served remind us that we have around 800,000 lives to explore, understand, and in some cases rescue from obscurity.

Chapter 6

Enlisted Men

This comes with my kind love to you hoping that these lines will find you in good health as the Lord me thank God for it – this it to inform you that that I got to Porchester on the same evening I left you and all whas well at the Regtm. I Hope when we meet again things will be more agreeable than when we met before. – I hope in a short time this Calamm [*sic*] war will End and then I hope we shall meet never to Part More – - I have rote down to my friends to inform them of our Marige but have not had one answer yet. But I hope you will Rite Back by Return of Post and let me know how you and the Child go on and by that time I hope to Rec'd a Letter from home …[1]

This letter from William Birchall, a private in Captain Horton's company of the Royal Lancashire Volunteers (a fencible regiment), to his wife Sarah Davis and their child reminds us that behind the statistics of the previous chapter were hundreds of thousands of human beings that deserve a richer appreciation of their lives. William's letter reveals a dim view of the war in 1798, just as his regiment was about to be sent to Ireland. Perhaps one of the saddest aspects of this intimate glimpse into a soldier's life is that his wife and child probably never got this letter. It was left at the Rose and Crown Inn in Brockenhurst, Hampshire, where it made its way into the records of the parish overseers and then into Hampshire Record Office. Despite William's misgivings about a military career, he served in the Royal Lancashire Volunteers between 1795 and 1800 and then exchanged into the 15th Foot in July 1800 whilst serving in Ireland, becoming a grenadier in the second battalion. He later transferred into the 15th's single battalion on the reduction of the regiment in 1802, continuing to serve in Ireland before the regiment went to the Caribbean in 1805. He died in Barbados on 29 August 1805, and his effects and credits (any money owed to him) went to his wife and child.[2]

The muster records through which William Birchall's career as a soldier were traced are an example of the extensive but sometimes opaque material that exists to explore the social history of the Army's enlisted men. Fortunately, we know a lot more about these men than we did for most of the twentieth century, when the Duke of Wellington's derogatory comments about the common soldier (which this author will not dignify with repeating again) were regarded as all that was needed to be said about them.[3] Assessments of who these men were, their experiences, identities and attitudes, needs to balance the different material we have, and juxtapose the individual and person material, like William Birchall's letter, with the information collected by the Army about its personnel. Likewise, care is needed not to conflate all soldiers in the period into one generic caricature. As we saw in Chapter 1, there were many different soldiers within the Army.

Pathways into the Army

Part of this diversity was the different ways of becoming a soldier. Enlisting into the Army in Britain and Ireland was a regulated and ritualized process that had barely changed in 100 years. Recruiting could only be undertaken under royal authority, which was granted through a beating order issued by the Secretary at War to each regimental colonel or officer. These officers then had the authority to send out small parties to recruit men. Typically composed of an officer or sergeant, plus drummers and occasionally other musicians to announce their presence, these recruiting parties toured areas enlisting men. The bounty – an upfront cash payment for joining up – played a very large part in recruitment, as Plate 7 makes clear, where three men gasp at the purse being held out to them as inducement to join up. This print was not exaggerating the sums, as the bounty could be as much as a labourer could earn in a year.[4] Taking this bounty started the transition between civilian and military life. Any enlistment was then subject to approval before a magistrate where the consent of the enlistee (or not if he was willing to pay back any bounty given to him) was established.[5] This process also left a documentary footprint: at this moment, a name, physical description, age, place of birth, occupation before enlisting and date of enlistment were recorded, which were then transferred to the 'description book' kept by each regiment.

Edward Coss' *All for the King's Shilling* provides the most recent and extensive study of recruitment. Based on a database of fourteen British infantry regiments, four cavalry regiments and a sample of artillery enlistments for the years 1790–1815 (with a noted emphasis on men recruited from 1800–15), Coss found that men generally enlisted when they were between 17 and 25 years old, and they described their occupation as labourers and specific artisan trades like weavers. Moreover, Coss' analysis detects a strong correlation between the broader economic situation and recruitment: when the economy contracted more men enlisted and vice versa.[6] This distant reading of the data provides a solid foundation to further explore recruitment but marginalizes other factors that were significant. Sometimes these could be so important that they counteracted any prevailing economic factors. The Army did not recruit large numbers in 1799–1801, despite, as Roger Well's *Wretched Faces* showed, massive economic and social distress in Britain and Ireland at the time.[7] By stepping down from the macro-level analysis, there are other economic factors involved. These are often thought about in terms of push and pull factors, with the economic situation of an area or an individual being the push and what the Army offered acting as the pull.

One of the biggest pull factors was the levy money for each recruit, of which the bounty was just part, and this was not static. Generally, the sums given to recruits increased over the period, dipping in the periods of European peace in 1802 and late 1814/early 1815 with both having a clear impact on recruitment in those periods. In January 1802, the levy money was reduced to just four guineas, rising to £22 8s for the infantry between September 1805 and October 1806, and peaking at £23 17s 6d for unlimited service between April 1808 and February 1813, over five times what it was in 1802.[8] A large proportion of this money went to the recruit as a cash reward, though it was also intended to provide 'necessaries' (in other words basic uniform and equipment) for the recruit. This was open to abuse through overcharging, and general orders became more explicit about what regiments had to provide and how much was allowed for it. From 1808 it was stipulated that out of the £23 17s 6d levy money, £12 1s went to the recruit.[9] The bounty also needed to be in cash to be attractive to a potential recruit, and poor recruiting results in the mid-1790s were partly due to cash-flow problems.[10] A further micro-economic factor was the financial incentives to recruiters. The levy money included a payment for each recruit to the recruiting party, the officer, and any other 'bringer' who was involved. Essentially a system of performance-based bonus pay, in February 1803 it increased from 10s 6d to the party to a guinea (£1 1s) and went up to three guineas for any bringer in 1808.[11]

For some recruits, there were very particular economic and social factors involved. This was case for many of the Highland regiments raised by clan lairds in the 1790s. The romanticized version of these, so prevalent in early regimental histories, places heavy emphasis on clan loyalty and traditions of military service that were harnessed by the Army though clan chiefs. We should not be too dismissive of the fealty between tenants and their lord in the Highlands. Nevertheless, the relationships were not just social and traditional, but underpinned by economic realities. Many of the Highland tenantry that became soldiers lived under the threat of eviction from the lands they toiled. Sending a male from the family, or finding someone who could serve, was a way of gaining favour with their landlord and so hopefully retaining their tenancy.

These calculations were even more acute in the 1790s with the relentless advance of the cheviot sheep as part of the Highland Clearances. The large numbers of men recruited in the Highlands were not, then, a reflection of the power of clan culture and identity, but the last desperate flourish of Highlanders trying to stay the demise of their society through military service.[12]

A solely economic analysis ignores the agency of those involved. The first of these agents was the Army itself. Throughout the wars the Army tweaked aspects of the system to increase or decrease enlistments, both deliberately and unwittingly. There was the simple factor of how many recruiting parties were operating in Britain and Ireland. Enlistments went up in relation to the number of recruiting parties, as was seen in 1793–5 and in 1807. The wholesale resetting of those recruiting in 1795 is another part of the explanation for declining enlistments in the mid-1790s. Conversely, to boost recruitment and champion the Talents government's short service scheme in 1806–07 over 1,100 recruiting parties were sent out and 19,000 men were enlisted from the UK. This was not sustainable, though. Much like the experience of 1793–5, surges in the number of recruiting parties had to be balanced against the loss of officers and NCOs from their units and the impact it could have on relations between the Army and society. By 1808 the number had reduced to more practical 800.[13]

The last part of the journey was the potential recruits' choice about *which* unit to join. The choices available varied with time and place. At a basic level, there were the different arms. Tall men may have recognized that their height carried a premium that meant they could join the better-paid cavalry, Foot Guards or artillery, provided that a recruiting party from those units was around to receive them. For the infantry there were options available too. In the early 1790s many potential recruits had the choice between joining a regiment of foot or one of the new fencible units. The success of the latter in raising men indicates that there was more to recruitment than raw economic factors, with likely service (and so chances of surviving) sitting alongside a keener territorial basis of recruiting that facilitated identity and community. This may explain why some fencible units filled their ranks so quickly.[14] There was also the militia too. Although based on a form of conscription, personal service could be avoided through substitutes serving instead. The price, effectively the bounty offered to a substitute, was unregulated and reflected the manpower demands of the militia, and a similar model operated for the Army of Reserve and Permanent Additional Force Act between 1803 to 1806. At moments of particularly high demand for men for the armed forces a potential recruit could get a higher bounty, better conditions of service, and would be less likely to be debilitated during his time as a soldier by choosing these other forces.[15] As we saw in Chapter 4, soldiers recruited for limited service then had opportunities to transfer to the line regiments, receiving another bounty.

There was also more to making the bargain between the individual, the army, and the regiment. Studies like Joe Cozens' have highlighted how there was a tangle of factors that influenced men to join beyond financial gain, including the promise of excitement, wanderlust, sexual conquest and notions of martial masculinity.[16] Recruiting posters and adverts in newspapers are an important sources about other influences on recruits. That regiments would spend money on these indicates their importance, and nor were they just for literate men as they could be read out (many have the same qualities as broadside ballads) and some were more visual. In effect regimental marketing, they made various appeals to adventure and glory, pay and conditions, and, as in the case of the poster for the Perthshire Fencible Cavalry, those who 'abhor the Tyranny and Cruelties of French Barbarians'. As Plate 8 shows, this message was made all the clearer through the vignette at the top of the poster of a cavalryman hunting down scrawny and ghoulish Frenchmen. Quite what made the 7th Light Dragoons 'The Old Saucy' is not clear from its recruiting poster, printed in Norwich in 1809, but it was certainly playing upon the potential attraction and sexualized swagger of some military uniforms, especially of hussars.[17] A little more muted was the advert that appeared each week between September to December 1794 in the *Reading Mercury*, which aimed to tap into local pride as it sought men with the 'noble and warlike spirit for which ENGLISHMEN are particularly distinguished, and which the LADS OF BERKSHIRE possess in the highest degree'.[18] Likewise, the ballad *Follow the Drum* recounts through song the impact a recruiting party would have on its travels:

> Soldiers through the town march'd gay
> The village flew to the sound of the drum
> From windows lasses look'd a score
> Neighbours met at every door
> Serjeant twirl'd his sash and story
> And talk'd of wounds, honor, and glory.[19]

In the tune that follow a ploughman, cobbler, and tailor all joined having had enough of their civilian lives, transferring their skills into ways of beating the French.[20] We should not dismiss these sources as rhetoric or fanciful, and just see potential recruits as driven into the Army through poverty. Ilya Berkovich's work has uncovered a far richer and deeper relationship of soldiers with military service in the late eighteenth and early nineteenth century.[21] It was not just the armies of Revolutionary France where men could have, or develop, martial and emotional bonds, and recruiting posters and newspapers adverts provide the evidence that the Army knew this and sought to use it.

There were other pathways to becoming a soldier outside of recruitment by bounty or transfers from other land forces. One of the most unsettling was the recruitment of boys. Some children were enlisted into the Army at a disturbingly young age to modern eyes to be entering a world characterized by violence, drink and the heavy physical burdens of marching and carrying their kit. Many of these very young boys were drummers, and their numbers were smaller than popular imagery supposed. Surveying unit inspection returns shows that only one in five musicians were under 18.[22] The recruitment of children was sometimes the result of certain circumstances, such as enlisting orphans or single-parent children of the regiment.[23] Outside these specific occasions, enlisting those under the age of 18 was increasingly regulated and restricted.[24] In 1807 boy recruits had to be at least 15 and 5ft 2in (1.57m) tall, and in 1812 the age limit was increased to 16 but the height lowered to 5ft (1.52m).[25] In comparison to broader notions of childhood and work, where boys could be apprenticed at 14 and children worked from six or seven, the Army was quite protective.[26] Initially, only units in South Asia were permitted to recruit boys, and this was extended to nineteen units in 1811 and then to forty-five in 1812, though in 1812 the numbers permitted per unit was reduced from one hundred to fifty.[27] Nor were they expected to be child soldiers, as the individuals were attached to second battalions or sent to units in India. In the latter case, we need to factor in the time spent getting to their point of departure, waiting for transport, and sailing time – in all at least six months. Many of the boys that enlisted were sons of serving soldiers or from the Royal Military Asylum, a coeducational boarding school established in 1801 for the children of soldiers.[28] Furthermore, the Duke of York encouraged boys to receive an education through regimental schools, with the hope that they would become NCOs in future. In all, figures presented to Parliament show that 13,700 boys were recruited from the UK into the Army between 1808 and 1815; a snapshot from 1808 shows that there were 2,600 boys in the Army, and it is unlikely that other years were that different.[29] From samples and statistical surveys about 4 per cent of the Army was under 18.[30]

Much of what has been said above about why men joined the Army in Britain and Ireland also applied to recruiting beyond those isles. The tendency, both at that time and afterwards, is to view these men as mercenaries, with all the pejorative associations that the term entails. As we have seen in previous chapters, there were substantial numbers of soldiers from western Europe in the Army. Like their British and Irish counterparts, it is worth exploring their agency and the opportunities that they had. Some had very little say in the matter, with units being rescued from disbandment by a commanding officer taking up an offer of British pay. New units made appeals to military service and financial gain. Generally, serving as a unit in British pay offered better terms and conditions, so in the 1790s the British Army's foreign corps were competitive in the German military labour market. Sometimes specific offers were made too. The Hompesch Hussars recruited for Caribbean service were told they were heading for a land of gold and silver. More tangible was the offer of land in Canada for those who joined the 7/60th in the latter stages of the Napoleonic Wars. Broadly, the British Army's foreign corps, especially those of the 1790s, were drawing upon established connections of eighteenth-century transnational European military labour. The sons of George III had royal status within the *Reich* as well as personal affiliations through their education in Germany. It was not just royalty either who had these links. There was a trans-European officer class who facilitated the recruitment of Europeans. Major Colin Halkett who formed the King's German Regiment that expanded into the King's German Legion was a former officer in the Dutch Guards.[31] New connections were added to these Anglo-German links through the emigration of officers from the French army in the 1790s. This bought Frenchmen, Swiss, more Germans, Italians and Irish Catholics into Britain as potential officers and recruiters to the Army. Nor should we forget the refugees from the French Revolution, some of them with military experience, who followed their officers or fled the Revolution for other reasons.[32]

There were also particular cases that expose other factors and motives. Both in the French Revolutionary and Napoleonic Wars there were European units that sought to preserve a military and political heritage in spite of European political changes wrought by the wars. The 5/60th, formed from many foreign corps in 1797, fostered and maintained a longer tradition of German light infantry service. Their cap badge of the Maltese Cross echoed the history of the Hompesch family and their relationship to the Knights of St John (itself a transnational military order). Perhaps the most evocative of these armies in exile were the Brunswick troops. Not only was their escape to the coast of North Germany to continue the fight against the Napoleonic Empire celebrated as romantic and heroic endeavour, their black uniforms and skull-and-crossbones on their caps was a stark indication of their commitment to their cause.[33] Of course, not everyone in these units will have subscribed to its avowed motives.

Against these units we can place soldiers who were recruited because they had little choice when the Army was so desperate for manpower. The men of the Waldeck regiment in Dutch service at the Cape of Good Hope were made prisoners and poorly treated to induce them to join the British Army.[34] Elsewhere around the globe practical realities meant it was a better choice for governors of newly-conquered territories to keep former enemy units on the payroll than have them disband, and so several Dutch units were incorporated into the Army through the 1790s and 1800s.[35] The need for manpower also drove the Army to recruit from prisoners of war. On one occasion, this had catastrophic results. In the run-up to the Quiberon expedition in 1795, some French émigré unit boosted their numbers by taking French prisoners of war. Back on their own soil some deserted, of which a few, perhaps keen to ensure their Republican convictions, revealed details of the Royalists' positions. The defences at Quiberon were compromised from the start and led to the destruction of the British army there.[36] By the 1810s, though, enlisting prisoners of war was perhaps a little safer. By then most of the soldiers of the Napoleonic Empire were conscripts and so the intense ideological commitment to their state of origin was less likely. Pay and conditions within the British Army were certainly better than in a prison camp, and from 1812 onwards there was a good chance they would be on the winning side and opportunities might come from fighting for the political order that likely would follow. There were, then, plenty of good reasons for them to enlist and for the British government to provide this opportunity.[37]

Like the recruitment of boys, the recruitment of criminals into the Army is often used as evidence of the Army's poor social standing. Yet the numbers were never as large as supposed and only a minority of offenders went into the Army.[38] Recruitment from prisons and from soldiers that had committed crimes was more tightly managed during the period. Handling military service overseas as a punishment was awkward for the Army, though it was routine business. In 1783 the Army withdrew its garrison company in West Africa that had functioned as a penal unit but sentencing soldiers to service in the Caribbean or South Asia was hardly fair on the soldiers already there for no other reason than being in a particular regiment of foot. Partly, this was solved by creating new units to receive prisoners or using those that were fixed to overseas service, such as the 3/ and 4/60th Foot (which were not permitted to return to Britain or Ireland), the New South Wales Corps in Australia, and the Queen's Rangers in North America.[39] The Royal African Corps was recreated in 1801 (later split into a unit serving in West Africa and one in the Caribbean), the York Light Infantry Volunteers were also sent offenders, and in 1813 the York Chasseurs were created for deserters from the Army.[40] These four units were not exclusively penal corps, however, as men could enlist for these regiments just as they could for any other, plus the Army instituted recruitment for 'General Service' at a lower physical standard than the regiments of foot and men recruited under these terms were often sent to such units.[41] Prisoners were not confined to these units. In the aftermath of the 1798 rebellion in Ireland and Emmet's rebellion of 1803, large numbers of Irish prisoners were sent to regiments already or on order for overseas service, a process that went on until 1804. Michel Durey estimates that 3,200 were sent to the Caribbean and distributed amongst units there, including the 60th Foot. When these units were moved elsewhere the men were drafted to the incoming regiments.[42]

As with the recruitment of children, we face questions about definitions and context in the recruitment of prisoners and criminals. A large proportion, especially in the 1800s and 1810s, were already soldiers in the Army who had transgressed military law as court-martial sentences could be commuted to service overseas.[43] Conditions in civilian prison hulks meant that many men there were not fit enough for the Army, and Horse Guards and military commanders knew that criminal-soldiers often caused more problems than they solved.[44] Then there were also the reasons why someone was a criminal or in prison at the time. The eighteenth-century penal code massively extended the range of offences that criminalized customary practices of survival of the rural poor, like poaching and gathering wood. Those that committed small-scale crimes that were often prompted by extreme deprivation and acts of a makeshift economy found themselves incarcerated. This was coupled with a decline in transportation as a punishment, and as a result the prison population in Britain and Ireland swelled. Moreover, those in prisons were not all convicted felons, as many were culprits: suspects waiting for trial. The Army specifically recruited from this population, betting on the individual taking their chance in the Army rather than a trial.[45] Some culprit and criminal recruits had a degree, however small, of choice about joining the Army.

There were significant numbers that were forced into the Army, almost all into the West India regiments. These units were intended to be raised from the Caribbean population, but this was frustrated by local colonial and plantation-owner opposition, and so the British Army resorted to purchasing newly arrived enslaved Africans to fill their ranks. Between 1795 and 1808 13,400 men were drafted into these units this way, making the Army one of the biggest individual purchasers in the British slave trade.[46] After the abolition of the slave trade in 1807 new means were adopted to continue the supply of personnel to the West India regiments. There were some Africans who volunteered to serve in them, receiving a bounty in the same way as any other recruit to the British Army. Through an 1808 Order in Council all illegally transported Africans that were captured by the Royal Navy in anti-slave trade patrols were assessed by an admiralty court in Sierra Leone. Those judged fit were then handed over to the British Army or Navy and so the forced enlistment and migration of Africans to the Caribbean for the Army continued.[47]

Material Lives

The recruits to the Army, whatever the pathway they took into it, faced a new social reality. The Army directed the lives of its soldiers in multiple ways and in almost every aspect. It regulated their basics of living, such as food, pay, clothing and accommodation. It sought to shape their behaviour, determining what was acceptable and what was not. The material life of soldiers was shaped and supplied by others, usually their officers, and alterations in its provision were mostly out of their hands. The enlisted man's experience was mediated through the unit – their new home and community – by the temperament and attitudes of those there to enforce these rules and norms. Primarily these were officers, but medical staff and NCOs (themselves drawn from the enlisted men) were important too. The impact of being in a world-wide Army affected individuals too as environment and circumstances changed. Routine was enforced as a soldier became more enmeshed in the structure of the Army. Whilst with a recruiting party, soldiers' initial experience was probably quite free, but as they were assimilated into the structure of the army in its battalions, troops of cavalry or company of artillery, and then into barracks, camps and armies in the field the Army sought increasingly to control their lives.

It was this structure into discrete units, most often regiments, that shaped the enlisted man's experience in what was a relatively self-contained community. An enlisted man's unit also provided new opportunities as they could be promoted to NCO rank, though only if there was a vacancy or the unit expanded. It is estimated that one man in six achieved an NCO rank, and a literate soldier had a higher chance.[48] A system of lance-corporals and lance-sergeants was instituted from 1804 to mark out potential soldiers for promotion, and further steps were added throughout the era with the addition of sergeant-majors and colour sergeants.[49] The proportion of soldiers that became NCOs was higher than the established structure of the Army would suggest, as there was regular turnover of men moving up and down the ranks. An examination of court-martial records by Danielle Coombes has found that NCOs were regularly being reduced in rank for infractions of the Army's rules and regulations, and then sometimes promoted again.[50] Within the infantry there were other ways of distinguishing themselves too, with men being selected from the entire unit to fill out the light and grenadier companies.

Alongside changes in status and position within a unit, there were also transfers from one unit to another. As we shall see later in this chapter, switching men around units could cause a lot of trouble for the Army, but it was deemed necessary to eke out manpower. There were moments of wholesale transfers, such as the reduction of infantry regiments in 1795 and their redistribution into the remaining regiments of foot and the disbanding of the fencible cavalry in 1800. Worn out and old soldiers were transferred to invalid and veteran units, and from around 1803 this was supplemented by the continued presence of second battalions for the infantry and depot troops for the cavalry, where new recruits were inducted into Army life and soldiers unfit for campaigning could be transferred back. Some soldiers would be transferred yet again into the Royal Veteran Battalions upon recommendation from their officers as deserving of this posting. The Garrison Battalions, which had been created to receive soldiers raised for limited service between 1803 and 1805, also became a means of keeping soldiers serving, by receiving men that were recovering from illness or otherwise unfit but not suitable for the veteran units.[51] These units were segregated, though, with a Royal Veteran Battalion allocated for the cavalry and Foot Guards, as well as one for Scottish soldiers (but not Irish), alongside separate black invalid companies stationed in the Caribbean for the West India regiments, and an Invalid company for the KGL. By the years of the Peninsular War, these layers of units had become a fairly well-established system, and so there was a constant flow of soldiers that largely was undertaken in the confines of a regiment so avoiding the problems of the 1790s.[52] This meant that many soldiers served in a variety of units across their careers.

All this lay in the future for the recruit. One aspect of Army life that will have struck him very quickly was its enforced communal living, which was more than just sharing accommodation and food. Recruits often found that their new-found wealth from the bounty was expected to be spent with and for their fellow soldiers. Soldier memoirs include tales where they bought drinks and food for fellow soldiers, usually in situations where they were left little choice, or other enlisted men taking on jobs like cleaning their uniform for a small fee or the expectation of standing them a loan later.[53] The new soldier also had to adjust to the physical accommodation that was provided to him. As the print *English Barracks* suggests (Plate 6), in a rather sanitised scene that was produced in contrast to an image of French barracks, all aspects of their lives were conducted together. The reality was much more cramped than this, even in barracks. Men shared beds, if they were not in hammocks where only 22–23in (56–58.5cm) was permitted per man.[54] Until the large barrack building programme of the 1790s most soldiers in England where billeted in inns, where cramped and poor facilities were only encouraged by the inadequate funding allocated for it by the government.[55] Life on campaign, or 'in the field' in other ways such as military camps, was similarly collective either by sharing lives in communities of tents or bivouacking around a fire.[56] Rarely were soldiers allowed private lives, with officially married men sometimes permitted to sleep outside quarters with their families.[57] This meant soldiers having to find somewhere. In the Caribbean, and probably other garrisons overseas too, enlisted men resorted to temporary huts.[58] It is telling, though, that Army regulations specified that soldiers avoid making separate berths on transport ships by hanging up blankets, suggesting that is exactly what they did. In some recognition for the need for a modicum of privacy, a kind of married quarters could be established, but which had to be cleared away by 7am.[59]

The Army also exerted more intimate control over soldiers' lives, as their bodies became at the service and control of military authorities. The increasing proscription of the process of recruitment included the inspection of new soldiers by surgeons. Surgeons were expected to examine recruits' bodies, looking for any infirmities, particularly skin ulcers.[60] More persistent was the Army's attempts to shape the bodies of soldiers. Dress was designed to encourage an erect posture by physically moulding the body of the wearer, and pride in physical appearance was encouraged. Hair was an example of this. Before 1808, it was soaped, covered in flour, and then shaped and pulled in such a way that head movements were difficult. These powdered pigtails were bad for the soldiers' health as they encouraged lice and vermin.[61] The leather stock worn around the neck was another example of physical restrictions imposed on their bodies, as it constricted the neck and forced a upright body shape. Physical punishment was the most significant form of military control over a soldier's body. Corporal punishment, especially through the brutal, ritualized, and public flogging of offenders with a cat o'nine tails in front of a punishment parade, exemplified how a soldiers' physical health was subject to the enforcement of military law.[62] Recent research by Zack White into court martials has shown that the Army was not wholly addicted to harsh discipline through the relentless flogging of its men (though some officers were), and that its incidence was dependent on a variety of factors. As such soldiers' experience of physical punishment varied considerably, but the threat encoded in military law and customary practice was ever present.[63]

Soldiers' lives were controlled through the rhythm of their day. Whilst in camp or garrisons, officers set their watches at headquarters at orderly time, and from this the chronology of a soldiers' day was largely set. Reveille was at daybreak in Britain and Ireland, whilst in tropical climates like the Caribbean soldiers were up at 5am for the first drills of the day before breakfast. On transports, bedding was to be bought up onto deck by 7am (later adjusted to 6am in 1804 regulations) and then the soldiers went to breakfast at 8am. Inspection followed at 9am. Lights out on transports was 8pm, but an hour later for soldiers in barracks. The retreat was at sunset, after which no trumpet or drum was to sound unless it was an alarm or for changing watches.[64] Any marches were usually done in the morning. The central feature of the day was the main meal just after midday. Alongside these, a soldier's daily conduct was set by regimental and garrison standing orders, plus any established by army commanders that were given out each day by the units' adjutant.[65] This meant that the tone of routine and discipline varied between units and places.

Cleanliness became one aspect where the Army prescribed activities for soldiers, especially on transport ships. These rules reflected the experience of the 1790s and the debilitating effect that cramped life on board ships had on the health of soldiers and was part of the wider medicalization of Army life discussed in Chapter 5. Feet were to be washed and hair combed every day. Men were to shave twice a week and wash once or twice a week. Shirts were to be cleaned with the same regularity.[66] The decks used as berths were to be aired every day, swept and scrubbed, but only washed once a week and then only when the weather was fine and the decks could dry.[67] Otherwise, Army regulations generally provided long lists of things that soldiers were not permitted to do, for instance no dogs in barracks (in Ireland 'Hawks or such like' were banned too), or prohibiting smoking between decks on transport ships. Some of these were clearly unenforceable, such as orders forbidding gaming in camp and cantonments.[68] It was in barracks where the Army's attempts to control soldiers' behaviour went furthest, with preserving the physical estate of government property above soldiers' comfort or practical use. Hooks or nails were not to be put into walls, despite the need for soldiers to store all their kit and keep it clean. Items in the barracks were not be re-used, for example sheets doubling as tablecloths. During the day, soldiers were not to sleep in barracks nor carry on trades there. On arrival in barracks, soldiers were faced with charges for the facilities: 3d for a pair of double sheets and 2d for a set of single sheets, which were changed once a month, alongside 1d a week for washing the round towel in each room.[69]

Charges against soldiers' pay, wherever he was stationed and whatever form of accommodation he was in, was an unremitting drain on their meagre finances. In the 1780s, the situation was dire as a soldier's total pay in a year amounted to £9 19s, out of which £7 16s was taken for food and a further charge £4 2s 4½d for his necessaries, meaning soldiers were in debt as soon as they enlisted. It took the worries about the susceptibility of soldiers to radicalism through literal bread and butter issues of work and pay for new regulations to be issued in 1792. This transferred the responsibility for the cost of food and necessaries to the state, so although soldiers were still paid 6d per day, they at least actually had a surplus each week.[70] From May 1797, pay was increased to 1s per day for infantry privates, with the stipulation that no more than 4s per week was to be deducted for food, 1s 6d per week for necessaries (taken monthly), leaving 1s 6d per week for the soldier. Cavalrymen's pay went up to 1s 3d per day, leaving them with 1s 7½d clear each week, and privates in the Horse Guards received 1s 11¼d per day.[71] Edward Coss' work allows us to make some comparisons of how this compared to civilian life. An agricultural labourer could get between 8s and 10s per week, whilst more skilled workers like carpenters and weavers could earn between 14s and 25s, and 'fine work' artisans earning as much as 44s.[72] Out of which, of course, workers had to find their own food, clothing, accommodation, any medical care they could afford, and in some trades the tools and material needed to earn money. Lastly, there was the uncertainty of being able to get employment. At least Army pay was continuously accounted for, if not regularly delivered, and they were shielded from high prices by mechanisms whereby the state stepped in if meat and bread became more expensive than the allotted funding.[73]

The deduction from his pay for food was meant to provide a daily ration of 1lb of meat, 1lb of biscuit (bread was issued in garrisons and in Britain and Ireland) and a third of a pint of spirits. Much of the food soldiers received was poor quality, as contractors were unable to preserve it, even if it was in a decent state in the first place. With all the transport and logistical problems of moving enormous volumes of foodstuffs, it was usual on campaigns for the commissariat to fail to provide soldiers even the basics.[74] This meant that soldiers acted themselves. In garrisons, soldiers' pay (if they got it) could be spent in local markets. In places like the Caribbean, where there was a well-established and largely fixed presence of the Army, soldiers could supplement their diet with locally-grown fruit and vegetables.[75] The bazaars that were established for the Army in India were intended to provide all of a soldier's needs.[76] On campaign in Iberia, as will be explored in more detail below, soldiers resorted to stealing food to survive.

Soldiers' uniform and equipment were a tangible manifestation of the administration of the Army discussed in Chapter 3. Any arms, such a musket, bayonet, and cartridge pouch for the infantry, were supplied by the Board of Ordnance. Most of the items of equipment needed for campaigning, such as knapsacks, cooking utensils, and the like, were purchased by the Treasury and then disbursed either through the commissariat or the storekeeper's department. The proprietorial management of clothing, where each regimental colonel or commandant personally received and disbursed funding for uniforms, coupled with a system of royal warrants to fix clothing design, meant that change came slowly and often only in response to catastrophic failures. The failure to adequately clothe soldiers in the campaigns of the 1793–5 in Flanders was well known, and the problem was still present in the Peninsular War over a decade later, with soldiers still going without shoes and wearing threadbare and patched uniforms.[77] The mini-ice age and terrible winters of the mid-

1790s exposed, literary, the inadequacy of uniforms to protect men from the weather. Greatcoats became a particular issue. The benefits of providing soldiers with these were obvious, but to address this the military administration had to find a way to work through existing systems that made new additions like this tricky. An attempt was made in the late 1790s to fund greatcoats for the infantry by reducing the length of the coat and using poorer-quality material for the waistcoat.[78] By 1808, greatcoats were provided by government contracts, bypassing the existing clothing arrangements for soldiers.[79] Like greatcoats, a public campaign to provide flannel clothing for soldiers in the winter of 1793/4 was yet more evidence of problems caused by the massive expansion of the Army in the 1790s.[80]

Behaviour and Identities

Like the reasons why men enlisted discussed earlier, it is important not to just see enlisted men as passive entities shaped and directed by an omnipotent Army. Despite having the hallmarks of a total institution through the publication of general orders, regulations, and regimental and garrison order books, those serving in the Army shaped it too. They bought into the Army their existing attitudes and their own senses of what was right and wrong. Most of the soldiers in the Army were drawn from a culture where ideas of a moral economy were still important. Service in the Army shaped the attitudes and behaviour of the enlisted men too. Peripatetic service explored in Chapter 2 gave individuals new experiences through encounters with different people and physical enviroments, and military communities forged new identities and behaviours. Sometimes, men protested and even rejected their condition through desertion, occasionally mutiny, and other infractions of the disciplinary code, particularly drunkenness but also theft of essentials simply to survive.

There were a variety of ways that enlisted men baulked at the regulation of their lives. The most overt of these were mutinies, but we need to be careful about what underpinned these events. The accusation of mutiny, and its punishment, was imposed on those involved in them by commanders of the Army that were sometimes desperate to maintain military authority. Looked at more closely though, and putting aside the terminology, these events were labour disputes. They were a militarized echo of collective bargaining accompanied by physical action that were the hallmarks of bread or wage riots that were part of the labouring and artisan life that most soldiers came from. John Prebble's work has highlighted Highlanders' resistance to changing terms and conditions that led some Scottish fencible regiments to mutiny in 1794–5, and again in 1803.[81] Although usually seen as peculiar to Highland regiments because of different attitudes to towards military service and pre-existing associations between the men, they were not as distinct as often portrayed. In 1783 a number of regiments refused orders to march to different quarters because they were due their discharge as limited-service soldiers at the end of the war.[82] There were a series of disturbances in 1795 when several units were ordered to be disbanded and the men drafted into the remaining regiments. Fearing, probably rightly, that they were to be sent to units known to be allocated for service in the Caribbean, they resisted the order.[83] But it was not just about the fear of overseas service. Reporting of events in Dublin in September 1795 showed the strength of feeling about changing their conditions of service, as men swore in public that they would 'sooner die than be drafted: they would go any where they might be commanded together till the war should end, but they would not go into other regiments'.[84] These sentiments were particularly expressed by the men of the 105th and 113th Foot in the same year to the point that an address was printed (reproduced in Plate 9). Hard treatment could also provoke mass response. Opposition to the draconian disciplinary regime introduced by the General Prince Edward, Duke of Kent, when he took over the command of the Gibraltar garrison in 1802 resulted in a mutiny and the Duke of Kent's recall.[85] Far more significant than all of these was the incident in the 2nd Dragoon Guards in August 1791. Joseph Cozens' close study of this event, when a group of troopers petitioned their colonel about unfair punishments but which intriguing included a request to be sent on foreign service, shows that it was fundamental in highlighting soldiers' meagre pay at home and led to Adjutant-General William Fawcett pressing for pay rises. Pay was not increased, but the provision of food and some equipment was changed to improve the soldiers' lot. Nor was this the last time the threat of direct action led to changes, as the pay rise given to soldiers in 1797 was a response to the growing agitation in the Army about pay, echoing the Naval mutinies of the time.[86]

Outside of collective action on a large scale more prevalent were smaller-scale or individual actions where soldiers rejected their lot. It contributed to desertion, although it was not the only reason soldiers deserted. In the 1780s, desertion was recognized as a problem although there were no official statistics about it. Low pay, debts, and boredom were seen as contributing factors.[87] As we saw in earlier chapters, desertion became an issue within the political debates about recruitment but viewed bottom-up several key features emerge. It was overwhelmingly new soldiers that deserted. The Duke of York estimated 10 per cent of recruits deserted, and recent detailed analysis of deserter records from the later parts of the Napoleonic Wars shows that 40 per cent of desertions occurred within twelve months of enlisting. Alongside these were a persistent number of desertions from longer-serving soldiers. There were myriad reasons for this, but a third to a half that returned to life as a soldier (most with their original unit) sometimes after very short periods away from the Army, indicating that desertion was a temporary withdrawal of labour. It is also evidence of a desire just to break the routine and gain a measure of control in their lives. Large numbers of desertions took place in 1814 and 1815, particularly amongst British and Irish units in the south of France that were under orders to serve in North America. We do not have direct testimony from these soldiers about their reasons, but we can reasonably infer that they were unhappy about continued service when many thought the war was over and so they were due their discharge. Unlike 1783 whole units were not composed of men enlisted for limited terms of service so there was less collective action.[88]

Desertion was a risky way of rejecting Army life. Punishments for it were extremely severe. Probably, soldiers were more likely to turn to other ways of expressing their boredom, disillusionment, annoyance, and even depression at military life. Soldiers feigning illness, malingering or just generally dawdling in the Peninsular War led to the moniker 'Belemites' or 'Belem Rangers' named after the hospital at Belem.[89] At the other end of the spectrum was self-harm to escape military life. This could range from encouraging illnesses to physical injury, and even suicide. Records about these, and particularly the causes of them, are sketchy, but present.[90] Then there were persistent infractions of the disciplinary code that fill up the records of courts martial at regimental level: not looking after equipment; not attending duties or drills; disrespecting those in positions of military authorities or refusing particular orders.[91] In examining these, we are largely in the hands of those who decided what was to be prosecuted and what evidence could be gathered, so conclusions based on the incidence of these infractions need to be circumspect. Nevertheless, the general picture is clear: the Army's disciplinary and regulatory regime was routinely challenged.

Alcohol repeatedly features in the records of the enforcement of military justice on enlisted men, and more generally drinking was a significant part of soldiers' lives. Before condemning soldiers for their drunkenness, it is worth highlighting the Army's contradictory position on alcohol. It provided it to enlisted men as a part of their provisions charged out of their own pay (and so more important than fruit and vegetables that the soldiers had to provide themselves) but then condemned its impact. To explore and explain this, alcohol and the Army needs to be considered as a social and cultural issue, as much as one about health. Without this context, scholars have tended to see alcohol in the Army just as abuse and frame it as a problem that should have been dealt with.[92] There were (and are) social functions to drinking. It is important as a social lubricant and features almost everywhere in human existence in celebrations.[93] Alcohol also had an important role in treating disease in the eighteenth and nineteenth centuries as well as perceived general medical properties.[94] Madeira wine was specifically recommended by the War Office for hospitals,[95] and rum was given legendary, though utterly false, powers to preserve the health of white soldiers in the Caribbean.[96] The background consumption of alcohol in society is important too. Enlisted men were probably already used to heavy drinking. Strong matured beer – porter – was the staple of labourers, and our best estimates are that labourers in London would have consumed at least ten pints a week of beer that had a strength of 20 to 12 per cent.[97] This was not just about intoxication either, as strong beer was seen as part of a labourer's diet: it was regarded as a food and essential for physical labour. Against this backdrop, it was improbable that the Army would offer fewer opportunities for alcohol consumption than in civilian life, and the Army used drink for specific purposes too. It was given as a reward and a stimulant, as well as medicine. Its largest function, though, was social. Although the Army sought to regulate time for soldiers it did not fill it for them. Soldiers had plenty of reasons to turn to drink when they had time on their hands. Boredom and alcohol as a relaxant featured heavily in the social lives of enlisted men. Whilst campaigning, it was also a mechanism to address stress and escape hardship, however temporarily. With all these additional factors added to drinking culture that soldiers bought with them into the Army, it is not surprising that Coss' analysis of soldiers in Spain and Portugal has shown the craving of soldiers for alcohol, their unerring ability to ferret it out from the Iberian population, and the risks they would take to get it.[98] Although drinking became a common vice of enlisted men, and there were certainly alcoholics in the Army, we should be aware of the cultural, social and military currents that pushed soldiers that way.

More pernicious in stimulating crime in the Army was the failure to provide adequate shelter, food and clothing, or the pay to address these things. Essentially soldiers were forced into poverty. Enlisted men responded to this in the different ways. On campaign in Portugal and Spain, Coss has shown how soldiers became accomplished and ingenious plunderers, but with a system of norms that had rules about what was acceptable to the group. Frequently on the verge of starvation, soldiers took what they could from the local population, yet acknowledged the harm that they were causing to people they took from, in part because they came from similar social backgrounds.[99] Outside the opportunities for plunder on campaign, soldiers turned to theft, either from each other, local communities or the military establishment. Items of equipment or stores were stolen and then sold on in black markets that emerged around military communities, ready to provide the means to turn goods into cash for soldiers.[100] In both these different scenarios soldiers were echoing the makeshift economy of their lives before they were soldiers, where crime was a necessary part of survival.[101]

Soldiers' behaviour was underpinned by their sense of identity and values. These are, however, tricky to ascertain. The evidence we have about what enlisted men thought about what they and others did is refracted through the literate British and Irish soldiers that wrote about their experiences, and the identities that were imposed by the Army. In terms of background, the Army only recognized four identities when units were inspected: English, Scottish, Irish and Foreign. All other identities were ignored though they will have existed, including (but not limited to) the language they spoke, religion, customs, the place they felt as home, family status and socio-economic position they may have occupied through trade. As soldiers were subsumed into the Army, it was the unit they joined that became their main identity. John Cookson has explored the full range of ways that regiments became the enlisted man's (and woman's too) world, as they were self-contained societies that by the Peninsular War had become increasingly fixed and formalized. This was not solely the imposition of ideas about paternalism by the Duke of York and unit commanders, as making units mean something as a community came from the soldiers themselves too. The unit became a collective scene for social activities, where men established reading clubs, funds for widows and children that echoed civilian friendly societies, Methodist meetings and missionary funds.[102] Underneath this level, the primary group was the mess, a group of six men that could form intensely close bonds of military comradeship to mitigate and navigate the challenges of life on military campaigns. As Andrew Bamford has explored, soldier memoirs provide much evidence of this rich regimental culture in the British and Irish units in Iberia, particularly the way that units jostled and defined themselves against each other through nicknames, traditions, and reputation (both good and bad).[103]

The multinational dimensions of the Army are understudied. Across all units, though, there was an ethos that was particularly emphasized from around 1800 to encourage an identity as a professional, and Christian, soldier that had a sense of what unit they served within, regardless of their previous identities. As Commander-in-Chief, the Duke of York sought to encourage pride in soldiers.[104] Unit identity, even without the opportunities to gain traditions and reputations through active service, was the fundamental vehicle for this. It was hard coded into the structure and material lives of soldiers explored earlier. Units were identified through their uniforms, each with distinctions sometimes greater for some units, like the hussars in their heavily braided jackets and pelisses or Highland regiments in kilts, to standardized distinctions between regiments of foot through the colours of their collars and cuffs (known as facings), and sometimes smaller, like the fine detail in lace that distinguished the yellow facings worn by both the 82nd and 84th Foot. All of this was captured in Anthony

Cardon's print *A View of the British Army* of 1803 (Plate 1) The fact that we have so much uniformology for this period reflects the importance it was given at the time, even if the reality on campaign was far from the official regulations.

Service in the Army fostered identities in other ways too. It was itself a mechanism for cross-cultural contact and comparison. This could both sharpen and broaden identities depending on the context and place. The Isle of Wight, for example, was home to the foreign depot that bought together recruits and otherwise detached soldiers from outside Britain and Ireland, and just in the title itself indicates a homogenization of British Army soldiers from western Europe into a single identity. In contrast, eastward along the coast at the depot in Bexhill in Sussex, the King's German Legion were able to more clearly define themselves as Hanoverian and the King's German subjects.[105] The Army's global commitments meant soldiers came into contact with different environments and people, presenting new contrasts to them and providing an 'other' against which their sense of self was shaped. Before even meeting anyone else, contemporary views about climate would have started to exert an influence. In the Caribbean, medical opinion about the inability of Europeans to cope with heat resulted in racial attitudes about soldiering. So European soldiers, regardless of their nationality, were excused from fatigue duties.[106] Similar can be said for South Asia, though there this process tended towards Britishness as, besides the De Meruon Regiment, there was no European component to the Army like there was in the Caribbean. Outside tropical climates, we await studies about that explore how soldiers were classified and utilized in Canada, southern Africa, Malta, and Sicily, to name four areas where the Army was stationed for some time. All had locally recruited units and auxiliaries and enough of a climatic difference which could have moulded identities.

Fortunately, we have two studies to draw upon: one for Iberia and the other on Egypt. For the enlisted men in Spain and Portugal, Gavin Daly's work has highlighted the cross-cultural encounters that it engendered. It bound soldiers together in hostility to the barbarity they witnessed between the French and the guerrillas, emphasized Britain's economic development, and yet romanticized the struggle of Spaniards and Portuguese just as some lusted after Iberian women who were perceived as more sexually receptive. Their experiences were both characterized by repugnance and exotic intrigue.[107] In Egypt, Simon Quinn's work has explored how even the relatively brief contact with this part of North Africa had important implications. Like Iberia, there was a religious dimension to this, as enlisted men bought with them some preconceptions of Egypt through biblical teachings. Echoing the soldierly professionalism that the Army was seeking to inculcate, soldiers evaluated their allies the Ottomans and Mamluks. The latter were particularly appreciated for their skill as swordsmen and horseman (though curiously this was not translated into recruiting them, in contrast to almost everywhere else in the world). Like the racial identities being entrenched the Caribbean, contact with the peoples of Egypt and the Ottoman Empire was a foundational moment in making tangible through experience the perception of distinctions between western Europe and these places, and then bringing these perceptions back into the Army and the British Isles through the 10,000 or so soldiers who served in this campaign.[108]

*   *   *

The differing responses of similar soldiers to environments in which they served highlights the diversity of the lives of enlisted men in the British Army. It brings out all the issues of the different sources we have to explore their lives and ways to approach them. So, Edward Coss' analysis of recruitment patterns holds true for those enlisted from Britain and Ireland through ordinary recruitment between 1808 and 1815, but it is less appropriate for all the other men who entered the Army in different ways and at different times. Their responses to these experiences were equally varied. They could take pride in identity as soldiers or their unit, but equally commit crimes to ensure their survival or to get some money. The structured and regulated life that the Army increasingly sought to impose on the enlisted men was intended to induce conformity and uniformity. It sought to re-frame the soldiers' material existence, changing their relationship to things by creating dependent relationships where the Army took responsibility for food, clothing, equipment and accommodation. The complexities of clothing, equipping, paying and feeding a soldier reflected the administration of the Army. This was all mediated, however, through others – especially officers but also contractors – and what the soldiers themselves saw as fair and appropriate. Underpinning these responses were attitudes they bought from their lives before enlisting and new norms that were created through military service. In all of this, enlisted men more fully emerge as humans, with all the complexities in psychology and culture that go with that. The history, then, of the enlisted men in the British Army is far more complex than the often-used quotes from Wellington about them. His pronouncement fails even as a broad approximation as it generalizes hundreds of thousands of people and offers no expertise or interest in their lives save for the prejudices of his class.

Chapter 7

Officers

From the humanity of your character & benevolent disposition & my feelings as the Mother of a large family has induced me to presume in taking this liberty of petitioning your interest, to favour me with an Ensigncy for my son Archibald Glenlyon Campbell who had the honor of a commission as Ensign in the 1st Breadalbane fencibles, served his Majesty while in Ireland, & also in Scotland, that has given him such a taste for the Army that were it convenient for his Father to provide for him in any other lyne there is none the young man is so partiall to.[1]

Mrs Sarah Campbell's petition on behalf her son to Henry Dundas in 1800 is just one of thousands of letters submitted to those in the administration of the Army seeking a commission. It is not certain if Archibald Campbell was ultimately successful; none of his namesakes in the 1801 and 1802 *Army Lists* fit the sketchy information that we have given in the letter. This is indicative of just how different the management of Army officers was to that of enlisted men covered in the previous chapter. The Army required minimal documentary information about officer entrants, often just recording a name and from 1783 a statement that they were over 16. There was no medical examination, no physical standards they had to meet, nor systematic record of their parish of birth, background and physical description. Unlike some other European armies in the eighteenth century, would-be officers were not required to provide proof of aristocratic lineage.[2] Like their enlisted fellow soldiers, though, the history of Army officers has been mired in stereotypes and beholden to a few individuals who have been taken to represent the whole. To undo this, what follows is underpinned by a survey of every British Army officer present at the Battle of Waterloo, totalling just over 2,400 people. They range from Ensign James Murphy of the 40th Foot who was commissioned on 8 June 1815 to Major Frederick W. Hoysted of the 59th Foot, whose career started in the 64th Foot thirty-eight years earlier, making him one of the longest-serving officers at Waterloo.

Entrants

Although patronage is usually deemed to dominate Army commissions, more correctly it was about the ability of individuals within the Army bureaucracy to either recommend, block or withhold nominations to the monarch. There were only a few situations where individuals had Army commissions in their gift that were guaranteed to be approved. In the 1780s and until 1793 all new officer appointments for the infantry and cavalry initially went to the Secretary at War who, if he had no objections, would pass them on the regimental agents for consideration by the candidate's potential colonel. If the commission was to be purchased – and not all were – then the money was deposited with the regimental agent. If the colonel approved, then all the paperwork was laid before the King, who would usually grant the commission. Duly signed, the commission was passed onto the new officer (who paid a fee to the regimental agents for the appointment), the name and date recorded, a public announcement made in *The London Gazette* (often then copied into other newspapers), and he would appear in subsequent *Army Lists*.[3] With the appointment of Amherst as Commander-in-Chief in 1793 the channel changed but the process remained the same.

This process, though, was not always so straightforward. Recommendations could come from multiple sources, each claiming the privilege to nominate a new officer. The creation of the 74th to 77th Regiments of Foot in 1787 illustrates this. The EIC successfully argued that half the appointments should be determined by them because these units were to be sent to South Asia. Sir George Younge, the Secretary at War, was progressing with nominating officers for the other part, when George III decided that the new colonels would have this patronage. This worked fine in three regiments, but in the 74th the new colonel was in Madras and so he gave the authority to make arrangements to his two brothers in Scotland. Alongside this, the Duke of Argyll claimed he had a right to nominate officers because so much of the recruiting was done on his land. The new lieutenant-colonel also insisted that he should provide names.[4] These sorts of difficulties were common as individuals sought patrons to support their application. So, the Irish Lord Lieutenant, government ministers, members of the royal family and those close to them, general officers holding a military command, and regimental colonels all held varying levels of sway in the process. Although in Ireland entrance and promotion into Irish Establishment units was used to ensure political support for the King's government,[5] generally political influence over officer appointments has been exaggerated. On average from 1784 to 1792 267 new officers were appointed into the Army, with only 168 in 1786. By the end of 1787 every single promotion had been by purchased, which was almost never blocked by anyone. The scope, then, for mass manipulation of officer appointments for political reasons was extremely limited.[6]

1793 to 1795 was a different matter, as Amherst was overawed by Pitt and Dundas as they took the reins of running the Army. Better filing of nominations, though, for officers started when Amherst came to office (all held in the WO31 series at The National Archives). The Duke of York's reforms on commissioning officers were outwardly quite modest but profound. He created the role of Military Secretary to the Commander-in-Chief: a single point of contact for officer appointments and responsible for making enquiries about potential officers and assessing their suitability.[7] Who was deemed suitable to recommend an officer was narrowed, with a candidate needing at least one reference from a major or higher rank.[8] Combined these changes resulted in fewer gatekeepers into the Army. This was taken further with standardized printed letters that could be obtained from regimental agents, filled out and then sent in. Guides for officers indicated that a recommendation from the regimental colonel was 'more acceptable'.[9]

Along with someone to recommend their name, there needed to be a vacancy. As we saw in Chapter 3, the numbers allowed in the Army were tightly managed and this was especially the case for officers, so appointments were driven by supply. In the 1780s, there were relatively few vacancies because of the over-officering of the Army relative to its size. This all changed between 1793 and 1795. The massive expansion both in size and number of units in the Army created a huge need for officers. The scale of the change is indicated by the raw figures: on 31 December 1792 there were 4,496 commissioned officers; by the late summer of 1795 the total was close to 8,500 (and there were 594 vacancies), including officers of the British and Irish Ordnance and around 850 officers in foreign corps.[10] The new regiments (regiments of foot above the 78th, the 21st Light Dragoons and above, and all the fencibles) meant new appointments at every level from lieutenant-colonel downwards in the military hierarchy. In a few circumstances officers were directly appointed to quite high rank, such as Henry, Lord Paget who was made lieutenant-colonel commandant of the 80th Foot without any previous service in the Army. New units, including the independent companies, had no colonels to consult and so nominations were more firmly in the hands of Henry Dundas and the Lord Lieutenant of Ireland.[11]

Officer appointments in the fencibles and other provincial units was a mixture of new and returning officers with some military experience. Often someone well connected was appointed directly as their commandant. The Sussex Fencible Cavalry, like many, was commanded by an Member of Parliament: George Thomas, baronet, MP for Arundel and whose wealth came from the Caribbean slave-plantation economy.[12] Under him was Lieutenant-Colonel

Christopher Teesdale, another man with Sussex connections but whose father, Colonel Christopher Teesdale, had served in the Army in the mid-eighteenth century.[13] Robert Hall, who commanded the Devon and Cornwall Fencibles, was a former ensign in the 72nd Foot.[14] Although there were no proscribed arrangements of social and economic position to military rank in the fencibles in the way that there was for the militia, there was some informal matching of two. John Poulett, 4th Earl Poulett, became colonel of the Somerset Fencible Cavalry as he was also the lord lieutenant of the county. John Berkely Burland, a lawyer, active magistrate, and whose family had owned the manor of Steyning in Somerset since the fourteenth century, was appointed major.[15] Outside of these social hierarchies, the British and Irish fencibles provided a means for aspiring officers to start a military career with lower risks and less scrutiny. Robert Nickle, who was with the 88th Foot in the Peninsular War and rose to major-general, started his long career in the Army in the Loyal Durham Fencibles at the age of 13.[16]

Direct entry was not the only pathway for new officers. As we saw in Chapter 4, the Duke of York as Commander-in-Chief largely eradicated recruiting for rank. It was replaced by recruiting for rank by militia officers. Part of the success of the 1799 militia transfers was down to the militia officers getting commissions in the Army. At Dundas' suggestion, when sixty men transferred from a militia unit and joined the same regiment of foot then one militia officer could go with them and get a commission as an ensign. This scheme was expanded further in the October 1799 transfer, when the offer was improved to a captaincy for eighty men.[17] After this, it came to be regular feature of militia transfers, with the ratio settling down at an ensigncy for every fifty militiamen that volunteered from a unit.[18] It also introduced new people into the commissioning process, as the recommendation for militia officers came from county lords lieutenant or the commander of the militia unit (who could be the same person). There was a lingering unease about this in the Army, especially the assumption that names would be accepted whatever, as Lieutenant-Colonel Henry Torrens (the Military Secretary in 1812) wrote that commissioning militia officers was the 'evil by which and acknowledged advantages of the Volunteering System have been purchased'.[19] Torrens' opinion does them some injustice, and their contribution to the Army was important and they came with some military service. Turning to our sample of Waterloo officer, seventy-two of them started their careers in the militia, plus a further six who were on the staff of units as paymasters, quartermasters and surgeons. Just over half were lieutenants, like Henry Martin of the 44th Foot who began his service in the Worcestershire Militia on 30 January 1809 as a captain, transferring to the Army as an ensign on 28 May 1812. There were a few army captains too, such as Edward Cole

Bowen (40th Foot) whose military career stretched back to 1795 when he joined the City of Cork Militia, rose to lieutenant, and then transferred to the 85th Foot in 1800 along with three other officers from his militia regiment; by 1811 he had been promoted a captain in the 40th Foot. He fought at seventeen battles, retired in 1823, and died at Swansea in 1842.[20] Former militia officers were a significant component of the officer corps, especially in the junior ranks. There are no definitive figures but based on the numbers of militiamen that transferred to the Army there would have been 1,000 former militia officers in the Army, and the total could run to 2,000.

A different group that bought some military experience with them were officer volunteers. These were men that served in the ranks as privates (but not enlisted) hoping to get a commission when a vacancy occurred.[21] Sometimes, it provided a means to maintain family obligations and networks, such as when Thomas Brereton went to the Caribbean with his uncle Captain Coghlan in 1797.[22] These men provided a useful pool of potential officers that were on hand for service immediately, usually stepping in to replace the dead. For example, two volunteers, Edwards and Gordon, were appointed ensigns in the 47th Foot after the casualties the unit sustained after siege of San Sebastián, and seven volunteers who were at Waterloo were commissioned after the battle.[23] Joining as a volunteer only made sense in units where there was a chance of a vacancy appearing. From the sample of officers at Waterloo, sixty started their careers as volunteers and their numbers are most noticeable in the 95th (seven officers), 28th (six), and 79th and 91st Foot (five in each) – all units regularly on active service in Europe and especially in Iberia. Volunteers needed connections, as was revealed in the *Military Memoirs of Four Brothers*. One was desperate to leave the Royal Marines and join the 95th Rifles. He used an introduction from one of his brothers in the Army to get approval from the commander of the 2/95th and Lord Wellington to join the Army whilst he waited on a vacant lieutenancy.[24] Their status as volunteers was not straightforward, however. Sometimes they were accepted as gentleman by the unit's officers, but it could also take time to overcome prejudices about serving in the ranks. There were probably far more who went out as volunteers but the realities of life in the Army, or not being accepted, meant they never obtained the commission that they sought.[25]

Promotion from the ranks provided a further source of officers with military experience. Some cases were famous as rewards for conspicuous gallantry, such as Sergeant Charles Ewart of the 2nd Dragoons for his capture at a regimental eagle of the *45e Régiment de Ligne* at the Battle of Waterloo.[26] Beyond such conspicuous appointments there was a small but steady flow of promoted NCOs.[27] There were eighty-one officers that had been promoted from the ranks in the Waterloo cohort, including nine captains, two majors and one lieutenant-colonel (in the Royal Waggon Train). They ranged across thirty-seven infantry and cavalry units including Captain John Whale of the 1st Life Guards, Lieutenant William Jones (51st Foot), to Cornet William Hemmings (23rd Light Dragoons). Some had very long service in the Army, often with the same unit. Captain John Haigh, who died at Waterloo, had been a quartermaster in the 33rd Foot since 1 January 1798. The KGL had a system of sergeant cadets which accounted for forty-three of these officers, so one in seven of the KGL's 567 officers present in June 1815 had served as an NCO or NCO cadet.

The sergeant cadet system was distinctive to the KGL, but the establishment of the Royal Military College (RMC) in 1802 created a cadet system for entry into the rest of the Army. The Junior College provided an educational establishment for 100 cadets (which was quadrupled in 1808) who were a mixture of the orphan sons of officers who had died in service, sons of serving officers that might not otherwise be able to afford an education, and those otherwise who were able to secure a place and pay its fees. The cadets joined between the ages of 13 and 15, had to be medically and physically fit and were required to pass certain educational standards in writing, grammar, and arithmetic. Cadets gained their commission after public examinations, and those who did not pass the exam after four years had to quit.[28] The RMC's cadets were diffused into the Army. Sixty-one cadets' careers took them to Waterloo, spread across twenty-nine units but with nine in the 1st Foot Guards and eight in the 52nd Foot. They include Hon. William Curzon, the third son of Nathaniel Curzon, Baron Scarsdale, who began his career in the Army in 1807, had been a captain in the 69th Foot since 17 December 1812 and was Deputy-Assistant Adjutant-General at Waterloo where he died.[29] Also present was Eaton Monins, aged 20, who purchased an ensigncy in 52nd Foot on 1 December 1814 and so was the second most junior officer in that unit at Waterloo.[30] Surviving the battle, he went on to be a captain in the 52nd by 1825, then exchanged into the 69th Foot, was eventually promoted to major-general and died, aged 66, at Walmer in 1861. His coffin was borne on the shoulders of sergeants from the 6th Depot Battalion at the wish of his widow, as Monins had 'spent his life amougst soldiers'.[31]

The Royal Military Academy (RMA) at Woolwich provided almost all the officers for the Royal Artillery and Royal Engineers. The RMA was very hard pressed to meet Royal Artillery's demands for officers, even though it expanded from sixty cadets in the 1780s to 100 in 1798 and to 248 by 1806.[32] The only way it could adapt to rapid expansion, like that of 1793–5, was to shorten the time cadets spent at the RMA and lower the standards they needed to attain. During the peace of 1783–93, selection was rigorous, and examinations often personally overseen by the Master-General the Duke of Richmond. In 1793 the examination for commission was dispensed with and entry qualifications were lowered too (they were restored in 1798). In lieu of examinations, the RMA's lieutenant-governor recommended who he thought were promising cadets for commissions. It was not until the 1810s that the capacity of the RMA better matched the artillery's vacancies. In 1810 the public examination for a commission was restored and in 1813 the public entrance examination was restored too.[33] By then, cadets were spending three to five years at the RMA. Of the twelve cadets commissioned on 11 September 1812 the most junior was Charles R. Danby who joined on 11 April 1809.[34] Peace in Europe in April 1814 led to complete stagnation at the RMA, as half-pay officers had first call on any vacancies in the Ordnance's units. By the end of 1815 the RMA was full of educated cadets with no prospects of a commission, and it was not until the late 1810s and early 1820s that this was remedied.[35] There were other pathways into the engineer and artillery units too. One hundred and twenty-eight of the 912 appointments between 1783 and 1815 listed in John Kane's *List of Officers of the Royal Regiment of Artillery* were not from the RMA.[36] Before 1797 there were some who had been 'gentleman attendants' of the RMA who paid the fee for the education but were not on the muster roll of the company. After 1797 there were often fifteen to twenty 'extra cadets' studying at private schools nearby to Woolwich.[37] A few more were promoted sergeants, like James Clark who was commissioned into the Artillery Invalid Battalion on 1 November 1805.[38] Many came into the Royal Artillery through other artillery and engineer units, particularly from the Royal Irish Artillery which was incorporated in 1801. Alongside these were the engineer and artillery officers of foreign corps raised in Europe, most of whom were eventually incorporated into the Royal Foreign Artillery. The establishment of the King's German Legion increased to include artillery companies and engineer officers, most of whom were transposed from the disbanded Hanoverian forces.

The King's German Legion was just one example of new units that bought officers with military experience into the Army. Baron Louis de Roll, for example, was a former officer of the French Swiss Guards who had fled France in 1789 and later raised the first Swiss unit taken into the British Army in 1794.[39] The biographical details of the officers of the Chasseurs Britanniques indicate the range of people and journeys they had into units like these. Some, like Rene Alexandre Joseph Le Thueur Le Chavalier de Combremont, were former officers of the pre-1789 French Army, who made their way into the British Army through other European emigre units. Others were men that these units recruited during its service, like Giacome Guiliani who joined as a private during the 1805 expedition in Naples and worked his way up through the ranks.[40]

The system for appointing medical officers, clerical staff and the clergy was different and became increasingly controlled by relevant specialist military departments. The largest contingent were the medical staff. After the reform of the Army's medical administration the Army Medical Board recommended all medical officers in the Army. Surgeons had to have a qualification from the College of Surgeons at London, Dublin and Edinburgh, and were examined by the Board too. Assistant-surgeons were commissioned after examination at Surgeons' Hall.[41] The new veterinary officers were covered in Chapter 5. It was the spiritual staff of the Army that went through the greatest change. By the mid-1790s chaplains were sinecures appointed by regimental colonels. Most never expected to go on service, mirroring the absenteeism in the Church, and there was a dismal turnout in the campaigns in Europe and the Caribbean between 1793 and 1796. Reform came quickly, with the appointment of a Chaplain-General heading a new department. Recruitment was slow, reflecting the unattractiveness of army chaplaincies compared to appointments in the Church. By the 1810s, though, a committee of the Archbishops of Canterbury and York with the Bishop of London selected non-parochial clergy for recommendation, based both on their religious abilities and their physical and mental strength to deal with military service.[42] Two other roles, paymasters and quartermasters, were not subject to such drastic changes. Through the 1790s and early 1800s both went through changes that shifted them from roles to commissioned appointments. Before 1798 paymasters – the unit's accountant – was usually held by an officer of the unit, but after criticism from the Parliamentary Select Committee on Finance a separate post of regimental paymaster was created. Although they were recommended by regimental colonels, they were required to provide sureties of £4,000 and were public servants acting under the authority of the Secretary at War.[43] Likewise, quartermasters, with a role than spanned all aspects of equipment, stores, quartering, and keeping facilities in good order, went from being the highest-ranking NCO to a commissioned officer. As they needed to be 'well skilled in the detail of the regiment', as the 1811 edition of *The Regimental Companion* put it, the role was mainly filled by senior NCOs.[44] Of our Waterloo sample thirty-nine of the fifty-one regimental quartermasters were former NCOs.

Outside quartermasters, officers were mostly from completely different social and economic backgrounds than the men that they commanded, but that does not mean that they were a homogeneous group. They were not all from the aristocracy; the number of officers that the Army required was just too many to be supplied from the relatively small number of titled families in Britain and Ireland. Nevertheless, the aristocracy was probably over-represented within the Army. In 1810 2 per cent of the officer corps had inherited titles (and it is worth remembering titles were the result of military service), and they were very unevenly distributed with just 0.5 per cent in the artillery compared to 17 per cent in the 1st Foot Guards.[45] For the majority of officers in the infantry and cavalry, their backgrounds reflected the shifting social status of relatively wealthy families outside the aristocracy who claimed, or wanted to claim, the status as gentleman. We lack a rigorous study of the background of Army officers to match the recent work on the Royal Navy.[46] Rory Muir's study of younger sons in the era, however, has shown that serving as an Army officer was one option for young men from the landed gentry, gentlemanly professions and families engaged in trade.[47] This mixture is confirmed in David Huf's close study of seventy-seven officers, although it is noteworthy that twenty-nine of them avoided discussing their backgrounds in their memoirs.[48] For these men, joining the Army was a way of preserving or gaining social status. This meant the officer corps was a mixture of junior sons of wealthy landowners who only received a small proportion of the family estate to set themselves up in a gentlemanly career, alongside the sons of bankers, merchants, farmers and all the other roles that made up the 'middling sort' in Georgian Britain and Ireland. The differing means and motives can be found in the *Oxford Dictionary of National Biography*. George Ridout Bingham was the fourth son in an old Dorset family, who joined the 69th Foot in 1793 aged 16 as an ensign, eventually commanding the 2/53rd in the Peninsula before going on to serve as senior officer of the St Helena garrison until 1819.[49] Collet Barker, from Hackney, Middlesex, was a son of a skinner and mercer on his father's side and a merchant family on his mother's. Aged 22 he was commissioned an ensign in the 39th Foot in 1806, and then went on to work in the colonial government of Australia and explored its interior.[50] There was one other major contributor to the Army's officers and that was sons of serving officers. Some military families were very well established, like the Beckwith family, of whom all the four sons of Major-General John Beckwith went into the Army.[51]

Family traditions of service were important, and some officers chose or were put into the Army by their family to maintain their status.[52] This status was based upon an increasing evocation of service and duty in the Army.[53] In the King's German Legion, and for other exiled officers from across Europe, the Army was probably essential for the living it offered just as much as preserving their status. Alongside livelihoods, however, a broader commitment to the European political order of the *ancien regime* played its part in officers from across western and southern Europe serving in the British Army. Many of the émigrés from France and the Netherlands (some of whom like the Irish Catholics from the pre-1789 French Irish regiments were from the British Isles themselves), and Germans, Poles, and Hungarians who became officers in the Army had good reason to transfer their allegiance to the British Army. This was eased as dechristianisation in France meant the religious character of the war was framed as a conflict between European Christians and an imperialist, atheist state.[54]

There were also other attractions to the serving as an Army officer. Huf's exploration of junior officers has shown how the pomp and glamour of military life was seductive to young men, and the most common age for them was 17. Showy uniforms were an outward reflection of their gentlemanly status. They projected masculinity, were well tailored, made of quality material, and often highly adorned.[55] Additionally, with leisure travel to the continent of Europe blocked through most of this period, service in the Army became a way to undertake a pseudo-Grand Tour, with all its connotations of reaching manhood, independence and cultivation of the self, an aspect played out in the memoirs and personal documents that form so much of our understanding of their lives.[56] Catriona Kennedy's study of diaries, letters and memoirs has highlighted how becoming an officer meant a break from family ties, and so the first steps from childhood into manhood. Moreover, it also meant moving beyond the immediate reliance on the family and existing domestic arrangements, which chimed with ideals of independence that were the hallmark of manliness in Georgian Britain.[57] Added to this was a chance for glory and recognition, to the point that Linda Colley has called this a cult of heroic sacrifice.[58] Service as an officer was a way of strengthening, testing, and affirming their inner character as a gentleman.

Careers

There was enormous complexity in how individual officers managed their careers. It was influenced by private convenience, political conscience, ideas of service, opportunities that were available, their network of contacts within the Army and influence with government, and their wealth – though the last not so much as is often supposed. Any kind of analysis risks generalizing their careers to the point that it loses a relationship to individual cases. Nevertheless, careerism stands out as a feature that characterizes most officers, judged by their length of service in the Army. John Houlding's research has determined the significant time that Army officers dedicated to their careers in the eighteenth century. In 1791, lieutenant-colonels of regiment of foot had on average been thirty years in the service, majors a little less at twenty-nine, captains eighteen years and lieutenants half this at nine years.[59] Predictably, the massive expansion of the Army reduced these figures, especially in 1794–5, and the full extent of this awaits exploration. Some examples give an indication of the scale of the change. Earlier, we met several officers who jumped into field rank when they raised units. More typical were officers that were promoted rapidly in 1794 and

1795, like Major-General William Ponsonby who started in an independent company on 22 October 1794 and made major in the Loyal Irish Fencibles by May 1795 with his commission backdated to December 1794 and permanent rank in the Army, which he was later able to bring into the 5th Dragoon Guards in March 1798.[60] Even more rapid was John Blair's career. Starting in September 1794 as an ensign in the 104th Foot, by October the following year he was in command of his own regiment of foot (the Loyal Liverpool Regiment) as lieutenant-colonel commandant with a commission backdated to February 1795, having passed through the 2/82nd, 113th and 32nd Foot.[61] By the Battle of Waterloo long service had been restored despite the continuing demand for officers: the service of all lieutenant-colonels stood at 18.5 years, majors 16.2, captains 10.7, lieutenants 5.3 and ensigns/cornets at 1.5 years. These figures hide some significant variations. Amongst them was Thomas Gerrard of the 23rd Light Dragoons, the longest-serving captain, who started out an ensign in the 108th Foot in August 1794 and made captain in March 1800.[62] His length of service to get to and remain in this rank even outdid the usually slow-paced promotion in the Royal Artillery. In contrast was Captain Mildmay Fane of the 44th, who only started his career in the Army in June 1812 and took just two years to become a captain.[63]

Careerism was a little more complicated with the Army' medical staff. For the surgeons and medical staff service in the Army could both be an alternative career to the civilian practice but also a way of developing and furthering medical knowledge, and so not every medical officer committed their entire career in the Army. As we saw in Chapter 5, the medical officers of the Army adopted increasingly militarized attitudes, but it was also imposed on them. Firstly, a career path from hospital mate to medical inspector was created through the restructuring of the medical staff and establishing their equivalent military rank, so doing away with the arrangements where medical officers were appointed directly to roles from civilian practice.[64] Secondly, expectations of service were enforced. When Staff-Surgeon John Gunning was ordered overseas in 1805 he tendered his resignation. This was refused, and his case was made public in newspapers. Later restored to service in 1808, he was Deputy-Inspector of Hospitals at Waterloo, and was the surgeon who amputated Lord FitzRoy Somerset's right arm.[65]

There were some fixed points that shaped their careerism. An officer's rank and the date they were appointed to that rank within their unit (their seniority) were fundamental as they set the precedence for promotion to the next rank. Seniority was the sole basis for promotion in the Royal Artillery and Royal Engineers, resulting in gradual, if not glacial, progress. Promotion in these units could only happen when a higher-ranking officer retired or died, or a new company or battalion was added. Major Robert Stephen Adye, for example, began his career in April 1793 and it took him ten years to become a captain then another ten be made a major. Adye's captaincy came from the cascade of promotions when the 73-year-old Colonel Alexander Shand died; his majority when Major Alexander Duncan died in an explosion in a powder magazine in Seville.[66] Promotion through seniority applied in the infantry and cavalry too, but there were additional channels through which officers could advance. One way was for vacancies to be filled by officers from outside the regiment at the behest of the King or Commander-in-Chief, which could vary in motive from political and social favours to genuine promotion on merit. The Duke of York kept a list of officers whose career he wanted to advance, checked against confidential reports on officers obtained through the system of regimental inspections and by inquiries by the Military Secretary. This system was stymied by Parliament's inquiry into the Duke of York in 1809 and his subsequent resignation. Understandably, Sir David Dundas as his successor stuck more rigidly to promotion by seniority and so rapid promotion of talented officers was rarely done.[67]

The other channel was through the purchase of commissions, which had a long history within the Army and by the 1780s had been codified though not always enforced. It was usual practice to offer the purchasable rank by seniority: so, a captain selling their commission would offer it to the most senior lieutenant in the unit, and if they did not have the money available for the transaction or did not want to be promoted then it would be offered to the next most senior lieutenant and so on. If all was agreeable, then the officer purchasing the rank would move to the bottom of the list of his new rank, and every else would move up a notch in the hierarchy. Only ranks below colonel could be purchased, and Viscount Barrington (Secretary at War between 1765 and 1778) had instigated a policy of only allowing commissions that had been purchased to be sold. This meant that the only opportunities to purchase a commission would have been if an officer who held their rank by purchase themselves purchased a higher rank, exchanged into a different unit (effectively buying into a different unit at the same rank), or sold their commission to retire.[68] This policy was undone by several factors. The King or Commander-in-Chief could give any officer permission to sell their commission, 'In particular circumstances' as *1811 General Regulations* put it, even if the officer concerned had never purchased it.[69] Generally, selling a commission under these terms was granted to officers of long service or in ill health, allowing them to retire and provide promotion opportunities for other officers. Additionally, the War Office had great difficulty keeping track of purchasable commissions as officers often mixed both purchased and non-purchased promotions in their careers.[70] The system became even more confused in the years 1793–5, when the government used purchase to finance recruiting in some units.[71]

Although purchasing commissions was a market, officially it was a regulated one. All purchases of commissions had to be approved by the Commander-in-Chief or the King, and the necessary statements required by regulations were sent to the Military Secretary. The price of purchasing a commission was fixed by royal warrants, ranging from £400 for an ensigncy in regiment of foot to £6700 for lieutenant-colonel in the Foot Guards.[72] There was, nevertheless, a black market that operated alongside the official transactions, as the fixed price did not always match their relative value. A commission in a unit that was staying in Britain, for example, could drive up the value and the reverse if it was rumoured to be sent overseas; an opportunity in a more senior unit would have additional value to officers serving in units at risk of being disbanded. There were pinch points in supply such as majorities in 1793 which were costing £1,600 to £2,000, even in new regiments, compared to the regulation price of £1,100 for the step from captain.[73]

The evidence for the additional illegal payments is sparse. Running the risk of the ire of the King in breaking regulations was not something to be done openly, and generally paying over-regulation prices in wartime was imprudent as officers were likely to get promoted anyway and their investment was at risk if they died.[74] Nevertheless, in 1804 general orders re-affirmed 1783 regulations prohibiting overpayment and the threat to remove any officer found doing it – good evidence that it was happening. At the same time, Horse Guards and the War Office made a concerted effort to tackle commission brokers. As the evidence against brokers mounted, particularly in 1804 and then with the Parliamentary inquiry into the Duke of York and Mary Ann Clarke (which largely showed brokerage as a sham as there was very little evidence of actual influence in buying and selling commissions), their services were specifically outlawed in the 1809 Brokerage Act, moving it from a breach of military regulations to a criminal offence.[75] More significant in managing purchase was the Commander-in-Chief's regulations about minimum terms of service in each rank before they could promoted, through whatever means. Captains had to have served six years before they could become eligible to be a major, and at least two years' service was necessary before an officer could become a captain, which was extended to three years to be a captain and seven to be major by 1811.[76] These arrangements were enforced through the process of appointments and a secondary system of checks through regimental inspections. Here, in pre-printed forms, the stages of an officer's career were laid out.

Although the purchase of rank frequently dominates discussion of the officer corps, its influence on officers' career diminished. Michael Glover's work shows that at least 2,000 purchase-free vacancies were created in 1804 and he estimates that by 1814 only 2,000 commissions had been purchased and during the Peninsular War 20 per cent of promotions were through purchase.[77] This proportion is echoed in our Waterloo list of officers, where 297 officers had purchased their rank from 1,376 that were eligible.[78] Purchase was unevenly distributed in the Army. Units that had expanded least and had suffered fewer officer casualties (purchased commissions were not property, and those of dead officers were only sold in rare circumstances) tended to have the highest proportion of purchasable commissions, which equated to the regiments of Foot Guards, the cavalry, and some single-battalion regiments of foot. In the 33rd Foot at Waterloo sixteen of thirty-seven officers had purchased their rank, mostly because it had been a single-battalion regiment throughout 1783 and 1815. In the 79th Foot, which was raised in 1793, rebuilt in the late 1790s and had two battalions from 1805, the ratio was only five officers from forty.[79] The legacy of purchase was also present in different ways. Two surgeons – John Bolton of the 6th Dragoons and David Irwin of the 7th Light Dragoons – purchased their position in the 1790s, a testament to their long service that meant the relic of system abolished twenty years before was still present in the Army.

Promotion prospects were affected by the context of the Army's establishment. As the number of units and their size varied so there were more or fewer vacancies in the Army's officer corps. The most disruptive changes occurred in the massive expansion of the Army between 1793–5. Not only was there a huge need for new entrants into the Army, but because so many new units were created there was a demands for officers all the way up to lieutenant-colonel. There was a mass movement of officers from existing units into new ones. In the wake of this the Duke of York kept on extra officers even as the Army shrank in size. In the autumn of 1795, the remaining regiments of foot were established at ten companies but with five field officers and twenty-one lieutenants (compared to the usual ten of the latter), and units in the Caribbean gained two extra captains.[80] These officers provided replacements for casualties but slowed down the rate of promotion. Just as significant in changing promotion prospects was removing field officers from the command of a company in 1803.[81] Before then regimental officers above the rank of captain still retained control of a company or troop, meaning a major was both a major and a captain. Changing this arrangement immediately created the need for more captains, but over the longer term created a bottleneck. Where once there had been seven captains and a captain-lieutenant in an infantry battalion in the promotion ladder behind a major, there were now ten captains.

All these structural and contingent factors affected officers' pathways through the Army. The Duke of Wellington's early career is often provided as an example of how rank could be quickly gained through purchase, in his case command of the 33rd Foot at the age of 24. Yet a more careful study of this phase of his career shows that it was not just about purchase but also the influence of his family and Irish political patronage. The resignations of the 33rd's major (William Gore) and then its lieutenant-colonel (John Yorke) within a few months of each other and in the right order for the young Arthur Wellesley were curiously convenient. Likewise, Wellington's early progress in the Army is marked by appointments to units that were changing or new. He went through the 41st just as it was reformed into a regiment of foot and all the existing officers were moved out, and then into the new 77th Foot.[82] The one unifying factor that shaped his career up to the rank of lieutenant-colonel was being on the Army's Irish Establishment, not purchase.

Horse Guards could make the system work to the advantage of those that they favoured. Horse Guards had direct control of a few regiments where the colonel was either the Commander-in-Chief or a member of his staff. The 60th Foot, for example, was used as a half-way house into which officers could be promoted from another regiment and then exchange (as swapping officers between units was known) at their new higher rank having overtaken their peers.[83] With the Commander-in-Chief's permission they could be granted leave and never actually serve with the 60th. Well-connected officers could use exchanges to their advantage too as it created opportunities for an officer prepared to jump around units. Of our Waterloo officers, William George Keith Elphinstone, the lieutenant-colonel of the 33rd Foot, was the most extreme example. He went through eleven different units with a mixture of exchanges, purchased ranks and promotion by seniority between April 1804 and September 1813.[84] How he came to make all the arrangements is unclear, but he was clearly well informed about which officers wanted to move and had the social and financial capital needed to make them happen.

William Keith Elphinstone's career was not typical, though, as Table 2 below demonstrates. The bulk of officers spent their time in one unit, and it was only at the rank of major or above that officers served in two units or more; even then 43 per cent of majors and 29 per cent of lieutenant-colonels at Waterloo had spent their careers in the same unit. These figures disguise short moves, either out of choice or forced on officers. Lieutenant-Colonel Alexander Hamilton of the 30th Foot, for example, was first commissioned in the 84th Foot for two months in 1784 until the unit was disbanded. He was on half pay through the 1780s until appointed to the 30th Foot during the 1787 mobilization, where he then spent the rest of his career with promotions coming through seniority until he made it to lieutenant-colonel in 1811.[85] Major John Hicks shows that purchase did not always speed up a career. His entire career was in the 32nd

Foot, which started in February 1786. He purchased both his lieutenant and captain ranks and became major in 1804 on augmentation of the regiment.[86] Typical of the career of captains was Charles Caddell of the 28th Foot, the only regiment he served in. He joined as ensign in September 1804 when an ensign was appointed to another regiment, gained his lieutenancy on augmentation in 1805, and purchased a captaincy in 1809 from William Forster Dalton who retired and was permitted to sell his commission after twenty-one years in the Army.[87] For longer-serving captains, the number of units they served in was not always a matter of choice. Captain James Henderson (71st Foot) was one of the longest-serving captains at Waterloo and served in four different units. He made it to lieutenant in the 92nd Foot by 1794 but was placed on half pay in the 60th Foot in 1800. Bought back to the 92nd in July 1803, he was then appointed to the 71st Foot in 1809 on the death of Captain George Sutherland. He was still the senior captain in the 71st Foot in 1830.[88]

Table 2: Summary of Officer Careers at Battle of Waterloo, 1815.

Number of units served in	Ensigns / Cornets	Lieutenants	Captains	Majors	Lieutenant-Colonels
1	365	741	259	70	19
2	51	176	85	46	13
3	7	45	38	16	12
4		11	31	14	7
5			18	7	4
6			6	6	3
7			2	1	4
8			2	1	1
9				1	1
10			1		
11					1
Total	423	973	442	162	65

Note: Figures exclude medical staff, paymasters, and commissariat officers. Officer's highest rank is used if they had brevet rank.

The frustrations of Army careers were ameliorated by brevet ranks. These were promotions in the Army as a whole and so outside of regimental rank and seniority. It accorded an officer a higher precedence and so improved their chances of further promotion and was a reward (although brevet rank did not give the pay of its rank unless they were employed at their brevet rank). Except in a very few cases, brevet rank was only acquired by majors or higher, and so the annual *Army Lists* started with list of officers from field marshal down to major providing their position within the whole Army. Generally, brevet ranks marched on by seniority, with the number of officers of general rank (major-general and above) residing with the King and Commander-in-Chief. However, stops could be made at points. An interesting case was the King refusing the Prince of Wales' promotion from brevet colonel to major-general, and so Prince George stayed the most senior colonel in the Army from 1793 all the way through the period.[89] When brevet ranks were to be awarded could become a scene of intense speculation. Amherst's 'monstrous brevet' of September 1794, as the Adjutant-General Sir William Fawcett termed it, was the most notorious example. Rumour of it circulated in the summer of 1794 which caused a surge in officers looking for any means to get a promotion before the brevet, and so gain a double step in a short time. Officers borrowed money, called in favours and the trafficking in places increased, only for their efforts to be undone by Amherst's decree that the brevet was antedated to 1 March 1793.[90] After this brevets were more carefully managed, often coming after significant military events and there was a large-scale brevet in June 1814 at the end of the war in Europe.[91]

There were careers for officers outside of their regiment too. The Army needed commanders and staff at garrisons and depots, administrators, inspectors, planners, liaison officers and intelligence-gatherers, as well as staff needed for the structure of the Army beyond regiments, battalions, companies and troops of cavalry. All these officers came from regiments. Each geographic and operational command mirrored the structure of the Commander-in-Chief's office, with adjutant-generals and quarter-master-generals, and some examples are provided in Appendix B. Staff were also assigned to brigades and divisions as they became formalized in the Army through the late 1790s and into the Peninsular War.[92] Each employed general was also permitted to appoint aide-de-camps (ADCs) and generals with the financial means could exceed the officially proscribed number permitted. An officer needed to catch the attention of a general to be considered for any of these roles, as there were far more eligible officers (in terms of rank) than available appointments. The positions often came with a brevet rank too, and Horse Guards sometimes filled vacancies in regiments to get officers the rank they needed to take on a role. One famous example was Wellington's Quarter-Master-General, Brigadier-General Sir George Murray, who was practically Wellington's chief of staff by 1813. He started his career in the Flanders campaigns of 1793–5 in the 3rd Foot Guards, where he met colonels Robert Anstruther and Alexander Hope. Both these officers understood the role that officers in the quarter-master-general's department could (indeed should) play in military operations, and in Murray they saw potential. Murray served as deputy to Anstruther, who was quarter-master-general in the 1799 campaign in Holland and again in Egypt in 1801. Murray studied at the senior branch of the Royal Military College during the Amiens Peace, and then was picked by the Quarter-Master-General of the Army Robert Brownrigg to serve in the department with the Commander-in-Chief. At this time, he was appointed Quarter-Master-General in Ireland, a position he retained until 1812. In 1807, Murray was appointed Quarter-Master-General to Lord Cathcart in the Copenhagen expedition; in 1808 he was in Moore's staff in the expedition to Sweden and then in Wellington's, continuing to serve in Portugal and Spain under Anstruther (again) in Moore's quarter-master-general's department. After four years of continuous service, Murray returned to the UK in 1811, but was back in the Iberian Peninsula by 1812.[93] By 1815, he was a major-general, Lieutenant-Governor of Edinburgh Castle, Knight Grand Cross of the Order of the Bath, and colonel-commandant in the 60th Foot. The latter rank was given to Murray when the 60th Foot was expanded with a seventh battalion in 1813; before then his regimental rank was captain and lieutenant-colonel (as he was a Foot Guard's officer), which he was appointed to on 5 August 1799.[94] Murray's career was particularly successful, a combination both of his abilities and contacts who were willing to advance him, and Horse Guards looking after an officer by finding them higher regimental rank when it became available.

Attitudes and Experience

The multitude of patterns in officers' careers reflected their attitudes towards service and the Army. The values and outlook of many officers were those of land-owning classes, even though, as we saw earlier, many were not from that background.[95] Bruce Collins has identified three broad types of officers.[96] For one group the Army provided a semi-occupation with some formal duties, pay, and provided a means to maintain their status or that of their families. These included 'court' officers wanting to secure access to royal or government social and political circles. For them, a commission was not just about sinecures, as it allowed some officers, especially in the Guards, to pursue military careers without long absences from centres of power and social activities like London and Dublin. Within this type we can also add those who sought to gain rank, preferment, status, and recognition through recruitment, mostly in 1794–5 but also at other periods, where an officer's commission, and particularly raising a unit, was part of wider ambitions of social advancement. In this category was William Earle Bulwer, who managed to become a captain in the 1780s by switching through regiments (as well as a captaincy in the Norfolk Militia) and exchanged onto half pay in 1792. He then raised an independent company in 1793 which was expanded into the 106th Foot in 1794, known as the Norwich Royal Regiment of Volunteers, reflecting his position in Norfolk where the family had long held an estate. He was placed on half pay after the unit was disbanded, became colonel of the Norfolk Provisional Cavalry in 1797, and progressed through brevet to the rank to general, and was expecting a peerage when he died in 1807.[97] A second group were the already well connected with the financial and political capital seeking high rank and commands in the Army, most famously Wellington but also Lord William Bentinck.[98]

By far the largest group were regimental officers. As we saw above, their career was often confined to a unit, with steady progress to become a captain. Their aspirations mostly focused on becoming a major or lieutenant-colonel. For these officers, a sense of duty and service pervades their writings and they closely identified with the Army and their unit. David Huf's detailed research on the writings of junior officers has shown how a distinct subaltern officer identity emerged in the Napoleonic Wars. They often shared the privations of the enlisted men and were exposed to extreme weather conditions and diseases just as much as them too. They lacked the political, social, and financial capital to cushion their military service, either through getting leave from certain postings or being able to afford some luxuries. Their identity was carved from a tension between the gentlemanly masculinity that emphasized independence, and the sacrifice these officers had made to defer or delay this through military service.[99] This identity also expressed itself in hostility to new officers who lacked dedication and collective spirit,[100] typified in the satirical poem *The Military Adventures of Johnny Newcome*, illustrated by Thomas Rowlandson, of 1815.[101]

Within this regimental context, wider identities were inserted and modified, none more so than gentlemanliness. This provides a model to understand officers' behaviour and identity, and as was discussed earlier was an important factor in many men becoming officers. Defining it, though, is not straightforward, as it was a web of attributes, manners, elegance, taste and sensibility that was not fixed and excess in any of these areas risked affectation and worse forgery.[102] Gentlemanliness manifested itself in the Army's officer corps in a focus on maintaining status through appearance, individual behaviour and social interactions. Attitudes towards officers promoted from the ranks highlight this, as they were accepted provided that they maintained gentlemanly status, but if they were absent, seen as shirking or behaved in an inappropriate way then this was attributed to their 'low' origins. The sociability of military gentlemanliness was focused on the mess. Eating and drinking together was important social bonding, and the egalitarianism of the mess was stressed. To make this work officers needed the social ease and mutual respect of gentlemen.[103] Officers demonstrated their status as gentlemen in other ways too, through polite accomplishments like tourism, hunting and fishing.[104] There was a stratification and hierarchy within the Army as regiments were like clubs, with each requiring different financial and social commitments to live as a gentleman within a unit to cover mess fees, own enough horses, and entertain fellow officers.[105] There was also a rough underbelly to gentlemanliness and masculinity of officers, in combinations of drinking, gambling, violence and misogyny. The mess itself could become a dissolute institution. Some officer embraced a blackguard reputation of anti-civility. From the studies we have, cultural superiority and anti-Catholicism led to incidents of violence against Portuguese and Spanish civilians.[106] In the Caribbean garrisons planter attitudes fused into the Army, typified by sexual licentiousness and dominance of mixed race and black enslaved people, complete dependence on the labour of the enslaved and perpetual social rounds.[107]

Military gentlemanliness was expressed through their material culture. Officers bought all their own equipment and uniform. Some parts were meant to conform to patterns deposited with the Comptrollers of the Army Account at Scotland Yard, London, but who they got it from, the fit, and the precise quality of the items were down to the officer. Other parts were individual choices and norms of the regiment, so some officers were required to wear a 'stock' of silk or black velvet for example. Kitting out an officer could cost £40–£60 for the infantry, and easily £300 in the cavalry and maybe as much as £500 in the more flamboyant or exacting units.[108] Conspicuous consumption formed part of the identity of a gentleman, and officers who could afford it not only expressed it through their uniform but also what they bought with them. Most officers would want to be equipped with tents, bedding, crockery and cutlery, candles and candlesticks, plus food that would keep like hams, cheese, tea, and sugar. Guards officers were the most flagrant, taking enough with them to be able to give a dinner for their fellow officers, which meant including a staff of cooks, servants and muleteers to move it all.[109] Its unseemliness was represented in *The Military Adventures of Johnny Newcome*, where in Plate 10 an officer goes shopping for food in front of starving civilians.

A symptom of tensions between service, gentlemanliness and officers' lives outside the Army was absenteeism. Officers being away from their units, both with and without permission, was pervasive in the 1780s through to the mid-1790s, with patterns often reflecting the risks and benefits of individual stations. In June 1789, 39 per cent of infantry and cavalry officers were absent (excluding troops on the Irish Establishment),[110] with the highest rate in the Leeward Islands at 47 per cent, an unsurprising pattern given the mortality in the Caribbean. The overall rate had improved a little by April 1793 to 33 per cent, where again the Leeward Islands were the worst, but the Army in

Holland was doing well with only twenty-four officers absent from 201.[111] By mid-1795, however, the situation was dire as 42 per cent of the Army's officers were absent, and in Jamaica just forty-four officers from 125 were present with their units. There, the 10th Foot had only nine officers present and twenty-nine absent. The 4/60th at Tobago had just three officers present with thirty-two absent, but the worst was the 39th Foot, stationed at Tynemouth, but then if its thirty-five officers had all been present (only three were) then they would have outnumbered the privates that were fit for duty. Generally, there were problems in the newly raised units, with only sixty-four officers spread between six units (120th, 121st, 122nd, 129th, 130th and 133rd Foot) and 176 absent.[112]

The extent of absenteeism resulted from the multiple sources that could grant leave, and the lack of measures to be able to check and address the issue. Regulations issued in the 1780s set a minimum number of officers per unit and required officers to join their unit within six months if it was in Britain else they would be listed as absent without leave.[113] The Duke of York, on becoming Commander-in-Chief, worked with Adjutant-General Fawcett to better detect absent officers and then tighten up regulations about leave. In 1795 officers were required to join their units or risk being superseded (the technical term used for being dismissed), and the system of returns was changed to indicate more clearly who was on leave and why. Armed with this information the Adjutant-General sent round a series of letters to regimental commanders in later 1795 and early 1796. In the wake of this officers complied, left or were superseded.[114] Later regulations strengthened authority over officers' leave. By 1804 new officers were given a month to join their units, or they would be dismissed,[115] and by 1811 any new or promoted officer needed to be with their unit or at the Army Depot on the Isle of Wight within a month. The system for leave was better channelled: applications were required to go through the unit's commanding officer, then to the unit's brigade general, and then to their general officer (either commanding the military district or local commander).[116] Leave on medical grounds could only be approved by a military medical officer, and then only up to three months after which special examinations would be made. Lastly, no leave of absence could be longer than six months if overseas, extended to a year for Australia and South Asia.[117]

This effort paid off. In June 1799 absenteeism in the infantry and cavalry on the British Establishment had been reduced to 29 per cent, though the rate in Caribbean remained much higher.[118] This proved to be a steady rate through the next two summers. Figures after 1802 are only available at unit level and are complicated by depots and additional battalions whereby officers could be listed as absent because they were serving in another part of the unit. For example, in June 1813 the 33rd Foot had four officers absent (three with leave and one without) out of forty-seven officers.[119] This indicates that there was a floor which overall the Army was unable to improve upon. Part of this was down to genuine needs of officers due to ill health and recovery from wounds, as well as breaks after particularly strenuous service. Staff officers needed leave from their units to take up their posts, and a few were prisoners of war too. More significant, though, was the recognition that officers had matters to attend to outside their military career, and the Army accepted these as appropriate reasons to be away from their units. The gentlemanliness of Army officers meant that not all of them could be with their units all the time. The three officers with leave from the 33rd Foot highlighted above were all granted it to attend their 'private affairs'. In this regard the artillery's much lower rate of absenteeism at just 14 per cent in June 1795 reflects the different ethos within the Ordnance units.[120]

Purchasing commissions was bound up with officers' attitudes and identity. The discussion earlier demonstrated that purchase was not on its own a great accelerant to officers' careers. As a financial arrangement, it was not very sound either. Purchase is usually portrayed as a quasi-pension scheme that did not require state funding to function as officers could retire on what they had accumulated through buying commissions.[121] Yet this analysis fails in several ways. Long service in the Army meant purchase was a long-term investment. The £3,500 held by army agents for a lieutenant-colonelcy in a regiment of foot for maybe as much as twenty years and returned when he sold his commission looks a very poor deal. While returns in investments varied in the era, 5 per cent per annum was a well-established expectation for a safe investment like government stock, so the officer would have lost £175 per year.[122] Officers who purchased would only gain a profit if they gained one or more step in rank for free and were then allowed to sell it, and this was usually only done after long service of over twenty years. Even then, retiring on a sold lieutenant-colonelcy was a long way short of the funds to live as a gentleman, where an annual income of £500 could work with some restraint, but £1,500 to £2,000 was reckoned for a family to live well. Less than £300 and a family would find it hard to maintain their gentility.[123] So the profits were poor and the pay-off not enough for most officers; factor in inflation and purchase was a bad financial arrangement. The risks were high too, as on death the whole fund was lost with potentially disastrous consequences for an officer's family. Captain Martin of the 1st Foot Guards, for example, 'sunk his fortune' to gain a captaincy but his sudden death put his family in a dire situation.[124] Officers persisted with purchase as it was the only way to advance in some regiments and it was a mark of financial independence. Yet because it was intertwined with the influence necessary to make it happen, promotion without purchase became a source of pride with officers without financial means. Promotion through seniority signalled an officer's commitment to service, and independence from external influence.[125]

* * *

Much like the enlisted men, it was the unit (usually a regiment) that shaped most officers' lives in the Army. The regimental system was fundamental to understanding and shaping their position as an officer. The Army only officially recorded a few things about an officer: the date of their commission to a rank, the unit that commission was in, and the name of the person. Such was the fixation on these pieces of information that even when *The Royal Military Calendar* pulled together information about all the general officers in the Army in 1815 and again in 1820, it was based around these pieces of information. Indeed, their background and relationships were very rarely mentioned. As a new entrant into a unit, an officer would be immediately placed in a hierarchy within that unit based on their rank and the date of their commission, so the most junior ensign, for example, was always last on this list. Until an officer reached field rank the only rank and position that he had was within that unit. This meant that for several years, if not his entire military career, where an officer was placed in that list shaped his perspective and prospects of promotion. Besides a very few exceptions, every officer in the Army from an ensign to a field marshal belonged to a regiment. In assessing officers' careers, identities and attitudes, the purchase of commissions had a much smaller imprint than is usually presented. The cut in the strength of the Army strengthened the forces keeping purchase as the pervasive mechanism for promotion in the 1780s, as it stultified the flow of officers out of the Army. When the Army expanded purchase was much less influential. Gentlemanliness was the defining feature of officers, with all its subtleties, nuances, and shifts that depended on context both socially but also culturally and geographically. Britain's global, multinational, and composite Army did not produce one hegemonic stereotype or model for officers.

Chapter 8

Soldiering

The army was never in such health, heart, and condition as at present, and is probably the most complete machine for its numbers now existing in Europe.[1]

A direct quote from Arthur Wellesley, Duke of Wellington, is probably overdue in a book about the history of the British Army, and Wellington had good grounds to make this judgement in November 1813. The Anglo-Portuguese army with its Spanish allies had won a spectacular success at Vittoria in the summer, effectively ending the French occupation of Iberia and harried the French army to the frontier of France. The Army had come a long way from its initial performance when it first faced the French Army in 1793–5 and was beaten and driven from the Netherlands at the start of this long conflict. This arc of the history of the effectiveness of the British Army, recounted by John Fortescue in his *History of the British Army* along with others, follows a well-trodden path. Underfinanced, undersized, and ill-equipped, the Army waned in the 1780s.[2] The government and the military command, itself shrivelled by the lack of a Commander-in-Chief, failed to effectively prepare the Army for war. A necessary period of expansion and reform followed that ultimately led to the British Army recovering its martial prowess and beating French armies in Iberia and finally at Waterloo. Such hindsight-driven views are evident in titles like Richard Glover's *Peninsular Preparation*,[3] and overarching judgements about the history of the Army in the period are not just the preserve of the twentieth-century historical profession. Sir Henry Bunbury, who as we saw in earlier chapters played a key role in the Army's management in the 1810s, was equally damning about the Army in 1793: 'Never was a kingdom less prepared for a stern and arduous conflict'.[4] Bunbury's statement, which has been echoed so frequently since, needs better locating in its time. His *Narratives of Some Passages in the Great War with France, from 1799 to 1810* was published as tensions with Russia escalated into the Crimean War, and, as he put it, the events of the last war 'afford a lesson which ought not to be forgotten'.[5] Fortescue too was writing a history lesson in the early twentieth century for ministers and military authorities. Nowhere was this clearer than in his 1909 publication *The County Lieutenancies and the Army*. As has been emphasized before in this book, the history of the Army needs to be better appreciated within its own context, and this is especially true when considering military effectiveness over the three decades the led up to Wellington judging the Army 'the most complete machine'.

Making Soldiers

If there was one feature that defined soldiering in the eighteenth and early nineteenth it was the intricate and heavily prescribed movements of close-order military drill that were the mainstay of military training, and which John Houlding's *Fit for Service* thoroughly covers for the Army up to 1795.[6] The publication of General David Dundas' *Principles of Military Movement* in 1788 and its subsequent adoption as the drill manual for infantry in the British Army in 1792 are regarded as pivotal moments in the regeneration of the Army. It codified the system of training and review (through which competency in drill was assessed by a general) to eighteen manoeuvres for battalions of infantry. It was followed by a training regime instituted by the Duke of York when he became Commander-in-Chief in 1795, whereby in Britain two days were allocated for battalion level exercises, two days as a brigade, and then one day for the whole force under a general's command.[7] In Richard Glover's opinion 'no one reform of our whole period did more to make the British Army an effective force than this steadily applied system of training'.[8] Certainly in the era of smoothbore flintlock muskets precision in infantry drill in close formations underpinned performance in many battles. This was more than just the ability to fire quickly and in unison. It was essential that infantry could manoeuvre on battlefields to bring maximum firepower to bear on an enemy, avoid confusion with friendly troops by maintaining sufficient distance between units and yet be close enough to support each other, and all the while be ready to change formation to face a cavalry attack that could be devastating against unprepared infantry.[9] Uniformity of practice between units, then, was important. In this regard, Wellington's comment used at the start of this chapter is intriguing as it conceptualises the Army on campaign and in battle as a machine, with component parts that all needed to be able to work together. A single drill book – a unifying language and practice – was central to this. Nor was this an abstract conceptualisation of battle and campaigning, or a justification for discipling troops. Some cases stand out where drill was important, if not crucial, to the outcome of military events. At the Battle of the River Côa on 24 July 1810 the Light Division under General Craufurd avoided disaster through the ability of the division's unit to undertake a withdrawal towards a single bridge whilst facing a superior French force.[10] Sir Charles Napier was effusive in his praise of the 'astonishing infantry' of the 4th Division under General Cole at the Battle of Albuera (16

1. Anthony Cardon, *A View of the British Army*, 1803. (*British Museum, 1917,1208.4132. © The Trustees of the British Museum*)

2. Anthony Cardon, *The British Army in Egypt*, 1806. (*Prints, Drawings and Watercolors from the Anne S.K. Brown Military Collection, Brown Digital Repository, Brown University Library*)

3. R. Temple, *View from the Deck of the Upton Castle Transport of the British Army Landing, 29th Nov 1810*, 1813. (*S.P. Lohia Hand Coloured Rare Book Collection*)

4. F. Nash, *The Admiralty and Horse Guards, Westminster*, 1814. (*Author's collection*)

London Pub August 20 1794 by G. Kinnersly   Corner of Tyler Street Carnaby Market

KIDDNAPING. or a Disgrace to Old England

5. Isaac Cruikshank, *Kidnapping, or a Disgrace to Old England*, 1794. (*British Museum, 1878,0511.1391.*
© The Trustees of the British Museum)

6. Thomas Rowlandson, *English Barracks*, 1788. (*Prints, Drawings and Watercolors from the Anne S.K. Brown*
Military Collection, Brown Digital Repository, Brown University Library)

7. Isaac Cruikshank, *A Recruiting Party*, 1797. (*Author's collection*)

TO DEFEND OUR OWN ISLAND,

And not to leave the Kingdom:

THREE TROOPS OF

Fencible Light Cavalry

COMMANDED BY

CHARLES MORAY, E∫q.

OF ABERCAIRNEY,

YOUNG MEN of Spirit and Character, who love their KING and COUNTRY, and who abhor the Tyranny and Cruelties of French Barbarians, are invited to Serve in this Corps, where the Intere∫t and Comfort of the Soldier will always be attended to.

N. B. As ∫uch an Opportunity of ∫erving in the DIGNIFIED Situation of

HORSEMEN,

And enjoying the hand∫ome Pay of LIGHT DRAGOONS, will ∫eldom be met with, none but Lads of good Figure and *known Character* need apply.

LONDON: Printed by H. REYNELL, No. 21, PICCADILLY, near the HAY-MARKET.

8. Perthshire Fencible Cavalry recruiting poster, c. 1795. (*National Records of Scotland, GD160/543/4*)

AN ADDRESS

From the 105th and 113th Regiments to the Public, and their Brothers in Arms.

Citizens and Fellow Soldiers.

IT is no longer time to fport with our Lives and trifle with our Credulity—We, too, have been Induftrious Citizens till a dreadful and atrocious War had dried up the channels of our Manufactures and caufed us to Roam at large, Idle and Dependent!—Neceffity, dire neceffity induced us to embark in a caufe which our fouls abhorred; but hunger has no Law; fooner than perifh, we had been tempted by large Sums (badly paid) to enrol ourfelves—We did fo, on condition of returning to our homes at the approach of Peace; but what now is the cafe? All faith is broken with us! We are led to be incorporated with Regiments that will never be reduced, except by a formidable enemy and the more formidable climate of the WEST-INDIES! And you, unfortunate and inflaved Natives of Africa, are you to feel our Steel? Are we to be made fhed your innocent blood with our Murderous Arms? Forbid it Heaven! Forbid it Juftice! No, no, perifh firft the man who dare embark for fo horrid a purpofe; Generous Citizens of Cork, do you not fympathife with us? Do you not pity us thus Crimped and Sold by unfaithful Officers? You furely muft; for you cannot be hardened to misfortunes.

As to our Brothers in Arms, they cannot, they will not unfheath the Sword to enforce an Aarbitrary and Unjuft Meafure, Our Fellow Soldiers, are fellow men, and cannot forget what they owe to themfelves—they muft *think,* and then we are all right. Yes, we will defend our Country, our Homes, our Wives and Children, to this we are pledged, and from this we fhall never Flinch.

CORK, September 4, 1795.

---

9. An Address From the 105th and 113th Regiments to the Public, and their Brothers in Arms. (National Army Museum 1968-07-370-42. Courtesy of the Council of the National Army Museum, London)

10. Thomas Rowlandson, *Johnny Newcome Going to Lay in Stock from The Military Adventures of Johnny Newcome*, 1815. (*The Met, 59.533.1623(3). The Elisha Whittelsey Collection, The Elisha Whittelsey Fund, 1959 The Met, New York, USA*)

11. Robert Dighton, *Triumph of the British Flag over the French Eagles & Colours, Taken by Our Brave Soldiers in Different Actions, as They Appear'd in the Park May 18th 1811*, 1811. (*Prints, Drawings and Watercolors from the Anne S.K. Brown Military Collection*)

May 1811) where the division advanced whilst threatened by French cavalry, then engaged and defeated a larger force of French infantry.[11]

The cavalry regiments of the British Army underwent a similar process of reform, albeit later than the infantry. Official regulations for cavalry dated back to 1728, prior to the establishment of (and vogue for) light cavalry in the army. In 1794–5 David Dundas was left in command of the cavalry force that had been sent to Flanders, and he worked with the officers there to establish a new system of manoeuvres. Using the standing orders of the 2nd Dragoon Guards, a new cavalry drill was developed and published as *Rules and Regulations for the Cavalry* in 1795, subsequently developed into a full system of cavalry drill in 1796, again after testing (this time at Weymouth in Dorset). Alongside this, Major John Gaspard Le Marchant developed a system of sword exercise, drawing upon expertise across the Allied armies in Flanders, that gave cavalry regiments the equivalent of the musket drill.[12] The artillery may seem behind both the infantry and cavalry in terms of official regulations, as they were under the Board of Ordnance's control so they were not subject to the same system of review as the infantry and cavalry. Although there was no equivalent set of regulations for firing and moving artillery, the need for a drill was just as necessary as it was in the infantry and cavalry. Artillerymen needed to be able to handle a range of ordnance as companies were not permanently assigned weaponry. There was, however, a well-established body of publications for this service. Artillery fire drill and tactics were covered in publications like Muller's *Treatise of Artillery*, which was in its third, enlarged, and corrected edition by 1780. This work was made much more accessible in Adye's *The Little Bombardier, and Pocket Gunner*, published in 1801.[13] In this there were details allocating each individual to specific roles with a particular calibre of gun for firing and moving, with adjustments depending on how many gunners were available as a crew.[14] These were supplemented by translations of text from across Europe on artillery, such as Major-General Allensandro Vittorio Papacino d'Antoni's *Service of Artillery*.[15]

The case for the importance of Dundas' drill books and the Duke of York's training regime looks pretty clear. These reforms, however, have a longer history than is often suggested. Far from coming to rescue the Army from its decrepit state in the 1780s, it was during that decade that work began on the Army's drill and training. The need for change was recognized as the Army's drill system had become confused in the 1770s. The *1768 Regulations* were the standard drill before 1792, but though these had been supplemented in 1778 they only applied in Britain. The rotation of units in and out of Britain meant that those infantry trained in the 1778 regulations moved on, and ones that came back did not know which drill set to use. By 1788 only three units attempted to use the 1778 regulations when they were reviewed. The problem was both which manual to use and the lack of authority to enforce it.[16] There was less variety in the cavalry in the 1780s. They drew on custom and practice built up across the eighteenth century and had not suffered so much from the confusion of interim regulations in the American War of Independence, and few units were deployed overseas in that war.[17] These problems began to be addressed in the 1780s. Interim infantry regulations were introduced in 1786 where techniques for movement were standardized, followed by some for the cavalry a year later. Dundas' 1788 *Principles* were tested in Ireland and led to the publication of an abridged version in 1789 for all infantry in Ireland.[18] Nor were Dundas' publications the end of the process. Explanations, commentaries, and revised editions of the infantry drill appeared throughout the 1790s and early 1800s. A simplified version was produced for subaltern officers and NCOs in 1801, along with pocketbook editions and others with fine plates to illustrate it all. Translations of the French *1791* and *1807 Regulations* appeared too, with those by John Macdonald including a commentary and comparison with British practice. The continuation with past drill practices is reinforced further by the limitations of infantry weapons in the era. Training of infantry was still broken down into elements, starting with the manual exercise that covered how an individual positioned their body, and held and used the musket, which then built up in successively larger groups of soldiers for firing and manoeuvring together.[19]

The *1792 Regulations* for the infantry and the *1796 Rules and Regulations for the Cavalry* may have provide the foundation for tactics in the British Army, but they did not provide advice and guidance about when to use what formation. The relevance and application of the drills and formations that soldiers learnt did not come from these books, but from custom, experience and the significant military book trade. There was a very active military literary world that published material that was full of observations and advice for officers. The value of these works was recognized in the Army too. Adjutant-General William Fawcett contributed (as an individual) to this world as an author and translator, and galvanized 600 subscribers from Army officers to publish a translation of Tielke's influential study of the Seven Years War.[20] The publishing firm of John and Thomas Egerton had a dedicated 'military library', offering forty-five different titles in 1795, which had expanded by nine more in 1799, and by 1811 they were publishing Wellington's General Orders for Spain and Portugal as a series of volumes.[21] Publications were supplemented by standing orders by generals for units they commanded, as well as those of units themselves. These books, treatises, orders, and practices reflected the wide and diverse range of roles and deployments of the Army that were explored in Chapter 2. Dundas' regulations for the infantry and cavalry were conceived for large-scale battles fought in relatively open terrain. It was a Eurocentric focus, though it was applicable to some battles in South Asia across the Deccan plateaus between the Western and Eastern Ghats, but the Army ranged much wider. Across the Caribbean, South Asia, southern Africa and in Australia the Army fought in a series of conflicts often referred to as wars on 'brigands' or 'bush wars' to impose, or re-impose, British colonial rule. These operations frequently took the Army into terrain and battle scenarios utterly unsuited to any of the eighteen manoeuvres in drill books. In Britain and Ireland the Army was involved in a range of security and police activities too, from chasing deserters, guarding prison camps and militarily and economically important buildings and sites, supporting magistrates in the execution of their duties, riot police, an anti-smuggling force, and in Ireland facing an actual insurrection. The Army was not just a military force to fight the French Army (or any other European army) but was also an imperial and domestic enforcer engaged in a series of counter-insurgencies.

Many of these military activities fell into the broad heading of *petite guerre*, the small-scale military actions outside of large battles and were viewed as the preserve of light troops, particularly light infantry. The Army understood the need for such troops and for its forces to adapt to the terrain they were fighting in. The American War of Independence had provided a further stock of memoirs and examples about light troops, with the publication of Simcoe's *Journal of the Queen's Rangers* and Tarleton's *History of the Southern Campaign* in the 1780s.[22] Until the 1790s those in command and with influence in the Army generally subscribed to ethno-cultural attitudes towards light troops, whereby some people were viewed as 'naturally' more adept at this kind of warfare. This echoed emerging discussions about national characteristics, which included evaluating perceived martial qualities. Germans (a broad definition that included Dutch, Swiss, Austrians and Poles as well as actual Germans) were particularly thought by the British to provide better light troops, and so were sought at the outbreak of the European war in 1793.[23] Such logic prompted Colonel Nesbitt in 1797 to advise keeping the Hompesch Light Infantry (who were armed with rifles), whilst other units recruited from western Europe were being reduced, as they were 'a kind of troop we never can possess by any other means'.[24] In the Napoleonic Wars too, Corsicans and Greeks were formed into light infantry units. Within Britain and Ireland, Scottish Highlanders and Irishmen had been seen as suitable stock for light infantry in the eighteenth century, and even in 1798 Sir John Sinclair thought highlanders made good light infantry as they were 'naturally active'.[25] Likewise, in the Caribbean black troops were believed to be better inured to the environment and the fatigues of fighting in tropical forests.[26] In this way, official manuals and training for British light infantry was not a priority, as the assumption was that there were better troops available that

Britain could use to do it. These beliefs were challenged in the 1790s. Firstly, there was a practical issue as German troops became increasingly hard to find due to French conquests. Just as important were intellectual developments, particularly the German idea of *Bildung* and pursuing learning with an emphasis on reason over superstition, which encouraged a scientific approach to soldiering against ideas of innate martial characteristics.[27] This was present in Baron Francis de Rottenburg's 1798 drill for riflemen and light infantry. This system of training, adopted in the 5/60th Foot when it was established as a rifle battalion in 1797,[28] made it possible to *make* light infantrymen. The story of the technical adoption and development of light infantry is covered in David Gates' *The British Light Infantry Arm*,[29] but it was more than a purely military reform for a specific military need. Training for light infantry, and the manuals and regulations that went with this, only made sense if good light infantryman could be created. It was tried and tested from 1797 onwards, with is ultimate proof in the Light Division in the Peninsular War.

The attention paid to training light infantry was not replicated to the same extent in the cavalry. As was mentioned above, new drill regulations were issued in 1796, accompanied by an excellent system of sword training developed by Le Marchant. Yet this did not address Wellington's justified complaint about the cavalry 'Galloping at Everything'.[30] As Paul Dawson has highlighted, equitation (the science and art of horse riding) was very poor in the Army.[31] In fact, specific training in military riding was practically non-existent. In the cavalry regiments a structure was in place to train new recruits (both enlisted men and officers) how to ride, as each regiment had a riding master who was assisted by rough riders, a kind of unofficial NCO rank. Rough riders were chosen from within the regiment from the best riders that had a good disciplinary record. They had, nominally, considerable authority during training sessions, but predictably their relationship with officers could be difficult. What they taught was largely based on custom and their own experience and so decided at a regimental level, and it was not until after 1815 that attempts were made to standardize military equitation. In particular, the complex combination of the saddle, stirrups, the cavalryman's bodily position and the ways these interacted with the horse that made up a rider's seat was particularly poor. The seat and a cavalryman's balance were fundamental as they had to wield a weapon, as so they controlled their horse with their left hand and through their legs.[32] Major William Tyndale of the 1st Life Guards was particularly scathing in his *Treatise on Military Equitation* (1797) of the 'young officer, who though he may have led the field with fox-hounds, and rode over turnpike gates in his native county, is in all probability, totally unacquainted with the method of riding which is necessarily adopted in regiments of cavalry'.[33] The one-hour riding lesson for five days a week for three months was barely enough to train someone to mount and sit on their horse, let alone control it well. There was an emphasis on speed, again drawing from the wider cultures of fox hunting and horse racing prevalent in Britain and Ireland in the era. The charge held an almost mystical place in the cavalry's military culture, with the devastating, all-out assault at the gallop celebrated. The cases of the 15th Light Dragoons at the Battle of Emsdorf in 1760 and then Villers-en-Cauchies in 1794 served as moments that cavalry officers aspired to.[34] It was emulated, stipulated in regulations, but seldom repeated. In fact, it was just as likely to be disastrous than a glorious success, with the battlefield history of the cavalry peppered with instances of out-of-control cavalrymen being severely mauled by French cavalry, most notably at the Battle of Waterloo.

The emphasis on the cavalry charge is a reminder that soldiering was more than just learning drill. Making soldiers involved psychological and physical dimensions, as facing battle they needed to overcome intense bodily responses to the potential lethal space they occupied as they stood and moved alongside their comrades. This was even more important given, as Edward Coss put it in *All for the King's Shilling*, infantry in a two-rank line was a 'lonely formation in which to fight'. Inherently the formation exposed soldiers to much more psychological stress than dense formations, plus it got worse as battle progressed and ranks were further thinned and gaps opened up.[35] Coss' work has uncovered more than any other the bonds that sustained soldiers, whereby small groups developed their own norms and behaviour that kept them going through combat and campaigning. As we saw in Chapter 6, the Army enforced collective living right from the start of the soldiers' military experience so inadvertently facilitating the development of these groups. Additionally, drill books and regulations instilled a transformation in the soldier that was designed to encourage steadiness under arms. Although the attention paid to bodily stance can be dismissed as a pedantic attempt to 'banish the air of the rustic',[36] as David Dundas put it in the *1792 Regulations*, its precision about the position of shoulders, feet, hands and elbows focused the soldier on how to stand in a certain way, building a form of muscle memory and also, once he was in the ranks with his comrades, a form an anonymity and collective security in all doing the same thing. A training regime of constant repetition of drill aimed to make soldiers greater than the sum of their parts, and to impart that sense to the men themselves. It is significant in the creation of a solider that both the infantry and cavalry learnt the same manual exercise first before specializing according to their arm. The repeated practice of these drill elements and the bodily control that it required underpinned a soldier's capacity to perform in battle, regardless of the particulars of the precise formation in which he was arranged. The relevance of this regimen, though, was not obvious until soldiers had been in combat, and it was generally enforced by a system of coercive compliance.

Becoming a soldier was a very different experience for an officer, but in one way they were like enlisted men. Outside of the officers of the Ordnance and those who had passed through the Royal Military College they, generally, had no military experience or education before they joined. As we saw in Chapter 7 it was not a requirement to know the duties, skills and attributes required to be an ensign, second lieutenant or cornet. The idea that officers needed training before they joined was not prevalent, and the first grades of officer ranks were seen as training positions. New officers developed through self-improvement and learning on the job.[37] The first task, then, was to ensure that new officers joined their regiments and stayed with them, and so the Duke of York's reforms to strengthen officers' careerism were important to improving their training, with the expectation set on commanding officers that within two years new officers should be able to command and exercise an infantry company or cavalry troop.[38] Some took this particularly seriously, and Huf's work on junior officers shows that some officers took to the ranks to learn the manual drill.[39] Probably more important was the inculcation of values that were considered important: stoicism, dedication to their career and collective spirit.[40] This was a normative system of discipline that was fundamentally distinct from that enforced on enlisted men. Although the courts-martial system was the same, the charges against officers were often framed around their honour and status, and punishments targeted these too. They pointedly did not involve physical punishment. Conversely, officers had a system or rewards; they could receive official public recognition through being mentioned in official despatches, awarded medals, honours and titles. We should not underestimate the power of these elements combined to shape an officers' outlook and attitudes (in a way providing some form of psychological preparation for combat) and it synchronized with gentlemanliness that underpinned officer's identity. It was possible, however, to circumvent and ignore as they were customary and much subject to the judgement of those around them – to the communities of company, troop, battalion, and regiment that they joined.

Structure

The personnel and the training that the Army gave them were managed through the Army's structure. Part of an exploration of the Army's military capability therefore involves discussing how it was arranged and changed. The Army was split into the different service arms of infantry, cavalry, artillery, and supporting services, and below these it was organized into units. Units (regiments, battalions, companies/troops) were the primary way that the human capital of the Army was arrayed. As we saw in Chapter 4, the Army expanded massively between the 1780s and 1810s but within this broad trend the patterns were not even. The Army's structure was set through the annual establishments that were explored in Chapter 3. The actual strength of the Army was different from the establishment set each year though. The Army is generally criticised for failing to match its strength to its establishment, but this misunderstands its purpose. The establishment provided the budget for the Army's manpower, and for the Army to expand it needed suitable finances. In effect, the Army's strength was always intended to be less than its establishment when it was growing. The technical details of the Army's establishments are complicated but not incomprehensible. Rather than adopt a fixed state for all units of a similar type (every infantry battalion having the same number of men, for example) the maximum size of an infantry unit was flexible and built around a building block of twenty men (one corporal and nineteen privates) that were then combined into companies and then into battalions or regiments. Likewise, cavalry had different-size establishments depending on their station and role. This system let the War Office adjust the size of units to suit the needs of its station and its likely strength, so hopefully avoiding unnecessary expense.[41]

Infantry formed the bulk of the Army. It routinely accounted for three-quarters of its strength and at times was close to 80 per cent. The permanent infantry component of the Army were the regiments of foot, most of which at least until 1803 comprised one battalion. In 1787, each infantry battalion of a regiment of foot was augmented from eight to ten companies, two of which were flank companies (one of grenadiers and one of light infantry).[42] This ten-company arrangement was the norm through the period, though recruiting companies were added at times. Between 1793 and 1815 individual company establishments varied from 60 to 120 men, depending on how well it was expected to recruit, its intended role, and the overall approved size of the Army. Superficially, the infantry seemed quite homogeneous. In the 1780s there were Foot Guard regiments, regiments of foot, plus the New South Wales Corps (in effect a small regiment of foot) and companies of invalid soldiers. The expansion of the 1790s was in both the size and the number of units. The three regiments of Foot Guards increased from 2,800 rank and file in 1793 to 8,900 by December 1814, boosted by its own recruiting and transfers from the militia, although this growth was half as much as the infantry overall. As we saw in Chapter 4, huge numbers of new units were added in 1793 to 1795. Appendix C provides a summary of these changes, and even these figures probably understate the changes in the organization of the Army, as they do not account for the hundreds of independent companies raised in 1793 to 1794 nor it is easy to pin down the number of *chasseur*, ranger, and volunteer units raised from enslaved Africans in Saint-Domingue during the British occupation. Details about the configuration of the foreign units the Army incorporated between 1793 and 1797 are not always available, as they were never formally established, but there was considerable variety. They range from small single-company formations of light troops to those that were arranged just like the regiments of foot.[43]

Probably the most celebrated transformation in the infantry were the regiments of light infantry, starting with the creation of the Rifle Corps in 1800 and then the retraining of the 43rd and 52nd Regiments of Foot in 1803. This bought specifically designated and trained light infantry into the establishment of the numbered regiments of foot, so making them as permanent as anything ever was in the Army at the time. Subsequently, three more regiments of foot (the 51st, 71st and 85th) were converted. As we saw above, the history of Britain's light infantry arm is more complicated than suggested by these changes. David Gates' work demonstrated that the 90th Foot was a unit of light infantry from its creation in 1794 until the end of the decade, largely at the behest of its commander.[44] Likewise, the Army had a large light infantry arm provided by units recruited in Europe and from enslaved Africans. Although without an official 'light infantry' designation, the West India regiments, and their predecessor ranger units, operated as light infantry in the Caribbean.[45]

As we saw in Chapter 2, one of the largest subsets of the infantry were men raised on geographically-limited terms of service, and up to 1805 there were successive waves of new units raised for these men. Fencible infantry in Britain expanded massively in the 1790s. In 1794 they numbered only 5,500, but a year later had already reached 17,400 men and forty-one units. These units had a more varied internal structure, with some small corps of a few companies and others, such as the Breadalbane Fencibles, reaching three battalions. More complex for the structure of the Army were the militia transfers of 1799, as these men enlisted for European service only. The regiments of foot that the militiamen transferred to were outwardly indistinguishable from other regiments but were legally restricted in where they could serve. More uniformity was established after the disbandment of the fencibles and the discharge of limited-service men in the Amiens Peace of 1802–03. The resumption of the war and the subsequent Army of Reserve and Permanent Additional Force Act massively increased the number of soldiers on limited service. The men procured by these two acts were only required to serve in the United Kingdom and the Channel Islands and between them accounted for 52,000. Whilst many transferred to unrestricted service, there were 20,700 soldiers who had not in January 1805.[46] Initially, these men were formed into specific sixteen Battalions of Reserve and second battalions of regiments of foot, but in February 1805 all those still serving under limited service were drafted into nine new garrison battalions (not to be confused with previous garrison battalions).

A critical transformation in the structure of the Army's infantry was the creation of second battalions in regiments of foot. These had existed episodically in the 1790s, with some units even having three battalions due to militia transfers in 1799, but they all proved to be temporary arrangements to cope with swelled numbers. Those created from 1803 were fundamentally different, as they were intended to provide a recruiting and training function for a sibling battalion of the regiment serving overseas.[47] This shifted expansion away from creating entirely new units from scratch to expanding existing ones. This process of growth from an existing base also manifested itself in other ways. The Battalions of Reserve created in 1803, although new units, drew their officers from existing units and half pay. Other new units also tended to spring from existing units, taking a core of officers and men with them, like the complicated history of the Royal African Corps, out of which was created the Royal West India Rangers, renamed the Royal York Rangers, and then split again to form a new Royal African Corps in 1808.[48] Alongside the creation of second battalions were more units to retain soldiers no longer fit for active duty but still able to man garrisons and fortresses. In the 1780s they were concentrated in the 41st Foot but this unit was transformed into a line infantry regiment after 1787 and was replaced by independent companies of invalids, which as they were without a regimental structure were cheaper to maintain than a regiment. The strength of these units gradually increased from 1,600 in 1789 to 7,175 in 1802.[49] The numbers in these units grew by drafting men from other units into them and by mobilizing Chelsea Pensioners, so releasing other soldiers for service elsewhere. A Royal Garrison Battalion was formed in 1795 from these invalid companies for service in Gibraltar. These companies were then reformed into five garrison battalions in 1802 which were then renamed royal veteran battalions in 1804, where they continued to expand reaching thirteen units by 1813 and increasing in strength from 4,700 in 1804 to 8,800 ten years later.[50] Smaller units of soldiers fit for garrison duty were also formed for European and black soldiers in the Caribbean, as well as from foreign corps. When combined with the royal veteran battalions these units totalled 12,000 men by 1811.

The cavalry was a small component of the Army compared to other European armies, averaging just 25,000 for the years 1794–1815, but this stability disguises shifts in its composition. After the re-designation of the Irish horse regiments in 1788 cavalry regiments were styled either dragoon guards, dragoons, or light dragoons. The gradual transformation of four regiments of light dragoons into hussars in the 1800s (officially granted in 1811 and backdated to 1807) was purely cosmetic but no less effective in encouraging a certain panache and self-styled superiority within them.[51] The Royal Horse Guards, a regiment of horse and the two regiments of Life Guards (themselves reformed from troops of Horse Guards and Horse Grenadier Guards) remained distinct. There was no difference between the regiments of dragoon guards and dragoons in their basic function and equipment as the Army's heavy cavalry arm (they were not the older meaning of dragoons as mounted infantry), except that dragoon guards were senior to the dragoons in the *Army List*. All cavalry units were organized into troops, two of which formed a squadron for tactical purposes, but the number of troops within a regiment could vary from four to as many as the twelve of the 1st Dragoon Guards (although this was unusual). From 1803 the cavalry were usually standardized to ten troops, and like the infantry the size of a unit varied through the establishments of their troops which for most units started at forty rank and file with increments of twenty men up to a maximum of 100.[52]

In terms of units and numbers, it was the light cavalry that expanded the most. Fourteen new regiments were raised in Britain and Ireland between 1793 to 1795, whilst one heavy cavalry regiment was disbanded in 1798. Alongside these were eleven regiments of light cavalry raised in Europe, most of which were reduced or amalgamated into others by 1797, and which bought the first units of hussars into the Army, most notably the York Hussars that served throughout the French Revolutionary Wars and had the unusual distinction of being placed on the establishment.[53] Even more significant were thirty-four fencible cavalry regiments raised between 1794 and 1795. In November 1794, they accounted for 4,700 rank and file out of a total of 16,750 (28 per cent) and nine months later they made up 35 per cent of the Army's cavalry arm.[54] There was much greater variety in the components of the foreign and fencible units, which ranged from units of a single troop to those with six. Anticipating the need for cavalry to face an invasion of Britain, the government also introduced a form of cavalry militia known as the provisional cavalry, and six regiments were formed in 1798.[55] The fencibles and provisional cavalry units' restricted terms of service, the small size of some of them, and a more secure military situation led to their disbandment in 1800.[56]

The arrangement of the Army's mounted arm was transformed from 1800. It shifted from creating new units to expanding existing ones, with waves of new troops being added to regiments. This was both a rationalization based on the experience of the 1790s and reflected the influence of the Peninsular War on the Army. Fencible cavalry regiments were not raised again in 1803, and by 1811 just six additional cavalry regiments (two heavy and four light) had been added, all composed of recruits from western Europe in the King's German Legion and Brunswick corps, plus there was a foreign troop attached to the 20th Light Dragoons in Sicily and a small corps of Ceylon Light Dragoons.

Overall, though, cavalry increased from 275 troops in 1803 to a peak of 410 in 1813.[57] As we saw in Chapter 2, transporting horses overseas was prohibitively costly, so maintaining a cavalry force outside of the UK was difficult. The cavalry force sent to Flanders in 1793 was made by combining squadrons from different regiments into brigades, but even then this meant that only 2,100 could be deployed.[58] Until the Peninsular War, the deployment of cavalry overseas was largely episodic, with units in South Asia, and part of one in Sicily the only continuous deployment. The early stages of the Peninsular War were not that different from earlier expeditions, but as the campaign became Britain's main military effort, so the need for cavalry grew both to maintain what was there and to increase it with new units.[59] Some means was needed to maintain the cavalry force overseas, and by 1811 this was addressed by regiments on overseas service increasing the number of troops they had and leaving two or four troops in Britain or Ireland. Alongside this was the creation of a cavalry depot at Canterbury and another at Radipole (just outside Weymouth) where small detachments of cavalrymen were brought together.[60] Although the cavalry depots were intended to facilitate training and administration they were far from efficient establishments, and supporting cavalry units outside the UK remained a problem throughout the wars.

Out of the three arms it was artillery that proportionally expanded the most, increasing from 4,100 (including the Royal Irish Artillery) in 1793 to 28,700 by 1814, close to a seven-fold increase. The basic arrangement of the Royal Artillery, though, remained the same. Artillery companies were the building blocks, which were formed into 'marching battalions' of ten companies that served a purely administrative function. On top of these were a small staff, a corps of invalids of artillerymen that were only fit for duty in garrisons, and the cadets at the Royal Military Academy (which counted as a distinct company). All these parts combined made up the Royal Regiment of Artillery. Before 1804 the battalions of artillery had different establishments, but these were standardized in that year into ten companies each of 144 men of all ranks.[61] A good part of the expansion of the artillery came from additional battalions in the Royal Regiment of Artillery. There were four in 1792, increased to five in 1794, then six in 1799, and the 7th battalion was formed from the former Royal Irish Artillery in 1800. The 8th, 9th, and 10th battalions followed in 1803, 1806, and 1808. In addition to these were the Royal Foreign Artillery, which formally appeared in Royal Artillery returns from 1799 but dated back to 1793,[62] and in 1806 the King's German Legion artillery (which itself included its own horse artillery) were added into the establishment too. Echoing the vogue for 'light' units in the infantry and cavalry, the addition of the Royal Horse Artillery was probably the most noted changes in the artillery.[63] Starting as two troops in

January 1793, it had increased to ten troops by 1801, in effect its own battalion. This expanded to twelve troops in 1806, and then a rocket detachment was added in 1813. Outside of the Royal Horse Artillery, artillery companies were not allocated specific weaponry or roles. Individual companies of artillery in the marching battalions (batteries in the modern sense) could be utilized as both field or garrison/static batteries, or before 1802 attached to regiments of foot to service regimental guns. As artillery companies were redeployed, they would have to adapt to their new role or ordnance, whether that be working with 6lb cannons that would be used as mobile artillery on campaign and in battles, large ordnance mounted in fortresses, or weaponry such as mortars and iron 18-pounder cannons used to besiege fortresses.[64] Gunners even served on board ships to man mortars in bomb-ketches.

This diverse range of roles and separation between gunners and their weapons meant that before 1794 the marching battalions did not include any transport service to move cannons and howitzers. Instead, teams of civilian drivers were hired as required. In 1794 a unit of gunner drivers was raised, which had various titles across the period, to provide the horsepower and drivers to move artillery on campaign. When combined with a company of foot artillery the formation was designated a brigade of artillery. As detailed in Table 3, these drivers made up a substantial part of the Royal Artillery (some 44 per cent). Much maligned as they were at the time, which is echoed in the histories of the artillery and the Army in general, they nevertheless were an improvement on the previous arrangements of hiring civilians. Part of the issues with the Royal Artillery Drivers were that although they had a military structure, discipline and *esprit de corps* was difficult to facilitate as they always served in small detachments and were attached to the companies of artillery as and when needed. In contrast to this, the Royal Horse Artillery was highly integrated and benefited from this cohesion between gunners and drivers. However, such an arrangement was not

Table 3: Strength of Departments within the Royal Artillery (officers and soldiers), 1 January 1814.

Marching Battalions and Company of Gentleman Cadets	15,333
Royal Horse Artillery	2,499
Military Medical Department	115
Corps of Royal Artillery Drivers and Riding House Department	6,801
King's German Artillery	1,168
Royal Foreign Artillery	499
Total	27,379

Source: TNA, WO 17/2562

possible in the rest of the artillery as not every company needed drivers, nor were there enough to match companies. Whilst artillery companies retained a universal role as gunners, the arrangements to move them were as good as they could have been.

This table also highlights the militarization of other roles in the Royal Artillery, like the Royal Artillery's own medical department and the Riding House Department for training horses. Alongside these troops, the Ordnance also oversaw the Royal Engineers. Like the artillery, they increased in number and by new additions. This process of the militarization of supporting and specialized military services began in the 1780s. Before 1787, the engineering capability of the Army only consisted of officers, but this changed with the formation of the Corps of Royal Military Artificers. This unit was established to maintain fortresses and build permanent defensive fortifications and was re-designated the Royal Sappers and Miners in 1813. The Military Artificers had their origins in a company of artificers raised in Gibraltar in 1772.[65] In terms of numbers again there was a considerable expansion from only a few hundred men to 2,700 by June 1814.[66] Other roles previously undertaken by civilians were also bought into the Army's structure. Tucked away in the figures for the cavalry was the Royal Wagon Train, raised in 1794 to provide a militarized transport service for the Army.[67] The creation and militarization of these units was not always straightforward, nor was their development a tale of gradual improvement and acceptance. It tended to be hidden as well, as logistical, engineering and other support units were included within the infantry or cavalry. One of these was the Royal Staff Corps raised in 1799 under the command of the Quarter-Master-General's department to provide capacity for field engineering outside the Ordnance's control. This unit, rather than being a progressive development, reflected the lack of engineering units for the Army in active campaigns and in the 'field' more generally.[68] The Royal Wagon Train had various guises across the era (and was separate from any transport hired by the Commissariat). It was created for the campaign in Flanders in 1793–4 and then disbanded, reformed in 1799 for the Helder campaign from drafts from the cavalry but only reached fourteen troops with an establishment of 1,596 men by February 1814.[69] Much like its sibling unit of drivers in the Royal Artillery, it was much maligned for poor discipline, and it operated in similarly small detachments. There is also evidence of a specialized medical unit for hospitals was created in the 1790s. Details of these units are incredibly sketchy, as they were never established in a formal way but show up in returns and correspondence as 'Hospital Corps'. It was probably a way providing a simpler system for paying and providing subsistence for soldiers who were detached from their units to provide medical orderlies and personnel for general hospitals.[70] As the debates about general versus regimental hospitals as the basis for medical treatment were thrashed out so the specialized hospital corps disappeared.

Effectiveness

It was from the training of soldiers and the arrangement into units that a military force was made, but judging the effectiveness of the Army needs to consider what it was asked to do. As we saw in Chapter 3, the Army was widely distributed across the globe and its activities in different places varied considerably. Predictably, it has been the big battles and campaigns within Europe that have caught the greatest share of historical attention, closely followed by the campaigns in South Asia. The predominant line within many of these studies suggests a steady and incremental improvement in the effectiveness of the Army, with the dire performance in Flanders in 1793–5 followed by a period of reform with the Army rebuilding and coming of age in the Egypt campaign of 1799 that then went on to improve yet again through the Peninsular War. This perspective all depends on where and when one looks, and a more holistic view shows that the Army made patchier progress. The British Army in South Asia achieved significant results in 1791–2 in the war against Mysore, which were then surpassed in 1799–1803, but the Army was less effective in the latter stages of the war against the Marathas.[71] As the Duke of Wellington was penning the lines that opened this chapter, the Army's force sent to Holland had a significant failure at Bergen-op-Zoom.[72] Conversely, the campaign in Caribbean in 1793–4 (with probably the best parts of Army at that moment) achieved considerable results, capturing Tobago, St. Lucia, Martinique and Guadeloupe.[73] This would have been a spectacular success if the war there was had not been transformed by the French Revolutionaries and the enslaved communities into a conflict that, when coupled with diseases, made the continuing occupation of these islands an almost insurmountable challenge. The capture of the Cape of Good Hope in 1795 may not have involved significant combat operations, nevertheless it showed the ability to project military power over very long distances at a moment when the Army is usually considered to be at its lowest ebb.

Operations against the army of another state were not all that the Army did, and to judge its preparation and effectiveness against these roles ignores a large part of what it did. The transformation of conflict in the Caribbean was echoed throughout Britain empire, and the Army was used in persistent conflicts to establish and maintain British rule in response to various forms of resistance. The memoirs and reports from officers about these operations frequently resort to labelling the people they fought as 'brigands' and echo the other war that the French fought to impose imperial rule across Europe.[74] (It is perhaps no coincidence that those most involved in the development of light infantry units in the Army had experience of these asymmetric conflicts.) The British state lacked the separate paramilitary police that Napoleonic states established for these duties, and so a significant role of the Army was as an imperial gendarmerie. It has been highlighted that the Army was unusually infantry-heavy for a European army, but this makes sense with its colonial role in mind and where it served. It was not completely the case that cavalry was functionally unimportant in terms of military power in the Caribbean, but there were really no circumstances for the mass cavalry charge that was a feature of some European battlefields. Where cavalry was considered useful in this context was as part of a small, combined-arms force, such as the legions that were created in Saint-Domingue, and where cavalry reverted to a mounted infantry role. Similarly in southern Africa the cavalry unit stationed there was used as mounted police and a rapid-response unit. Different again was the British Army campaign in the Adriatic between 1809 to 1814, where for most of the time a single infantry unit (the 35th Foot) conducted highly successful amphibious operations.

The variable performance of the Army is not a particular surprise considering all the factors that could affect its performance. These range from the political and strategic, through supplies, equipment and weaponry, and on into the specific abilities of individuals in command roles to manage the military force under the charge and make decisions. It is worth reiterating the communication problems posed by the geographic scale of the Army's operations. This meant that ministers could not control nor provide advice on operations, and so generals appointed as commanders-in-chief of expeditions or theatres were given wide-ranging powers. Instructions came from the Secretary for War (once this position was created in 1794), but the length of time that communications took meant that these instructions were often open ended, mentioning a number of options.[75] If they were too focused they could cause problems and restrict the operational choices of the military commander. It was adaptable and gave commanders scope to use their initiative. This could work well, for example Major-General Brent Spencer took a force from Gibraltar in 1808 to join the army in Portugal, but equally it could result in the government losing control of events, such as the invasion of South America from the force sent to the Cape of Good Hope in 1806.[76] Though the *Army List* may have included a long list of generals in the Army, those that were suited for these roles was much fewer. Despite the lack of formal training for officers, this does not mean that any general officer could be appointed to a command role. There were informal ways that competence was judged and discussed through political, social and kin networks, and suitability often also had to involve considering their diplomatic skills and standing.[77] This, for example, goes a long way in explaining the appointment of the Duke of York to command in Flanders in 1793–5 over the more senior, and more experienced, Duke of Richmond. Decisions like this then effected subsequent choices, as only general officers that were junior to the commander in the *Army List* could then be appointed as subordinates. In this regard, the Army was no different from the Royal Navy, nor other European armies. There was no individual responsible for making decisions about appointing commanders, as it was a discussion between politicians and the king (who formally commissioned the commander), made within the precedents and structures of the officer corps. This meant that there was considerable continuity in commanders. The careers of those who held roles in the 1790s stretched back in the 1760s and 1770s (like Cornwallis and Abercromby) with active service in North America or India, and those that came to the fore in early 1800s had experience in the Caribbean, South Asia, and Europe from the 1790s (like Sir John Moore).

Command of a military force involved a host of tasks that were broadly undertaken by a military staff. The suggestion that British armies had *no* staff in the 1790s is another myth of the era based on unrepresentative evidence. As commander of forces, a general was provided with a staff to mirror the Commander-in-Chief: they were allocated an adjutant-general and quarter-master-general (often each with assistants depending on the size of the force), a chief engineer and artillery officer (responsible to the Board of Ordnance), along with a commissary and medical staff and a judge advocate-general. The question, then, is if the structure was efficient and those in these roles effective.[78] More generally, there is a criticism that the Army lacked a general staff. Besides this being anachronistic, as it was in this era that the idea of a modern general staff took shape and then only in the specific instance of the Prussian Army planning for the future war with France, like other parts of the Army this is a question of where this function was undertaken rather identifying it structurally. Planning for future operations was dispersed across the Quarter-Master-General's department, individual officers in staff roles, and government ministers. Military planning for the British Army was focused on anti-invasion planning (which we explored in Chapter 3). Outside of this, operations were too dependent on political circumstances and opportunities for meaningful planning to take place. Britain's main war was with the French from 1793 but how that war would be fought and where were not obvious.

The British Army also seemed out of sync with its European counterparts in not adopting permanent operation-level formations like combined-arms divisions and corps.[79] Again, the context of what the Army expected to do is important. Divisions made no sense when units were shuffled around garrisons in the 1780s, and in the 1790s expeditions and territorial-based commands were the operational structures around which the Army was organized. Below this were brigade-sized organization that matched the scale of its operations. However, brigades were not suitable for multi-axis operations within a theatre, and this was recognized when it was needed. Andrew Bamford in *Sickness, Suffering, and the Sword* has unearthed the plans for divisions in Portugal right from the start of the war in Iberia, but which were overtaken by the complications of rank and command in the army in the wake of the victories at Roliça and Vimiero, and then the recall of the army's commanding officers for the inquiry into the Convention of Cintra.[80]

Once deployed, the effectiveness of the British Army was persistently tugged at the seams. As we saw in Chapter 5, the health of troops was a significant problem. This could be exacerbated by supply problems. Officially, the Army relied upon a system of depots and magazines to supply the army, which for food and forage themselves were supplied through contracts. Running alongside this were commissaries who could purchase what they could get hold of locally. Coss' *All for the King's Shilling* has demonstrated just how inadequate official rations were in the Army, both in terms of overall calorie count compared to the work they did and in key nutrients for health. The reality, then, was that soldiers needed a supplementary source of supplies to keep themselves going and to vary the carbohydrate-based diet offered by the Army. How – and if – this was achieved depended a lot on the place and circumstances. A regular military presence, such as in the Caribbean, could stimulate local markets and provide troops with a more varied diet. Conversely, in retreat (and sometimes in rapid advances) soldiers were completely devoid of even basic rations as the supply network of wagon or mule trains was disrupted and unable to be reconfigured. The Army needed considerable management during operations to maintain its fighting strength and was heavily dependent on officers commanding units. Some officers were able to maintain the strength and efficiency of a unit, often termed 'internal economy', yet the same unit could fall away quickly in the hands of a new commander.[81] The structural changes outlined above made their job a little easier as it separated the tasks of recruiting and training new soldiers, a function also taken over by the militia as they provided more and more drafts to the Army. This meant that in most cases, in the 1800s and 1810s, the Army was able to maintain units in the field for prolonged periods in ways that it was unable to do in the 1790s where units were sent out on service, were worn down by casualties, and then had to be taken out of service to recruit and rebuild.

The military effectiveness of a unit faced its ultimate test in battle. Pitched battles, usually lasting a day, were key moments in the military operations of the day. The fighting ability of the Army depended on so many factors that any summary risks generalization or being unrepresentative. The most detailed analysis of combat psychology of the Army has, predictably, focused on the Peninsular War, which showed that there was a close alignment between the Army's tactics based on close-order infantry drill in lines and aggressive counter-attacking with the chances of survival of the soldiers involved. This alignment motivated soldiers in combat.[82] There was differences, though, that we should recognize. The experience of killing varied between arms and roles. The infantry firing in mass volleys or artillerymen firing cannons both that produced great discharges of smoke would have very little sense of fighting individuals. Riflemen, though, were different and their combat experience of taking aim and deliberately try to kill individuals resulted in fairness or self-preservation featuring in the way they dealt with combat.[83] Cavalry combat, where both sides engaged in hand-to-hand fighting, was not as common as one might think. Here, the instinctual responses that sword drill was intended to instil came into play, and it is telling that generally British cavalrymen were considered superior individual fighters. Nor should we ignore the fact that once in battle the soldier's military community could motivate troops. Many officers took on a cult of heroism and sacrifice that meant demonstrations of physical courage were important in their persona as an officer. Casualty figures for officers bear this out, for example 50 per cent of the majors and lieutenant-colonels at Waterloo were wounded or killed.[84]

* * *

Soldiering in the British Army was a varied business, but its basis was rooted in the discipline intended to be instilled through close-order drill. The precision and repetitiveness of this drill makes the training of the Army seem detached from the reality of combat in the era. There was only so far that the Army could go in preparing for war without actual experience of it, especially when what form that combat could take was so dependent on what they were going to be asked to do. Besides adjusting the nature of the conflict that they were going to engage in, for actual operations to be successful a whole host of factors and influences needed to align, be managed or nullified. Part of the improvement in the Army came from structural changes that separated out some functions of military service. Fewer new units were raised after 1803 and existing units were expanded. Second battalions, depot troops and companies, and militia played an increasing part in improving the sustainability of the Army by handling recruitment and training. This transformed the British Army from a single-shot weapon where expeditions were mounted for a particular purpose (which was either achieved or not) after which a new force needed to be built to 'reload' the weapon, into a force that could sustain a military commitment over a series of years. It still then took capable military commanders to wield Britain's military force, in whatever form it took, effectively. The sustained military conflict then provided that experience and practice such that Wellington was able to claim that the part he managed was 'the most complete machine'. Others may not have got quite to the same level of efficiency, and the effectiveness of the Army was patchy but it persisted.

Chapter 9

Army, Society and Culture

Leaving old Glasgow once more, I returned to the south. Coming up in the London smack, two hours after leaving Leith, one of the passengers entered into a conversation with me, inquiring if I had been at Walcheren, the number of my regiment, whether I would like best to be a sailor or a soldier, and such like chit-chat. The steward at this time calling the passengers to tea, the stranger went down among them, but soon came up again, carrying a porringer of tea and a roll – these he politely forced me to accept.[1]

This little vignette of the interaction between a soldier of the 71st Foot returning from furlough in Glasgow (granted to him to recover from illnesses after Walcheren) shows how despite the separation between the military and civilian worlds there could be close ties between the two, even if it just extended to acknowledging in the small gift of some food and drink all that a soldier had suffered. Of course, not all such interactions between soldiers and the communities, either those they came from or those they met, were so amicable. Nor was the relationship always so direct and personal. Nevertheless, there was a continuing dialogue between the Army, society and culture, and as the Army increasingly became an overseas force and more of it was housed in barracks, so its representation in print and visual arts took on more significance in shaping the relationship between soldiers and civilians, both at the time and subsequently.

Populations and the Army

Before we get to the details of the interactions between the Army, society and culture, a sense of scale can be explored through demographics. As we saw in Chapters 3 and 5, the statistical-mindedness within Army provided a much clearer sense of the size of the Army, and this reflected the broader shift within European intellectual thinking that increasingly valued the study of populations through numerical data as a science with practical social applications.[2] This was emphasized by the first census taken in Britain in 1801, and every ten years thereafter. These figures provide us with the male population in Britain, which when coupled with estimates for Ireland can contextualize the number of people who went into the Army. The Army totalled 209,000 men in 1801, from which we need to deduct the foreign soldiers (about 15,000), meaning 2.5 per cent of the UK male population was in the Army. By 1811, when we can be surer about the part of the Army raised in Britain and Ireland, the proportion had increased slightly to 2.7 per cent.[3] The Army focused on quite a narrow age range of the entire male population enumerated in the census, and its physical standards were relatively exclusive. In 1802, regulations stipulated that only men up to 25 could be enlisted, which increased to 30 for the infantry in February 1803. Recruits for the infantry had to be at least 5ft 6in (1.67m) tall, which was reduced to 5ft 5in (1.65m) in 1803 and reduced by another inch in 1812.[4] The lowering of the height standard echoed the falling height of the population generally (as much as an inch every ten years) and the maximum height of individuals was often not reached until the early 20s. The average height of an 18-year-old was around 5ft 4in (1.63m), and only by 21 would young men start to meet the height standard for the infantry, which provided a further cause for the age range to being extended to 30.[5] Outside the infantry, height requirements were even more limiting: heavy cavalrymen needed to be at least 5ft 7in (1.7m) and 3in taller still for the Life Guards; militia volunteers for the Foot Guards and artillery (when these were permitted) had to be at least 5ft 8in (1.73m).[6]

With these standards in mind, more useful comparisons can be made with richer demographic information. Tony Wrigley and Roger Schofield's *The Population History of England* calculated the demography of England in the eighteenth and nineteenth century based on back-projection and family reconstitution, but their approach and findings have been re-appraised by Peter Razzell, leading to questions about their accuracy.[7] Fortunately, we have an underused set of information collected for Defence Acts in the summer of 1803 and published in 1804 that determined the available manpower in Britain of military age.[8] This legislation required all the counties in Britain to list the male population aged between 17 and 55. The Army was even more restrictive than this age group, and the 1803 Defence Act returns classified the male population even further. Divided into classes by age and number of children, the first two are relevant for a comparison to the Army as they encompassed men ages 17 to 30, almost matching the Army's recruiting standard of 18 to 30. Men in these classes totalled 1.07 million in 1803 for Britain. Using this as a base, we can calculate the potential pool of military manpower that could have joined the Army between 1803 and 1815: a figure of 3.25 million.

The population that was permitted to enlist was also affected by the religious basis on the Army. Officially, only Protestants could be soldiers, but the enlistment of Catholics had been an accepted reality of wartime recruitment since the Seven

Years War, although it was limited in the American War of Independence over concerns of using Catholics to quell Protestant Americans.[9] Catholic recruitment was explicitly approved through Catholic Relief Acts, particularly Ireland's 1793 law, which allowed Catholics to hold officers' commissions.[10] Moreover, the Army sought to improve the situation of Catholics in the Army, permitting them to practice their religion openly and officially. A series of general orders gave approval to Catholics in the Army, and by 1811 there was full religious toleration for soldiers.[11] Yet the issue was still contentious enough for George III that, as we saw in Chapter 3, when the Talents ministry tried to assimilate Irish and British law on Catholics in the Army in 1807 it led to their dismissal.[12] We lack a religious census of the Army to make statistically robust accounts of the impact of Catholic recruitment, but both Pitt and Dundas saw it as a vital element in meeting the military demands of the wars.[13] Besides Army recruitment in Ireland, Pitt sought to encourage Irish Catholic enlistments by creating specific Catholic regiments, partially reconstituting the Irish Brigade formerly in French service.[14] Additionally, a substantial number of men joined the Army from the predominately Catholic Irish militia. Nor should we just assume that Catholics recruitment was limited to Ireland. In 1794 the Macdonnells, a Catholic clan in Scotland, raised the Glengarry Fencibles which included Father Alexander Macdonnell as their chaplain, the first Catholic chaplain since the Reformation.[15]

The final factor restricting the proportion of the population that could join the Army was health. This is far harder to judge retrospectively, and we are left in the hands of surgeons from the period about defining who was healthy enough to be a soldier. Nonetheless, some evidence appears for the generally poor health of the population and the ever-decreasing proportion of men who would have qualified to be soldiers in the era. These particularly came out in inspections of new regiments of foot in 1795, so before they had seen any active operation or indeed much service. In the 107th Foot 173 men out of 539 were judged unfit for military service; fifty-one had incurably lame or sore legs; fifty-three had rheumatism, palsy or other nervous disorders; and nineteen had 'useless hands and arms'.[16] The combination of age and physical standards led to half of the soldiers in the 126th Foot being declared as unfit for service in 1795.[17] These figures may not be typical, as they were both inspected by the same team of a surgeon and Brigadier-General Hunter in February 1795 who may have been more exacting than others. Still, the frenzy of recruiting in those years certainly led to recruiters hustling any man they could get into the Army, and that may inadvertently mean these inspections were representative of the population. As such, as many as a third of the 17–30 age group may not have been healthy enough to pass inspections by military surgeons.

The proportion of men that went into the Army from the population of Britain and Ireland that met the age, height and health standards of the Army can only be estimated. Certainly, standards about age and health were evaded. Yet equipped with the data above we can still give a range. Some 365,000 men were raised for the Army from Britain and Ireland between 1803 and 1815. These were drawn from a male population aged 17 to 30 that over the same period totalled 3.25 million, meaning that one man in nine from this age group served in the Army. It is unlikely all of them would have met the physical standards for the Army due to their height or physical condition, for which we could deduct a third (1.08 million). This shortens the proportion to about one man in six from Britain and Ireland of military age, height and health serving in the Army.

These figures about the UK population and the Army can be broken down further to explore a breakdown by nations. What we know about the Army before 1794 suggests that its Protestant basis meant it tended towards Anglo-Scottish as Highland regiments were steadily added in the Seven Years War and American War of Independence. For John Cookson in *The British Armed Nation*, a new Scots-Irish emphasis in the Army sprang into being in 1794 which carried on into the Victorian era's well-recognized and larger 'Celtic' component in the Army.[18] It is easy to highlight the Scottish and Irish contribution to the Army in the 1790s through the number of new infantry units raised by them. Scottish fencibles, for example, accounted for over 15,000 men in the 1790s. Heavy recruiting in Ireland at the start of the French Revolutionary War, with twenty-two new regiments of foot raised on the Irish Establishment plus recruiting for existing units, meant about one-third of the Army's soldiers were Irish.[19] These patterns, though, were not consistent through the 1790s and early 1800s. A more extensive sample of inspection returns of the infantry and cavalry, which delineated the number of English, Irish, Scots and foreigners in each unit (Wales was subsumed into English in the eyes of the Army), shows that the national breakdown of infantry and cavalry was very similar to the population ratios of the UK calculated in 1811 when Ireland's population made up 33 per cent of the UK, Scotland 10 per cent, and England 57 per cent. The pathways into the Army were different though. There were more direct recruits from Ireland and Scotland (especially the Highlands) but this was balanced by a higher proportion of English militiamen going into the Army. The Scottish militia were particularly resistant to volunteering into the Army, perhaps a symptom of the much tighter age groups that enlisted or were balloted into that force. Militia volunteers allow us to look at Wales in more detail, and they provided fewer men in proportion than English regiments, but more than Scottish.[20] These figures exclude the Ordnance's units, and the samples we have show that the Royal Artillery was overwhelmingly English at 69 per cent, Scotland provided a higher proportion than its population with 18 per cent, and Ireland was under-represented with 12 per cent.[21] Factoring this breakdown with the size of the artillery arm in 1813 further emphasizes how the Army had come to more closely represent the national composition of the UK.

There were further distinctions at a regional level too. Generally, urban areas provided a higher proportion of men for the Army. Statistics created by the Army in 1809 based on the recruiting districts that divided up Britain indicate that the London, Birmingham and Manchester districts provided high numbers of recruits. The Highlands of Scotland, roughly equivalent to the Inverness recruiting district, saw an exceptional effort to raise men, so much so that it provided 50 per cent more men per capita than London. This was achieved by an exceptional concentration of recruiting parties. In the Inverness district there were forty-four recruiting parties that enlisted 371 men (just over eight men per party); in contrast the ratio per recruiting parties in the Manchester district was over almost three times more productive at twenty-three men. At the other end of the scale were the two recruiting districts that covered Wales, Herefordshire, and Shropshire, where not only were very few recruiting parties sent by they were not very successful either.[22] Contemporary analysis of recruiting in Ireland also shows regional variation, with communities in and around Dublin, north Leinster, Ulster, and Connaught providing a higher proportion of soldiers for the Army than the rest of Ireland.[23]

These regional variations were played out in the Army's units in strikingly different ways. At one end of the spectrum were highly national regiments. Most famous of these were the Highland regiments. Close to nine out of ten men in the 42nd Foot were Scottish when it was inspected in 1807 and 1808, and the 78th, 79th, 92nd and 93rd Foot regularly had over 80 per cent of their soldiers from Scotland. The 18th, 27th, 87th and 88th Foot had a similarly high proportion of Irishmen. Less well known were the English regiments, such as both battalions of the 24th Foot in 1807 where over 90 per cent of its soldiers were English and the 36th Foot in which three-quarters or more of its soldiers were English. Some cavalry regiments were particularly national too. The 2nd and 3rd Dragoon Guards and the 7th Light Dragoons were consistently English; a rare inspection of the 4th and 5th Dragoons Guards in 1810 show that they still retained their Irish connections, having been units of Irish horse that were converted in 1788. A noted absence, outside of the 2nd Dragoons, were Scottish cavalry regiments. These units need to be put alongside the rest of the Army that was much more of a melting pot of the nations and regions of Britain and Ireland. The 8th and 28th Foot can be categorized as Anglo-Irish; the 26th a combination of Scots and English, with Scots just making a majority. Where we have a series of inspections to compare, shifts in composition are precipitable as units changed where they recruited and how many militia volunteers they attracted. The 85th Foot, for example, went from an Irish–English unit (68 per cent and 26 per cent respectively) to becoming a more equal mixture of the two nations. One consistent feature, though, was that units rarely matched the population breakdown of Britain and Ireland. The 1/3rd Foot came close in 1812 with 63 per cent English, 7 per cent Scottish, and 27 per cent Irish.[24] All these patterns and trends were an aggregation of individuals who joined the Army. Their motives and circumstances we explored in Chapter 6, and the varied composition of individual units reflected the history of their recruiting efforts and links that came about through government recruiting initiatives like the Army of Reserve and militia volunteers. The regimental description books that each unit was required to maintain (and of which a good few have survived) reveals many future recruits migrating from rural areas to town and cities where they enlisted, accounting for the emphasis of urban areas in the recruitment for the Army.[25]

The Presence of the Army

The regional composition of the Army reflected its varied geographical presence in Britain and Ireland. The form it took was significantly changed by the massive barrack-building programme in the 1790s that continued well in the first decade of the 1800s. In 1794 there was barrack accommodation for 18,000 men in Britain, which by 1807 had increased more than eightfold to a little short of 150,000, with barracks for a further 11,000 in the Channel Islands and 33,000 in Ireland.[26] The scale of the change was most noticeable in Kent and Sussex, which accounted for nearly one-third of Britain's entire barrack accommodation, followed by Suffolk and Essex. For some places, this was an expansion of existing military infrastructure, but for other places having a military force permanently close by was a new phenomenon. Some towns like Colchester and Winchester became garrison towns. A good few places were dwarfed by these new military bases. Woodbridge in Suffolk, for example, was a small town (the parish had 3,020 people in 1801) and had a barracks for 4,469 men and 290 horses; Bexhill in Sussex (population 1,091 in 1801) was home to 3,954 soldiers and 521 horses. The experience of Bexhill's population was yet more jarring as most of the soldiers stationed there were from the KGL.

Just as noticeable was the increased fortification of Britain and Ireland, particularly of the coast. Probably most famous of these were the Martello Towers, squat, round fortifications with a cannon at the top that could swivel through 360 degrees, erected along the coast of Britain at likely landing points. Alongside these were numerous batteries and other fortifications from a few guns to large defensive structures. In Ireland, artillery batteries were set up to guard bridges across the river Shannon and new and enlarged fortifications were added to Cork and Dublin harbours. From 1807, Martello Towers were built around Ireland at principal anchorages.[27] Outside of Britain and Ireland there was an intensification of the British Army's presence. As we saw in Chapter 3, the size of the British Army increased almost everywhere it was stationed over the period. Accommodation for soldiers, however, failed to keep up. In the Caribbean this led to significant overcrowding in what were already poor-quality barracks. They were austere, damp, and dark, and enlisted men had to sleep in hammocks at 22–23in per man. Faced with this, married enlisted men built huts, usually of earth plus other material they could gather around barracks, so they could live with their wives and children with some degree of privacy.[28]

Barracks and fortifications were designed to separate the Army from the surrounding civilian population. This was, in part, the principal objections to building barracks in England before the 1790s as there was a fear that barracks would facilitate military despotism. Certainly, there was an uneasy balance between barracks being a source of protection and security (and even pride) for local communities and them representing an occupation. Barracks in Ireland had always been part of the coercive machinery of state power, and the upsurge in barrack capacity in the 1790s and through the 1800s re-affirmed the Army's role there as an occupying force. The first round of barrack-building in England that began in 1792 was prompted by nervous magistrates wanting troops close by to deal with strikes, riots and any other social and economic disorders, part of a longer trend in the use of the military as a public order force.[29] In Scotland, which itself had undergone a military occupation from the 1740s with the building of military roads, new fortifications and blockhouses, the garrison there was turned into a base for Scottish regiments.[30] Whatever the perceived status of a local military garrison, they were rarely sealed off from their surrounding communities. As garrisons were supplied by contract, a military presence represented trade opportunities for local merchants and the prospect of increased prices for those producing foodstuffs and especially purveyors of alcohol. Though there is some truth in soldiers spending a lot of their time in idleness (and so vice), some were industrious and supplemented their pay by practising trades they had before enlisting or providing labour during the harvest.[31] For officers, cultures of gentlemanliness helped maintain bonds between the Army and society. Officers attended local balls and events, as interacting with women was part of the polite accomplishments expected of them.[32] Marriage, and the independence that this signified, was an important part of officers' status.[33] More generally, women were sought out for companionship as well as sexual relationships.[34]

Soldiers sometimes turned on the civilians around them, which was all the more troubling as they were equipped with deadly weapons. Soldiers used violence to get money or alcohol; rape and sexual assault appear in records of military justice, and there were some exceedingly disturbing cases including child sexual assault.[35] We cannot ignore the incidents of violent crime by soldiers, but it did not characterize most of the interactions between the Army and society. Property crime was a persistent problem as soldiers supplemented their meagre rations, for example taking root vegetables from fields near barracks and camps.[36] What was just as common were crimes associated with black markets that accompanied soldiers wherever they went. Danielle Coombs' research into crime and the soldiers exposed this shadowy world glimpsed through court-martial records. From these sources we find an informal economy that dealt in illicit alcohol, trading stolen goods (usually soldiers' necessaries, the collective term for about twenty-five items provided freely by the state or at a fixed price), second-hand clothing, pawning, moneylending and fraud. These exchanges and relationships emerged in semi-settled military communities, but could also pop up when opportunities arose, such as the plunder market after the siege of Badajoz in 1812 or the stores of food and drink offered by Spanish civilians at inflated prices after the Battle of Vittoria in 1813. These activities were recognizable as part of wider makeshift economies for survival of the working poor. There were nefarious practices on both the military and civilian side. In the Peninsular War we know about soldiers scamming civilians by selling items that were then discovered by a soldier playing sergeant and, in the confusion, flattened uniform buttons were passed back instead of coins, with the soldiers keeping the money and the civilian probably feeling lucky that they had avoided a brush with military law. Civilians would undervalue items when soldiers were desperate to move illicit goods on or could encourage selling necessaries through their own shops.[37]

The Army's encounters with people across the globe drew out a range of responses and shifting relationships with the societies it passed through. Within Britain and Ireland, the Army's role as a police force meant that if blood was spilt during a riot, it would be vilified by the population for years. After the Irish rising in 1798 and the attempted coup in 1803, Irish regiments were stigmatized, leading to clashes.[38] All these relationships with civilians were complicated yet further still when it involved encounters between different cultures and peoples. This was most pronounced when the Army moved into places where the contrast and the circumstances made these difference starker. This was not just about simple definitions of enemies and allies. Soldiers of all ranks bought with them attitudes and prejudices from their lives before joining the Army. For many the cultural framework of Protestantism and anti-Catholicism shaped the way they saw others, and for encounters outside Europe the reference points for enlisted men were usually biblical (like Egypt) or travel writing that was infused with Enlightenment ideas about human difference that were racist. Gavin Daly's studies of the British soldier in the Peninsular War shows how the Portuguese and Spanish were generally seen as backward and uncivilized, cruel and savage.[39] These sentiments were also expressed when the British Army campaigned in Egypt, not just of local populations but also Ottoman soldiers and generals.[40] Yet there, particular praise was singled out for Mamluks, the military caste of warriors that governed Egypt, for their martial skill.[41] The recognition of military skill by soldiers in the British Army extended to the French too, where soldiers particularly in the Peninsular War found they had more in common with Frenchmen as strangers in 'barbarous' lands, leading to fraternization and live and let live agreements outside battles.

Studies by Edward Coss and Alice Parker on the Peninsular War highlight the complicated relationship between British Army soldiers and Portuguese and Spanish civilians within spheres of active military operations. The British Army was in Iberia to support the liberation of Portugal and Spain, but poor rations and supply failures drove soldiers to steal food, drink and money from the population alongside other destructive behaviour like breaking into buildings for shelter or ripping them up for firewood. Yet soldiers were generally restrained in the behaviour; paying for things when they could or only taking what they needed. All of this was backed by strong and communally enforced norms and unwritten rules about what was fair.[42] But then there were the atrocities after the sieges of Ciudad Rodrigo, Badajoz and San Sebastian, to which we can also add Seringapatam in 1799. The exact extent of the scale of the violence against civilians at these places is coloured by the sources that we have and who created them. Undoubtedly, though, violence on a scale wholly outside usual parameters took place. With sieges, context can help explain this, as siege warfare was dangerous work that put soldiers under prolonged psychological stress that can be likened to trench warfare in the First World War. The crisis point was the actual storming of a fortress, when men had to charge through a hail of musket and canister fire, cross physical obstacles designed to funnel and channel them into killing zones, and then face assaulting a breach that artillery fire had blasted through the wall or scrabbling up vertical walls on flimsy ladders. The experience would have seemed like the entering the gates of hell as it was lit up by cannon and musket fire that spat out death to them and their comrades around them. In these moments of utter sensory overload, and almost certainly overwhelmed by the physical response to stress that pumped their body full of adrenaline, restraint was ever going to be difficult.[43] The practice of sacking towns (the deliberate plundering and physical assault of the population within a fortress that was stormed after surrender terms were rejected) was recognized in the contemporary practice of war. Indeed, there is some evidence that plunder was offered as motivation by officers to enlisted men.[44] Gavin Daly's study of the siege of Montevideo, though, shows the complexities of these practices, as the fortress was stormed but, unlike the sieges in the Peninsular War and elsewhere, the sack of the town did not follow, a contrast stranger still as at the time Spaniards were the enemy rather than allies. The restraint shown cannot be attributed to a single factor, nor is a full explanation ever likely given the sources that have come down to us, but it nevertheless stands as an example of how the behaviour of British Army soldiers towards civilians was far more complex than often portrayed.[45]

Former Soldiers

As we saw in Chapter 5, for a many soldiers there was no life after soldiering. Death from disease and wounds means that the remains of Britain's soldiers are present across the globe, sometimes in marked graves close to garrisons but in most cases in unmarked gravesites that occasionally come to light. Like much of the Army, there is a divide between officers and enlisted men, where even if the physical remains of an officer did not make it back to a community, his death was often memorialized. Nevertheless, for a larger number of soldiers there was some life after soldiering and a return, in some way, to a civilian community and civilian life. There were different ways that this could happen. Enlisted men deserted or were discharged, and in the latter group there is a distinction between those who were discharged due to ill health or wounds and those who left the when the Army's numbers were reduced.

Around 115,000 enlisted men deserted from the Army between 1793 and 1815. The reasons for desertion were explored in Chapter 7, and although some returned to the Army, either by surrendering themselves or through recapture, desertion for many was a break from their lives as a soldier. It was also usually one that occurred very early on in a soldier's career. Registers of deserted soldiers created between 1811 and 1815 show that over 40 per cent of all desertions occurred within one year of enlistment. Opportunities outside the Army also encouraged enlisted men to consider their situation, with a notable spike in desertions in the south of France and North America during 1814. A large proportion of deserters were historically silent, in that after deserting there were no further records of their actions unless they were caught and were taken to trial or, as in the unusual case of Charles O'Neil, decided to talk about it in a memoir. From these snippets, we get the sense that deserters often figured in the fringes of society. They would have to find new clothes through theft, pawning or exchange, the first part of changing their identity that often involved taking on pseudonyms. Deserting in, or moving to, cities offered opportunities to start afresh. They would take on labouring jobs that offered some anonymity but risked being exploited if their real identity became known, which then might lead to further crimes to protect their identity. For many, though, there was simply a desire to get back home to family and friends, and perhaps the safety of a known community that would protect them.[46]

Most enlisted men who had lives after the Army were discharged. At the time, the Army made no distinction within its statistics about the reasons for ejecting men from the Army, but reasonable assumptions can be made between the mass discharges of men in 1802 and then again from 1814 until 1817 (which can be seen in Appendix D), and the persistent movement of enlisted men out of the Army due to health issues. These figures overlap though, as what was considered a healthy soldier and so worth retaining in the Army changed over time. The criteria, such that can be discerned from practice rather than any official policy, was that men on limited service (either by terms of place or time) were discharged first and the most useful, which was a subjective combination of experience, health, and likely length of service, were kept with a series of gradations beyond that where an enlisted man might or might not be discharged according to the number of men that the unit needed to shed. Outside of these moments, the Army always kept men who were not fit for active service but still could perform some duty in specific garrison units. Between 1803 and 1815, a system was developed that worked the other way, by which enlisted men that were not deemed fit enough for active service were gradually moved through tiers of units. They were moved back to units deployed for garrison duty in active combat zones or to second battalions or depot squadrons in British and Ireland. From these some then went to the Royal Veteran Battalions that had been created in 1802 for deserving soldiers recommended by their officers.[47] This system significantly changed the volume of discharges from the Army before and after 1803, so that after 1803 (and outside demobilizations and major restructuring) roughly half as many men were discharged each year as had been between 1793 and 1801.

The men who made it to the veteran battalions could expect to become Chelsea Pensioners, along with those who were directly discharged from their units with a recommendation from their officers. For most pensioners, this meant being an 'out-pensioner' as the number of places within Chelsea Hospital was extremely limited. Through Caroline Nielsen's research on pensioners in the eighteenth and early nineteenth century we know a lot more that we did about these men. The system of military pensions for enlisted men was overhauled as part of Windham's reforms to the Army in 1806. Under the short service scheme every soldier was entitled to a pension, and the system was adapted again when service for life was reintroduced in 1808. Potential pensioners were subject to a series of examinations of their case by the commissioners and surgeons of Chelsea Hospital. Length of service was established as the primary qualification for a pension and its amount, which was usually set at either 5d, 9d, or 1s per day though up to 2s a day could be claimed. Disability was considered too, as was the recommendation from the soldier's officer.[48] The number of pensioners, which had been relatively steady through the eighteenth century, varying between 15,000 and just over 20,000 from 1784 to 1802, jumped to slightly higher range of 20,000 to 25,000 between 1803 and 1813. Predictably, it was from 1814 when the number of pensioners grew massively, with 36,700 in 1815 and a peak of 62,200 by 1820 after the big reductions in the Army's size following the disbandment of the army of occupation in France.[49] Their presence, then, within the Britain and Ireland would have been common in some areas, to the extent that a specific cultural representation of a veteran soldier became well established. He was an old soldier, recognized as such by the community in which he lived, and had endured the physical and psychological effects of service, sometimes quite visibly through scars or lost limbs, and so they fitted into the category of 'deserving' poor. The literary and cultural representations focused on them as symbols in their community of military service, where their tales to family members and others could inspire the next generation of soldiers. This idealized image became so pervasive from the 1810s that those who did not fit this image could be marginalized and excluded.[50] There were plenty in this category, as the mass discharge of enlisted men from 1814 meant that there were many young former soldiers without obvious signs of their military service.

For former soldiers the stereotype, often echoed in prints and stories, was of their inability to adapt to civilian life, leading to begging, turning to crime to survive, and where their military experience encouraged restlessness and violence. Though this was undoubtedly true for some, it is not true for all, nor even the majority. Because the Army kept ties to Chelsea Pensioners, it is this group of discharged soldiers that we know most about, and studies of their lives after the Army show that they settled back into communities, often where they had previously had strong ties to family or friends. John Cookson's study of Scottish pensioners showed that 90 per cent of them returned to Scotland. They were more like sojourning workers, where the Army was a period of temporary emigration for employment and just a part of the pattern of their lives. They then married, had children and worked. They led settled lives that largely conformed to social norms for the era, with a tendency to live in towns where they, and their family, could do a variety of jobs and there were opportunities in positions of trust and responsibility, like stewards, bailiffs or town sergeants, and, once it had been established, in the police. They were far from law breakers.[51]

In some ways, the reality of the lives of discharged enlisted men from the Army was not that different for officers but with some significant differences. Desertion technically did not exist as a means of leaving the Army for officers (though they could be absent) and they had more control over the moment of leaving as they could resign, retire or move onto half pay. Like the enlisted men they too were subject to changes in the size of the Army with large-scale reductions in the officer corps in 1783, 1802, 1814 and then through 1815 to 1820. When whole units were disbanded or were reduced in size officers were placed on half pay where they kept their rank, received a much-reduced salary but were not employed on any duty in the Army (officers that held temporary rank were not entitled to half pay). This provided the Army with a list of officers (but not always how to contact them) that it could draw upon in any future expansion in the Army. In 1803, 319 captains, 498 lieutenants, and 79 ensigns (or equivalent) were bought back into the Army from half pay.[52] It also created opportunities for officers to exchange between employment and half pay if a suitable pairing could be found. Major changes to the list of half-pay officers matched alterations in the structure of the Army. The demobilizations of 1783–4, 1802 and 1814 significantly expanded the list. With the massive reduction in the number of units in the Army in 1795 there should have been a matching surge in the half-pay lists, but Horse Guards maintained officers that it could not relocate to other units on full pay.

Settling those who would be put on half pay was usually determined by an officer's position within their rank, working up from the most junior officer until enough officers were shed to match the new establishment. This could frustrate the career plans of officers. For example, Ensign Henry Powell was promoted to lieutenant in the 9th Foot on 8 December 1801, only to be reduced on 25 June 1802; yet as he had been the regiment's most senior ensign he would have stayed in the regiment if he had not been promoted.[53] A period of half pay was a common occurrence in officers' careers. Some 150 officers at Waterloo had had a spell on half pay. They include Lieutenant-Colonel Charles Morice of the 69th Foot, who was half-pay major of 15th Foot when that unit was reduced in 1802 and returned to the Army via the 2nd Ceylon Regiment in 1803;[54] and Major John Wilkins (95th Rifles), who made his way through the 31st, the 85th and MacDonnell's Foot between 1794–5, was then placed on half pay in 1795 for five years until he was bought back into the 85th Foot as a captain in 1800, and subsequently promoted into the 95th in 1809.[55] After 1815, the opportunities to resume a military career from half pay were much more limited. Like the enlisted men, officers on half pay married, had children and settled into communities. Like the enlisted men, some sought new careers in official roles with some having particularly notable careers in Britain's empire and significant influence over, for example, British colonies in Australia.[56] Like it did for the Chelsea out-pensioners, the Army undertook periodic audits of half-pay officers, which have yet to be examined in the way that John Cookson has done for enlisted men in Scotland.

Army and Culture

The Army's relationship with society was wider than the personal and individual, as it had a presence within British and Irish culture, particularly in the print culture of the era. Gauging the reach and engagement of material about the Army in newspapers, prints, books and artwork is tricky but more significant in the history of the Army was what was being represented, and consequences that this had on the way that the Army was viewed. Representation of the Army were driven by events, people and units (usually regiments). All these were present in the newspapers of the era, whether it was the dailies produced in London or in the burgeoning provincial press across the British Isles.[57] Indeed, the press bought the first news about the Army's activities. Usually leading the way was *The London Gazette* in which official dispatches from the Army's commanders were published, which were then reprinted, and sometimes commented upon, by other newspapers. Commentary, when it appeared, followed the inclinations of the newspaper, its editors, readers and funders. The *Morning Chronicle*, for example, tended to take a hostile view to the Duke of Wellington, echoing its loose association with the Whig party when they were in opposition to the government. As Zack White has shown in his study of popular opinions about the Peninsular War, perceptions were affected just as much by political stance and situation as the military events. One particular feature of newspaper reporting of the Army's campaign were 'croakers' (as the Duke of Wellington termed them) – officers writing back home whose letters and views were then published anonymously in newspapers.[58] The phenomenon was not peculiar to the Peninsular War, as there was an unofficial 'back channel' about the Duke of York and the campaign in Flanders between 1793 and 1795.[59] Yet it is easy to overplay the political nature of reporting about the Army. There was careful and detailed reporting of what the Army was doing on campaign and some papers were exceptionally well informed about European politics.[60] Alongside these were publications of maps that meant the interested reader could follow and interpret the movements and actions themselves.[61] More broadly, promotions, appointments and changes in the officer corps were all tracked in newspapers from *The London Gazette*. Also tucked in away in the pages of most newspapers were the comings and goings of regiments, especially in Britain and Ireland, a reflection of the connections that some units had to certain locations, but also the advent of a change in the local social scene as officers of a unit left and new ones came in.

This interest in the military extended to 'scarlet fever', a phenomenon explored by Louise Carter. Her work shows that images about women and soldiers reflected broader social and cultural concerns and views just as much as newspapers reflected political ones.[62] Social commentary of the Army, like the barrack and recruiting party prints reproduced in this book's plates, were less numerous than the prints about contentious events, particularly where the Army was bought into disrepute or when the Army's activities were a means to make broader criticisms of the military and the government. Some moments stand out, most notably the failure of the British Army in Buenos Aires in 1807 and then the Convention of Cintra following closely in 1808. In both these cases, it was the subsequent inquiries that prints and the press criticised. These sat alongside a more celebratory prints of battles or notable events appearing soon after they had taken place. These needed the Army to be successful, so the Egyptian campaign of 1801 featured, with a lull between 1802 and 1808, and then there were regular images of the battles appearing (and a selection of these appear on the cover to this book). The Army seeped into contemporary culture in other ways too. Theatres turned to established repositories to explore themes of martial masculinity, responses to war and national identities, mixed with both new and old plays that explored and represented Spain, Portugal and South America. The succession of victories for Britain's armies in Iberia from 1810 led to representation of these events in London's theatres. *The Siege and Capture of Badajoz* was staged at London's Amphitheatre in May 1812, a month after its capture. Sieges translated particularly well to the theatre, as they focused on an event with dramatic set pieces and a formalized structure. Representation of the Army was extended in *The Battle of Salamanca*, performed at Sadler's Wells theatre in 1812, which included a bayonet charge with actual soldiers as actors. After the Battle of Vitoria in 1813, the newly-titled Marquess Wellington was increasingly valorised as a national hero in theatres.[63]

The Army created and staged its own performances too. The military camps in the American War of Independence had established these as public spectacles,[64] and military display continued in the 1780s, albeit to a much more limited extent, through field days in London by the Foot Guards and similar in Dublin by its garrison. The new drill regulations of 1792 were followed up by camps that were also public events. The *Reading Mercury* claimed 200,000 people viewed Bagshot camp in August 1792.[65] Through the French Revolutionary and Napoleonic Wars, military camp tourism was replaced with the Army's own performances, ceremonies, and involvement in local events. There were public displays of military manoeuvres, like sham fights and mock invasions.[66] The Army was paraded before the public too, and many of these events were enhanced by the military bands that were becoming a more conspicuous part of military spectacle and regimental identity. The range of instruments they used expanded in the era allowing a bigger repertoire. Serpents and bass horn instruments were used more frequently in the early 1800s, giving a wider range of tone and potential tunes that could be laid over practical functions of drumming to maintain the rhythm of military step. This facilitated the emergence of 'military music', with marches dedicated to individuals or units. It also built association between bands, particular units and certain tunes.[67]

Contemporary print culture, military ceremony, military music and public display were sometimes deliberately combined. A particular example was the depositing of captured French Eagles (the totemic standard personally presented by Emperor Napoleon to each French regiment) and other captured colours at the Royal Chapel in Whitehall in May 1811. The was a carefully choreographed event and involved six Eagles including that of the *8e Ligne* captured at the Battle of Barossa by Sergeant Masterson only two months earlier. (The other five Eagles were all taken in the Caribbean during the capture of Martinique and Guadeloupe in 1809 and 1810.) Appearing in 'full dress' of bearskins and white gaiters, the uniforms themselves were evidence of the military's awareness that appearance was part of the theatre of the event. The parade of guardsmen was witnessed by 'many thousand spectators' in London as it processed from St James' Park to Whitehall. All of this was accompanied by a combined band of the 1st and Coldstream Foot Guards, playing 'martial music appropriate to the occasion'.[68] Alongside details in newspapers, the event was then recorded in a print by 'Dighton' (Plate 11, and probably meaning a combined effort between Robert and his sons) available from their studio and shop in London. The colours and Eagles remained on either side of the Royal Chapel until they were moved to the Great Hall of the Royal Hospital Chelsea in 1835.[69]

Denis Dighton, Robert's son, went on to publicize Sergeant Masterson's capture of the Eagle at Barossa in a watercolour in 1812.[70] Denis Dighton served in the Army and then was appointed military painter to HRH the Prince Regent, evidence that, like music, there was a strand of military art that emerged in this era.[71] The military was already the subject of significant artworks in the 1780s, particularly with John Singleton Copley's works about the American War of Independence. Though about events preceding the time frame of this book, they were on public display in the late 1780s and early 1790s. Copley's *The Defeat of the Spanish Batteries at Gibraltar* was put in a one-work exhibition in a temporary pavilion in Green Park in London, with an admission fee of one shilling that included a printed guide. There was an option to subscribe for an engraved copy of the painting for a further fee.[72] The artworks of the 1780s tended to explore themes of masculinity and martial prowess and provided a sentimental diversion much in tune with cultural trends of the era. Through the 1790s and early 1800s, artwork furthered themes of heroic sacrifice, a trend that stretched back to the Seven Years War and Benjamin West's *Death of General Wolfe*, but with added impact as the Army lost important commanders in battle like Ralph Abercromby in the Battle of Aboukir in 1801 and General Sir John Moore at Corunna in 1809. The Army was also the subject of artistic practice more generally. For example, Samuel Drummond, who is more famous for his large oil paintings of British maritime history, produced a striking and eerie study of an soldier in the 1810s.[73] The Army featured in bigger, more theatrical, and more public displays. Public entertainment in London and Dublin was punctuated with huge panoramas of battles and military events. The storming of Seringapatam, shown in 1800, was an enormous 360-degree structure covering 2,550ft.[74] The impressive panorama of the Battle of Alexandria, said to been 22ft x 135ft, was exhibited at the Lyceum in the Strand, London in 1802 and then Dublin in 1803 but was lost in a shipwreck in the mouth of the Mersey.[75] Panoramas emphasized accuracy and presented a frozen moment in time for the visitor to step into. Viewers were placed in the scene rather than in front of it, in a position like a military commander.[76] Art to engender an emotional response was made through representation of suffering, especially in painting and prints in the immediate aftermath of the Battle of Waterloo. The battles and events of the Hundred Days were important to Romantic culture.[77] It is significant too what was marginalized in British military art. The horrors of conflict that the British Army endured, perpetrated, and witnessed were seldom represented; there was no equivalent of Francisco Goya recording the conflicts in the Caribbean, Ireland or South Asia.

The panoramas, theatres, displays of artwork, parades in London, Dublin, Edinburgh and military towns necessarily meant that the public who engaged with the Army through these forms was limited by geography. More widespread were printed literary works, and these often quickly followed on from newspaper reporting of British Army events. During the eighteenth century writing about war had tended to be campaign narratives, sometimes to justify or criticise commanders, but in the 1780s a shift began where writers included some personal experiences or stories within a larger narrative. Publications about the 1793–5 campaign in Flanders and then in Egypt in 1799–1801 followed in this vein.[78] The volume of them, particularly on the Egyptian campaign, was significant as it is evidence of continuing interest in the Army's campaigns. Like newspaper reports and art, the history of the British Army was being shaped by the interests of readers and publishers in the 1790s and early 1800s. This was especially the case with the Peninsular War and the emergence of a new form of war writing in the military autobiography or memoir, especially of junior officers and enlisted men. Writing on the Peninsular War reflected the interest in this conflict that spanned the political spectrum in Britain and Ireland, as well as an interest in war as an ultimate experience of intense emotions and a means to link civilian readers and military writers through explorations of suffering and sentimentalism. The publication of the *Journal of a Soldier of the Seventy-First* in 1819 was a pivotal moment in establishing military memoirs as a genre, and it was hugely influential on subsequent publications. Rather than Southey's much-anticipated *History of the Peninsular War* of 1822, military memoirs were the main mechanism to commemorate the wars after 1815.[79] In creating this form of history of the British Army, Matilda Greig's careful research into this outpouring of military writing has shown how soldiers were not accidental authors, and that their publications were not passive testimony. They were attuned to their audience, the moment of their writing and publication, and subject to interventions by editors and publishers. And many of these books were popular. The modesty authors often showed in the opening paragraphs was a literary device to help establish authenticity, and the published text hid all the edits, changes, clashes between authors and publisher, and shaping that went into a finished product designed for a reading market. The war writing that appeared just after events and then as memoirs through the nineteenth century were interventions in the debate about the past.[80]

As soldier veterans were more active in shaping the history of the British Army so was the Army itself influencing the way its activities were presented to the public. Crucial to this was fostering regimental traditions and culture within the Army and then to the public. Some units in the Army already had strong senses of a collective identity, but the 1810s institutionalized this culture so that all regiments should have it. Elsewhere in this book we have already covered how regiments came to dominate the organization of the Army. From around 1805 the Army began to internally capture records of each unit in a set of volumes that now are WO 380 in The National Archives. At a unit level, in 1811 orders were issued to regiments to keep a 'Record Book' that was a forerunner of regimental histories. These forms of institutional memory were built upon from the 1820s, where alongside the personal military memoir or campaign narrative, a systematic publication of regimental histories was started. The first, a history of the 26th Foot, was 'unofficial' even though it was supported by the Commander-in-Chief. In 1835 the first volume of Richard Canon's *Historical Records of the British Army* was published, and seventy more volumes followed.[81]

Linked to publications about regiments, a second strand to the Army's influence on the history and memory of the period was through battle honours. These were names of battles and events added to the colours of the regiments and were prestigious recognition of events. Before 1815, the award of battle honours was very sparse. Up to the American War of Independence the Army had only two battle honours each only issued to one unit; a few units received the Gibraltar honour in 1784 in recognition of their participation in the four-year siege from 1779. In 1801 'Minden' was awarded to five units, and more significantly the 'Egypt' award (along with a sphinx image) given in 1802. Through the first decade of the 1800s a few more were given: Assaye, Maida, Hindoostan, India and Barrosa. Some were awarded a significant time afterwards, like Lincelles given to the Foot Guards regiments in 1811 for the battle of 1793. It was after the wars that retrospective awards massively increased, both units being awarded existing honours or new battle honours. Orthes (27 February 1814), for example, was not awarded to the 13th Hussars (heirs of the 13th Light Dragoons) until 1890.[82] These shaped what events were deemed significant and important and, just as importantly, who they applied to, as it excluded units that had been disbanded.

*   *   *

These different strands of representations of the Army were present in Napier's *History of the Peninsular War*. Its success reflected the combination of the literary and cultural trends that had been shaping the history of the wars and the British Army up until it publication. Firstly, there was the subject; secondly, the author as a military man involved in the events was important (and set a trend for soldier-authors claiming a privileged position within military history). Thirdly, was the way the history was written as a heroic tale, mixing information about individual achievements, highlighting regiments and units, and concentrating on battles and big events like sieges.[83] These events were – and still are – important in the historical culture of the British Army, but they also relegated the broader history of the Army both in Iberia and beyond it. The success of Napier's *Histories* could also be attributed to increasing separation between the Army and civilian society that historians have argued characterized civil-military relations from around 1800. Representation either in art or literature had replaced the day-to-day contact between soldiers and communities and soldiers who were now barracked and led a distinct, opaque life. As was shown in the first part of this chapter, soldiers continued to have close relationships with the communities in which they lived, though they were shaped by accommodation and the changing regulation of soldiering. The increasing representation of the Army in culture in news, prints, art and literature overlay existing and persistent civil-military relations. Moreover, the Army and soldiers were not just being represented in these mediums by others, they were active participants and agents in their creation. From the 1810s and 1820s, soldiers of the British Army, but not all of them and certainly not representative of all of them, shaped the making of the history of the Army in the years 1783 and 1815.

Conclusion

Napoleons do not so frequently appear that the downfall of them and of the power that they have wielded can readily lose significance. By a happy coincidence it occurred simultaneously to the Commanders-in-Chief in the field and at the Horse Guards that so heroic a fight and so momentous an occasion should be commemorated, for the first time since Dunbar, by the issue of a medal to every man in the army who had been present; and this medal is still the possession most highly treasured alike in the highest and the humblest of English homes. The design is of little merit, yet it is unique, and worthily unique, among British military medals, for it bears on the reverse, besides the name and date of the battle, the name of him without whom there would have been no victory – the one word Wellington.[1]

These words finished Sir John Fortescue's volume of the *History of the British Army* that covered up to 1815. Within this quote there are many things that we could point to as hallmarks of the 'old' military history and the historical focus of the early twentieth century. For example, the great men in Napoleon and Wellington stand tall as *the* individuals worthy of mention; and the multinational British Army at Waterloo has been conflated with the 'English'. In many ways, this book has been in a dialogue – antidote even – to Fortescue's work and the operationally-focused histories of these wars. It has sought to take a global view of Britain's military commitments; explore and understand the people who served within it; and consider the Army's relationship to politics, the societies it drew from and encountered, its own culture and its representation. In doing this, though, acknowledgement needs to be made of the contribution of Napier, Fortescue and Oman (to name just three) in providing us, within certain parameters, a clear sense of what the Army did: the who, where and whens without which a book like this risks being detached from the chronology of the Army's history.

The years of peace and war covered in this book give a more measured judgement about the central plot lines of the British Army between 1783 and 1815. The Army in the 1780s has been used as a foil to its proficiency in 1810s, so emphasizing the reforms of the late 1790s and early 1800s that rendered the Army capable of facing and beating the military forces of the Napoleonic

Empire. This is the military equivalent of the Whig interpretation of history – a grand narrative of progress that looks back from its the end point. Yet military preparations were not completely ignored between 1783 and 1793. The Irish and British military establishments were assimilated; greater attention bought to bear on recruitment; the Household Cavalry were transformed into viable units; reforms in drill and training were begun. They may seem small-scale, but they are evidence enough that the Army had not completely atrophied. Also, the composite nature of Britain's military power meant that changes within any land forces affected the other parts and so potential military force. Significant changes took place outside of the British Army in the 1780s. By 1787 two things had improved Britain's military situation. Firstly, the various Militia Acts passed from 1767 were combined and reduced into a single piece of legislation. Although not introduced by ministers (it was initiated by Charles Marsham, MP for Kent) it was nevertheless adopted by the government and received its support.[2] The 1786 Militia Act did not increase the size of the militia in England and Wales, but it did enact annual training for twenty-eight days and by providing a single set of procedures and rules for the militia made the force potentially more efficient and certainly easier to mobilize.[3] This potentially freed the Army as an expeditionary force. Secondly, treaties with Hesse-Kassel provided Britain with a 'go-to' auxiliary force. It is also important to make clear the criteria by which we should judge the Army in the 1780s. The 1790s witnessed a revolution in warfare for which all European armies were ill-adapted. That the British Army may have been especially poor in its response was partly due to its existing global commitments, the structural difficulties these caused, and the limited resources that it had.

It was the period 1793–6 that massively damaged the Army, and it was more than just its encounter with the military forces of Revolutionary France. The readjustment in British politics as Pitt's ministry coalesced with the Portland Whigs destabilized the military bureaucracy just as the Army rapidly expanded. The administration of the Army was flexible (or ill-defined from a structural viewpoint), and positions were malleable and responded to the persons holding other posts around them. In the years 1793 to 1796 the Army's senior posts (essentially the staff at Horse Guards) were subservient and bypassed by ministerial and political appointments. No more so than in management of the expansion and the recruitment of the Army. The massive increase in the number of units, which has hints that it was part of a wider effort to build a political coalition to face the French Revolution, was catastrophic for the management and efficiency of the Army. The British state's military machinery was fundamentally unable to cope with the scale of the change in the number of administrative entities (units and their commanders) that it had to deal with. These issues were the result of political choices that did not recognize the fundamental arrangements of Britain's military at the time. That the problems of the early stages of the war with Revolutionary France were particular to those years (and those decisions) is confirmed by the second phase of expansion and political turbulence between 1803 and 1811, when the Army grew just as much, though less quickly, whilst there were repeated changes in the people involved in running the Army. In the first half of the Napoleonic Wars, the Army was much better able to absorb increases in its strength and less buffeted by political changes. An important part of this resilience, and a fundamental change from previous practices, was the government shifting from personally brokering the expansion of the Army through deals with individuals to legislation that provided the manpower that the Army then used in ways that it saw fit. The transition was not a sharp one, but it took place between 1796 and 1808.

Better management of the human resources of the Army was essential because of its commitments. A stronger appreciation of geographic range is an important part of the framework for understanding and exploring the Army. The result of the web of conflicts across the globe was the continuing deployment of troops thousands of miles away from the war in Europe, even in the final few years of the Napoleonic Wars. The commitment to the Iberian Peninsula was but one in several theatres for the British Army. Despite criticisms from Britain's First Coalition partners about sending troops outside Europe, there were more of Britain's soldiers in Western Europe (principally Flanders) than there were in the Caribbean in 1794. It was after the First Coalition broke up that more of the British Army was employed outside Europe. Viewed within the context of all deployments, it was only from January 1811 that the forces in Spain and Portugal were consistently the largest overseas force (finally outnumbering those stationed elsewhere in southern Europe), but it still just accounted for a quarter of all Britain's soldiers. The units outside Europe needed a manpower base to draw upon for reinforcements and replacements and so it was relatively late that in early 1814 that there were finally more troops in Spain than were in Britain, Ireland and the Channel Islands.

Outside of planning to counter an invasion and the day-to-day running of the Army, Horse Guards and relevant ministers increasingly focused on the strategic management of the Army's limited resources. The limits of sail- and horse-based communications meant that military commanders could not be closely managed, nor was operational planning from London practicable, though that is not to say that it was not attempted sometimes. Decisions at this level were best focused on the choice of commander, what force to allocate to them, and broad objectives. Britain's military staff in Horse Guards focused on gathering information about the Army's strength, and to a lesser extent its quality. It became a more sustainable military force, and just good enough for all the different tasks allocated to it. It tracked the number of men and casualties. This was a manifestation of care for soldiers (not for nothing was the Duke of York appreciated as the soldier's friend, as were other commanders) but it was other forces that drove this. It was partly the political impetus from Parliament for accounts from the Army of its resources and their use; it was partly the Army's own quest to know itself better, drawing on statistical thinking and the rise of professional bureaucrats within and outside the Army that were able to process and interpret the figures. It was also driven by the fact that disease was the persistent foe to the Army: although we do not have direct figures to compare, it is completely plausible that more soldiers died from yellow fever than died in battles with the French Empire. One significant feature of this focus on numbers was the emergence of racial theories about soldiering and climate. A distinct military medicine developed that fused eighteenth-century ideas about human difference with medical theories about climate and disease. The result was categorizing soldiers of different heritages according to their suitability to serve in certain places and undertake different duties. As a result, and despite the British Army's very stretched manpower resources, there were no West India regiments at the Battle of Waterloo, for example. Yet the Army's global commitments meant that its units across the world were intertwined with the forces in Europe. Put simply, if the West India regiments had not existed there would have been at least eight fewer units in Flanders on 18 June 1815.

A substantial proportion of the British Army's manpower was from outside Britain and Ireland. Alongside Englishmen, Welsh, Scots and Irish, the Army's soldiers included: West and East Africans, and Afro-Caribbeans; Southern Africans; North Americans; French, Germans, Swiss, Italians, Greeks and Maltese. Utilizing foreign and colonial troops to such an extent was contentious. The concerns of Caribbean plantation owners of utilizing black soldiers to defend the slave system may have been specific to the region, but the broader social and political ramifications of foreign enlistment were not. Foreigners in the British Army or in the pay of the British government was fraught with constitutional ramifications for many politicians, and suspicions were further aroused by the opaque arrangements and finances compared to the rest of the Army. The history of the British Army tends to replicate political attitudes and discourse from the eighteenth century that viewed foreign soldiers with suspicion and unease;[4] worst still is branding them mercenaries. Though perhaps more exaggerated in Britain, this trend was not peculiar to Britons especially as armies became essential components in ideas of the nation state in the nineteenth and twentieth century.[5] These soldiers, and the other units outside the numbered regiments like the fencibles, deserve much greater prominence in the history of the Army. Labelling them as foreign or auxiliaries suggests an outsider status that is not deserved. A much better way to consider Britain's foreign and colonial troops is to frame them as transnational soldiers. Although not a term recognized at the time, borrowing it from the world of corporate multinationals better represents what these units were: soldiers from different states who moved between political boundaries for military service. The Army spread its soldiers around the globe in defence and furtherance of the interests of the British state. Indeed, it is not too far a stretch to consider the whole of the British Army as a multinational security force managed by the British state.

The multinational dimensions of the British Army needed rediscovering as there has been an uneven process of remembering and forgetting across different parts of the Army. An element of this was the newspaper reporting at the time and then the immediate post-war memoir boom, all of which focused on the line regiments and especially those that fought in Iberia and at Waterloo. As the two chapters on the social history of enlisted men and officers revealed, though, there is a lot more that we can do by going beyond these sources to explore experience in the Army. They revealed that although soldiers were separate from society, they were not divorced from it. The Army was supported by and relied upon a much wider labour pool that included women and local labour (especially enslaved Africans). Soldiers bought into their military experience attitudes and behaviour from their previous lives, whether it be gentlemanliness, a sense of contractual obligations, commitments to family and friends, or drinking alcohol. They learnt to survive and seek opportunities in the Army, even exploit it, in ways that echoed civilian life even if the social and economic environment was different. Hopefully, we can finally put to rest damming and generalized comments about soldiers of all ranks in the period. They may not fit our expectations of standards of soldierly professionalism, but they deserve understanding in their own terms.

The Army's relationship with society and culture was closer than has been appreciated. The Army was already being represented by others in print, visual arts and the written word, but it began to intervene and shape these representations. It is a shame that items like the panorama of the Battle of Alexandria have been lost, as it is the visual culture of the Victorian era that has tended to dominate representations of the British Army, such as Lady Butler's paintings *Scotland Forever* and the *28th at Quatre Bras*. A perusal of book covers about the British Army, the Peninsular War, and Waterloo make this very clear. There is something odd about this though; it is equivalent to works on the First World War using media produced in the 1980s and 1990s on their covers. This Victorian artwork was produced in the post-Crimean War and post-Cardwell era, when there was a renewed focus national martial identities played out through individual regiments. Only a portion of the units that made up the British Army between 1783 and 1815 were still in existence then, and fewer still were former soldiers who were alive to tell their tales. This book, then, stands to give a better voice to the three-quarters of a million members of the Army that passed through the Army between 1783 and 1815, and in the hopeful expectation that they continue to receive and capture historical attention in the future.

Appendices

Appendix A

Deployment of the British Army, 1783–1815

Date	Britain, Ireland and the Channel Islands	Western and Northern Europe	Southern Europe	Iberian Peninsula	Northern America	Caribbean	South America	Africa	South Asia	Southeast and East Asia, Australia	In transit and unknowns	Grand Total
Dec/83	13,632		3,506		9,889	4,145		152	4,800		2,092	38,216
Jun/84	13,468		2,462		4,882	3,194			5,759		2,014	31,779
Nov/84	16,344		3,184		4,359	2,619			5,580			32,086
Jul/85	13,715		3,231		4,379	3,325			4,093			28,743
Nov/85	14,471		3,744		3,939	3,064			3,810			29,028
Jan/86	14,943		3,556		3,950	2,999			2,923		175	28,546
Jul/86	14,223		3,682		4,256	3,845			3,455			29,461
Jan/87	15,671		3,471		4,111	3,043			3,505			29,801
Jul/87	12,876		3,100		4,783	2,543			3,530			26,832
Dec/87	16,009		3,446		4,181	2,917			3,473			30,026
Feb/88	17,753		3,362		4,175	4,083			3,085		786	33,244
Jun/88	15,008		3,536		4,175	4,134			5,270		2,022	34,145
Feb/89	17,338		3,557		4,409	5,422			5,623		1,778	38,127
Jun/89	15,547		3,509		5,478	5,332			6,447		801	37,114
Dec/89	13,631		3,607		4,520	5,086			6,376	266	1,018	34,504
Jun/90	13,989		3,250		4,625	5,111			7,232			34,207
Jun/91	14,199		3,991		4,511	4,996			9,533	350		37,580
Jun/92	13,152		3,380		5,348	4,774			9,647	316		36,617
Apr/93	26,703	3,730	3,309		4,340	6,327			6,887	337	1,401	53,034
Aug/93	41,561	6,816	3,256		3,449	7,169			6,122	397	2,116	70,886
Dec/93	42,814	7,351	3,250		3,592	7,022			6,052	397	9,063	79,541
Jun/94	45,867	17,690	6,724		4,040	14,346			5,633	468	11,345	106,113
Dec/94	63,748	35,086	6,892		3,358	11,140			5,668	447	9,516	135,855
Jun/95	102,704	17,338	6,551		3,412	14,077			5,434	472	4,967	154,955
Dec/95	73,071	6,117	8,721		4,289	14,482		3,075	5,297	443	23,538	139,033
Jun/96	68,303	14	9,825		4,185	22,512	201	2,887	6,058	433	30,053	144,471

Date	Britain, Ireland and the Channel Islands	Western and Northern Europe	Southern Europe	Iberian Peninsula	Northern America	Caribbean	South America	Africa	South Asia	Southeast and East Asia, Australia	In transit and unknowns	Grand Total
Feb/97	62,825	14	7,937	2,283	4,329	33,870	1,842	4,634	5,270	433	10,303	133,740
Jun/97	66,685	13	7,374	2,327	4,794	22,153	1,809	4,623	5,362	433	7,755	123,328
Feb/98	73010	9	5,643	5,331	5,458	13,875	854	4,497	11,264	475	265	120,681
Jun/98	81,520	9	4,602	5,328	5,451	15,916	1,463	4,684	11,376	475	221	131,045
Feb/99	97,523	14	7,417	4,655	4,803	13,864	1,372	3,678	13,916	532	435	148,209
Jun/99	98,157	14	7,549	5,332	4,437	13,377	1,118	3,711	13,541	532	169	147,937
Dec/99	123,596	14	10,448	2,761	5,794	12,658	1,915	2,881	15,343	466	895	176,771
Jun/00	116,004	14	11,951	2,915	7,394	13,996	2,578	4,235	14,783	484	219	174,573
Feb/01	101,314	21	13,512	3,508	5,205	18,848	2,750	6,539	14,803	484	16,240	183,224
Jun/01	101,901	896	15,044	3,186	4,913	18,333	2,889	25,291	14,801	484	670	188,408
Feb/02	92,812	12	19,670	3,478	3,987	17,242	2,982	21,556	12,586	484	22	174,831
Jun/02	84,124		17,274	2,472	3,789	19,596	2,924	12,341	12,611	549	543	156,223
Dec/02	56,639		9,302		3,634	15,142	2,240	11,435	12,868	563	745	112,568
Jun/03	59,932		8,374		3,037	14,424		191	15,981	496	7,384	109,819
Jan/04	101,035		8,844		3,375	14,377		120	16,194	496	6,078	150,519
Jun/04	102,950		9,286		3,904	17,402		1,360	19,243	500	1,947	156,592
Jan/05	108,398		10,458		4,276	16,240		344	19,043	490	3,938	163,187
Jun/05	108,238		15,861		4,368	18,254		282	19,125	490	9,053	175,671
Jan/06	91,723	569	16,848		5,523	17,380		5,044	21,091	482	1,315	159,975
Jun/06	113,597		18,770		5,087	18,759	818	5,026	21,594	506	719	184,876
Jan/07	102,726		28,497		5,324	17,567	8,966	3,597	21,952	521	1,412	190,562
Jun/07	96,033		21,330		5,226	19,718	9,328	10,781	21,440	513	597	184,966
Jan/08	124,654	308	21,274		5,879	18,591		9,080	21,879	531	5,999	208,195
Jun/08	104,789	1,167	24,601		9,889	23,684		8,811	22,357	520	5,054	200,872
Jan/09	123,430	311	26,233	17,501	7,594	21,799		8,056	25,679	714	208	231,525
Jun/09	118,933	295	24,366	8,696	10,045	22,791		8,365	25,803	767	346	220,407
Jan/10	112,827	342	27,288	34,611	6,969	24,649		8,028	24,687	1,524	445	241,370
Jun/10	97,804	328	36,071	35,740	9,426	24,159		7,218	27,512	1,146	569	239,973
Jan/11	93,701	464	36,104	46,041	8,447	21,528		9,152	24,036	1,173	801	241,447
Jun/11	87,358	450	26,254	51,727	8,372	22,197		9,025	20,926	5,961	1,348	233,618
Jan/12	84,768	481	38,943	58,729	9,266	20,908		10,158	22,750	3,952	344	250,299

Date	Britain, Ireland and the Channel Islands	Western and Northern Europe	Southern Europe	Iberian Peninsula	Northern America	Caribbean	South America	Africa	South Asia	Southeast and East Asia, Australia	In transit and unknowns	Grand Total
Jun/12	87,718	467	39,911	62,147	10,015	22,057		10,235	23,007	3,748	32	259,337
Jan/13	79,977	756	40,772	65,859	13,652	23,459		10,796	23,319	3,677	312	262,579
Jun/13	83,509	1,140	37,661	65,066	17,149	22,789		10,921	23,250	3,639	2,675	267,799
Jan/14	66,968	3,440	31,970	67,341	17,895	22,080		11,500	24,080	2,916	2,937	251,127
Jun/14	73,808	2,943	26,852	43,921	23,010	21,317		10,752	24,549	2,385	2,812	232,349
Jan/15	78,569	20,984	6,822	440	45,669	19,441		9,930	25,139	2,034	2,916	211,944
Jun/15	58,003	46,850	10,459	9	15,406	19,991		9,080	24,769	1,956	3,121	189,644
Jan/16	79,855	39,858	12,486	4	13,097	20,990		8,854	25,876	631	2,277	203,928

Notes

Figures are for rank and file (soldiers up to the rank of corporal) for the infantry and cavalry, but for the artillery include all soldiers (gunners, drivers, NCOs and officers).

The total for Africa includes small detachments in Asia Minor. The total for the Caribbean includes Honduras and occasionally Bermuda.

Notable gaps in returns are: Ireland before 1793; newly-raised European units in 1793 and 1794; Saint-Domingue between 1793 and 1798; and generally the early months of newly-raised transnational units, e.g. Chasseurs Britanniques in 1801.

Sources

TNA: AO 3/56; WO 1/170-171, 1/899; WO 12/11627, /11951; WO 17/804, /811, /838-839, /845, /1504-1507, /1156-1161, /1744-48, /1757-1758, /1987-1989, / 1992, /2118, /2237-2240, /2460-2463, /2484-2493, /2555-2562, /2813-2814.

Irish State Paper Office, 620/50/56.

Henry John Temple, 3rd Viscount Palmerston, 'An Account of the Effective Numbers, and Established Strength, of Regiments of Cavalry, Guards, and Infantry, Borne on the British Establishment, and the General Distribution of the Said Forces,--in the Years 1788,--1789,--1790,--1791,--& 1792.', *Commons Journals*, 1814 vol. 70, 599.

William Windham, 'Return of Emigrant and Foreign Forces, on the 1st August 1795', *Commons Sessional Papers* vol. 100, pp. 49–52.

'Papers, Presented to the House of Commons, Respecting the Royal Regiment of Artillery; the Corps of Royal Engineers, and Military Artificers; and Royal Artillery Drivers; &c.', *Commons Papers*, 1806 vol. 10, p. 5.

J. Maclean and R. Morse, 'Papers from the Ordnance-Office, Relating to the Royal Regiment of Artillery, the Brigade of Royal House Artillery, Drivers, &c.', *Commons Papers*, 1807 vol. 4, p. 195.

Rt Moorsom and R. Ward, 'Return of the Effective Strength of the Royal Regiment of Artillery; Corps of Royal Artillery Drivers; Artillery of the King's German Legion; Royal Foreign Artillery; Corps of Royal Engineers; and Corps of Royal Military Artificers, or Sappers and Miners;--on the 25th June 1812.', *Commons Papers*, 1813 vol. 13, p. 23b.

R.H. Crew, 'Returns Relating to the Artillery, &c.', *Commons Papers*, 1814 vol. 11, p. 333.

Gother Mann, 'Return of the Effective Strength of the Corps of Royal Military Artificers, or, Sappers and Miners; on 25th June and 25th December 1814:--Distinguishing, Those Enlisted for Life, or for a Term of Years; and, Specifying the Numbers Serving at Home and Abroad.', *Commons Papers*, 1815 vol. 9, p. 303.

H. Oakes and others, 'Return of the Effective Strength of the Corps of Royal Engineers, and of the Corps of Royal Sappers and Miners; on the 25th June, and 25th December, 1815', *Commons Papers*, 1816 vol. 12, p. 401.

C.T. Atkinson, 'Foreign Regiments in The British Army, 1793-1802: Part VI—Notes on Each Corps or Regiment', *Journal of the Society for Army Historical Research*, 22.89 (1944), pp. 187–97; 22.90 (1944), pp. 234–50; 22.91 (1944), pp. 265–76; 22.92 (1944), pp. 313–24.

Appendix B

Principal Offices in the Military Administration

Secretary of State for War (and the Colonies from August 1801)

11 July 1794	Henry Dundas
17 March 1801	Robert Hobart, Lord Hobart
14 May 1804	John Jeffreys Pratt, 2nd Earl Camden
10 July 1805	Robert Stewart, Viscount Castlereagh
5 February 1806	William Windham
25 March 1807	Robert Stewart, Viscount Castlereagh
1 November 1809	Robert Banks Jenkinson, 2nd Earl Liverpool
11 June 1812	Henry Bathurst, 3rd Earl Bathurst

Undersecretary

11 July 1794	Evan Nepean
1 March 1795	William Huskisson
18 March 1801	John Sullivan
15 May 1804	Edward Cooke
16 February 1806	Sir George Shee
25 March 1807	Edward Cooke
2 November 1809	Charles Cecil Cope Jenkinson
10 June 1810	Robert Peel
20 August 1812	Henry Goulbourn

Military Undersecretary

27 November 1806	Sir James Cockburn
25 March 1807	Brigadier-General Charles Stewart
1 May 1809	Frederick John Robinson
1 November 1809	Colonel Henry Bunbury

War Office

Secretary at War

11 April 1783	Richard Fitzpatrick
6 January 1784	Sir George Yonge
11 July 1794	William Windham
February 1801	Charles Philip Yorke
17 August 1803	Charles Bragge

12 May 1804	William Dundas
8 February 1806	General Richard Fitzpatrick
31 March 1807	General Sir James Murray Pulteney
1 July 1809	Lord Granville Leveson Gower
28 October 1809	Henry John Temple, 3rd Viscount Palmerston

Deputy Secretary-at-War

1 December 1775	Matthew Lewis
22 August 1803	Francis Moore
19 December 1809	William Merry

Ordnance Office

Master-General of the Ordnance

5 January 1784	General Charles Lennox, 3rd Duke of Richmond
23 February 1795	General Charles Cornwallis, 1st Marquess Cornwallis
28 August 1801	General John Pitt, 2nd Earl of Chatham
8 February 1806	General Francis Rawdon-Hastings, 2nd Earl of Moira
4 April 1807	General John Pitt, 2nd Earl of Chatham
5 May 1810	General Henry Phipps, 1st Earl Mulgrave

Lieutenant-General

6 May 1782	General Sir William Howe (later Viscount Howe)
22 November 1804	General Sir Thomas Trigge
1 February 1814	Lieutenant-General Sir Hildebrand Oakes

Military Staff

Commander-in-Chief

25 January 1793	General Jeffery Amherst, 1st Baron Amherst (with title of General on the Staff of Britain)
13 February 1795	Field Marshal Frederick, Duke of York (with title of Field Marshal on the Staff)
(3 April 1798	Title changed to Commander-in-Chief of all His Majesty's Forces in the kingdom of Great Britain)
(4 September 1799	Title changed to Captain-General of the Forces in Great Britain and all Forces Employed in the Continent of Europe)
(9 June 1801	Commander-in-Chief of all His Majesty's Land-Forces in the United Kingdom of Great Britain and Ireland)
18 March 1809	General Sir David Dundas
26 May 1811	Field Marshal Frederick, Duke of York

Military Secretary

February 1795	Lieutenant-Colonel Robert Brownrigg
14 March 1803	Colonel William Henry Clinton
4 August 1804	Lieutenant-Colonel James Willoughby Gordon
2 October 1809	Lieutenant-Colonel Henry Torrens

Adjutant-General to His Majesty's Forces
(in the War Office before 1793)

10 July 1781	Major-General William Fawcett (lieutenant-general 20 November 1782; general 3 May 1796)
9 January 1799	Colonel Harry Calvert (major-general 25 September 1803; lieutenant-general 25 July 1810)

Quarter-Master-General to the Forces
(in the War Office before 1793)

11 November 1761	Lieutenant-Colonel George Morrison (lieutenant-general 20 November 1782)
8 November 1796	Major-General David Dundas (lieutenant-general 26 January 1797; general 29 April 1802)
15 March 1803	Major-General Robert Brownrigg (lieutenant-general 25 April 1808)
10 August 1811	Colonel James Willoughby Gordon (major-general 4 June 1813)

Inspector-General of the Recruiting Service

24 January 1778	Lieutenant-Colonel Samuel Townsend (major-general 20 November 1782; lieutenant-general 12 October 1793; died 17 May 1794)
21 October 1795	Major-General Hon. Henry Fox
10 August 1799	Major-General George Hewett
22 November 1804	Major-General John Whitelocke

Office abolished in March 1807 and duties transferred to the Adjutant-General to His Majesty's Forces

Ireland
Lord Lieutenant

31 July 1782	George Nugent-Temple-Grenville, 3rd Earl Temple
3 May 1783	Robert Henley, 2nd Earl of Northington
11 February 1784	Charles Manners, 4th Duke of Rutland
27 October 1787	George Nugent-Temple-Grenville, 1st Marquess of Buckingham
24 October 1789	John Fane, 10th Earl of Westmorland
13 December 1794	William Wentworth Fitzwilliam, 2nd Earl Fitzwilliam
13 March 1795	John Jeffreys Pratt, 2nd Earl Camden
14 June 1798	General Charles Cornwallis, 1st Marquis Cornwallis
27 April 1801	Philip Yorke, 3rd Earl of Hardwicke

(Edward Clive, 1st Earl Powis was appointed on 21 November 1805, but did not go to Ireland and Hardwicke continued in office)

12 March 1806	John Russell, 6th Duke of Bedford
1 April 1807	Charles Lennox, 4th Duke of Richmond

3 June 1815	Charles Whitworth, Viscount Whitworth (3 June 1813, lieutenant-general and general governor of Ireland)

Under-Secretary in the Military Department
Sometimes referred to as Secretaryship at War

June 1782	Charles Francis Sheridan
7 April 1789	Edward Cooke
7 June 1796	William Elliot
February 1801	Lieutenant-Colonel Edward Baker Littlehales

Irish Military Staff
Commander-in-Chief of the Forces in Ireland (Commander of the Forces in Ireland from 1801)

16 March 1782	Lieutenant-General John Burgoyne
13 February 1784	Lieutenant-General William Augustus Pitt
16 December 1791	Lieutenant-General George Warde
14 May 1793	Lieutenant-General Robert Cunninghame
10 October 1796	General Henry Lawes Luttrell, 2nd Earl of Carhampton
12 December 1797	Lieutenant-General Sir Ralph Abercromby
25 April 1798	Lieutenant-General Gerard Lake
20 June 1798	General Charles Cornwallis, 1st Marquis Cornwallis
5 May 1801	General Sir William Meadows
9 May 1803	Lieutenant-General Henry Fox
20 October 1803	Lieutenant-General William Lord Cathcart
30 October 1805	General Charles Stanhope, 3rd Earl of Harrington
3 January 1812	Lieutenant-General Sir John Hope
5 October 1813	General Sir George Hewett

Adjutant-General to the Forces in Ireland

6 October 1770	Lieutenant-Colonel Henry Lawes Luttrell
6 May 1783	Lieutenant-Colonel Henry Pigott
June 1787	Lieutenant-Colonel William Fawcett
23 June 1789	Colonel David Dundas (major-general 28 April 1790; gave up role on 2 April 1791)
16 December 1791	Lieutenant-Colonel George Hewett (colonel 1 March 1794; major-general 3 May 1796)
17 August 1799	Major-General George Nugent
26 May 1801	Colonel Hon. Alexander Hope
25 April 1802	Lieutenant-Colonel Robert Anstruther
28 January 1809	Brigadier-General Henry Clinton
12 May 1812	Major-General George Murray
26 September 1812	Major-General James Hay
16 June 1814	Major-General George Murray

31 December 1814   Major-General Matthew Whitworth-Aylmer, 5th Baron
                    Aylmer

Quarter-Master-General to the Forces in Ireland
31 December 1778   Lieutenant-Colonel David Dundas (colonel 14 February 1782)
23 June 1789   Lieutenant-Colonel William Fawcett
21 September 1792   Lieutenant Colonel John Francis Craddock (exchanged
                    with Fawcett) (colonel, 26 February 1795; major-general, 1
                    January 1798)
31 July 1804   Colonel William Henry Clinton (major-general 25
                    April 1808)
25 December 1813   Major-General George Airey

Other Military Departments
Army Medical Offices

Physician General
May 1740   Sir Edward Wilmot, Bart.
5 December 1786   Sir Clifton Wintringham, Bart., M.D.
15 January 1794   Sir Lucas Pepys, Bart.

Surgeon General
1748   David Middleton
4 January 1786   Robert Adair
17 March 1790   John Hunter
17 October 1793   John Gunning
10 March 1798   Thomas Keate

Inspector-General of Regimental Infirmaries (Inspector-General of Army Hospitals in 1801)
1748   David Middleton
4 January 1786   Robert Adair
17 March 1790   John Hunter
17 October 1793   Thomas Keate
10 March 1798   John Rush
29 December 1801   Francis Knight

On Sir Lucas Pepys' appointment as Physician General in 1794 the Army Medical
Board was formed of him, the surgeon general, and the inspector-general of
regimental infirmaries. On the death of John Gunning the Board was discontinued.

Apothecary General
1763   George Charles Garnier

Army Medical Board
In 1810 this new board replaced the above four military medical appointments.

Director-General
27 February 1810   John Weir
13 June 1815   Sir James McGrigor

Principal Inspectors
27 February 1810   Theodore Gordon and Charles Kerr

Barrack Department
Superintendent-General of Barracks
1 January 1793   Colonel Oliver de Lancey
In 1794 this role became:

Barrack-Master-General
30 May 1794   Colonel Oliver de Lancey (promoted major-general on 3
                      October 1794; lieutenant-general 1 January 1800)
10 November 1804   Lieutenant-General George Hewett

Deputy Barrack-Master-General
16 May 1795   Lieutenant-Colonel Richard Taylor (Tayler)
13 November 1798   Colonel Edward Hewgill
7 January 1804   Lieutenant-Colonel Willougby Gordon

The barrack-master general and deputy-barrack-master general were abolished
and replaced with:

**Commissioners for the General Superintendence and Management of the
Barrack Department**
19 December 1807   Osborn Markham, John Fisher, and Alexander Loraine

Chaplain General to the Forces
Position created in 1796.
4 October 1796   John Gamble
10 March 1810   Rev. Archdeacon John Owens

Commissary-in-Chief
Office created in 1809, but did not cover Ireland and India. Before 1809 Commissary
Generals were appointed for different areas or armies.

30 September 1809   Lieutenant-Colonel James Willoughby Gordon
1 October 1811   John Charles Herries

Principal Veterinary Surgeon to the Cavalry
Created in 1796
27 September 1796   Edward Colemen

Judge Advocate General
1771   Sir Charles Gould (known as Sir Charles Morgan from 1792)
8 March 1806   Nathaniel Bond

Sources
https://www.british-history.ac.uk/search/series/office-holders
Army Lists.
Stockdale's New Companion to the London and Royal Calendars Or Court and City Register, for the Year 1798: Being a List of All the Changes in Administration, from the Accession of the Present King, in October 1760, to the Present Time.
The Dublin Gazette.
The Edinburgh Almanack.
The London Gazette.
The New Annual Register, or General repository of history, politics, and literature.
The Royal Military Calendar, or Army Service and Commission Book: Containing the Services and Progress of Promotion of the Generals, Lieutenant-generals, Major-generals, Colonels, Lieutenant-colonels, and Majors of the Army, According to Seniority: with Details of the Principal Military Events of the Last Century (1820).

Appendix C
Structure of the British Army

The following table lists the changes in the number units (regiments or corps) in the Army for each year.

Year	Change	Numbered Cavalry Regiment	British and Irish limited-service cavalry	Transnational Cavalry	Numbered Regiment of Foot	Unnumbered Regiment of Foot	British and Irish limited-service infantry	Transnational Infantry	Transnational Artillery
1783	Formed						1		
1785	Disbanded				4				
1787	Formed				4				
1787	Reformed						1		
1789	Formed					1			
1790	Disbanded						1		
1791	Formed	1						1	
1793	Formed			3	18		10	11	
1794	Formed	10	33	5	41	10	28	25	
1794	Disbanded							1	
1795	Formed	3	1	2		2	3	28	1
1795	Disbanded			4	39	10		17	
1795	Merged							2	
1796	Formed				1		1	5	
1796	Disbanded	4			3	3		5	
1796	Merged		2					1	
1797	Formed							1	
1797	Disbanded			2			2	10	

Year	Change	Numbered Cavalry Regiment	British and Irish limited-service cavalry	Transnational Cavalry	Numbered Regiment of Foot	Unnumbered Regiment of Foot	British and Irish limited-service infantry	Transnational Infantry	Transnational Artillery
1798	Formed						14	6	
	Disbanded					1		9	
	Merged							3	
	Reformed							1	
1799	Formed						1	6	
	Disbanded						8		
	Merged							1	
1800	Formed			1	1			4	
	Disbanded		28				2		
1801	Formed							4	
	Disbanded							2	
1802	Formed				1		7		
	Disbanded	4	3	3			44	18	1
1803	Formed			3		1	17	11	
	Merged							1	
1804	Formed				3	1	1	5	
1805	Formed			3	1		4	4	
	Disbanded					1	16		
1806	Formed						7	4	
1807	Formed						1		
	Disbanded							1	
1808	Formed				2		1	1	
	Reformed				2		1		
1809	Formed			2				1	
1810	Formed				1			2	
	Disbanded						2		
	Reformed							1	

Year	Change	Numbered Cavalry Regiment	British and Irish limited-service cavalry	Transnational Cavalry	Numbered Regiment of Foot	Unnumbered Regiment of Foot	British and Irish limited-service infantry	Transnational Infantry	Transnational Artillery
1811	Formed							2	
	Disbanded						1	1	
1812	Formed							5	
1813	Formed					1	1	2	
1814	Formed						1	2	
	Disbanded			1			10	4	
1815	Formed						7		
	Disbanded						5	4	

Recruitment and Casualties in the British Army

Recruitment, 1801–1815

In the year	Ordinary recruitment in Britain and Ireland	Recruitment legislation	Ordnance recruitment	Foreign and colonial corps
1801	17,413		1,175	
1802	7,403		281	
1803	11,253	34,982	4,251	*7,600*
1804	11,088	3,812	4,029	*8,200*
1805	11,677	21,868	3,488	*6,100*
1806	11,875	8,802	*1,000*	*12,800*
1807	19,114	29,108	*6,000*	*4,400*
1808	12,963		*3,400*	*3,400*
1809	11,720	23,358	*2,800*	*4,400*
1810	9,095		*1,400*	*5,600*
1811	11,472	11,453	*2,500*	*8,800*
1812	14,432	9,927	*3,500*	11,327
1813	14,698	19,245	*3,600*	5,282
1814	7,989	3,243		5,575
1815	15,279			
Total	18,7471	165,798	37,524	83,484

Notes

Figures in italics are calculations based on other figures, thus:

- Ordnance Recruitment: net gains in overall strength between the start and end of the year plus casualties for the year based on average casualty rates from a sample of months.
- Foreign and Colonial Corps: net gains in overall strength plus casualty figures for that year.

In both cases the figures have been rounded to the nearest hundred.

Recruitment legislation include the Army of Reserve, Additional Force Act, and militia transfers. The figures for 1807/08 and 1809/10 were not disaggregated by year in the returns.

Ordnance units underwent significant reductions their strength in 1814 and 1815; no returns of recruitment were collated, and calculations based on strength and casualties are not possible for those years.

Sources

Ordinary Recruitment in Britain and Ireland:

Harry Calvert, 'Return of the Total Number of Men Raised in Great Britain and Ireland, for Unlimited Service; since 1st January 1801 to the 28th February 1806', *Commons Papers*, 1806 vol. 10, p. 221.

Harry Calvert, 'Return of the Number of Men Raised for the Regular Army, Exclusive of Foreign and Colonial Corps, by Ordinary Recruiting, and by Transfers from the Militia, &c.;--during the Last Ten Years', *Commons Papers*, 1813 vol. 11, p. 263. (Also covers recruitment legislation yield between 1805 and 1812.)

Harry Calvert, 'Return of the Number of Recruits Raised Monthly, for the Regular Army, between 25th December 1812 and 25th December 1813, by the Ordinary Modes of Recruiting (Exclusive of Foreign and Colonial Corps); Distinguishing Men and Boys, and Those Enlisted for Life or for a Term of Years', *Commons Papers*, 1814 vol. 11, p. 273.

Harry Calvert, 'Return of the Number of Recruits Raised Monthly, from 25th December 1813, to 25th December 1814, by the Ordinary Modes of Recruiting, Exclusive of Foreign and Colonial Corps; Distinguishing Men and Boys, and Those Enlisted for Life or for a Term of Years', *Commons Papers*, 1815 vol. 11, p. 309.

Harry Calvert, 'Return of the Number of Recruits Raised Monthly, from the 25th December 1811, to the 25th December 1815; Distinguishing Men and Boys, and Those Enlisted for Life or for a Term of Years', *Commons Papers*, 1816 vol. 12, p. 423.

Recruitment Legislation

Inspector-General's Office, 'Accounts Presented to the House of Commons of Men Raised for the Royal Army of Reserve, in Each Month to the First May 1804, since the Commencement of the Act Passed for That Purpose', *Commons Papers*, 1804 vol. 11, p. 30.

Harry Calvert, 'Return of the Number of Volunteers from the Different Regiments of Militia, English, Irish and Scotch, That Have Enlisted into the

Regular Army, from the 25th December 1811 to the 24th December 1812: Distinguishing, Men and Boys, and Those Enlisted for Life or for a Term of Years', *Commons Papers*, 1813 vol. 13, p. 3.

Harry Calvert, 'Return of the Number of Volunteers from the Militia to the Regular Army, since the 25th December 1812; Distinguishing Those Enlisted for Life, or for a Term of Years', *Commons Papers*, 1814 vol 11, p. 271.

Harry Calvert, 'Return of the Number of Volunteers from the Militia, English, Irish and Scotch, That Have Enlisted into the Regular Army, from the 25th December 1813, to the 25th December 1814; Distinguishing Men and Boys, and Those Enlisted for Life, or for a Term of Years', *Commons Papers*, 1815 vol. 9, p. 327.

Ordnance Troops

TNA, WO 17/2560, /2561, /2562, / 2563.

J. MacLeod, 'Papers, Presented to the House of Commons, Respecting the Royal Regiment of Artillery; the Corps of Royal Engineers, and Military Artificers; and Royal Artillery Drivers; &c.', *Commons Papers*, 1806 vol. 10, p. 5.

J. MacLeod, 'Return of the Effective Strength of the Royal Regiment of Artillery, Corps of Royal Artillery Drivers, Artillery of the King's German Legion, and Royal Foreign Artillery; on 25th June and 25th December 1814', *Commons Papers*, 1815 vol. 9, p. 301

Foreign and Colonial Corps

Harry Calvert, 'Return of the Several Foreign and Colonial Corps in His Majesty's Service on the 1st January 1806, 1807, 1808, 1809, and 1810: Specifying the Effective Strength and Establishment of Each Corps', *Commons Papers*, 1810 vol. 13, p. 431.

Harry Calvert, 'Return of the Number of Foreign and Colonial Recruits, That Have Been Added to the Regular Army, from the 25th of December 1811, to the Latest Period the Same Can Be Made Up', *Commons Papers*, 1813 vol. 13, p. 9.

Harry Calvert, 'Return of the Number of Casualties Which Have Occurred in the British Army, during the Last Ten Years, by Deaths, Discharges, and Desertions;--Distinguishing British from Foreign and Colonial Corps', *Commons Papers*, 1813 vol. 11, p. 261.

Harry Calvert, 'Return of the Number of Foreign and Colonial Troops That Have Been Added to the Regular Army, from the 25th December 1813, to the 25th December 1814, as Well as Their Present Effective Strength, so Far as the Same Can Be Made Up', *Commons Papers*, 1815 vol. 9

Casualties 1793–1815

Year	British Corps			Foreign and Colonial Corps			Total Infantry and Cavalry			Ordnance units' casualties	Casualties from Irish Establishment before 1801	Foreign and Colonial casualties before 1803	Total
	Deaths	Discharges	Desertions	Deaths	Discharges	Desertions	Deaths	Discharges	Desertions				
1793							2,059	2,234	1,700	300	1,500		7,793
1794							8,596	4,229	2,500	400	2,700	200	18,625
1795							11,870	26,005	4,100	600	2,000	1,700	46,275
1796							9,858	14,634	4,200	1300	2,900	1,600	34,492
1797							5,967	7,981	3,800	700	2,800	11,880	33,128
1798							4,008	7,772	3,700	700	3,000	600	19,780
1799							5,071	8,734	4,600	800	3,500	700	23,405
1800							1,542	4,321	4,100	900	2,100	700	13,663
1801							8,175	9,229	3,196	1,800		2,500	24,900
1802							4,417	27,139	3,383	1,600		6,600	43,139
1803	4,591	4,627	4,178	617	1,831	226	5,208	6,458	4,404	900			16,970
1804	4,861	3,634	4,852	1,258	964	616	6,119	4,598	5,468	1,300			17,485
1805	5,888	3,685	6,497	945	915	584	6,833	4,600	7,081	1,600			20,114
1806	6,141	3,836	4,466	914	879	1,282	7,055	4,715	5,748	1,700			19,218
1807	6,379	3,170	5,021	1,553	708	707	7,932	3,878	5,728	1,700			19,238
1808	7,994	4,131	5,059	1,292	859	1,582	9,286	4,990	6,641	2,100			23,017
1809	14,486	2,968	4,188	1,867	355	715	16,353	3,323	4,903	2,200			26,779
1810	11,576	3,945	3,995	2,037	683	735	13,613	4,628	4,730	2,200			25,171
1811	11,679	3,289	4,060	1,778	697	966	13,457	3,986	5,026	2,200			24,669
1812	14,113	2,561	4,372	2,489	1,222	1,689	16,602	3,783	6,061	2,200			28,646
1813	16,148	2,738	4,284	2,678	1,613	2,179	18,826	4,351	6,463	2,300			31,940
1814	12,305	25,910	4,985	2,254	8,631	4,358	14,559	34,541	9,343	6,700			65,143
1815	7,925	13,355	5,307	1,908	13,955	2,625	9,833	2,7310	7,932	1,800			46,875

Grand total: 630,456
Adjustment for transfers between 1793 and 1800: -37,550
Adjusted total = 592,906

Notes
The total infantry and cavalry for 1800 only cover up to November of that year.

The totals do not include 9,700 struck off regimental lists between 1809 and 1812 who were captured or made prisoners of war.

The figures for discharges before about 1803 will include some transfers to other units.

Sources
Harry Calvert, 'Return of the Number of Men Who Have Been Discharged from the Service of the Army, on Account of Wounds or Bodily Infirmity, since the Commencement of the Present War; as Far as the Can Be Made up from Documents in the Adjutant-General's Office', *Parliamentary Register*, vol. 14, p. 594.

Harry Calvert, 'Return of the Number of Casualties in the British Army since the Year 1801, Inclusive; Distinguishing Each Year, and the Casualties in the Army at Home from Those in the Army Abroad, to the Latest Periods in the Year 1805, for Which Returns Have Been Received from the Several Stations Abroad', *Commons Papers*, 1805 vol. 10, p. 225

Figures for 1806–15 are compiled from TNA, WO 17/2814.

Notes

Introduction

1. 'London, Dec 11', *Saunders's News-Letter*, 16 December 1789, p. 1.
2. *The Parliamentary History of England from the Earliest Period to the Year 1803*, 36 vols (London: T. C. Hansard, 1816), vol. 28, col. 353.
3. T.C.W. Blanning, *The Origins of the French Revolutionary Wars* (London: Longman, 1986); see also Charles J. Esdaile, *The Wars of the French Revolution: 1792-1801* (London; New York, NY: Routledge, 2018).
4. James Michael Villalard, 'A Re-Assessment of the Strategic Role of the Channel Islands during the Great French War (1792-1815)' (unpublished Ph.D., University of Exeter, 2017).
5. Geert van Uythoven, *The Secret Expedition: The Anglo-Russian Invasion of Holland 1799* (Warwick: Helion, 2018).

Chapter 1: A Composite Army

1. 'London. Thursday 22 June 1815. Great and Glorious News', *Morning Post*, 22 June 1815, p. 3.
2. Brian Cathcart, *The News from Waterloo: The Race to Tell Britain of Wellington's Victory* (London: Faber & Faber, 2016), pp. 227–40.
3. Alan Forrest, *Waterloo* (Oxford: Oxford University Press, 2015).
4. Publications about the Waterloo campaign reached a crescendo in 2015, such that a bibliography of the battle would now be its own book. Some key texts include: Paul L. Dawson, *Waterloo: The Truth at Last: Why Napoleon Lost the Great Battle* (Barnsley: Frontline Books, 2018); Gareth Glover, *Waterloo: The Defeat of Napoleon's Imperial Guard; Henry Clinton, the 2nd Division and the End of a 200-Year-Old Controversy* (Barnsley: Frontline Books, 2015); Peter Hofschröer, *1815, the Waterloo Campaign: Wellington, His German Allies and the Battles of Ligny and Quatre Bras* (London: Greenhill, 1998); Peter Hofschröer, *1815: The Waterloo Campaign: The German Victory* (London: Greenhill, 1999); William Siborne, *History of the War in France and Belgium, in 1815*, 2 vols (London: T. and W. Boone, 1844).
5. Richard Glover, *Peninsular Preparation: The Reform of the British Army, 1795-1809* (Cambridge: University Press, 1963), p. 6.
6. Harry Calvert, 'Return of the Number of Effective Men in the British Army, from the 1st January 1793 to the 1st January 1801; Distinguishing Each Year:--As Far as the Same Can Be Made up from Documents in the Adjutant General's Office.', *House of Commons Papers*, 1806, vol. 10, p. 397.
7. *Parliamentary History*, vol. 26, cols. 1257–1264.
8. L. von Sichart, *Geschichte Der Könglich-Hannoverschen Armee*, 4 vols (Hanover: Hahn'sche Hofbuchhandel, 1871), vol. 4, p. 12.
9. Its full title was *A List of the Officers of the Army and Marines*.
10. Gareth Cole, *Arming the Royal Navy, 1793-1815: The Office of Ordnance and the State* (London: Pickering and Chatto, 2012).
11. Michael Mann, 'The Corps of Invalids', *Journal of the Society for Army Historical Research*, 66 (1988), pp. 5–19.

12. Keith John Bartlett, 'The Development of the British Army during the Wars with France, 1793-1815' (Ph.D., Durham University, 1998), p. 191.
13. War Office, *A List of All the Officers of the Army and Royal Marines on Full and Half-Pay: With an Index* (London: C. Roworth, 1812), p. 493.
14. For the King's refusal to send the Guards to the West Indies in 1795, see Roger Norman Buckley, *Slaves in Red Coats: The British West India Regiments, 1795-1815* (New Haven; London: Yale University Press, 1979), p. 37.
15. J.L. Pimlott, 'The Administration of the British Army, 1783-1793' (Ph.D., University of Leicester, 1975), p. 104.
16. The National Archives (TNA), London, WO 380/2.
17. Pimlott, 'Administration of the British Army', p. 179.
18. George Arthur, *The Story of the Household Cavalry*, 2 vols (London: A. Constable, 1909), vol. 2, pp. 545–60.
19. 'Army Estimates, 8 February 1785', *Journals of the House of Commons*, vol. 40, pp. 491–501.
20. Pimlott, 'Administration of the British Army', p. 283.
21. 'Army Estimates, 9 January 1795', *Commons Journals*, vol. 50, pp. 32–50.
22. Harry Calvert, 'Return of the Number of Regiments and Effective Strength of the Royal Veteran Battalions; Specifying Whether Abroad or at Home, and the Length of Time Each Regiment Has Been on Foreign Service', *Commons Papers*, 1813–14 vol. 11, p. 281.
23. The units were the three battalions of the 9th Foot, 2/27th, 31st, and 1/ & 2/52nd; Richard Cannon, *Historical Record of the Thirty-First, or, the Huntingdonshire Regiment of Foot*, Historical Records of the British Army (London, England: Parker, Furnivall and Parker, 1850), p. 61.
24. Kevin Linch, *Britain and Wellington's Army: Recruitment, Society and Tradition, 1807-15* (Houndmills, Basingstoke, Hampshire; New York: Palgrave Macmillan, 2011), p. 107.
25. Harry Calvert, 'State of the British Army, Distinguishing the Number of Men and Boys Who Are Engaged for Limited Service Only, from Those Who Are Engaged for Service for Life', *Commons Papers*, 1808 vol. 7, p. 185.
26. Pimlott, 'Administration of the British Army', p. 228.
27. Linch, *Britain and Wellington's Army*, p. 145.
28. Kevin Linch, 'Making New Soldiers', in *Britain's Soldiers: Rethinking War and Society, 1715-1815*, ed. Kevin Linch and Matthew McCormack (Liverpool: Liverpool University Press, 2014), pp. 209–12.
29. Fencibles accounted for 28,428 from a total of 137,440: William Windham, 'Return of His Majesty's Land Forces, Consisting of Regular Cavalry and Infantry, Fencible Cavalry and Infantry, Independent Corps, Militia, Volunteers and Yeomanry Cavalry and Infantry; as They Were Effective 1st August 1795', *House of Commons Sessional Papers of the Eighteenth Century*, ed. Sheila Lambert, 147 vols, (Wilmington, Del.: Scholarly Resources, 1795), vol. 100, pp. 25–6. Rory Butcher, "By Beat of Drum or Otherwise': Assessing Recruitment to the Fencible Regiments, 1793-1802', in *One Hundred Years of Army Historical Research: Proceedings of the SAHR Centenary Conference*, ed. by Andrew Bamford (Warwick: Helion, 2022), pp. 103–28.
30. L. Homfray Irving, *Officers of the British Forces in Canada during the War of 1812-15* ([Welland], 1908), pp. 25–6; W.Y. Baldry and A.S. White, 'Disbanded Regiments. The New Brunswick Fencibles—Afterwards The 104th Foot', *Journal of the Society for Army Historical Research* 1, (1922), pp. 90–2; Bertram Edward Sargeaunt, *The Royal Manx Fencibles* (Aldershot: Gale & Polden, 1947).
31. John Randle Western, *The English Militia in the Eighteenth Century: The Story of a Political Issue 1660-1802* (London: Routledge & Kegan Paul, 1965), pp. 127–61.
32. '26 Geo. 3 c. 107, An Act for Amending, and Reducing into One Act of Parliament, the Laws Relating to the Militia, in That Part of Great Britain Called England [1786]', *The*

Statutes at Large, from Magna Charta to the End of the Eleventh Parliament of Great Britain, Anno 1761, vol. 35 (Cambridge: Printed by John Archdeacon, 1786), pp. 869–70.

33. J.E. Cookson, *The British Armed Nation, 1793-1815* (Oxford: Clarendon, 1997), p. 104; Ivan V. Nelson, *The Irish Militia, 1793-1802: Ireland's Forgotten Army* (Dublin: Four Courts Press Ltd, 2007); Western, *English Militia*, pp. 237–40.

34. J.W. Fortescue, *The County Lieutenancies and the Army, 1803-1814* (London: Macmillan and Co., limited, 1909), p. 14.

35. Harry Calvert, 'Return of the Effective Strength of the British Army, in Rank and File, in Each Year from the Year 1804 to the Year 1813, Inclusive;--Distinguishing Cavalry, Artillery, Infantry, and Militia, and British from Foreign and Colonial Corps', *Commons Papers*, 1813, vol. 11, p. 269; Nelson, *Irish Militia*; for the Scottish militia, see Cookson, *British Armed Nation*, pp. 105–08.

36. *List of the Officers of the Several Regiments and Corps of Fencible Cavalry and Infantry; of the Officers of the Militia; of the Corps and Troops of Gentlemen and Yeomanry: And of the Corps and Companies of Volunteer Infantry* (London: War Office, 1795).

37. Austin Gee, *The British Volunteer Movement, 1794-1814* (Oxford; New York: Clarendon Press; Oxford University Press, 2003), pp. 26–8.

38. Ibid., pp. 53–4.

39. Cookson, *British Armed Nation*, pp. 71, 73.

40. Edwin Parks, *The Royal Guernsey Militia: A Short History and List of Officers* (St. Peter Port: La Societé guernesiaise, 1992); Villalard, 'A Re-Assessment of the Strategic Role of the Channel Islands during the Great French War, pp. 47–52.

41. John Robert Elting, *Amateurs, to Arms!: A Military History of the War of 1812* (Chapel Hill, N.C.: Algonquin Books of Chapel Hill, 1991); Kenneth William Grundy, *Soldiers without Politics: Blacks in the South African Armed Forces* (Berkeley: University of California Press, 1983), pp. 33–4; Randolph T. Jones, 'The Trinidad Militia, 1801-38', *Journal of the Society for Army Historical Research* 82 (2004), pp. 132–54; George F. G. Stanley, 'The Canadian Militia during the Colonial Period', *Journal of the Society for Army Historical Research* 24 (1946), pp. 30–41; Roger Buckley, *The British Army in the West Indies: Society and the Military in the Revolutionary Age* (Gainesville, Fla: University Press of Florida, 1998), pp. 51–6.

42. Charles James, 'Volunteer', in *A New and Enlarged Military Dictionary, or, Alphabetical Explanation of Technical Terms: Containing, among Other Matter, a Succinet Account of the Different Systems of Fortification, Tactics, &c. Also the Various French Phrases and Words That Have an Immediate, or Relative, Connection with the British Service, or May Tend to Give General Information on Military Subjects in Either Language* (London: T. Egerton, 1805).

43. TNA, WO 380/4, fol. 81; S. Rogers, *Historical Record of the Eighty-First Regiment, or Loyal Lincoln Volunteers; Containing an Account of the Formation of the Regiment in 1793, and of Its Subsequent Services to 1872* (Gibraltar: Printed by the Twenty-Eighth Regimental Press, 1872), pp. 2–5.

44. For an example of the advert for the unit promising a large bounty, see 'Old England Forever', *Stamford Mercury*, 1 November 1793.

45. J. R. Western, 'The Recruitment of the Land Forces in Great Britain, 1793-99' (PhD, University of Edinburgh, 1953), p. 20; 'General Orders for the Security of Great Britain, Whitehall, 14th March 1794', in *A Collection of State Papers, Relative to the War against France Now Carrying on by Great-Britain and the Several Other European Powers, Containing Authentic Copies of Treaties, Conventions, Proclamations, Manifestoes, Declarations, Memorials, … , vol. 2* (London: J. Debrett, 1795), p. 85.

46. Fortescue, *County Lieutenancies*, pp. 27–8.

47. Ibid., pp. 16–17.

48. J.A. Houlding, *Fit for Service: The Training of the British Army, 1715-1795* (Oxford: Clarendon, 1981), p. 103.

49. *A List of the Officers of the Army and Marines* (War Office, 1797), p. 267.

50. Bruce Collins, *War and Empire: The Expansion of Britain, 1790-1830* (London: Routledge, 2014), pp. 156–7, 467–8; Kaushik Roy, 'The Hybrid Military Establishment of the East India Company in South Asia: 1750–1849', *Journal of Global History* 6, pp. 195–218.

51. Pimlott, 'Administration of the British Army', pp. 20–1. The Act was '21 Geo. 3 c 65, An Act for Establishing an Agreement with the United Company of Merchants of England Trading to the East Indies, … [1781]', *Statutes at Large*, vol. 33, pp. 414–35.

52. J. L. Pimlott, 'The Raising of Four Regiments for India, 1787-8', *Journal of the Society for Army Historical Research*, 52 (1974), pp. 68–88; Pimlott, ' Administration of the British Army', pp. 20–1.

53. Steve Brown, *By Fire and Bayonet: Grey's West Indies Campaign of 1794* (Warwick: Helion & Company, 2018), pp. 78, 92, 129–30.

54. John D. Grainger, *British Campaigns in the South Atlantic 1805-1807: Operations in the Cape and the River Plate and Their Consequences* (Barnsley: Pen & Sword Military, 2014), p. 11.

55. N.A.M. Rodger, *The Command of the Ocean* (London: HarperCollins, 1997), p. 435.

56. Pimlott, 'Administration of the British Army', pp. 56–76; Kenneth Patrick Ferguson, 'The Army in Ireland from the Restoration to the Act of Union' (PhD, Dublin, Ireland, Trinity College, 1981).

57. Pimlott, 'Administration of the British Army', p. 63.

58. Ibid., pp. 288–90.

59. Ibid., p. 286

60. Ibid., pp. 283, 287–8.

61. Allan Blackstock, 'The Union and the Military, 1801-c.1830', *Transactions of the Royal Historical Society* 10 (2000), pp. 329–51.

62. Villalard, 'A Re-Assessment of the Strategic Role of the Channel Islands during the Great French War', pp. 16–20.

63. Kevin Linch, 'The Politics of Foreign Recruitment in Britain during the French Revolutionary and Napoleonic Wars', in *Transnational Soldiers: Foreign Military Enlistment in the Modern Era*, ed. Nir Arielli and Bruce Collins (Basingstoke: Palgrave Macmillan, 2012), pp. 50–66.

64. Mark Wishon, *German Forces and the British Army: Interactions and Perceptions, 1742-1815* (Basingstoke (GB); New York: Palgrave Macmillan, 2013), pp. 81–5.

65. Thomas Agostini, '"The Provincials Will Work like Giants": British Imperialism, American Colonial Troops, and Trans-Atlantic Labor Economics during the Seven Years' War', *Early American Studies: An Interdisciplinary Journal* 15 (2017), pp. 64–98; Philip R.N. Katcher, *Encyclopedia of British, Provincial, and German Army Units 1775-1783* (Harrisburg: Stackpole, 1973); Paul H. Smith, 'The American Loyalists: Notes on Their Organization and Numerical Strength', *The William and Mary Quarterly* 25 (1968), pp. 259–77.

66. Uythoven, *The Secret Expedition*, p. 375.

67. William Henry Flayhart, *Counterpoint to Trafalgar: the Anglo-Russian Invasion of Naples, 1805-1806* (Gainesville: University Press of Florida, 2004); Piers Mackesy, *The War in the Mediterranean, 1803-1810* (London: Longmans, 1957).

68. Robert K. Sutclife, *British Expeditionary Warfare and the Defeat of Napoleon 1793-1815* (Woodbridge: Boydell & Brewer Ltd., 2014), p. 11.

69. Thomas Munch-Petersen, *Defying Napoleon: How Britain Bombarded Copenhagen and Seized the Danish Fleet in 1807* (Stroud: Sutton, 2007); Andy Phillipson, 'The Raid on Ostend 1798: Combined Operations against Revolutionary France', *Journal of the Society for Army Historical Research* 81 (2003), pp. 31–46.

70. Christopher D. Hall, *British Strategy in the Napoleonic War, 1803-15* (Manchester: Manchester University Press, 1992), pp. 118–22, 157–63; Rory Muir, *Britain and the Defeat of Napoleon, 1807-1815* (New Haven (CT) and London: Yale University Press, 1996).

71. Gordon C. Bond, *The Grand Expedition: The British Invasion of Holland in 1809* (Athens: University of Georgia Press, 1979).
72. Charles William Chadwick Oman, *A History of the Peninsular War*, 7 vols (Oxford: Clarendon Press, 1902), vol. 5, pp. 750–2.
73. Desmond Gregory, *Sicily: The Insecure Base: A History of the British Occupation of Sicily, 1806–1815* (London: Associated University Press, 1988).
74. Andrew Bamford, *A Bold and Ambitious Enterprise: The British Army in the Low Countries, 1813–1814* (Barnsley: Frontline Books, 2013).
75. Alexander V. Campbell, *The Royal American Regiment: An Atlantic Microcosm, 1755–1772* (Norman: University of Oklahoma Press, 2010).
76. Robert Griffith, *Riflemen: The History of the 5th Battalion, 60th (Royal American) Regiment - 1797-1818.* (Warwick: Helion & Company, 2021).
77. 'War-Office, 19th June 1824 Memorandum', *The London Gazette*, 26 June 1824.
78. Harry Calvert, 'Returns, from the Adjutant General's Office, of the Number of Effective Men in Foreign and Provincial Corps, in the Service of Great Britain; and of the Number of Recruits Raised in Great Britain and Ireland, for Unlimited Service; &c.', *Commons Papers*, 1806, vol. 10, p. 373; Henry John Temple, 3rd Viscount Palmerston, 'Estimates Presented to the House of Commons, of Army Services, for the Year 1813', *Commons Papers*, 1812-13 vol. 12; D. S. Gray, '"Prisoners, Wanderers and Deserters": Recruiting for the King's German Legion, 1803-1815', *Journal of the Society for Army Historical Research* 53 (1975), pp. 148–58; Wishon, *German Forces and the British Army*.
79. C. T. Atkinson, 'Foreign Regiments in The British Army, 1793-1802: Part VI—Notes on Each Corps or Regiment, Section II—Du Dressnay's to Maclean's Chasseurs', *Journal of the Society for Army Historical Research* 22 (1944), pp. 234–50.
80. TNA, WO 6/5, fols. 20-113 (for Saint-Domingue); WO 1/633, fol. 193-201 (Cape of Good Hope); WO 4/277, fol. 207 (Nova Scotia); WO 1/629, fols. 387 & 391 (Maltese provincials).
81. *Commons Journal*, vol. 51, p. 704; *List of the Officers of His Majesty's Foreign Corps under the Inspection of Colonel Nesbit, Inspector General of Foreign Troops* (Southampton, 1796); *List of the Officers of His Majesty's Foreign Corps, under the Inspection of Colonel Nesbitt, Inspector General of Foreign Troops, Shewing the Dates of Their Commissions and Role in the British Service* (Southampton, 1797).
82. Linch, 'The Politics of Foreign Recruitment', p. 60.
83. Atkinson, 'Foreign Regiments in The British Army, 1793-1802: Part VI—Notes on Each Corps or Regiment, Section II—Du Dressnay's to Maclean's Chasseurs', *Journal of the Society for Army Historical Research*, 22.90 (1944), pp. 243–6.
84. Charles Mathew Clode, *The Military Forces of the Crown: Their Administration and Government*, 2 vol. (London: J. Murray, 1869), vol. 1, pp. 89–92.
85. '34 Geo. 3 c. 43, An Act to Enable Subjects of France to Enlist as Soldiers in Regiments to Serve on the Continent of Europe, and in Certain Other Places; and to Enable His Majesty to Grant Commissions to Subjects of France, to Serve and Receive Pay as Officers in Such Regiments, or as Engineers under Certain Conditions [May 9, 1794]', *Statutes at Large*, vol. 39, part 2, pp. 531–3; '38 Geo. 3 c. 13, To Amend an Act, Made in the Twenty-Ninth Year of the Reign of His Late Majesty King George the Second, Intituled, *An Act to Enable His Majesty to Grant Commissions to a Certain Number of Foreign Protestants, Who Have Served Abroad as Officers of Engineers, to Act and Rank as Officers or Engineers in American Only, under Certain Restrictions and Qualifications* [Dec. 30, 1797]', *Statutes at Large*, vol. 41, pp. 533–4; '44 Geo. 3 c. 75, An Act for Enabling Subjects of Foreign States to Enlist as Soldiers in His Majesty's Service, and for Enabling His Majesty to Grant Commissions to Subjects of Foreign States to Serve as Officers or as Engineers, under Certain Restrictions, and to Indemnify All Persons Who May Have Advised His Majesty to Enlist Any Such Soldiers, or Grant Any Such Commissions as Aforesaid [14 July 1804]', *Statutes of the United*

Kingdom of Great Britain and Ireland (London: George Eyre and Andrew Strahan, 1807), vol. 2, pp. 150–1; '46 Geo. 3 c. 23, An Act to Extend the Provisions of an Act Passed in the Forty-Fourth Year of the Reign of His Present Majesty, for Enabling Subjects of Foreign States to Enlist as Soldiers in His Majesty's Service; and to Indemnify Those Who Have Advised His Majesty to Land Such Soldiers in This Kingdom [22 March 1806]', *Statutes of the United Kingdom*, vol. 2, pp. 616–17; '54 Geo. 3 c. 12, An Act to Enable His Majesty to Augment the Sixtieth Regiment of Foot to Ten Battalions, by Enlistment of Foreigners [6 December 1813]', *Statutes of the United Kingdom*, vol. 22.

86. Guy de Meuron, *Le régiment Meuron, 1781-1816* (Lausanne: Le Forum historique, 1982), pp. 279–86.

87. Buckley, *Slaves in Red Coats*, pp. 28–30; Peter D. G. Thomas, 'Vaughan, Sir John (c. 1731–1795)', in *Oxford Dictionary of National Biography* (Oxford University Press, 2008), https://doi.org/10.1093/ref:odnb/28136.

88. Maria Alessandra Bollettino, '"Of Equal or of More Service": Black Soldiers and the British Empire in the Mid-Eighteenth-Century Caribbean', *Slavery & Abolition* 38 (2017), pp. 510–33.

89. Alan Gilbert, *Black Patriots and Loyalists: Fighting for Emancipation in the War for Independence* (Chicago (IL): Chicago University Press, 2012); Gerald Horne, *Negro Comrades of the Crown: African Americans and the British Empire Fight the U.S. before Emancipation* (New York: Yale University Press, 2016).

90. Buckley, *Slaves in Red Coats*, pp. 131, 156–7.

91. TNA, WO 1/648, fol. 349-355, Col. Torrens to Lt. Col. Bunbury, 1 August 1811; WO 380/4.

92. For example, the British Army recruiting Spaniards into 'British' regiments see Andrew Bamford, *Sickness, Suffering, and the Sword: The British Regiment on Campaign, 1808-1815* (Norman, OK: University of Oklahoma Press, 2013), pp. 166–8. Also see TNA, WO 4/306, fol. 241, about Africans in units at the Cape of Good Hope.

93. '26 Geo. 3 c. 107, An Act for Amending, and Reducing into One Act of Parliament, the Laws Relating to the Militia, in That Part of Great Britain Called England [1786]', *Statutes at Large*, vol. 35, pp. 902–03.

94. For distribution of forces into districts, see: TNA, HO 50/383, fols. 845-851, Sir George Younge to Home Office, 29 December 1792; for an example of staff appointments: TNA, WO 3/13, fols. 177-178 Circular to General Sir William Pitt and Lord George Lennox, Sir William Howe, etc., 23 April 1795.

95. TNA, WO 3/17, fol. 66, Circular to Generals commanding Military Districts, 17 February 1797; WO 3/31, fols. 10-12, Circular to Officers Commanding Districts, 17 February 1797.

96. '34 Geo. 3 c. 31, An Act for Encouraging and Disciplining Such Corps or Companies of Men, as Shall Voluntarily Inroll Themselves for the Defence of Their Counties, Towns, or Coasts, or for the General Defence of the Kingdom, during the Present War [April 17 1794]', *Statutes at Large*, vol. 39, part 2, pp. 508–10.

97. Thomas Bartlett, 'Defence, Counter-Insurgency and Rebellion: Ireland, 1793-1803', in *A Military History of Ireland*, ed. Thomas Bartlett and Jeffery Keith (Cambridge: Cambridge University Press, 1996), pp. 249, 259–63.

98. Allan Blackstock, *An Ascendancy Army: The Irish Yeomanry, 1796-1834* (Dublin: Four Courts Press, 1998), pp. 144–5; for the arrangement of brigades see Ferguson, 'Army in Ireland', p. 154.

99. Ian Soulsby, 'The Irish Military Establishment 1796-1798. A Study in the Evolution of Military Effectiveness' (MA, Cork, National University of Ireland, 2018).

100. '38 Geo. 3 c. 27, An Act to Enable His Majesty More Effectually to Provide for the Defence and Security of the Realm during the Present War; and for Indemnifying Persons Who May Suffer in Their Property by Such Measures as May Be Necessary for That Purpose [April 5, 1798]', *Statutes at Large*, vol. 41, pp. 594–602.

101. See a copy of the circular letter sent to Lord Lieutenants in 1798: 'Defence of the Country', *Manchester Mercury*, 24 April 1798, p. 2. Sir Charles Grey, for example, attended a meeting of the Sussex Lieutenancy: 'Lewes, April 21', *Kentish Weekly Post or Canterbury Journal*, 24 April 1798, p. 4; a summary of meetings was produced too, see WO 1/831, fols. 77-128, 145-208.

102. 'Returns, Presented to the House of Commons, of the Volunteer Corps of Cavalry, Infantry, and Artillery, in Great Britain; Discipline, the Effective Strength of Each Corps, Together with Their State of Discipline and Fitness for Service; as Reported by the General Officers and Inspecting Field Officers of the Different Districts throughout the Kingdom, in Their Last Returns; and Also, the Names of the Officers by Whom Such Returns Have Been Signed', *Commons Papers*, 1806 vol. 10, pp. 229–331; Philip Haythornthwaite, '1353 Inspectors of Yeomanry and Volunteers', *Journal of the Society for Army Historical Research* 70, no. 284 (1992), pp. 270–1.

103. Cookson, *British Armed Nation*, pp. 43–8.

104. Collins, *War and Empire*, pp. 153–222.

105. Jac Weller, *Wellington in India* (London: Greenhill Books, 1993), pp. 301–03.

106. Villalard, 'A Re-Assessment of the Strategic Role of the Channel Islands during the Great French War'.

107. Captain John Le Couture, from half-pay of the late 100th Regiment, was appointed their brigade major, 'War Office, February 23', *The London Gazette*, 23 February 1793.

108. Desmond Gregory, *The Beneficent Usurpers: A History of the British in Madeira* (Rutherford, [N.J: Fairleigh Dickinson University Press, 1988), pp. 45–64.

109. Donald E. Graves, *Where Right and Glory Lead!: The Battle of Lundy's Lane, 1814* (Toronto: Robin Brass Studio, 2000), pp. 261–2.

110. Western, 'Recruitment of the Land Forces', pp. 291–3.

111. Ibid., pp. 299–301.

112. Western, *English Militia*, p. 232; Cookson, *British Armed Nation*, pp. 116–19.

113. Linch, *Britain and Wellington's Army*, pp. 46–8.

114. Ibid, pp. 107–08.

115. '51 Geo. 3 c. 118, An Act to Permit the Interchange of the British and Irish Militias Respectively [1st July 1811]', *Statutes at Large*, vol. 51, pp. 355–60; '51 Geo. 3 c. 128, An Act to Explain an Act Passed in This Present Session of Parliament, Intituled, An Act to Permit the Interchange of the British and Irish Militias Respectively [24th July 1811]', *Statutes at Large*, vol. 51, p. 435.

116. '54 Geo. 3 c. 1, An Act to Enable His Majesty to Accept the Services of a Proportion of the Militia out of the United Kingdom, for the Vigorous Prosecution of the War [24th November 1813]', *Statutes at Large*, vol. 54, pp. 1–7.

117. '54 Geo. 3 c. 19, An Act to Enable His Majesty to Accept the Services of the Local Militia out of Their Counties, under Certain Restrictions, and until the Twenty Fifth Day of March One Thousand Eight Hundred and Fifteen [10th December 1813]', *Statutes at Large*, vol. 54, pp. 34–5.

118. Fortescue, *County Lieutenancies*, pp. 277–80.

119. Simon Quinn, 'Orientalists in Uniform?: British Military Encounters and Experiences in Egypt, c.1798-1801' (Ph.D., University of York, 2017), p. 33.

120. Royal Commission on Historical Manuscripts (ed.), *The Manuscripts of J. B. Fortescue, Esq. Preserved at Dropmore* (London: H.M.S.O., 1912), vol. 8, pp. 157, 159, 415–16, 418–20; for context on the British government's invasion plans for South American, see Hall, *British Strategy*, pp. 143–8.

121. Amita Das, *Defending British India against Napoleon: The Foreign Policy of Governor-General Lord Minto, 1807-13*, ed. Aditya Das (Woodbridge: The Boydell Press, 2016), pp. 153–69, 193–222; Premansukumar Bandyopadhyay, *Sepoys in the British Overseas Expeditions* (Kolkata: K P Bagchi & Co., 2011).

122. *Frontier and Overseas Expeditions from India*, vol. 6 (Calcutta: Superintendent Government Printing India, 1911), pp. 325–6.

123. Edward Dodwell and James Samuel Miles, *Alphabetical List of the Officers of the Indian Army: With the Dates of Their Respective Promotion, Retirement, Resignation, or Death, Whether in India or in Europe, from the Year 1760 to the Year 1834 Inclusive, Corrected to September 30, 1837* (London: Longman, Orme, Brown, 1838).

124. Bamford, *Sickness, Suffering, and the Sword*, pp. 187–216; full details of the arrangements can be found in Appendix II of Sir Charles William Chadwick Oman, *Wellington's Army, 1809-1814* (London: E. Arnold, 1912).

125. Andrew Bamford, '"Infamous", or Incomplete? The Origins and Structure of Wellington's 1815 Field Army', *Journal of the Society for Army Historical Research*, 93 (2015), pp. 102–19.

126. *A List of the Officers of the Army, and Marines* (London, 1786).

127. *A List of All the Officers of the Army and Royal Marines* (London, 1818). For the penal units, see Linch, *Britain and Wellington's Army*, p. 145.

Chapter 2: A Global Army and Global Conflicts

1. John Tams, *Over the Hills and Far Away* (England: EMI Music Distribution/Virgin, 1996).

2. George Farquhar, *The Recruiting Officer. A Comedy. As It Is Acted at the Theatre Royal in Drury-Lane, by Her Majesty's Servants. Written by Mr. Farquhar* (London, 1706), p. 21; Shirley Strum Kenny, 'Farquhar, George (1676/7–1707)', *Oxford Dictionary of National Biography*, 2004 <https://doi.org/10.1093/ref:odnb/9178>.

3. Aeneas Anderson, *A Narrative of the British Embassy to China in the Years 1792, 1793, and 1794; Containing the Various Circumstances of the Embassy, with Accounts of Customs and Manners of the Chinese and a Description of the Country, Towns, Cities &c. &c* (London: J. Debrett, 1795).

4. Collins, *War and Empire*, p. 487.

5. Daniel A. Baugh, *The Global Seven Years War, 1754-1763: Britain and France in a Great Power Contest* (Harlow, England; New York: Longman, 2011).

6. Piers Mackesy, *The War for America 1775-1783* (London: Longman, 1964), pp. 524–5.

7. Christopher D. Hall, *British Strategy in the Napoleonic War, 1803-15* (Manchester: Manchester University Press, 1992).

8. Collins, *War and Empire*, pp. 176–81.

9. Das, *Defending British India against Napoleon*, pp. 223–4. R.A. Huttenback, 'The French Threat to India and British Relations with Sind, 1799-1809', *The English Historical Review*, 76.301 (1961), pp. 590–9.

10. George Ward Hunt, 'Accounts of Net Public Income and Expenditure of Great Britain and Ireland, 1688-1800; Receipts and Issues from Exchequer; Accounts of Gross Public Income and Expenditure, 1801-69', *Commons Papers*, 1867 vol. 35, pp. 1155–7.

11. Pimlott, 'Administration of the British Army', pp. 18–19.

12. Patrick Crowhurst, *The Defence of British Trade, 1689-1815* (Folkestone: Dawson, 1977).

13. Hall, *British Strategy*, p. 87.

14. John McAleer, '"The Key to India": Troop Movements, Southern Africa, and Britain's Indian Ocean World, 1795–1820', *The International History Review*, 35.2 (2013), pp. 294–316.

15. Christopher Alan Bayly, *Imperial Meridian: The British Empire and the World 1780-1830* (London: Longman, 1989), pp. 103–05.

16. For a discussion of this, McAleer, '"The Key to India"', p. 294.

17. Roger Knight, *Britain against Napoleon: The Organization of Victory, 1793-1815* (London: Allen Lane an imprint of Penguin Books, 2013), pp. 405–09. For the wider debate about banknotes, specie, and inflation, see Emir Phillips, 'The Bank of England and Parliament Were Monetarily Adroit during the Napoleonic Wars', *Journal of Post Keynesian Economics*, 41.4 (2018), pp. 620–47.

18. J. Sperling, 'The International Payments Mechanism in the Seventeenth and Eighteenth Centuries', *The Economic History Review*, 14.3 (1962), pp. 446–68.

19. Muir, *Britain and the Defeat of Napoleon*, p. 118.

20. 'The Ninth Report of the Commissioners of Military Enquiry', *Commons Papers*, 1809 vol. 5, p. 269.

21. Michael Craton, *Testing the Chains: Resistance to Slavery in the British West Indies* (Ithaca N.Y.: Cornell University Press), p. 199.

22. For the wider history of rumours and resistance to slavery, see Wim Klooster, 'Slave Revolts, Royal Justice, and a Ubiquitous Rumor in the Age of Revolutions', *The William and Mary Quarterly*, 71.3 (2014), pp. 401–24.

23. Craton, *Testing the Chains*, chaps. 15, 16, 17, 18; Kit Candlin, 'The Role of the Enslaved in the "Fedon Rebellion" of 1795', *Slavery & Abolition*, 39.4 (2018), pp. 685–707; Wim Klooster, 'Slave Revolts', *The William and Mary Quarterly*, 71.3 (2014), pp. 401–24; Nicole Ulrich, 'Abolition from below: The 1808 Revolt in the Cape Colony', in *Humanitarian Intervention and Changing Labor Relations: The Long-Term Consequences of the Abolition of the Slave Trade* (Leiden: Brill, 2011), pp. 193–222; David Geggus, 'The Enigma of Jamaica in the 1790s: New Light on the Causes of Slave Rebellions', *The William and Mary Quarterly*, 44.2 (1987), pp. 274–99; David Geggus, *Slavery, War, and Revolution: The British Occupation of Saint Domingue, 1793-1798* (New York and Oxford, 1982).

24. Buckley, *Slaves in Red Coats*, p. 86.

25. Ibid., p. 86.

26. Julia Gaffield, *Haitian Connections in the Atlantic World: Recognition after Revolution* (Chapel Hill: University of North Carolina Press, 2015).

27. TNA, WO 25/3224, Prince Frederick, Duke of York and Albany, to Lord Liverpool, 7 December 1811.

28. Donald R. Hickey, *The War of 1812: A Forgotten Conflict* (Urbana: University of Illinois Press, 1989), p. 97.

29. TNA, WO 25/3225, Prince Frederick, Duke of York and Albany, to Lord Bathurst, 31 January 1813.

30. Jon E. Wilson, *India Conquered: Britain's Raj and the Chaos of Empire* (London: Simon & Schuster, 2016); Randolf G.S. Cooper, *The Anglo-Maratha Campaigns and the Contest for India: The Struggle for Control of the South Asian Military Economy* (Cambridge: University Press, 2007).

31. Sashi Bhusan Chaudhuri, *Civil Disturbances During the British Rule In India (1765-1857)* (Calcutta: The World Press, 1955).

32. Devedas Moodley, 'Vellore 1806: The Meanings of Mutiny', in *Rebellion, Repression, Reinvention: Mutiny in Comparative Perspective*, ed. by Jane Hathaway (Westport, Conn: Praeger, 2001), pp. 87–102; Richard Cannon, *Historical Record of the Fifty-Sixth, or the West Essex Regiment of Foot: Containing an Account of the Formation of the Regiment in 1755, and of Its Subsequent Services to 1844*, Historical Records of the British Army (London: Parker, Furnivall, and Parker, 1844).

33. V.C.P. Hodson, *List of the Officers of the Bengal Army 1758-1834*, 4 vols (Constable, London, 1927); Chris Bayley, 'The British Military-Fiscal State and Indigenous Resistance. India 1750-1820', in *An Imperial State at War: Britain from 1689 to 1815*, ed. by Lawrence Stone (London: Routledge, 1994), pp. 322–54.

34. Denver A. Webb, 'War, Racism, and the Taking of Heads: Revisiting Military Conflict in the Cape Colony and Western Xhosaland in the Nineteenth Century', *Journal of African History*, 56.1 (2015), pp. 37–55.

35. Nigel Worden, 'Armed with Swords and Ostrich Feathers: Militarism and Cultural Revolution in the Cape Slave Uprising of 1808', in *War, Empire and Slavery, 1770–1830*,

ed. by Richard Bessel, Nicholas Guyatt, and Jane Rendall, (London: Palgrave Macmillan UK, 2010), pp. 121–38.

36. Geoffrey Powell, *The Kandyan Wars: The British Army in Ceylon, 1803-1818* (New Delhi: Navrang, 1984); Sujit Sivasundaram, 'Tales of the Land: British Geography and Kandyan Resistance in Sri Lanka, c. 1803-1850', *Modern Asian Studies*, 41.5 (2007), pp. 925–65.

37. John Connor, *The Australian Frontier Wars, 1788-1838* (UNSW Press, 2002); Stephen Gapps, *The Sydney Wars: Conflict in the Early Colony, 1788-1817* (Sydney, NSW: University of New South Wales Press, 2018).

38. Robert S. Allen, *His Majesty's Indian Allies: British Indian Policy in the Defence of Canada, 1774-1815* (Toronto [Ont.]: Dundurn Press, 1992), chap. 4; Michael Duffy, *Soldiers, Sugar, and Seapower: The British Expeditions to the West Indies and the War against Revolutionary France* (Oxford [Oxfordshire]; New York: Clarendon Press; Oxford University Press, 1987), pp. 103–04.

39. Robert Stewart Castlereagh, *Memoirs and Correspondence of Viscount Castlereagh, Second Marquess of Londonderry*, ed. by Charles William Vane Londonderry, 12 vols (London: H. Colburn, 1850), vol. 8, p. 104.

40. TNA, WO 30/80, 'Defence Report', 1811.

41. Hall, *British Strategy*, pp. 41–2.

42. Robert K. Sutclife, *British Expeditionary Warfare and the Defeat of Napoleon 1793-1815* (Woodbridge: Boydell & Brewer Ltd., 2014), pp. 13–14.

43. Ibid., p. 89.

44. Ibid., p. 241.

45. Hall, *British Strategy*, p. 46; Sutclife, *British Expeditionary Warfare*, pp. 190–1.

46. TNA, WO 380/2.

47. Richard Cannon, *Historical Record of the Sixth Regiment of Dragoon Guards, or the Carabineers: Containing an Account of the Formation of the Regiment in 1685, and of Its Subsequent Services to 1839* (London: Longman, Orme; Clowes, 1839), p. 81.

48. Sutclife, *British Expeditionary Warfare*, p. 240.

49. David G. Chandler, *The Campaigns of Napoleon* (London: Weidenfeld and Nicolson, 1967).

50. Pimlott, 'Administration of the British Army', pp. 21 and 262–3.

51. Ibid., pp. 288–311, 321, 345.

52. Duffy, *Soldiers, Sugar, and Seapower*, pp. 137–9

53. Ibid., pp. 183–204.

54. Sutclife, *British Expeditionary Warfare*, pp. 208–09.

55. TNA, WO 380/3, fols. 97, 99.

56. TNA, WO 17/2814, fols. 68-9.

57. For the decision to evacuate Egypt, see Mackesy, *The War in the Mediterranean*, pp. 205–06. The orders were sent to General Fox, but he was replaced by Moore.

58. Hall, *British Strategy*, pp. 74–5.

59. Das, *Defending British India against Napoleon*, pp. 162–70.

60. The National Army Museum, Nam 1960-05-35, 1971-02-33-501, 1971-02-33-500, 1972-09-19, and 1982-04-88.

61. Pimlott, 'Administration of the British Army', pp. 306–11.

62. W.B. Rowbotham, 'Soldiers in Lieu of Marines', *Journal of the Society for Army Historical Research*, 33.133 (1955), pp. 26–34.

63. Richard Glover, *Peninsular Preparation*, pp. 184–5.

64. TNA, WO 17/142, returns for February and March 1812.

65. Houlding, *Fit for Service*, pp. 20–2; Pimlott, 'Administration of the Army', pp. 48–9.

66. Richard Cannon, *Historical Record of the Fourteenth, or the Buckinghamshire Regiment of Foot: Containing an Account of the Formation of the Regiment in 1685, and of Its Subsequent*

Services to 1845, Historical Records of the British Army (London: Parker, Furnivall, and Parker, 1845), pp. 36 and 38.

67. Richard Cannon, *Historical Record of the Seventy-Third Regiment: Containing an Account of the Formation of the Regiment from the Period of Its Being Raised as the Second Battalion of the Forty-Second Royal Highlanders in 1870 and of Its Subsequent Services to 1851*, Historical Records of the British Army (London: Parker, Furnivall, and Parker, 1850), p. 6; TNA, WO 380/4, fol. 49.

68. Richard Cannon, *Historical Record of the Twelfth, or the East Suffolk, Regiment of Foot: Containing an Account of the Formation of the Regiment in 1685, and of Its Subsequent Services to 1847*, Historical Records of the British Army (London: Parker, Furnivall, and Parker, 1848), p. 57; TNA, WO 380/4, fol. 49.

69. Steve Brown, 'British Artillery Regiments and the Men Who Led Them 1793-1815', *Napoleon Series*, 2015 <https://www.napoleon-series.org/military-info/organization/Britain/Artillery/c_ArtilleryRegimentsIntro.html>; M.E.S. Laws, *Battery Records of the Royal Artillery, 1716-1859* (Woolwich, Eng.: Royal Artillery Institute, 1952).

70. Jacqueline Reiter, 'Citizen Soldiers: "Military Spirit" and Recruitment in Britain during the Wars against France, 1793–1815', in *Redcoats to Tommies: The Experience of the British Soldier from the Eighteenth Century*, ed. by Kevin Linch and Matthew Lord (Woodbridge: Boydell Press, 2021), pp. 22–3; F.J. McLynn, *Invasion: From the Armada to Hitler, 1588-1945* (London: Routledge & Kegan Paul, 1987), pp. 97–112.

71. John A. Murphy, *The French Are in the Bay: The Expedition to Bantry Bay, 1796* (Cork and Dublin: Mercier Press, 1997).

72. TNA, WO 30/80, Defence Report, 1 January 1811.

73. Richard Glover, 'The French Fleet, 1807-1814; Britain's Problem; and Madison's Opportunity', *The Journal of Modern History*, 39.3 (1967), pp. 233–52.

74. Houlding, *Fit for Service*, pp. 128–9.

75. TNA, WO 17/1156, 'General Returns, 1783 to 1785', fol. 26; Henry John Temple, 3rd Viscount Palmerston, 'An Account of the Effective Numbers, and Established Strength, of Regiments of Cavalry, Guards, and Infantry, Borne on the British Establishment, and the General Distribution of the Said Forces,--in the Years 1788,--1789,--1790,--1791,--& 1792.', *Commons Journals*, 1814 vol. 70, p. 599.

76. J.R. Western, 'The County Fencibles and Militia Augmentation of 1794', *Journal of the Society for Army Historical Research*, 34.137 (1956), pp. 3–4.

77. TNA, WO 17/1159.

78. Cookson, *The British Armed Nation*, pp. 38–40.

79. TNA, WO 1/617, fols. 239-241, Frederick, Duke of York, 'According the Last Returns, the Actual Force in England Consists Of …', 24 February 1795; WO 1/617, fol. 311, 'Number and Disposition of the Force Required for North Britain in 1795', 12 March 1795.

80. TNA, WO 25/3224, Prince Frederick, Duke of York and Albany to Lord Hobart, 13 January 1804.

81. Roger Wells, *Insurrection: The British Experience 1795-1803* (Gloucester: Alan Sutton, 1983); E.P. Thompson, *The Making of the English Working Class* (London: Penguin Books, 2013); Linda Colley, *Britons: Forging the Nation 1707-1837* (London: Pimlico, 2003).

82. Western, *English Militia*, p. 374.

83. Joseph Thomas Cozens, 'The Experience of Soldiering: Civil-Military Relations and Popular Protest in England, 1790-1805' (unpublished Ph.D., University of Essex, 2016), pp. 168–226.

84. Cookson, *British Armed Nation*, pp. 189–90.

85. John Stevenson, *Popular Disturbances in England, 1700-1832*, 2nd edn. (London; New York: Longman, 1992); John Bohstedt, *Riots and Community Politics in England and Wales, 1790-1810* (Cambridge, Mass.: Harvard University Press, 1983); TNA, WO 3/595, Dispositions

of troops around London were sent to the Home Secretary: Henry Torrens to Richard Ryder, 2 April 1810.

86. Cookson, *British Armed Nation*, p. 55; H.M. Chichester and S. Kinross, 'Hope, Sir Alexander (1769–1837), Army Officer', in *Oxford Dictionary of National Biography* (Oxford University Press, 2008) <https://0-doi-org.wam.leeds.ac.uk/10.1093/ref:odnb/13712>.

87. Jacqueline Suzanne Marie Jeanne Faulkner, 'The Role of National Defence in British Political Debate, 1794-1812' (unpublished PhD, University of Cambridge, 2006), p. 49.

88. Ruan O'Donnell, *Aftermath: Post-Rebellion Insurgency in Wicklow, 1799–1803* (Dublin; Portland, OR: Irish Academic Press Ltd, 1999).

89. TNA, WO 25/3224, Prince Frederick, Duke of York and Albany, to Lord Hobart, 13 January 1804.

90. TNA, WO 1/612, Wellesley to Lord Castlereagh, 9 December 1807, including memorandum, fols. 215–299.

91. Clive Emsley, 'Political Disaffection and the British Army in 1792', *Historical Research*, 48.118 (1975), pp. 230–45.

92. Ferguson, 'Army in Ireland', pp. 171–7.

93. John R. Breihan, 'Army Barracks in the North East in the Era of the French Revolution', *Archaeologia Aeliana*, 5th Series, 18 (1990), pp. 165–76; Joseph Thomas Cozens, 'The Experience of Soldiering: Civil-Military Relations and Popular Protest in England, 1790-1805' (unpublished Ph.D., University of Essex, 2016), p. 184; James Douet, *British Barracks 1600-1914: Their Architecture and Role in Society* (London: Stationery Office, 1998).

94. Cozens, 'The Experience of Soldiering', pp. 127–8.

95. William Windham, *The Windham Papers: The Life and Correspondence of the Rt. Hon. William Windham, 1750-1810 … Including Hitherto Unpublished Letters from George III, the Dukes of York and Gloucester, Pitt, Fox, Burke, Canning … Etc. ; with an Introduction by the Earl of Rosebery*, 2 vols (Boston, 1913), vol. 2, p. 50.

96. '37 Geo. 3 c. 70, An Act for the Better Prevention and Punishment of Attempts to Seduce Person Serving in His Majesty's Forces by Sea or Land, from Their Duty and Allegiance to His Majesty, or to Incite Them to Mutiny of Disobedience [June 6, 1797]', *Statutes at Large*, vol. 41, pp. 270–1.

97. Ferguson, 'Army in Ireland', pp. 171–7.

98. Ibid., pp. 176–7; Walter Temple Willcox, *The Historical Records of the Fifth (Royal Irish) Lancers from Their Foundation as Wynne's Dragoons (in 1689) to the Present Day* (London: A. Doubleday & co., 1908), pp. 148–52.

99. Fortescue, *County Lieutenancies*, pp. 310–11.

100. TNA, WO 17/1159, fol. 28, 'General Returns, 1793 to 1795'.

101. TNA, WO 25/3224, 'Return of the British Army', 1810.

102. TNA, WO 27/99, Inspection Return of the 65th Foot, 14 March 1810.

103. TNA, WO 1/637, James Willougby Gordon to Steward, 21 March 1808.

104. Bamford, *Sickness, Suffering, and the Sword*, pp. 88–92, 144–56.

105. TNA, WO 3/595, Henry Torrens to Henry Edward Bunbury, 10 January 1810.

106. TNA, WO 3/595, Henry Torrens to Henry Edward Bunbury, 8 March 1810.

107. TNA, WO 3/598, Henry Torrens to Lord Liverpool, 17 October 1810.

108. Pimlott, 'Administration of the British Army', pp. 116–18.

109. For an example of the dispersal of cavalry across Dorset, see David Clammer, 'Soldiers and Civilians: Troops in Dorset, 1793 – 1805', *Journal of the Society for Army Historical Research*, 93.375 (2015), pp. 214–30; TNA, WO 3/195, William Wynyard, 'Wynyard to Taylor', 30 July 1808.

110. TNA, WO 380/2; Richard Cannon, *Historical Record of the First, or King's Regiment of Dragoon Guards: Containing an Account of the Formation of the Regiment in the Year 1685*

and of Its Subsequent Services to 1836, Historical Records of the British Army (London: William Clowes and Sons, 1837), pp. 81–2.

111. Surrey History Centre, BR/QS/5/32, 'List of Quarters of Captain Alexander Gordon's Troop at Guildford', 1809.

112. TNA, WO 1/636, Prince Frederick, Duke of York and Albany, to Robert Stewart, Viscount Castlereagh, 1 September 1807.

Chapter 3: Authority and Control

1. 'Jan. 27, Conduct of the Duke of York', *The Parliamentary Debates from the Year 1803 to the Present Time*, 41 vols (London: T. C. Hansard, 1812), vol. 12, p. 179; David R. Fisher, 'Wardle, Gwyllym Lloyd (?1761-1833), of Hartsheath, Nr. Mold, Flints.', *History of Parliament Online* <https://www.historyofparliamentonline.org/volume/1790-1820/member/wardle-gwyllym-lloyd-1761-1833>.

2. Philip Harling, 'The Duke of York Affair (1809) and the Complexities of Wartime Patriotism', *Historical Journal*, 39 (1996), pp. 963–84; H.M. Stephens and John Van der Kiste. 'Frederick, Prince, duke of York and Albany (1763–1827), army officer and bishop of Osnabrück.', *Oxford Dictionary of National Biography*, 23 Sep. 2004.

3. 'London, Monday, January 23', *The Morning Post*, 23 January 1809, pp. 2–3; Rory Muir, *Britain and the Defeat of Napoleon, 1807-1815* (New Haven (CT) and London: Yale University Press, 1996), pp. 53–9, 77.

4. Houlding, *Fit for Service*, p. 153.

5. Richard Glover, *Peninsular Preparation*, p. 14.

6. *Parliamentary Debates*, vol. 12, cols. 23–27.

7. *Parliamentary Debates*, vol. 27, col. 245.

8. John Childs, *The British Army of William III, 1689-1702* (Manchester: Manchester University Press, 1987), pp. 19–21, 84–8; Stephen Brumwell, *Redcoats: The British Soldier and War in the Americas, 1755-1763* (Cambridge: Cambridge University Press, 2002), p. 55.

9. Charles Mathew Clode, *The Military Forces of the Crown: Their Administration and Government*, 2 vols (London: J. Murray, 1869), vol. 1, pp. 144–5.

10. '22 Geo. 3 c. 4, An Act for Punishing Mutiny and Desertion, and for the Better Payment of the Army and Their Quarters [1782]', *Statutes at Large*, vol. 34, pp. 4–8; *An Act for Punishing Mutiny and Desertion and for the Better Payment of the Army and Their Quarters. With an Index. Also, Rules and Articles for the Better Government of All His Majesty's Forces* (London: Printed by G. Eyre and a. Strahan, printers to the King's most Excellent Majesty, 1809), p. 5.

11. Clode, *Military Forces*, vol. 1.

12. *Parliamentary History*, vol. 27, cols. 163–168 and 639–642.

13. *Parliamentary Debates*, vol. 3, cols. 640–641, 707–709, 857–861; vol. 10, cols. 922–923, 980–991, 1080–1088, 1179–1184 ; vol. 11, cols. 811–815, 1115–1122; vol. 19, cols. 350–356, 360–365, 367–377; vol. 21, cols. 1201–1209, 1264–1292; vol. 25, cols. 125–137; vol. 27, cols. 215–217, 244–246; vol. 30, cols. 45–52.

14. *Parliamentary Debates*, vol. 9, col. 63.

15. *Parliamentary Debates*, vol. 8, cols. 961–962, 1073–1074; A.D. Harvey, 'The Ministry of All the Talents: The Whigs in Office, February 1806 to March 1807', *The Historical Journal*, 15.4 (1972), pp. 643–5.

16. The dates can be followed through the indexes of *Commons Journals*, vols. 39–70.

17. '23 Geo. 3 c. 17, An Act for Punishing Mutiny and Desertion; and for the Better Payment of the Army and Their Quarters [1783]', *Statutes at Large*, vol. 34, p. 223; '23 Geo. 3 c. 24, An Act for Punishing Mutiny and Desertion; and for the Better Payment of the Army and Their Quarters [1783]', *Statutes at Large*, vol. 34, pp. 254–55; '23 Geo. 3 c. 52, An Act

for Punishing Mutiny and Desertion; and for the Better Payment of the Army and Their Quarters [1783]', *Statutes at Large*, vol. 34, p. 299.

18. *Parliamentary History*, vol. 24, cols. 719–720.

19. Ibid., cols. 303, 682–684, 719–733, 744–755; John Ehrman, *The Younger Pitt*, 3 vols (London: Constable, 1996), vol. 1, pp. 125, 142; Paul Kelly, 'British Politics 1783-4: The Emergence and Triumph of the Younger Pitt's Administration', *Bulletin of the Institute of Historical Research*, 54.129 (1981), pp. 62–78.

20. *Parliamentary Debates*, vol. 7, col. 439.

21. Ibid., col. 457.

22. *Parliamentary Debates*, vol. 19, cols 369–370.

23. Ibid., cols 356, 361.

24. *An Act for Punishing Mutiny and Desertion: And for the Better Payment of the Army and Their Quarters, with an Index: Also, Rules and Articles for the Better Government of All His Majesty's Forces* (London: G. Eyre and A. Straham, 1813); *An Act for Punishing Mutiny and Desertion; and for the Better Payment of the Army and Their Quarters* (London: printed by C. Eyre and the executors of W. Strahan, Printers to the King's most Excellent Majesty, 1786); for Palmerston's time at the War Office, see Michael Stephen Partridge, 'Palmerston and the War Office, 1809-1828', in *Palmerston Studies II*, ed. by Miles Taylor and David Brown ([Southampton]: Hartley Institute, University of Southampton, 2007), pp. 1–23; Kenneth Bourne, *Palmerston: The Early Years 1784-1841* (London: Allen Lane, 1982).

25. *Parliamentary History*, vol. 31, cols. 830–831.

26. E.A. Reitan, *Politics, Finance, and the People: Economical Reform in England in the Age of the American Revolution, 1770-92* (Basingstoke: Palgrave Macmillan, 2007); Warwick Funnell, 'The 'Proper Trust of Liberty': Economical Reform, the English Constitution and the Protections of Accounting during the American War of Independence', *Accounting History*, 13.1 (2008), pp. 7–32.

27. Knight, *Britain against Napoleon*, pp. 115–17.

28. W.H. Greenleaf, 'The Commission of Military Enquiry, 1805-12', *Journal of the Society for Army Historical Research*, 41.168 (1963), pp. 171–81; Knight, *Britain against Napoleon*, pp. 512–15.

29. Figures abstracted from *Commons Journals*, vols. 39 to 70.

30. Harry Calvert, 'Return of the Number of Desertions from the Regular Army at Home; from 1st January 1807, to the 24th December 1809', *Commons Papers*, 1810 vol. 13, pp. 381–82.

31. *Commons Journals*, vol. 56, p. 564; *Parliamentary Debates*, vol. 7, cols 1252–1260.

32. *Commons Journals*, vol. 65, p. 104; vol. 66, p. 118; vol. 67, p. 115; vol. 68, p. 148; in 1814 the returns were presented in March and April, *Commons Journals*, vol. 69, pp. 144, 208.

33. Clode, *Military Forces*, vol. 1, pp. 93–109.

34. Bartlett, 'Development of the British Army', pp. 67–70.

35. George Ward Hunt, 'Accounts of Net Public Income and Expenditure of Great Britain and Ireland, 1688-1800; Receipts and Issues from Exchequer; Accounts of Gross Public Income and Expenditure, 1801-69', *Commons Papers*, 1867 vol. 35, p. 700.

36. Pimlott, 'Administration of the British Army', pp. 121–50.

37. Ibid., pp. 159, 164–65, 171–73; '23 Geo. 3 c. 50, An Act for the Better Regulation of the Office of the Paymaster General of His Majesty's Force, and the More Regular Payment of the Army and to Repeal and Act Made in the Last Session of Parliament, Intitules, An Act for the Better Regulation of the Office of Paymaster of His Majesty's Forces [1783].', *Statutes at Large*, vol. 34, pp. 284–99.

38. Reitan, *Politics, Finance, and the People*, p. 199.

39. Pimlott, 'Administration of the Army', pp. 153–67.

40. Clode, *Military Forces*, vol. 1, pp. 140–1 and vol. 2, p. 335.

41. Hunt, 'Accounts of Net Public Income and Expenditure of Great Britain and Ireland', *Commons Papers*, 1867 vol. 35, p. 483.

42. 'An Account of the Extraordinary Expenses of the Army, for 1815', *Commons Papers*, 1816 vol. 12, 225.

43. 'An Account of the Extraordinary Expenses of the Army, for 1814', *Commons Papers*, 1815 vol. 9, p. 233.

44. J. L. Pimlott, 'The Reformation of The Life Guards, 1788', *Journal of the Society for Army Historical Research*, 53.216 (1975), pp. 194–209.

45. Muir, *Britain and the Defeat of Napoleon*, pp. 110–13.

46. Knight, *Britain against Napoleon*, p. 407.

47. *Parliamentary Debates*, vol. 15, cols. 606–632 and 657–672.

48. *Parliamentary Debates*, vol. 5, cols. 649–701; for Craufurd's role as a politician, see Michael J. Durey, '"Black Bob" Craufurd and Ireland, 1798-1804', *War in History*, 16.2 (2009), pp. 133–56.

49. 'Return of the Number of Men Wanting to Complete the Establishment of the Regular Army, on the 1st January 1805, 1806, & 1807; Distinguishing the British from the Foreign Troops, and the Cavalry from the Infantry', *Commons Papers*, 1807 vol. 4, pp. 297–8.

50. J.D. Turner, 'Army Agency', *Journal of the Society for Army Historical Research*, 13.49 (1934), p. 29.

51. Bartlett, 'Development of the British Army', pp. 82–7.

52. 'The Sixth Report of the Commissioners of Military Enquiry: Appointed by Act of 45 Geo. III. Cap. 47. Office of the Secretary at War. The Establishment of the War-Office; Regimental Accounts; Agency; and, Clothing. With a Supplement to the Fifth Report.', *Commons Papers*, 1808 vol. 5, p. 335.

53. *A Collection of Orders, Regulations, and Instructions, for the Army; on Matters of Finance and Points of Discipline Immediately Connected Therewith* (London: Sold by T. Egerton, 1807), p. 47.

54. 'The Sixth Report of the Commissioners of Military Enquiry', p. 338.

55. Ibid., p. 359.

56. 'Sunday's Post', *Bury and Norwich Post*, 28 March 1804, p. 4.

57. Edward Erastus Deacon, Edward Chitty, and Great Britain Court of Review, *Reports of Cases in Bankruptcy: Argued and Determined in the Court of Review, and on Appeal Before the Lord Chancellor* (Saunders and Benning, 1837); 'Report from the Select Committee on Army and Ordnance Expenditure; Together with the Proceedings of the Committee, Minutes of Evidence, Appendix, and Index', *Commons Papers*, 1850 vol. 10, p. 662.

58. K.R. Jones, 'Richard Cox, Army Agent and Banker', *Journal of the Society for Army Historical Research*, 34.140 (1956), pp. 178–81; K.R. Jones, 'Cox and Co.: Army Agents Craig's Court: The Nineteenth Century', *Journal of the Society for Army Historical Research*, 40.164 (1962), pp. 178–86.

59. 'Statement of Monies Paid by Paymaster General to Army Agents on Establishment of Great Britain, 1811', *Commons Papers*, 1812–13 vol. 12, p. 199.

60. 'Sixth Report of the Commissioners of Military Enquiry', pp. 334, 348.

61. Turner. 'Army Agency'.

62. Pimlott, 'Administration of the British Army', pp. 32, 49–55.

63. *Parliamentary History*, vol. 27, cols. 1310–1318.

64. Clode, *Military Forces*, vol. 2, pp. 263–4.

65. Ibid., pp. 338–46.

66. TNA, WO 4/156, Circular from the War Office, 13 February 1795; Clode, *Military Forces*, vol. 2, pp. 339.

67. Faulkner, 'The Role of National Defence', p. 41.

68. Pimlott, 'Administration of the British Army', p. 35; for the longer history of the King's Closet and governance, see Edward Raymond Turner and Gaudens Megaro, 'The King's Closet in the Eighteenth Century', *The American Historical Review*, 45.4 (1940), pp. 761–76.
69. Ehrman, *The Younger Pitt*, vol. 1, pp. 170–1.
70. Western, 'Recruitment of the Land Forces', p. 46.
71. *HMC Dropmore*, vol. 8, p. 8.
72. Faulkner, 'The Role of National Defence', pp. 86–8.
73. Ibid., pp. 45–6.
74. Pimlott, 'Administration of the British Army', pp. 99–100.
75. Ibid., p. 42.
76. Clode, *Military Forces*, vol. 2, p. 204.
77. Pimlott, 'Administration of the British Army', p. 46.
78. Clode, *Military Forces*, vol. 2, pp. 327–8.
79. Faulkner, 'The Role of National Defence', p. 164.
80. Pimlott, 'Administration of the British Army', pp. 65–70.
81. Ferguson, 'The Army in Ireland', pp. 64–7.
82. Pimlott, 'Administration of the British Army', pp. 39, 56–7.
83. Clode, *Military Forces*, vol. 2, p. 206.
84. Ibid, pp. 204–52.
85. Muir, *Britain and the Defeat of Napoleon*, pp. 277, 354.
86. Cole, *Arming the Royal Navy*, chap. 1.
87. Clode, *Military Forces*, vol. 2, p. 256; Olive Anderson, 'The Constitutional Position of the Secretary at War, 1642-1855', *Journal of the Society for Army Historical Research*, 36.148 (1958), pp. 165–9.
88. *Parliamentary History*, vol. 27, col. 1312.
89. Pimlott, 'Administration of the British Army', pp. 77, 109, 114.
90. The volumes are TNA, WO 1/1018 to /1136.
91. Chris Cook, *British Historical Facts, 1760-1830* (London: Macmillan, 1980), pp. 15–18.
92. Clode, *Military Forces*, vol. 2, pp. 258–9, 265.
93. Ibid., p. 710
94. For example: War Office, *A Collection of Orders, Regulations, and Instructions, for the Army; on Matters of Finance and Points of Discipline Immediately Connected Therewith* (London: Sold by T. Egerton, 1807); Adjutant-General's Office, *General Regulations and Orders* (London; Quebec: G. Roworth, Printer … ; Reprinted by John Neilson, 1804); *General Regulations and Orders for the Army: Adjutant General's Office, Horse-Guards, 12th August, 1811* (London: W. Clowes, 1811).
95. Bartlett, 'Development of the British Army', p. 32.
96. Faulkner, 'The Role of National Defence', p. 33.
97. Clode, *Military Forces*, vol. 2, p. 320.
98. J.R. Western, 'Recruitment of the Land Forces', p. 29; Cookson, *British Armed Nation*, p. 63.
99. Catherine Kelly, *War and the Militarisation of British Army Medicine, 1793-1830* (London: Pickering & Chatto, 2011); Roy David Burley, 'An Age of Negligence? British Army Chaplaincy, 1796–1844' (unpublished MPhil, University of Birmingham, 2013), pp. 35–44; for clothing see 'The Sixth Report of the Commissioners of Military Enquiry: Appointed by Act of 45 Geo. III. Cap. 47. Office of the Secretary at War. The Establishment of the War-Office; Regimental Accounts; Agency; and, Clothing. With a Supplement to the Fifth Report', *Commons Papers*, 1808 vol. 5, pp. 366–88.
100. Hunt, 'Accounts of Net Public Income and Expenditure of Great Britain and Ireland, 1688-1800', *Commons Papers*, 1867 vol. 35, pp. 700–02. The figures are for total Grants to the Army and Ordnance, including ordinary and extraordinary charges; it excludes funds for the militia, volunteer, and subsidies to allies.

101. Knight, *Britain against Napoleon*, p. 97.
102. See TNA, WO 2/36 for summaries in the 1790s; Pimlott, 'Administration of the British Army', p. 120.
103. Arthur Aspanall, 'The Cabinet Council, 1783-1835', *Proceedings of the British Academy*, 38 (1954), pp. 145–252.
104. Pimlott, 'Administration of the British Army,', p. 36
105. Cole, *Arming the Royal Navy*, pp. 16–17.
106. Pimlott, 'Administration of the British Army', pp. 35–9.
107. Knight, *Britain against Napoleon*, pp. 53–3.
108. Ibid., pp. 42–3; William C. Lowe, 'Lennox, Charles, Third Duke of Richmond, Third Duke of Lennox, and Duke of Aubigny in the French Nobility (1735–1806)', *Oxford Dictionary of National Biography*, 2013 <https://doi.org/10.1093/ref:odnb/16451>.
109. Windham, *Windham Papers*, vol. 2, p. 46.
110. David Wilkinson, 'Windham, William (1750–1810)', *Oxford Dictionary of National Biography*, 2008 <https://doi.org/10.1093/ref:odnb/29725>.
111. Faulkner, 'Role of National Defence', p. 30.
112. Ibid., pp. 33–4.
113. Ibid., p. 29.
114. Knight, *Britain against Napoleon*, pp. 99–100.
115. Muir, *Britain and the Defeat of Napoleon*, pp. 84–7.
116. Hall, *British Strategy*, pp. 105–25.
117. Ibid., pp. 138, 145.
118. Huw J. Davies, *Spying for Wellington British Military Intelligence in the Peninsular War* (Norman (OK): University of Oklahoma Press, 2018), pp. 52–6; Hall, *British Strategy*, pp. 153–8.
119. Hall, *British Strategy*, p. 191; Muir, *Britain and the Defeat of Napoleon*, pt. 1.
120. Cookson, *British Armed Nation*, pp. 81–85.
121. S.M. Farrell, 'Pratt, John Jeffreys, First Marquess Camden (1759–1840), Politician', *Oxford Dictionary of National Biography* (Oxford University Press, 2008) <https://doi.org/10.1093/ref:odnb/22705>.
122. D.R. Fisher, 'Fitzpatrick, Richard (1748–1813)', *Oxford Dictionary of National Biography*, 2008 <https://doi.org/10.1093/ref:odnb/9624>.
123. Muir, *Britain and the Defeat of Napoleon*, pp. 105–6.
124. Hall, *British Strategy*, p. 179.
125. Muir, *Britain and the Defeat of Napoleon*, pp. 107–13, 137–43, 157–62, 193–8, 216–19.
126. Brown, *By Fire and Bayonet*, pp. 137–8.
127. Knight, *Britain against Napoleon*, p. 104.
128. *Castlereagh Correspondence*, vol. 8, pp. 6–8.
129. Faulkner, 'Role of National Defence', pp. 25–6.
130. TNA, WO 1/617, fol. 169-171, Jeffery Amherst, 1st Baron Amherst to Henry Dundas, 17 November 1794.
131. TNA, WO 1/617, fol. 177-179, Jeffery Amherst, 1st Baron Amherst to Henry Dundas, 4 December 1794.
132. Knight, *Britain against Napoleon*, p. 105.
133. 'War Office, December 23, 1809', *The London Gazette* 23 December 1809; *The Royal Kalendar (Calendar) Or, Complete and Correct Annual Register, for England, Scotland, Ireland, and America, for the Year 1807 (Etc.)* (Stockdale, 1807), p. 213. For a summary of his career see Louis F. Peck, *A Life of Matthew G. Lewis* (Cambridge, 1961), pp. 1–4.
134. Linch, *Britain and Wellington's Army*, pp. 117–19.
135. Knight, *Britain against Napoleon*, p. 335.
136. Davies, *Spying for Wellington*, pp. 40–1.

137. Michael Durey, *William Wickham, Master Spy: The Secret War against the French Revolution* (London: Pickering & Chatto, 2009).

138. Knight, *Britain against Napoleon*, pp. 122–30.

139. Davies, *Spying for Wellington*.

140. Knight, *Britain against Napoleon*, pp. 475–503; the following offices are included in the total: Comptrollers of Army Accounts, Commissariat, Secretary for War, Commander-in-Chief, Army Pay Office, Ordnance Office, Irish Army.

141. 'The Sixth Report of the Commissioners of Military Enquiry: Appointed by Act of 45 Geo. III. Cap. 47. Office of the Secretary at War. The Establishment of the War-Office; Regimental Accounts; Agency; and, Clothing. With a Supplement to the Fifth Report', *Commons Papers*, 1808 vol. 5, pp. 436–7.

142. 'Further Army Regimental Accounts: Viz: (1.)--List of Regimental Accounts, for Periods Previous to the 25th June 1798, Which Have Been Received, and Settled, since the 10th of June 1811. (2.)--List of Miscellaneous Accounts Which Have Been Received, and Settled, since the 10th of June 1811. (3.)--Statement of the Progress Made in the Examination of Regimental Accounts, for the 10 Years from 1784 to 1794, since the 10th of June 1811; Together with the Number of Accounts Delivered for Any of the Said Years Subsequent to That Date', *Commons Papers*, 1814–15 vol. 9, p. 375; 'Return of Number of Regimental and Militia Accounts Received and Settled, 1812-14', *Commons Papers*, 1814–15 vol. 9, p. 371.

Chapter 4: Waning and Waxing

1. 'Friday, June 13 Army Estimates', *Stamford Mercury*, 19 June 1783, p. 2.

2. Pimlott, 'Administration of the British Army', pp. 2–5.

3. Stephen Conway, *War, State, and Society in Mid-Eighteenth-Century Britain and Ireland* (Oxford: Oxford University Press, 2006), pp. 69–75; Stephen Conway, *The British Isles and the War of American Independence* (Oxford: Oxford University Press, 2000), pp. 15–19.

4. Pimlott, 'Administration of the British Army', p. 166.

5. John Brooke, 'The House of Commons', *History of Parliament Online* <http://www.historyofparliamentonline.org/volume/1754-1790/survey/iv-house-commons>.

6. Knight, *Britain against Napoleon*, pp. 43–4.

7. Western, 'Recruitment of the Land Forces', p. 41.

8. Pimlott, 'Administration of the British Army', pp. 268–9.

9. Pimlott, 'The Raising of Four Regiments for India, 1787-8', *Journal of the Society for Army Historical Research*, 52.210 (1974), pp. 68–88.

10. Pimlott, 'Administration of the British Army', pp. 298–9, 326–8.

11. Western, 'Recruitment of the Land Forces', p. 42.

12. 'War Office', *The London Gazette*, 25 February 1794.

13. Western, 'Recruitment of the Land Forces', pp. 35–7.

14. Ibid., pp. 36–7, 54.

15. Western, 'The County Fencibles and Militia Augmentation of 1794', *Journal of the Society for Army Historical Research*, 34.137 (1956), pp. 3–11.

16. Western, 'Recruitment of the Land Forces', pp. 33–4.

17. Ibid., p. 35.

18. Ronald M. Sunter, 'Raising the 97th (Inverness-Shire) Highland Regiment of Foot', *Journal of the Society for Army Historical Research*, 76.306 (1998), pp. 93–110.

19. TNA, WO 1/617, fol. 83-87, Jeffery Amherst, 1st Baron Amherst to Henry Dundas, 15 August 1794.

20. Ibid.; Western, 'Recruitment of the Land Forces', pp. 52–6.

21. 'Friday's Post', *The Ipswich Journal*, 12 April 1794, p. 2.

22. Cozens, 'The Experience of Soldiering', pp. 44–6; Arthur N. Gilbert, 'An Analysis of Some Eighteenth Century Army Recruiting Records', *Journal of the Society for Army Historical Research*, 54.217 (1976), p. 42.

23. 'CRIMPS and KIDNAPPERS', *Dublin Evening Post* (Dublin, 6 September 1794), p. 3.

24. Western, 'Recruitment of the Land Forces', p. 37; Christine Lodge, 'Gordon [Née Maxwell], Jane, Duchess of Gordon (1748/9–1812)', *Oxford Dictionary of National Biography*, 2007 <https://doi.org/10.1093/ref:odnb/11059>.

25. Cozens, 'The Experience of Soldiering', pp. 44–55.

26. John Stevenson, 'The London "Crimp" Riots of 1794', *International Review of Social History*, 16 (1971), pp. 40–58.

27. 'RIOTS', *Hereford Journal*, 27 August 1794, p. 1; 'CRIMPING', *The Scots Magazine*, 1 September 1794, p. 59.

28. 'RIOTS', *Caledonian Mercury*, 18 July 1795, p. 3; 'London', *Cambridge Intelligencer*, 17 January 1795, pp. 1–2; Cozens, 'The Experience of Soldiering', pp. 47–55.

29. Wishon, *German Forces and the British Army*, p. 148; Peter H. Wilson, 'The German "Soldier Trade" of the Seventeenth and Eighteenth Centuries: A Reassessment', *The International History Review*, 18.4 (1996), pp. 757–92.

30. Atkinson, 'Foreign Regiments in The British Army, 1793-1802: Part VI—Notes on Each Corps or Regiment, Section IV—Royal Louis to York Rangers', *Journal of the Society for Army Historical Research*, 22.92 (1944), pp. 322–4.

31. Atkinson, 'Foreign Regiments in The British Army, 1793-1802: Part VI—Notes on Each Corps or Regiment, Section I—Albanian Regiment to Dillon's', *Journal of the Society for Army Historical Research*, 22.89 (1944), pp. 188–90.

32. Linch, 'Politics of Foreign Recruitment', *Transnational Soldiers*, pp. 50–66.

33. TNA, WO 6/131, fols. 529-561, Frederick, Duke of York to Henry Dundas, 29 July 1795.

34. 'House of Commons, Wednesday, Jan. 21', *Reading Mercury*, 26 January 1795, p. 2; 'House of Commons, Thursday, Jan. 22', *Chester Chronicle*, 30 January 1795, p. 1.

35. TNA, WO 1/617, fol. 231, Frederick, Duke of York to Henry Dundas, 17 February 1795; WO 4/156, fol. 427: Circular, War Office, 21 February 1795.

36. 'War-Office, Dublin Castle, 30th March 1795', *Saunders's News-Letter*, 2 April 1795, p. 3; 'Recruiting Service', *Kentish Weekly Post or Canterbury Journal*, 3 April 1795, p. 2; 'Sunday's Post', *Ipswich Journal*, 4 April 1795, p. 1.

37. TNA, WO 6/131, fols. 529-561, Frederick, Duke of York to Henry Dundas, 29 July 1795. In 1795 all units above the 100th Foot were disbanded along with the 91st to 94th, 96th, and 97th Foot; in 1796 the 95th, and 99th Foot were disbanded. The 98th Foot was renumbered 91st and the 100th renumbered the 92nd.

38. Western, 'Recruitment of the Land Forces', pp. 46–9.

39. *Regulations and Instructions for Carrying on the Recruiting Service for His Majesty's Forces Stationed Abroad* (London: War Office printed; and sold by J. Walter, 1796).

40. Pimlott, 'Administration of the British Army', pp. 246–54.

41. *Instructions for Officers on the Recruiting Service of Regiments on Foreign Stations* (London, 1792).

42. Linch, *Britain and Wellington's Army*, pp. 85–6.

43. TNA, WO 2/1, fol. 246, A regiment of infantry commanded by Capt. Thomas Steele.

44. TNA, WO 2/1, fol. 281, Colonel Lofts Corps of Foot; R. G. Thorne, 'Loft, John Henry (?1769-1849), of Camby House, Louth and Healing House, Nr. Grimsby, Lincs.', *History of Parliament Online* <http://www.historyofparliamentonline.org/volume/1790-1820/member/loft-john-henry-1769-1849>.

45. 'A Statement of the Proceedings of the War-Office, with Reference to the Accounts of John Ogle, Esquire, Formerly a Lieutenant Colonel in the Army', *Commons Papers*, 1809 vol. 10, p. 197.

46. Fortescue, *County Lieutenancies*, p. 127; Cookson, *The British Armed Nation*, pp. 113–14.

47. Harry Calvert, 'Returns Presented to the House of Commons, by Mr. Secretary at War, Respecting Foreign Levies, Recruits, &c. Raised for General Service, and State of the British Forces, &c. &c', *Commons Papers*, 1805 vol. 8, p. 47.

48. *Parliamentary Debates*, vol. 3, cols. 141–142.

49. *Parliamentary Debates*, vol. 13, cols. 266–267.

50. Ibid., cols. 12–16.

51. Linch, *Britain and Wellington's Army*, pp. 108–09.

52. James Pulteney, 'Return of the Number of Men for Whom Bounty Has Been Drawn, as Enlisted at the Head Quarters of Regiments in Great Britain, during Each Half Year of the Years 1805, 1806, and 1807', *Commons Papers*, 1808 vol. 7, p. 139.

53. Linch, *Britain and Wellington's Army*, pp. 70–1.

54. Ibid., pp. 71–2.

55. See for example T.H. McGuffie, 'The Short Life and Sudden Death of an English Regiment of Foot: An Account of the Raising, Recruiting, Mutiny and Disbandment of the 113th Regiment of Foot, or "Royal Birmingham Volunteers" (April, 1794, to September, 1795)', *Journal of the Society for Army Historical Research*, 33.133 (1955), pp. 16–25.

56. TNA, WO 1/617, fol. 177-179, Jeffery Amherst, 1st Baron Amherst to Henry Dundas, 4 December 1794.

57. John Prebble, *Mutiny: Highland Regiments in Revolt, 1743-1804* (London: Secker & Warburg, 1975), pp. 263–391.

58. Western, 'Recruitment of the Land Forces', pp. 295–6.

59. Ibid., pp. 296–7.

60. Ibid., pp. 291–7.

61. Atkinson, 'Foreign Regiments in The British Army, 1793-1802: Part VI, Section IV', *Journal of the Society for Army Historical Research*, 22.92 (1944), pp. 316–19.

62. Atkinson, 'Foreign Regiments in The British Army: Part VI, Section II', *Journal of the Society for Army Historical Research*, 22.90 (1944), pp. 234–6.

63. R. L. Yaple, 'The Auxiliaries; Foreign and Miscellaneous Regiments in The British Army 1802-1817', *Journal of the Society for Army Historical Research*, 50.201 (1972), pp. 10–28.

64. Knight, *Britain against Napoleon*, pp. 142–3; Meuron, *Le régiment Meuron, 1781-1816*.

65. Many of these can be tracked in TNA, WO 6/20-22, e.g.: TNA, WO 6/20, fols. 107-117 Henry Dundas to Lieutenant General Trigge, 14 June 1799.

66. Atkinson, 'Foreign Regiments in The British Army, 1793-1802: Part IV, Section II', *Journal of the Society for Army Historical Research* 22.90 (1944), p. 313; Atkinson, 'Foreign Regiments in The British Army, 1793-1802: Part IV, Section IV', *Journal of the Society for Army Historical Research* 22.92 (1944), p. 250.

67. Yaple, 'The Auxiliaries', *Journal of the Society for Army Historical Research* 50.201 (1972), p. 19.

68. Laurent Dubois, *Avengers of the New World: the Story of the Haitian Revolution* (Cambridge, Mass.: Belknap, 2005), pp. 152–3.

69. C. T. Atkinson, 'Foreign Regiments in The British Army, 1793-1802: Part IV—The West Indies', *Journal of the Society for Army Historical Research*, 22.87 (1943), pp. 107–15.

70. TNA, WO 380/4, 'Cape Regiment', 1803.

71. René Chartrand, 'Black Corps in the British West Indies, 1793-1815', *Journal of the Society for Army Historical Research*, 76.308 (1998), p. 253.

72. Gray, 'Recruiting for the King's German Legion', *Journal of the Society for Army Historical Research*, 53 (1975), pp. 148–58.

73. Wishon, *German Forces and the British Army*, p. 142.

74. TNA, WO 1/916, Alexander Levy (Transport Office) to Goulbum, 21 October 1813; Maj. Baurenis (60th Foot) to Torrens, 26 December 1813; Torrens to Baurenis, 3 December 1813.

75. See *Army List* for 1795, 1803, and 1804.

76. Some returns are in TNA, WO 1/612, WO 1/170, WO 1/171, and WO 1/899.
77. Cookson, *British Armed Nation*, pp. 28–35.
78. Western, *English Militia*, p. 221; H. M. Stephens and S. Kinross, 'Anstruther, Robert (1768–1809)', *Oxford Dictionary of National Biography* <https://doi.org/10.1093/ref:odnb/588>.
79. Hertford Museum, HETFM/Military/6242.4, Poster Recruiting for the Army at All Saints Church, Hertford, 1796.
80. '37 Geo. 3 c. 4, For Raising a Certain Number of Men in the Several Counties in England for the Service of His Majesty's Army and Navy [Nov. 11, 1796]', *Statutes at Large*, vol. 41, pp. 20–63; Western, 'Recruitment of Land Forces', pp. 204–09.
81. Western, *English Militia*; Matthew McCormack, *Embodying the Militia in Georgian England* (Oxford: Oxford University Press, 2015).
82. Western, 'Recruitment of the Land Forces', pp. 307–08.
83. '26 Geo. 3 c. 107, An Act for Amending, and Reducing into One Act of Parliament, the Laws Relating to the Militia, in That Part of Great Britain Called England [1786]', *Statutes at Large*, vol. 35, pp. 860–917; Western, *English Militia*, p. 265.
84. 'House of Commons, April 11', *Caledonian Mercury*, 15 April 1793, p. 2; 'House of Commons, Thursday, April 16', *Hereford Journal*, 24 April 1793, p. 4; R. G. Thorne, 'Feilding, William Robert, Visct. Feilding (1760-99), of Chesterfield Street, Mdx.', *The History of Parliament* <http://www.historyofparliamentonline.org/volume/1790-1820/member/feilding-william-robert-1760-99>.
85. '35 Geo. 3 c. 83, An Act for Augmenting the Royal Corps of Artillery, and Providing Seafaring Men for the Service of the Navy, out of the Private Men Now Serving in the Militia; and to Amend an Act, Passed in the Twenty-Six Year of the Reign of His Present Majesty, Intituled *An Act for Amending, and Reducing into One Act of Parliament, the Laws Relating to the Militia in That Part of Great Britain Called England* [June 2, 1795]', *Statutes at Large*, vol. 40, pp. 285–93.
86. TNA, WO 3/31, fols. 111-115, William Fawcett, Circular to officers commanding 5th, 9th, 20th, 31st, 35th, 44th, 46th, 48th, 55th, 62nd, and 85th Foot, 23 January 1798.
87. '38 Geo. 3 c. 17, For Allowing, during the Continuance of the Present War, a Certain Proportion of Men, Raised in Pursuance of the Two Acts of the Last Session of Parliament for Augmenting the Militia, to Enlist in His Majesty's Other Forces, and to Serve until Six Months after the Conclusion of a General Peace [Jan. 12, 1798]', *Statutes at Large*, vol. 41, pp. 581–2; Western, 'Recruitment of the Land Forces', pp. 309–14.
88. Piers Mackesy, *Statesmen at War: The Strategy of Overthrow, 1798-1799* (London; New York: Longman, 1974).
89. Cookson, *British Armed Nation*, pp. 116–17; Western, 'The Recruitment of the Land Forces', p. 316.
90. TNA, WO 6/188, fols. 218-229, Dundas, Circulars to Lord Lieutenants of Counties, 13 July 1799.
91. WO 6/188, fols. 230-1, Dundas to Duke of York, 18 July 1799.
92. Western, 'Recruitment of the Land Forces', pp. 317–18, 322; '39 Geo. 3 c. 106, An Act for the Reduction of the Militia Forces, at the Time and in the Manner Therein Limited; for Enabling His Majesty More Effectualy to Increase His Regular Forces, for the Vigorous Prosecution of the War, and for Amending Law Relating to the Militia [July 12, 1799]', *Statutes at Large*, vol. 42, pp. 393–410; '39 & 40 Geo. 3 c. 1, For Enabling His Majesty to Accept the Services of an Additional Number of Volunteers from the Militia, under Certain Restrictions [October 8, 1799]', *Statutes at Large*, vol. 42, pp. 463–73.
93. '40 Geo. 3 c. 1 (Ireland), An Act for Enabling His Majesty to Accept the Services of Volunteers from the Militia under Certain Restrictions, and for Amending the Law Relative to the Militia of Ireland [24 March 1800]', *Statutes at Large, Passed in the Parliaments Held in*

Ireland :From the Third Year of Edward the Second, A.D. 1310, to the Twenty Sixth-[Fortieth] Year of George the Third, A.D. 1786-[A.D. 1800], Inclusive : With Marginal Notes, and a Compleat Index to the Whole … , 20 vols (Dublin: Printed by George Grierson, 1801), vol. 20, pp. 1–12.

94. '45 Geo. 3 c. 31, An Act for Allowing a Certain Proportion of the Militia of Great Britain Voluntarily to Enlist into His Majesty's Regular Forces and Royal Marines [10 April 1805]', *Statutes of the United Kingdom*, vol. 2, pp. 358–61; '47 Geo. 3, Sess. 2, c. 55, An Act for Allowing a Certain Proportion of the Militia of Ireland, Voluntarily to Enlist His Majesty's Regular Forces [13 August 1807]', *Statutes of the United Kingdom, 47 George III*, pp. 397–8; '47 Geo. 3, Sess. 2, c. 57, An Act for Allowing a Certain Proportion of the Militia of Great Britain, Voluntarily to Enlist His Majesty's Regular Forces [13 August 1807]', *Statutes of the United Kingdom, 47 George III*, pp. 405–06; '49 Geo. 3 c. 4, An Act to Allow a Certain Proportion of the Militia of Great Britain to Enlist Voluntarily into the Regular Forces [13 March 1809]', *Statutes of the United Kingdom, 49 George III*, pp. 21–2; '49 Geo. 3 c. 5, An Act to Allow a Certain Proportion of the Militia in Ireland Voluntarily to Enlist into the Regular Forces [13 March 1809]', *Statutes of the United Kingdom, 49 George III*, pp. 22–3.

95. Fortescue, *County Lieutenancies*, pp. 146, 182.

96. Linch, *Britain and Wellington's Army*, pp. 48–52, 79–81.

97. '43 Geo. 3 c. 82, An Act To Enable His Majesty More Effectually to Raise and Assemble in England, an Additional Military Force, for the Better Defence and Security of the United Kingdom, and for the More Vigorous Prosecution of the War [6 July 1803]', *Statutes of the United Kingdom*, vol. 1, pp. 888–96; '43 Geo. 3 c. 83, An Act To Enable His Majesty More Effectually to Raise and Assemble in Scotland, an Additional Military Force, for the Better Defence and Security of the United Kingdom, and for the More Vigorous Prosecution of the War [6 July 1803]', *Statutes of the United Kingdom*, vol. 1, pp. 896–900; '43 Geo. 3 c. 85, An Act to Enable His Majesty More Effectually to Raise and Assemble in Ireland, an Additional Military Force, for the Better Defence and Security of the United Kingdom, and for the More Vigorous Prosecution of the War [6 July 1803]', *Statutes of the United Kingdom*, vol. 1, pp. 910–17; '43 Geo. 3 c. 101, An Act for Raising in the City of London, a Certain Number of Men as an Additional Military Force, for the Better Defence and Security of the United Kingdom, and for the More Vigorous Prosecution of the War [27 July 1803]', *Statutes of the United Kingdom*, vol. 1, pp. 980–3.

98. Fortescue, *County Lieutenancies*, pp. 27–30.

99. Inspector-General's Office, 'Accounts Presented to the House of Commons of Men Raised for the Royal Army of Reserve, in Each Month to the First May 1804, since the Commencement of the Act Passed for That Purpose', *Commons Papers*, 1804 vol. 11, p. 301; Joseph Cozens, "The Blackest Perjury': Desertion, Military Justice, and Popular Politics in England, 1803-1805', *Labour History Review*, 79.3 (2014), pp. 255–80.

100. 'Imperial Parliament', *Morning Post*, 29 March 1804, pp. 1–3; *Commons Journals*, vol. 59, p. 189; *Parliamentary Debates*, vol. 2, cols. 143, 174–9, 265–320, 322–3; Fortescue, *County Lieutenancies*, p. 126.

101. *Castlereagh Correspondence*, vol. 8, p. 80.

102. Fortescue, *County Lieutenancies*, pp. 132–4; '44 Geo. 3 c. 56, An Act for Establishing and Maintaining a Permanent Additional Force for the Defence of the Realm, and to Provide for Augmenting His Majesty's Regular Forces; and for the Gradual Reduction of the Militia in England [29 June 1804]', *Statutes of the United Kingdom*, vol. 2, pp. 106–17; '44 Geo. 3 c. 66, An Act for Establishing and Maintaining a Permanent Additional Force for the Defence of the Realm, and to Provide for Augmenting His Majesty's Regular Forces; and for the Gradual Reduction of the Militia of Scotland [10 July 1804]', *Statutes of the United Kingdom*, vol. 2, pp. 124–9; '44 Geo. 3 c. 74, An Act for Establishing and Maintaining a

Permanent Additional Force in Ireland for the Defence of the Realm, and to Provide for Augmenting His Majesty's Regular Forces [14 July 1804]', *Statutes of the United Kingdom*, vol. 2, pp. 143–9; '44 Geo. 3 c. 96, An Act to Alter, Amend, and Render More Effectual, an Act, Passed in the Present Session of Parliament, Intituled, *An Act for Establishing and Maintaining a Permanent Additional Force for the Defence of the Realm, and to Provide for Augmenting His Majesty's Regular Forces; and for the Gradual Reduction of the Militia of England*; so Far as the Same Related to the City of London [28 July 1804]', *Statutes of the United Kingdom*, vol. 2, 174–5.

103. Fortescue, *County Lieutenancies*, pp. 129–30.

104. Ibid., pp. 299–301.

105. Cookson, *British Armed Nation*, pp. 114–16.

106. '46 Geo. 3 c. 51, An Act to Repeal Several Acts Passed in the Forty-Third and Forty-Fourth Years Respectively of His Present Majesty's Reign, for the Raising and Establishing an Additional Force for the Defence of the Realm [23 May 1806]', *Statutes of the United Kingdom*, vol. 2, 633–4.

107. *Castlereagh Correspondence*, vol. 8, p. 55.

108. '46 Geo. 3 c. 66, An Act for Punishing Mutiny and Desertion; and for the Better Payment of the Army and Their Quarters [20 June 1806]', *Statutes of the United Kingdom*, vol. 2 , pp. 743–7; Fortescue, *County Lieutenancies*, pp. 159–65.

109. Cookson, *British Armed Nation*, p. 123.

110. 'Army Estimates, 21 January 1807', *Hansard: UK Parliament*, <https://bit.ly/3b4bBqa>; 'Army Estimates, 23 January 1807', *Hansard* <https://bit.ly/35w60bl>; 'Mutiny Bill, 12 March 1807', *Hansard* <https://bit.ly/2YvUKKj>.

111. Windham, *Windham Papers*, vol. 2, p. 357.

112. Harry Calvert, 'Return of the Number of Men Who Extended Their Services from the Militia to the Regular Army, during the Years 1807, 1808, and 1809', *Commons Papers*, 1810 vol. 13, p. 383; Harry Calvert, 'Return of the Number of Recruits Raised Quarterly, and Finally Approved for the Regular Army, in the Years 1807--1808--& 1809', *Commons Papers*, 1810, vol. 13, p. 377; Harry Calvert, 'Return of Number of Men Extending Service from Militia to Regular Army, 1807-09', *Commons Papers*, 1810, vol, 13, p. 383; W. Wynyard, 'Return of the Number of Recruits Raised for the Regular Army, by Other than the Ordinary Modes of Recruiting,--(Exclusive of Foreign and Colonial Corps)--in the Year 1811: Distinguishing Men and Boys, and Those Enlisted for Life, or for a Term of Years.', *Commons Papers*, 1812 vol. 9, p. 197; Harry Calvert, 'Return of the Number of Volunteers from the Different Regiments of Militia, English, Irish and Scotch, That Have Enlisted into the Regular Army, from the 25th December 1811 to the 24th December 1812: Distinguishing, Men and Boys, and Those Enlisted for Life or for a Term of Years', *Commons Papers*, 1813 vol. 13, p. 3; Harry Calvert, 'Return of the Number of Volunteers from the Militia to the Regular Army, since the 25th December 1812; Distinguishing Those Enlisted for Life, or for a Term of Years', *Commons Papers*, 1814 vol. 11, p. 271; see returns in TNA, WO 25/3224 and /3225.

113. '51 Geo. 3 c. 20, An Act to Allow a Certain Proportion of the Militia of *Great Britain* to Enlist Annually into the Regular Forces; and to Provide for the Gradual Reduction of the Said Militia [11 April 1811]', *Statutes of the United Kingdom, 51 George III*, pp. 78–89; '51 Geo. 3 c. 30, An Act to Amend the Several Acts for Enabling His Majesty to Accept the Services of Volunteers from the Militia of *Ireland* [25 May 1811]', *Statutes of the United Kingdom, 51 George III*, pp. 102–04.

114. Kevin Barry Linch, 'The Recruitment of the British Army 1807-1815' (unpublished PhD, University of Leeds, 2001), pp. 56–7.

Chapter 5: Numbers

1. 'Eleventh Report of the Commissioners of Military Enquiry: Departments of the Adjutant General and Quarter-Master General', in *Report of the Commissioners of Military Enquiry*, 6 vols (1806–1812), vol. 4, p. 49.

2. Bamford, *Sickness, Suffering, and the Sword*.

3. Harry Calvert, 'Return of the Number of Effective Men in the British Army, from the 1st January 1793 to the 1st January 1801; Distinguishing Each Year:--As Far as the Same Can Be Made up from Documents in the Adjutant General's Office.', *Commons Papers*, 1806 vol. 10, p. 397.

4. J.W. Fortescue, *A History of the British Army*, 13 vols (London; New York: Macmillan and Co.; Macmillan Co., 1899), vol. 4, part II, p. 940; Fortescue, *County Lieutenancies*, p. 293.

5. Charles James, *The Regimental Companion: Containing the Relative Duties of Every Officer in the British Army; … By Charles James, … A New and Enlarged Edition. In Two Volumes*, 2 vols (London: printed for T. Egerton [by C. Roworth], 1800), vol. 2, p. 521.

6. Pimlott, 'Administration of the British Army', pp. 179, 182–3.

7. The series are: TNA, WO 17/1156-1161 and WO 17/2813 and /2814.

8. TNA, WO 17/1159, fol. 15.

9. Harry Calvert, 'Return of the Number of Casualties Which Have Occurred in the British Regular Army, from the 25th December 1813, to the 25th December 1814, (as Far as the Same Can Be Made up) by Deaths, Discharges, and Desertions; Distinguishing British from Foreign and Colonial Corps', *Commons Papers*, 1815 vol. 9, p. 313.

10. TNA, WO 17/2814.

11. 'Eleventh Report of the Commissioners of Military Enquiry: Departments of the Adjutant General and Quarter-Master General'.

12. Ferguson, 'The Army in Ireland', p. 149.

13. Stephen Freemantle, 'Abstract of the Number of Troops That Were in This Kingdom on the 29th Day of September, 1786', *The Journals of the House of Commons, of the Kingdom of Ireland, from the Eighteenth Day of May, 1613 [-1794]*, 31 vols (Dublin: printed by J. King, and A.B. King, 1787), vol. 24, p. 34.

14. J.J. Crooks, *History of the Royal Irish Regiment of Artillery* (Dublin: Browne and Nolan, 1914), pp. 241, 279, 328.

15. TNA, WO 17/2555-2563.

16. Harry Calvert, 'Return of the Effective Strength of the British Army, in Rank and File, in Each Year from the Year 1804 to the Year 1813, Inclusive;--Distinguishing Cavalry, Artillery, Infantry, and Militia, and British from Foreign and Colonial Corps', *Commons Papers*, 1813 vol. 11, p. 269.

17. The four units are: Dutch Troops (WO 17/804, 1800-1803); Hompesch Dragoons (WO 17/809, 1802); York Hussars (WO 17/810, 1796-1802); York Fusiliers (WO 17/810, 1796).

18. TNA, WO 17/2460-2463, Portugal and Spain; WO 17/844 Jersey.

19. WO 17/1987 and /1988.

20. J.A. Houlding, 'The Number of Commissioned British Military Officers, 1725-1792', *Journal of the Society for Army Historical Research*, 91.366 (2013), pp. 92–7.

21. TNA, WO 17/1159, 'General Returns, 1793 to 1795'; Henry John Temple, 3rd Viscount Palmerston, 'Number of Regimental Officers of His Majesty's Regular Army, and Such of the Staff as Are under the Cognizance of the War Office; Arranged According to Rank;--Distinguishing Those upon Full Pay, and Half Pay, and the Rank on Which They Receive the above Pay', *Commons Papers*, 1814 vol. 11, pp. 285–9.

22. TNA, WO 17/1159, 'General Returns, 1793 to 1795'; TNA, WO 17/1161, 'General Return, 1800 to 1802'.

23. 'Army Estimates of Effective and Non-Effective Services, for the Year 1912-13, Together with Statements of the Variations of the Numbers of His Majesty's British Forces; Explanations

of the Increases and Decreases in the Estimates; the Amounts Provided for Each Arm of the Service and for Various Miscellaneous Establishments; the Amounts Included for the Colonies and Egypt; and the Net Army Expenditure for Ten Years', *Commons Papers*, 1912–13 vol. 50, p. 11.

24. Harry Calvert, 'Return of the Number of Recruits Raised for the Service of the Army, from the 1st of January 1793 to the 1st of January 1801', *Commons Papers*, 1806 vol. 10, p. 381.

25. Ibid.

26. Western, 'Recruitment of the Land Forces', p. 233.

27. William Barwick Hodge, 'On the Mortality Arising from Military Operations', *Journal of the Statistical Society of London*, 19.3 (1856), p. 232.

28. Cookson, *The British Armed Nation*, p. 112.

29. Calvert, 'Return of Number of Recruits Raised for Regular Army: 1793-1801', *Commons Papers*, 1806 vol. 10, p. 381; Harry Calvert, 'Return of the Number of Men Who Volunteered from the English Militia, for Limited Service, into the Regular Army, under the Act of the 39th of Geo. III. c. 106. and 39 and 40 of Geo. III. c. I', *Commons Papers*, 1806 vol. 10, p. 389.

30. Harry Calvert, 'Return of the Number of Men Who Have Been Killed in Action, or Who Have Died in the Service of the Army, since the Commencement of the Present War; as Far as the Can Be Made up from Documents in the Adjutant-General's Office', *The Parliamentary Register; Or, History of the Proceedings and Debates of the House of Commons [and House of Lords] Containing an Account of the Most Interesting Speeches and Motions: Accurate Copies of the Most Remarkable Letters and Papers; of the Most Material Evidence, Petitions, Etc. Laid Before, and Offered to the House* (London: Oriental Press, by Wilson and Co., 1800), vol. 14, p. 594.

31. Harry Calvert, 'Return of the Number of Men Who Have Been Discharged from the Service of the Army, on Account of Wounds or Bodily Infirmity, since the Commencement of the Present War; as Far as the Can Be Made up from Documents in the Adjutant-General's Office', *Parliamentary Register*, vol. 14, p. 594.

32. TNA, WO 25/700, fols. 14-22, 'Return of the General and Staff Officers and Officers of the Hospitals (including Garrison Officers and the several Persons employed in the Military Departments) attached to the Forces serving in Nova Scotia and its Dependencies from the 25th of December 1802 to 24th of June 1803 inclusive'.

33. TNA, WO 17/1760, Monthly Return France 1815

34. Mesrob Vartavarian, 'An Open Military Economy: The British Conquest of South India Reconsidered, 1780-1799', *Journal of the Economic and Social History of the Orient*, 57.4 (2014), p. 500.

35. Buckley, *The British Army in the West Indies*, pp. 128–35.

36. Jennine Hurl-Eamon, *Marriage and the British Army in the Long Eighteenth Century : 'The Girl I Left behind Me'* (Oxford: Oxford University Press, 2014). See also John A. Lynn, 'Essential Women, Necessary Wives, and Exemplary Soldiers: The Military Reality and Cultural Representation of Women's Military Participation (1600–1815)', in *A Companion to Women's Military History*, ed. by Barton Hacker and Margaret Vining (Brill, 2012), pp. 93–136; Charles J. Esdaile, *Women in the Peninsular War* (Norman: University of Oklahoma Press, 2014); and F.C.G. Page, *Following the Drum: Women in Wellington's Wars* (London: Andre Deutsch, 1986).

37. TNA, WO 380/3, entry for 4th Royal Veteran Battalion.

38. Fortescue, *History of the British Army*, vol. 4 part 1, pp. 493–4.

39. Archibald Forbes, *The 'Black Watch': The Record of an Historic Regiment* (London: Cassell and Company, 1896), p. 157.

40. Hurl-Eamon, *Marriage and the British Army*, pp. 22–6; Richard Glover, *Peninsular Preparation*, p. 221.

41. Bamford, *Sickness, Suffering, and the Sword*, pp. 263–4.

42. Arthur Wellesley, *Supplementary Despatches and Memoranda of Field Marshal Arthur, Duke of Wellington, K. G.* , ed. by Arthur Richard Wellesley, 15 vols (London: J. Murray, 1858), vol. 1, pp. 125–6, 203–05.

43. Paul L. Dawson, *Boots and Saddles!: Horses and Riders of Wellington's Army* (Stockton-on-Tees: Black Tent Publications, 2014), pp. 62–75.

44. Andrew Bamford, 'British Army Unit Strengths: 1808-1815', *The Napoleon Series* <https://www.napoleonseries.org/military/organization/Britain/Strength/Bamford/c_BritishArmyStrengthStudyIndividualUnitsCavalry.html>; TNA, WO 17/11 Monthly Returns 3 Dragoon Guards, 1799-1812; TNA, WO 17/255, Monthly Returns 1 Life Guards-2 Dragoons, 1813; TNA, WO 17/271, Monthly Returns 1 Life Guards-9 Dragoons, 1814.

45. Bamford, *Sickness, Suffering, and the Sword*, p. 266.

46. Ibid.

47. Harry Calvert, 'Return of the Effective Strength of the British Army, in Rank and File, in Each Year from the Year 1804 to the Year 1813, Inclusive;--Distinguishing Cavalry, Artillery, Infantry, and Militia, and British from Foreign and Colonial Corps', *Commons Papers*, 1813 vol. 11, p. 269.

48. TNA, WO 17/2560.

49. Dawson, *Boots and Saddles!* , p. 184.

50. *Commons Journals*, vol. 50, cols. 162–163 & 446–448 and vol. 51, cols. 667–668; *8th Report of the Commissioners of Military Enquiry*, pp. 221–6.

51. Bamford, *Sickness, Suffering, and the Sword*, pp. 220–1 and 235.

52. TNA, WO 17/2814, 'Monthly Summaries and Annual Abstracts of Effectives and Casualties of British and Foreign Corps at Home and Abroad, 1805-1816'.

53. Bamford, *Sickness, Suffering, and the Sword*.

54. Martin R. Howard, 'Walcheren 1809: A Medical Catastrophe', *British Medical Journal*, 319.7225 (1999), pp. 1642–5.

55. TNA, WO 17/1159, 'General Returns, 1793 to 1795'; Catherine Kelly, *War and the Militarization of British Army Medicine, 1793-1830* (London: Pickering & Chatto, 2011), pp. 21–4.

56. Kelly, *War and the Militarization of British Army Medicine*, pp. 81–8.

57. Mark Harrison, 'Disease and Medicine in the Armies of British India, 1750-1830: The Treatment of Fevers and the Emergence of Tropical Therapeutics', in *British Military and Naval Medicine, 1600-1830* (Amsterdam; New York: Rodopi, 2007), pp. 87–119; Douglas M. Peers, 'Imperial Vice: Sex, Drink and the Health of British Troops in North Indian Cantonments, 1800-1858', in *Guardians of Empire: The Armed Forces of the Colonial Powers c.1700-1964* (Manchester: Manchester University Press, 1999), pp. 25–52.

58. Duffy, *Soldiers, Sugar, and Seapower*, p. 333.

59. Buckley, *British Army in the West Indies*, p. 276.

60. In 1802 there were 1,350 deaths: Buckley, *British Army in the West Indies*, p. 276; there were 2,630 deaths in 1803 and 1804: Robert Jackson, *A Sketch of the History and Cure of Febrile Diseases: More Particularly as They Appear in the West-Indies Among the Soldiers of the British Army* (Stockton: T. and H. Eeles, 1817), p. 586.

61. Sheldon Watts, 'Yellow Fever Immunities in West Africa and the Americas in the Age of Slavery and beyond: A Reappraisal', *Journal of Social History*, 34.4 (2001), pp. 955–67.

62. Rana A. Hogarth, 'An African Corps in a Most Distressed and Sickly Condition: Yellow Fever in the West Indies', in *Medicalizing Blackness, Making Racial Difference in the Atlantic World, 1780-1840* (University of North Carolina Press, 2017), pp. 48–78.

63. Michael Joseph, 'Military Officers, Tropical Medicine, and Racial Thought in the Formation of the West India Regiments, 1793–1802', *Journal of the History of Medicine and Allied Sciences*, 72.2 (2017), pp. 142–65.

64. James McGrigor, *Medical Sketches of the Expedition to Egypt from India* (London: Printed for John Murray, 32, Fleet-Street; Edinburgh: Bell and Bradfute; Dublin: Gilbert and Hodges, 1804).

65. Enslaved Africans served in all the Ceylon Regiments, and were concentrated into the 3rd and 4th Ceylon Regiment by 1811: G. Tylden, 'The Ceylon Regiments, 1796 to 1874', *Journal of the Society for Army Historical Research*, 30.123 (1952), pp. 124–5; Enslaved East Africans were purchased for the Bourbon Regiment in French Mauritius: Randolph Jones, 'The Bourbon Regiment and the Barbados Slave Revolt of 1816', *Journal of the Society for Army Historical Research*, 78.313 (2000), pp. 3–5.

66. TNA, WO 40/19, W.H. Clinton to Matthew Lewis, 19 July 1806; WO 26/39, fol. 196, Warrant for York Rangers.

67. TNA, WO 380/1, fol. 259. There were fifty recruits in Nova Scotia who were discharged and given an allowance of 14 days' pay after disbanding.

68. Bamford, *Sickness, Suffering, and the Sword*, pp. 142–56.

69. Ibid., pp. 86–126.

70. Neil Cantlie, *A History of the Army Medical Department*, 2 vols (Edinburgh: Churchill Livingstone, 1974); Richard L. Blanco, *Wellington's Surgeon General: Sir James McGrigor* (Durham (NC), 1974); Martin Howard, *Wellington's Doctors: The British Army Medical Services in the Napoleonic Wars* (Staplehurst: Spellmount, 2002); Marcus Ackroyd and others, *Advancing with the Army : Medicine, the Professions, and Social Mobility in the British Isles, 1790-1850* (Oxford: Oxford University Press, 2006); Buckley, *British Army in the West Indies*, chap. 8.

71. Robert P. Hudson, *Disease and Its Control: The Shaping of Modern Thought* (New York: Praeger, 1983).

72. Kelly, *War and the Militarization of British Army Medicine*, pp. 13–17.

73. Ibid., pp. 18, 21–50.

74. *The Fifth Report of the Commissioners of Military Enquiry: Army Medical Department*, (1808); Kelly, *War and the Militarization of British Army Medicine*, pp. 36–50.

75. Kelly, *War and the Militarization of British Army Medicine*, pp. 42–3.

76. Buckley, *British Army in the West Indies*, pp. 298–302.

77. Peter H. Niebyl, 'The English Bloodletting Revolution, or Modern Medicine before 1850', *Bulletin of the History of Medicine; Baltimore, Md.*, 51.3 (1977), pp. 464–83; Buckley, *British Army in the West Indies*, p. 280.

78. Linch, *Britain and Wellington's Army*, p. 112; Cantlie, *Army Medical Department*, vol. 1, p. 275.

Chapter 6: Enlisted Men

1. Hampshire Record Office, 4M81/PO40/2, William Birchall to His wife and child, 19 March 1798.

2. TNA, WO 13/3875 to /3877; WO 12/3294 to /3296, /3234 to /3297.

3. For a longer discussion about this quote, see Edward J. Coss, *All for the King's Shilling: The British Soldier under Wellington, 1808-1814* (Norman: University of Oklahoma Press, 2010), pp. 29–49.

4. Cozens, 'The Experience of Soldiering', pp. 90–1.

5. Clode, *Military Forces of the Crown*, vol. 2, pp. 1–8.

6. Coss, *All for the King's Shilling*, pp. 50–85.

7. Roger A. Wells, *Wretched Faces: Famine in Wartime England, 1793-1801* (Gloucester: Sutton, 1988).

8. TNA, WO 17/2813, 'Scale of Bounty', 1802.

9. TNA, WO 123/117, Harry Calvert, 'General Orders', 1808.

10. Western, 'The Recruitment of the Land Forces, pp. 9–10.

11. TNA, WO 123/117, Harry Calvert, 'General Orders', 1803, and 1808.

12. Western, 'The Recruitment of the Land Forces, pp. 104–11. See also: Andrew Mackillop, *More Fruitful than the Soil: Army, Empire, and the Scottish Highlands, 1715-1815* (East Linton: Tuckwell, 2000), chap. 5; Prebble, *Mutiny*, esp. chaps 3–5.

13. Linch, *Britain and Wellington's Army*, pp. 64–7.

14. Western, 'The County Fencibles and Militia Augmentation of 1794', *Journal of the Society for Army Historical Research*, 34.137 (1956), pp. 3–11.

15. Western, 'The Recruitment of the Land Forces', p. 148; Fortescue, *The County Lieutenancies*, pp. 40–57, 70–4; Linch, *Britain and Wellington's Army*, p. 58.

16. Cozens, 'The Experience of Soldiering, pp. 70–84; Linch, *Britain and Wellington's Army*, pp. 90–8.

17. National Army Museum, NAM. 1976-06-21-1, *The Old Saucy Seventh, or Queen's Own Regt of Lt. Dragoons*, 1809.

18. 'The Loyal Berkshire Volunteers', *Reading Mercury*, 17 November 1794, p. 3.

19. 'Follow the Drum', 1797, Broadside Ballads Online, Bod1582 <http://ballads.bodleian.ox.ac.uk/static/images/sheets/15000/13664.gif>.

20. Ibid.

21. Ilya Berkovich, *Motivation in War: The Experience of Common Soldiers in Old-Regime Europe* (Cambridge, United Kingdom ; Cambridge University Press, 2017), chap. 4.

22. Linch, 'The Recruitment of the British Army', pp. 195–6.

23. Patricia Y. C. E. Lin, 'Caring for the Nation's Families : British Soldiers' and Sailors' Families and the State, 1793-1815', in *Soldiers, Citizens and Civilians: Experiences and Perceptions of the Revolutionary and Napoleonic Wars, 1790-1820* (Basingstoke: Palgrave Macmillan, 2009), pp. 111–13.

24. Zeta Mary Moore, 'Army Recruitment and the Uncertainties of the "fiscal-Military" State in Britain, 1793-1815' (unpublished Ph.D., Royal Holloway, University of London, 2006), pp. 116–24.

25. Linch, 'The Recruitment of the British Army', pp. 130–1.

26. See, for example, Katrina Honeyman, *Child Workers in England, 1780-1820: Parish Apprentices and the Making of the Early Industrial Labour Force*, Studies in Labour History (Aldershot: Ashgate, 2007).

27. Linch, 'The Recruitment of the British Army', pp. 129–30.

28. T.A. Bowyer-Bower, 'A Pioneer of Army Education: The Royal Military Asylum, Chelsea, 1801-1821', *British Journal of Educational Studies*, 2.2 (1954), pp. 122–32; A. W. Cockerill, 'The Royal Military Asylum (1803-15)', *Journal of the Society for Army Historical Research*, 79.317 (2001), pp. 25–44.

29. Harry Calvert, 'State of the British Army, Distinguishing the Number of Men and Boys Who Are Engaged for Limited Service Only, from Those Who Are Engaged for Service for Life', *Commons Papers*, 1808 vol. 7, p. 185; Harry Calvert, 'Return of the Number of Men Raised for the Regular Army, Exclusive of Foreign and Colonial Corps, by Ordinary Recruiting, and by Transfers from the Militia, &c.;--during the Last Ten Years', *Commons Papers*, 1813 vol. 11, p. 263; Harry Calvert, 'Return of the Number of Recruits Raised Monthly, for the Regular Army, between 25th December 1812 and 25th December 1813, by the Ordinary Modes of Recruiting (Exclusive of Foreign and Colonial Corps); Distinguishing Men and Boys, and Those Enlisted for Life or for a Term of Years', *Commons Papers*, 1814 vol. 11, p. 273; Harry Calvert, 'Return of the Number of Recruits Raised Monthly, from 25th December 1813, to 25th December 1814, by the Ordinary Modes of Recruiting, Exclusive of Foreign and Colonial Corps; Distinguishing Men and Boys, and Those Enlisted for Life or for a Term of Years', *Commons Papers*, 1815 vol. 11, p. 309; Harry Calvert, 'Return of the Number of Recruits Raised Monthly, from the 25th December 1811, to the 25th December 1815; Distinguishing Men and Boys, and Those Enlisted for Life or for a Term of Years', *Commons Papers*, 1816 vol. 12, p. 423.

30. Linch, 'The Recruitment of the British Army', pp. 195–6.

31. Wishon, *German Forces and the British Army*, pp. 143–54.

32. For the broader history of emigration to Britain in response to the French Revolution, see Juliette Reboul, *French Emigration to Great Britain in Response to the French Revolution* (Basingstoke: Palgrave Macmillan, 2017); R.J.W. Mills, '"L'Île Des Bannis": Jersey, Britain and the French Emigration 1789–1815', *European Review of History: Revue Européenne d'histoire*, 28.1 (2021), pp. 99–123. For a study of a unit, see Hughes de Bazouges and Alistair Nichols, *For God and King: A History of the Damas Legion* (Helion and Company, 2021).

33. Wishon, *German Forces and the British Army*, pp. 157–8.

34. Grainger, *British Campaigns in the South Atlantic*, p. 34.

35. C. T. Atkinson, 'Foreign Regiments in The British Army, 1793-1802: Part VI, Section II', *Journal of the Society for Army Historical Research*, 22.90 (1944), 234–50. For Surinam, see Griffith, *Riflemen*, pp. 77–8.

36. C.T. Atkinson, 'Foreign Regiments in The British Army, 1793-1802: Part III—Quiberon', *Journal of the Society for Army Historical Research*, 22.86 (1943), pp. 45–52.

37. Linch, 'The Politics of Foreign Recruitment', *Transnational Soldiers*, pp. 50–66.

38. Cozens, 'The Experience of Soldiering', p. 63.

39. Pimlott, 'The Administration of the British Army', pp. 225–30.

40. Linch, *Britain and Wellington's Army*, p. 145.

41. The Royal West India Rangers minimum height standard was even lower at 5ft 1in (1.55m), 5in shorter than it was for the rest of the infantry; TNA, WO 380/4.

42. Michael Durey, 'White Slaves: Irish Rebel Prisoners and The British Army in The West Indies 1799-1804', *Journal of the Society for Army Historical Research*, 80.324 (2002), pp. 296–312.

43. Richard Glover, *Peninsular Preparation*, pp. 183–5.

44. Cozens, 'The Experience of Soldiering', p. 65.

45. Buckley, *British Army in the West Indies*, pp. 93–9; James J. Willis, 'Transportation versus Imprisonment in Eighteenth- and Nineteenth-Century Britain: Penal Power, Liberty, and the State', *Law & Society Review*, 39.1 (2005), pp. 171–210.

46. Buckley, *Slaves in Red Coats*, pp. 55–6.

47. Ibid., pp. 130–4.

48. John E. Cookson, 'Regimental Worlds: Interpreting the Experience of British Soldiers during the Napoleonic Wars', in *Soldiers, Citizens and Civilians: Experiences and Perceptions of the French Wars, 1790-1820*, ed. by Alan Forrest, Karen Hagemann, and Jane Rendall (Basingstoke: Palgrave Macmillan, 2009), pp. 32–6.

49. Adjutant-General's Office, *General Regulations and Orders* (London; Quebec: G. Roworth, Printer ...; Reprinted by John Neilson, 1804), p. 28.

50. Danielle S.E. Coombs, 'Crime and the Soldier: Identifying a Soldier-Specific Experience of Crime in the British Army, 1740-1830' (unpublished Ph.D., University of Leeds, 2015), pp. 185–217.

51. Linch, 'The Recruitment of the British Army', pp. 29–30; A. S. White, 'Garrison, Reserve and Veteran Battalions and Companies', *Journal of the Society for Army Historical Research*, 38.156 (1960), pp. 156–67.

52. Bamford, *Sickness, Suffering, and the Sword*, pp. 114–26.

53. Coss, *All for the King's Shilling*, pp. 86–7.

54. Buckley, *British Army in the West Indies*, pp. 327–32.

55. Stephen Conway, *The British Army, 1714–1783: An Institutional History* (Pen & Sword Military, 2021), p. 6. For the barrack-building programme, see Cozens, 'The Experience of Soldiering'.

56. Bamford, *Sickness, Suffering, and the Sword*, pp. 241–2.

57. Adjutant-General's Office, *General Regulations and Orders* (London; Quebec: G. Roworth, Printer …; Reprinted by John Neilson, 1804), p. 26

58. Buckley, *British Army in the West Indies*, p. 332.

59. *General Regulations and Orders for the Conduct of His Majesty's Forces in Great Britain* ([London], 1799), p. 176.

60. Linch, 'The Recruitment of the British Army', p. 109.

61. Oman, *Wellington's Army*, p. 294

62. Coss, *All for the King's Shilling*, pp. 135–44.

63. Zack White, 'Pragmatism & Discretion: Discipline in the British Army, 1808-1818' (unpublished PhD, University of Southampton, 2022).

64. *General Regulations and Orders for the Conduct of His Majesty's Forces in Great Britain* ([London], 1799), pp. 15, 61, 74, 174–7; *General Regulations and Orders* (London; Quebec: G. Roworth, Printer …; Reprinted by John Neilson, 1804), pp. 19 and 53.

65. G. A. Steppler, 'British Military Law, Discipline, and the Conduct of Regimental Courts Martial in the Later Eighteenth Century', *The English Historical Review*, 102.405 (1987), pp. 862–3.

66. *General Regulations and Orders for the Conduct of His Majesty's Forces in Great Britain* ([London], 1799), pp. 174–7.

67. *General Regulations and Orders* (London; Quebec: G. Roworth, Printer …; Reprinted by John Neilson, 1804), p. 53.

68. *General Regulations and Orders for the Conduct of His Majesty's Forces in Great Britain* ([London], 1799), pp. 26, 74, 173; *Standing Orders and Regulations for the Army in Ireland* (Dublin, 1794), p. 3.

69. *General Regulations and Orders for the Conduct of His Majesty's Forces in Great Britain* ([London], 1799), p. 7

70. Pimlott, 'The Administration of the British Army', pp. 199–201.

71. *General Regulations and Orders for the Conduct of His Majesty's Forces in Great Britain* ([London], 1799), pp. 143–56.

72. Coss, *All for the King's Shilling*, pp. 73–4.

73. Cozens, 'The Experience of Soldiering', p. 111.

74. Coss, *All for the King's Shilling*, pp. 91–4.

75. Buckley, *British Army in the West Indies*, pp. 350–1.

76. Neema Cherian, 'Spaces for Races: Ordering of Camp Followers in the Military Cantonments, Madras Presidency, c. 1800-64', *Social Scientist*, 32.5–6 (2004), pp. 32–50.

77. Coss, *All for the King's Shilling*, pp. 89–91.

78. TNA, WO 3/19, fols. 152-153, Harry Calvert to Lieutenant General Garth, 22 January 1799.

79. TNA, WO 4/206, fols. 231-235, J. Pulteney, Circular, 12 August 1808.

80. Cantlie, *A History of the Army Medical Department*, vol. 1, p. 202; R.N.W Thomas, *No Want of Courage: The British Army in Flanders, 1793-1795* (Warwick: Helion & Co Ltd, 2022), pp. 163–4.

81. Prebble, *Mutiny*.

82. Pimlott, 'The Administration of the British Army, pp. 1–5.

83. Clive Emsley, 'The Military and Popular Disorder in England 1790-1801 (Continued)', *Journal of the Society for Army Historical Research*, 61.246 (1983), pp. 96–112.

84. 'Mutiny in Ireland', *Kentish Gazette*, 1 September 1795, p. 3.

85. Elizabeth Longford, 'Edward, Prince, Duke of Kent and Strathearn (1767–1820)', *Oxford Dictionary of National Biography* <https://doi.org/10.1093/ref:odnb/8526>.

86. Cozens, 'The Experience of Soldiering', pp. 103–06 and 114–17.

87. Pimlott, 'The Administration of the British Army', p. 223.

88. Kevin Linch, 'Desertion from the British Army during the Napoleonic Wars', *Journal of Social History*, 49.4 (2016), pp. 808–28.

89. Bamford, *Sickness, Suffering, and the Sword*, p. 243.
90. Coombs, 'Crime and the Soldier', pp. 69–80.
91. Ibid., pp. 85–93.
92. Paul E. Kopperman, '"The Cheapest Pay": Alcohol Abuse in the Eighteenth-Century British Army', *Journal of Military History*, 60.3 (1996), pp. 445–70.
93. *Constructive Drinking: Perspectives on Drink from Anthropology*, ed. by Mary Douglas (Abingdon, Oxon: Routledge, 2003), pp. 4–5.
94. Jonathan Reinarz and Rebecca Wynter, 'The Spirit of Medicine: The Use of Alcohol in Nineteenth-Century Medical Practice', in *Drink in the Eighteenth and Nineteenth Centuries*, ed. by Barbara Schmidt-Haberkamp and Susanne Schmid (Pickering & Chatto), pp. 127–40.
95. TNA, WO 2/1, index entry for 'Madeira'.
96. Buckley, *The British Army in the West Indies*, pp. 284–5.
97. Paul Jennings, *A History of Drink and the English, 1500-2000* (London: Routledge, 2016), chap. 1.
98. Coss, *All for the King's Shilling*, pp. 117–19.
99. Ibid., pp. 94–111.
100. Coombs, 'Crime and the Soldier', pp. 147–83 and 218–47.
101. J.M. Beattie, *Crime and the Courts in England, 1660-1800* (Clarendon Press, 1986), p. 187; Matt Neale, 'Making Crime Pay in Late Eighteenth-Century Bristol: Stolen Goods, the Informal Economy and the Negotiation of Risk', *Continuity and Change*, 26.3 (2011), pp. 439–59.
102. Cookson, 'Regimental Worlds', *Soldiers, Citizens and Civilians*, pp. 23–42.
103. Bamford, *Sickness, Suffering, and the Sword*, pp. 44–60.
104. Cookson, 'Regimental Worlds', *Soldiers, Citizens and Civilians*, p. 26.
105. Wishon, *German Forces and the British Army*, pp. 183–90.
106. Buckley, *British Army in the West Indies*, pp. 1–40.
107. Gavin Daly, *The British Soldier in the Peninsular War: Encounters with Spain and Portugal, 1808-1814* (Houndmills, Basingstoke; New York: Palgrave Macmillan, 2013).
108. Simon Quinn, 'British Military Orientalism: Cross-Cultural Contact with the Mamluks during the Egyptian Campaign, 1801', *War in History*, 28.2 (2019), pp. 263–82; Simon Quinn, 'Orientalists in Uniform?: British Military Encounters and Experiences in Egypt, *c.*1798-1801' (unpublished Ph.D., University of York, 2017).

Chapter 7: Officers

1. National Records Scotland, GD51/6/557, Mrs Sarah Campbell to Henry Dundas, 8 May 1800.
2. For the French Army, see Rafe Blaufarb, 'Noble Privilege and Absolutist State Building: French Military Administration after the Seven Years' War', *French Historical Studies*, 24.2 (2001), pp. 223–46; for Spain see Graciela Iglesias Rogers, *British Liberators in the Age of Napoleon; Volunteering under the Spanish Flag in the Peninsular War* (London; New York: Bloomsbury, 2013), pp. 21–2.
3. Pimlott, 'The Administration of the British Army', pp. 85–6.
4. Pimlott, 'The Raising of Four Regiments for India, 1787-8', *Journal of the Society for Army Historical Research*, 52.210 (1974), pp. 68–88.
5. Pimlott, 'The Administration of the British Army', p. 64.
6. Ibid., p. 97; Houlding, 'The Number of Commissioned British Military Officers, 1725-1792', *Journal of the Society for Army Historical Research*, 91.366 (2013), pp. 92–7.
7. Details about this office emerged during the 1809 Inquiry into Duke of York's conduct: 'Minutes of Evidence, Taken before the Committee of the Whole House, upon the Conduct of His Royal Highness the Commander in Chief', *Commons Papers*, 1809 vol. 2, p. 504.
8. Richard Glover, *Peninsular Preparation*, pp. 146–7.

9. James, *The Regimental Companion*, 1800, vol. 1, pp. 27–8.

10. Houlding, 'The Number of Commissioned British Military Officers, 1725-1792', *Journal of the Society for Army Historical Research*, 91.366 (2013), p. 95; TNA, WO 17/1159, June 1795; WO 17/2558, June 1795; William Windham, 'Return of Emigrant and Foreign Forces, on the 1st August 1795', *House of Commons Sessional Papers*, vol. 100, pp. 49–52.

11. Western, 'Recruitment of the Land Forces', pp. 39, 42–3.

12. M. H. Port, 'Thomas, Sir George, 3rd Bt. (c.1748–1815), of Dale Park, Nr. Arundel, Suss.', *History of Parliament Online* <http://www.historyofparliamentonline.org/volume/1790-1820/member/thomas-sir-george-1748-1815>.

13. 'Christopher Teesdale', *Westminster Abbey* <https://www.westminster-abbey.org/abbey-commemorations/commemorations/christopher-teesdale>.

14. Peter Mandler, 'Hall, Samuel Carter (1800–1889), Journal Editor and Writer', *Oxford Dictionary of National Biography*, 2008 <https://doi.org/10.1093/ref:odnb/11987>.

15. David R. Fisher, 'Burland, John Berkeley (1754–1804), of Steyning, Stogursey, Som. and Stock House, Stock Gaylard, Dorset', *History of Parliament Online* <http://www.historyofparliamentonline.org/volume/1790-1820/member/burland-john-berkeley-1754-1804>.

16. C.A. Harris, 'Nickle, Sir Robert (1786–1855), Army Officer', *Oxford Dictionary of National Biography*, 2004 <https://doi.org/10.1093/ref:odnb/20158>.

17. Western, 'Recruitment of the Land Forces', pp. 318–26.

18. Linch, *Britain and Wellington's Army*, p. 78.

19. TNA, WO 3/604, Lieutenant-Colonel Henry Torrens to Henry Addington, 28 December 1812.

20. Martin's career: TNA, WO 65/64, p. 255; TNA, WO 65/62, p. 197; *The London Gazette*, 11 February 1809, issue 16228, p. 193. Bowen's: *By Permission of His Excellency the Lord Lieutenant. A List of the Officers of the Several Regiments of Fencible Cavalry and Infantry, and of the Several Regiments and Battalions of Militia, with the Dates of Their Respective Commissions upon the Establishment of Ireland, (with an Alphabetical Index.)* (Dublin: Printed by James King and Abraham Bradley King, printers to the Honourable the House of Commons, No. 72, Dame-Street, 1796), p. 36; *The London Gazette*, 1 March 1800, issue 15235, p. 216; TNA, WO 65/61, p. 175; TNA, WO 65/55, p. 170; TNA, WO 65/55, p. 333; TNA, WO 65/50, p. 286; TNA, WO 65/50, p. 287; 'Deaths', *Bristol Times and Mirror*, 24 April 1842, p. 4.

21. Houlding, *Fit for Service*, p. 103.

22. Elizabeth Baigent, 'Brereton, Thomas (1782–1832), Army Officer', *Oxford Dictionary of National Biography* <https://doi.org/10.1093/ref:odnb/3331>.

23. *The London Gazette*, 2 October 1813, p. 1961. For the appointments in the immediate aftermath of Waterloo, see: *The London Gazette*, 1 July 1815, issue 17032, p. 1278; *The London Gazette*, 8 July 1815, issue 17037, p. 1353; *The London Gazette*, 29 July 1815, issue 17045, p. 1538 and p. 1540; *The London Gazette*, 26 August 1815, issue 17055, p. 1738.

24. In the end, he received a commission before he served as a volunteer. Thomas Fernyhough, Robert Fernyhough, and John Fernyhough, *Military Memoirs of Four Brothers, (Natives of Staffordshire) Engaged in the Service of Their Country, as Well in the New World and Africa, as on the Continent of Europe* (London: W. Sams, 1829), pp. 152–85.

25. David Huf, 'The Junior British Army Officer: Experience and Identity, 1793-1815' (unpublished PhD, University of Tasmania, 2017), p. 47.

26. For his obituary, see 'Deaths', *Manchester Courier*, 1 April 1846, p. 6.

27. For a list of some, see Steve Brown, 'Wellington's Sharpes: British Army Ranker Officers 1793-1815' <https://www.napoleon-series.org/research/biographies/GreatBritain/c_Wellington'sSharpes.html>.

28. Richard Glover, *Peninsular Preparation*, pp. 205–10.

29. Charles Dalton, *The Waterloo Roll Call. With Biographical Notes and Anecdotes*, 2nd edn (London: Eyre and Spottiswoode, 1904), p. 32.

30. Ibid., pp. 170, 174.

31. TNA, WO 76/244; 'Walmer', *Kentish Gazette*, 25 June 1861, p. 6.

32. Frederick Gordon Guggisberg, *'The Shop'; the Story of the Royal Military Academy.* (London, New York: Cassell, 1902), p. 12, 13, 42; Richard Glover, *Peninsular Preparation*, pp. 191–3.

33. Ibid., pp. 44 and 75.

34. John Kane, *List of Officers of the Royal Regiment of Artillery, as They Stood in the Year 1763, with a Continuation to the Present Time ... with a List of the Officers of the Corps of Royal Artillery Drivers ... and of the Officers of the Military Medical Department of the Ordnance, since 1763; with a List of the Chief Commissaries ...* (Greenwich: printed by Elizabeth Delahoy, Albion Printing Office, 1815), pp. 48–51.

35. Guggisberg, *'The Shop'*, p. 76.

36. Kane, *List of Officers of the Royal Regiment of Artillery*.

37. Guggisberg, *'The Shop'*, pp. 13 and 42.

38. Kane, *List of Officers of the Royal Regiment of Artillery*.

39. C.T. Atkinson, 'Foreign Regiments in The British Army, 1793-1802: Part VI, Section III', *Journal of the Society for Army Historical Research*, 22.91 (1944), pp. 273–6.

40. Alistair Nichols, *Wellington's Mongrel Regiment: A History of the Chasseurs Britanniques Regiment 1801-1814* (Staplehurst: Spellmount, 2005), pp. 185–204.

41. Charles James, *The Regimental Companion: Containing the Pay, Allowances and Relative Duties of Every Officer in the British Service*, 4 vols (London: Printed for T. Egerton ... by C. Roworth ..., 1811), vol. 2, pp. 20–4 and 51.

42. Burley, 'An Age of Negligence? British Army Chaplaincy', pp. 36–68.

43. Bartlett, 'The Development of the British Army', pp. 78–81.

44. Charles James, *The Regimental Companion* (London: printed for T. Egerton [by C. Roworth], 1800), vol. 1, pp. 101–02; Charles James, *The Regimental Companion* (London: Printed for T. Egerton ... by C. Roworth ..., 1811), vol. 3, pp. 354–56.

45. P. E. Razzell, 'Social Origins of Officers in the Indian and British Home Army: 1758-1962', *The British Journal of Sociology*, 14.3 (1963), p. 255.

46. Evan Wilson, *A Social History of British Naval Officers, 1775-1815* (Woodbridge, Suffolk: The Boydell Press, 2017).

47. Rory Muir, *Gentlemen of Uncertain Fortune: How Younger Sons Made Their Way in Jane Austen's England* (New Haven: Yale University Press, 2019), pp. 242–58.

48. Huf, 'The Junior British Army Officer', p. 19

49. H.M. Chichester, 'Bingham, Sir George Ridout (1777–1833), Army Officer', *Oxford Dictionary of National Biography*, 2011 <https://doi.org/10.1093/ref:odnb/2408>.

50. Ronald Bayne and Elizabeth Baigent, 'Barker, Collet (1784–1831), Army Officer and Explorer', *Oxford Dictionary of National Biography*, 2004 <https://doi.org/10.1093/ref:odnb/1391>.

51. Jonathan Spain, 'Beckwith, Sir George (1752/3–1823), Army Officer and Colonial Governor', *Oxford Dictionary of National Biography*, 2008 <https://doi.org/10.1093/ref:odnb/1911>; H. M. Stephens and Roger T. Stearn, 'Beckwith, Sir Thomas Sydney (1772–1831), Army Officer', *Oxford Dictionary of National Biography*, 2004 <https://doi.org/10.1093/ref:odnb/1915>. John Beckwith's grandson also served in the Army: H. M. Stephens and James Lunt, 'Beckwith, John Charles (1789–1862), Army Officer and Missionary', *Oxford Dictionary of National Biography*, 2008 <https://doi.org/10.1093/ref:odnb/1912>.

52. Huf, 'The Junior British Army Officer', p. 77.

53. J.E. Cookson, 'Service without Politics? Army, Militia and Volunteers in Britain during the American and French Revolutionary Wars', *War in History*, 10.4 (2003), pp. 381–97.

54. Catriona Kennedy, *Narratives of the Revolutionary and Napoleonic Wars: Military and Civilian Experience in Britain and Ireland* (Basingstoke: Palgrave Macmillan, 2013), pp. 55–6.

55. Huf, 'The Junior British Army Officer', pp. 74–7; Cookson, 'Service without Politics', *War in History*, 10.4 (2003), pp. 381–97.

56. Daly, *The British Soldier in the Peninsular War*, pp. 60–90; Gavin Daly, 'Liberators and Tourists: British Soldiers in Madrid during the Peninsular War', in *Soldiering in Britain and Ireland, 1750-1850: Men of Arms*, ed. by Catriona Kennedy and Matthew McCormack (Palgrave Macmillan, 2013), pp. 117–35.

57. Kennedy, *Narratives of the Revolutionary and Napoleonic Wars*, pp. 40–1; Matthew McCormack, *The Independent Man: Citizenship and Gender Politics in Georgian England* (Manchester, U.K.; New York: Manchester University Press, 2011).

58. Colley, *Britons*, pp. 177–92.

59. Houlding, *Fit for Service*, pp. 108–15.

60. TNA, WO 65/44, im. 150. *Dublin Gazette*, 4 November 1794, issue 6088, p. 1825; TNA, WO 65/44, im. 150. *The London Gazette*, 9 December 1794, issue 13730, p. 1211; *The London Gazette*, 2 May 1795, issue 13775, p. 411; TNA, WO 65/48, im. 39.

61. *The London Gazette*, 27 September 1794, issue 13708, p. 985; TNA, WO 65/43, im. 283; WO 65/45, im. 111; *The London Gazette*, 8 September 1795, issue 13812, p. 929; *The London Gazette*, 27 October 1795, issue 13826, p. 1115.

62. *The London Gazette*, 27 September 1794, issue 13708, p. 988; *The London Gazette*, 16 December 1794, issue 13732, p. 1241; TNA, WO 65/49, p. 62; WO 65/50, p. 60.

63. TNA, WO 65/62, p. 232; WO 65/63, p. 245; WO 65/64, p. 294, WO 65/65, p. 245

64. 'New Plan of Arrangement for the Medical Staff', *Evening Mail*, 2 April 1804, p. 3. See also Ackroyd and others, *Advancing with the Army*.

65. 'Gunning, John (1773–1863)', *Plarr's Lives of the Fellows* <https:// livesonline.rcseng.ac.uk/client/en_GB/lives/search/results?qu=%22RCS: E000405%22&rt=false|||IDENTIFIER|||Resource+Identifier>; *Public Ledger and Daily Advertiser*, 15 August 1805, p. 1.

66. Adye's career: *The London Gazette*, 29 December 1812, issue 16687, p. 2; 24 July 1810, issue 16390, p. 1095; 10 May 1803, issue 15583, p. 551; 10 November 1798, issue 15079, p. 1072; 7 January 1794, issue 13611, p. 23; 23 April 1793, issue 13522, p. 332. For Shand's death, *Aberdeen Press and Journal*, 20 April 1803, p. 4. For Duncan's death: Kane, *List of Officers of the Royal Regiment of Artillery*, p. 20.

67. Richard Glover, *Peninsular Preparation*, pp. 158–60.

68. A.P.C. Bruce, *The Purchase System in the British Army, 1660-1871* (London: Royal Historical Society, 1980), pp. 36–7.

69. *General Regulations and Orders for the Army* (London: W. Clowes, 1811), p. 31.

70. Bruce, *The Purchase System*, pp. 38–9.

71. Western, 'The Recruitment of the Land Forces', pp. 64–5.

72. Charles James, *The Regimental Companion* (London: Printed for T. Egerton ... by C. Roworth ..., 1811), vol. 1, pp. 66–7.

73. Western, 'The Recruitment of the Land Forces', p. 70.

74. Bruce, *The Purchase System*, pp. 50–1.

75. Ibid., pp. 53, 58–61.

76. Michael Glover, *Wellington's Army: In the Peninsula, 1808-1814* (Newton Abbot: David & Charles, 1977), p. 153; *General Regulations and Orders for the Army* (London: W. Clowes, 1811), p. 37.

77. Michael Glover, 'The Purchase of Commissions: A Reappraisal', *Journal of the Society for Army Historical Research*, 58.236 (1980), pp. 223–35.

78. Those that were not eligible were: officers of the King's German Legion and the Ordnance units; any rank above lieutenant-colonel; medical staff, paymasters, and commissaries.

79. Robert Jameson, *Historical Record of the Seventy-Ninth Regiment of Foot: Or Cameron Highlanders* (Edinburgh; London: William Blackwood, 1863), pp. 1–17.

80. Western, 'The Recruitment of the Land Forces', p. 47.

81. 'War Office, June 7 1803', *The London Gazette*, 4 June 1803, pp. 666–9.

82. For Wellington's early life in these years see Rory Muir, *Wellington the Path to Victory, 1769–1814* (New Haven: Yale University Press, 2013), pp. 10–26. His promotions and exchanges are recorded in the *Army Lists:* WO 65/37 (73rd and 41st Foot; 12th Light Dragoons), /41 (58th Foot), /42 (18th Light Dragoons), /43 (33rd Foot).

83. Charles James, *The Regimental Companion* (London: printed for T. Egerton [by C. Roworth], 1800), vol. 1, p. 57.

84. TNA, WO 65/63, p. 202; WO 65/62, p. 79; WO 65/61, p. 347; WO 65/61, p. 47; WO 65/59, p. 88; WO 65/59, p. 217; WO 65/57, p. 101; WO 65/56, p. 295; *The London Gazette*, 21 June 1806, issue 15930, p. 783; WO 65/54, p. 160; WO 65/54, p. 190; WO65/54, p. 143.

85. TNA, WO 65/61, p. 179; WO 65/54, p. 144; *The London Gazette*, 19 September 1795, issue 13815, p. 970; WO 65/41, im. 80; WO 65/37, im. 85; WO 65/33, p. 160; WO 65/33, p. 160; Dalton, *The Waterloo Roll Call*, p. 30. He died on 4 June 1838: *The Gentleman's Magazine*, ed. by Sylvanus Urban (London: William Pickering; John Bowyer and Son, 1838), vol. 10, pp. 102–03.

86. *The London Gazette*, 14 August 1804, issue 15728, p. 999; *The London Gazette*, 24 February 1795, issue 13755, p. 187; TNA, WO 65/39, im. 87; WO 65/36, im. 87. He eventually made lieutenant-general and died in 1862: Dalton, *The Waterloo Roll Call*, p. 146.

87. TNA, WO 65/58, p. 143; TNA, WO 65/55, p. 138; TNA, WO 65/54, p. 117. Dalton's first commission: *The London Gazette*, 26 September 1789, issue 3135, p. 625.

88. TNA, WO 65/59, p. 238; *The London Gazette*, 20 September 1803, issue 15622, p. 1266; TNA, WO 65/50, p. 300; *The London Gazette*, 7 October 1794, issue 13711, p. 1020; *The London Gazette*, 16 September 1794, issue 13704, p. 943; Dalton, *The Waterloo Roll Call*, p. 18.

89. *The London Gazette*, 26 January 1793, issue 13497, p. 82. His appointment was backdated to 19 November 1782. His request for promotion through the government was turned down in 1795; see Royal Collections Trust, GEO/MAIN/39054-39055, Henry Dundas to George, Prince of Wales, 5 March 1795.

90. Michael Glover, *Wellington's Army*, pp. 150–1.

91. For two large brevets, see 'War Office, June 7, 1813', *The London Gazette*, 5 June 1813, pp. 1099–1100; 'War-Office, June 7, 1814', *The London Gazette*, 7 June 1814, pp. 1180–7.

92. Bamford, *Sickness, Suffering, and the Sword*, pp. 177–204.

93. Davies, *Spying for Wellington*, pp. 220–1; S.G.P. Ward, 'Murray, Sir George (1772–1846)', *Oxford Dictionary of National Biography*, 2008 <https://doi.org/10.1093/ref:odnb/19608>.

94. TNA, WO 65/65, p. 294, *1815 Army List*; WO 65/63, pp. 121, 265; *1813 Army List*.

95. Cookson, 'Regimental Worlds', *Soldiers, Citizens and Civilians*, pp. 23–42.

96. Bruce Collins, 'Effectiveness and the British Officer Corps, 1793-1815', in *Britain's Soldiers: Rethinking War and Society, 1715-1815*, ed. by Kevin Linch and Matthew McCormack (Liverpool: Liverpool University Press, 2014), pp. 57–76.

97. Andrew Brown, 'Lytton, Edward George Earle Lytton Bulwer [Formerly Edward George Earle Lytton Bulwer], First Baron Lytton (1803–73), Writer and Politician', *Oxford Dictionary of National Biography*, 2004 <https://doi.org/10.1093/ref:odnb/17314>. For his military career: Ensign, 40th Foot: 15 July 1784: TNA, WO 65/34, p. 102; Lieutenant, 68th Foot, 6 October 1784: TNA, WO 65/34, p. 132; Captain, Norfolk Militia: *The London Gazette*, 5 June 1787, issue 12892, p. 274; Captain, 65th Foot, 24 December 1787: TNA, WO 65/37, p. 128; Captain, 34th Foot 11 November 1788: from half pay, 65th Foot, 11 Nov 1789, TNA, WO 65/39, p. 110; Captain, half-pay of Independent Companies: *The London Gazette*, 28 June 1792, issue 13431, p. 480; Captain, Independent Company of Foot: *The London Gazette*, 15 March 1794, issue 13632, p. 239; Major-commandant 106th Foot: *The*

London Gazette, 23 September 1794, issue 13707, p. 974; Lieutenant-colonel commandant, 106th Foot: *The London Gazette*, 14 March 1795, issue 13760, p. 243; Colonel, Norfolk Provisional Cavalry: *The London Gazette*, 25 July 1797, issue 14031, p. 700.

98. Douglas M. Peers, 'Bentinck, Lord William Henry Cavendish [Known as Lord William Bentinck] (1774–1839), Army Officer, Diplomatist, and Governor-General of India', *Oxford Dictionary of National Biography* <https://doi.org/10.1093/ref:odnb/2161>.

99. Huf, 'The Junior British Army Officer', pp. 81–7.

100. Ibid, pp. 95–8.

101. David Roberts and Thomas Rowlandson, *The Military Adventures of Johnny Newcome, with an Account of His Campaign on the Peninsula and in Pall Mall and Notes, by an Officer. With Fifteen Coloured Sketches by T. Rowlandson* (London, Methuen and co., 1904).

102. Lawrence E. Klein, 'Politeness and the Interpretation of the British Eighteenth Century', *The Historical Journal*, 45.4 (2002), pp. 869–98.

103. Huf, 'The Junior British Army Officer', pp. 48–54.

104. Daly, *The British Soldier in the Peninsular War*, pp. 60–75 and 101–02.

105. Cookson, 'Regimental Worlds', in *Soldiers, Citizens and Civilians*, pp. 23–42.

106. Daly, *The British Soldier in the Peninsular War*, pp. 115–18 and 174–9.

107. Buckley, *British Army in the West Indies*, pp. 339–48.

108. Muir, *Gentlemen of Uncertain Fortune*, p. 260.

109. Huf, 'The Junior British Army Officer', pp. 62–6.

110. TNA, WO 17/1158, Return June 1789.

111. TNA, WO 17/1159, Return April 1793.

112. TNA, WO 65/1159, Return June 1795.

113. Pimlott, 'The Administration of the British Army', pp. 211–20.

114. Richard Glover, *Peninsular Preparation*, pp. 167–8.

115. Adjutant-General's Office, *General Regulations and Orders* (London; Quebec: G. Roworth, Printer ...; Reprinted by John Neilson, 1804), pp. 40–1.

116. *General Regulations and Orders for the Army* (London: W. Clowes, 1811), pp. 43–51.

117. Ibid., pp. 55–7.

118. TNA, WO 17/1160, Return June 1799.

119. TNA, WO 17/261, Return 33rd Foot, 25 June 1813.

120. TNA, WO 17/2558, Return June 1795.

121. Richard Glover, *Peninsular Preparation*, pp. 145–6.

122. Muir, *Gentlemen of Uncertain Fortune*, p. 24.

123. Ibid., pp. 25–6, 32.

124. Orlando Bridgeman, *A Young Gentleman at War: The Letters of Captain Orlando Bridgeman 1st Foot Guards in the Peninsula and at Waterloo 1812-15*, ed. by Gareth Glover (Ken Trotman: Huntingdon, 2008), p. 169.

125. Huf, 'The Junior British Army Office', pp. 93–4.

Chapter 8: Soldiering

1. *The Dispatches of Field Marshal the Duke of Wellington: During His Various Campaigns in India, Denmark, Portugal, Spain, the Low Countries, and France, from 1799 to 1818*, ed. by John Gurwood, 13 vols (London: J. Murray, 1838), vol. 11, p. 303.

2. Fortescue, *County Lieutenancies*, p. 3.

3. Richard Glover, *Peninsular Preparation*.

4. Sir Henry Bunbury, *Narratives of Some Passages in the Great War with France, from 1799 to 1810* (London: R. Bentley, 1854), p. vii.

5. Ibid., p. xi.

6. Houlding, *Fit for Service*.

7. Richard Glover, *Peninsular Preparation*, pp. 115–21.

8. Ibid., p. 122.

9. For three different approaches to the study of battle in the era, see George Nafziger, *Imperial Bayonets: Tactics of the Napoleonic Battery, Battalion and Brigade as Found in … Contemporary Regulations* (Warwick: Helion and Company, 2021); Brent Nosworthy, *Battle Tactics of Napoleon and His Enemies* (London: Constable, 1995); Rory Muir, *Tactics and the Experience of Battle in the Age of Napoleon* (New Haven, Conn.: Yale University Press, 1998).

10. Oman, *A History of the Peninsular War*, vol. 3, pp. 257–67.

11. William Francis Patrick Napier, *History of the War in the Peninsula and in the South of France from the Year 1807 to the Year 1814*, 6 vols (London: John William, 1836), vol. 3, p. 170; Guy C. Dempsey, *Albuera, 1811: The Bloodiest Battle of the Peninsular War* (Barnsley, South Yorkshire: Frontline Books, 2011).

12. Houlding, *Fit for Service*, pp. 249–51; Richard Glover, *Peninsular Preparation*, pp. 135–41; R.H. Thoumine, *Scientific Soldier: A Life of General Le Marchant 1766-1812* (London: Oxford University Press, 1968); *Rules and Regulations for the Cavalry* (London, 1795); *Rules and Regulations for the Sword Exercise of the Cavalry* (Whitehall: War Office, printed; and sold by T. Egerton, Military Library, 1796).

13. Houlding, *Fit for Service*, pp. 253–6. John Muller, *A Treatise of Artillery* … (London: printed for John Millan, Whitehall, 1780).

14. Ralph Willett Adye, *The Little Bombardier, and Pocket Gunner* (T. Egerton, Military Library, Whitehall, 1801), pp. 72–88.

15. Alessandro Vittorio Papacino d'Antoni, *A Treatise on Gun-Powder; a Treatise on Fire-Arms; and a Treatise on the Service of Artillery in Time of War*, trans. by Captain Thomson (London: sold by T. and J. Egerton, at the Military Library, Whitehall, 1789).

16. Houlding, *Fit for Service*, pp. 226–32 and 243–8.

17. Ibid., pp. 228–30

18. Ibid., pp. 231–2.

19. Ibid., pp. 160–3.

20. Ibid., pp. 161–71.

21. 'Thomas Egerton and the Publication History', in *Pride and Prejudice*, ed. by Jane Austen and Pat Rogers, The Cambridge Edition of the Works of Jane Austen (Cambridge: Cambridge University Press, 2006), pp. 437–40; Thomas Egerton, *Military Books, Printed for T. Egerton, at the Military Library, Whitehall* (London: s.n., 1795); John Williamson, *A Treatise on Military Finance; Containing the Pay of the Forces on the British and Irish Establishment; with the Allowances in Camp, Garrison and Quarters, &c.* (London: Printed for T. Egerton, at the Military Library, near Whitehall., 1799), pp. 172–5; *General Orders: Spain and Portugal, January 2nd to December 29th 1810* (Whitehall: T. Egerton, 1811), vol. 2.

22. David Gates, *The British Light Infantry Arm c. 1790-1815: Its Creation, Training and Operational Role* (London: Batsford, 1987), pp. 45–6.

23. Wishon, *German Forces and the British Army*, pp. 21–33 and 50–1.

24. TNA, WO 1/900, fol. 103-105, Col. Nesbitt, 'Foreign Corps', 1797.

25. Gates, *The British Light Infantry Arm*, p. 56.

26. Buckley, *Slaves in Red Coats*.

27. Wishon, *German Forces and the British Army*, pp. 35–6.

28. Griffith, *Riflemen*.

29. Gates, *The British Light Infantry Arm*.

30. Ian Fletcher, *Galloping at Everything: The British Cavalry in the Peninsular War and Waterloo Campaign 1808-15* (Staplehurst: Spellmount, 1999).

31. Dawson, *Boots and Saddles!*.

32. Ibid., pp. 98–119.

33. William Tyndale, *A Treatise on Military Equitation. By W. Tyndale, Lieut. Col. And Major Of The First Regiment Of Life Guards* (London: printed for the author, and sold by T. Egerton, Military Library, Near Whitehall, 1797), p. 60.

34. Fletcher, *Galloping at Everything*, pp. 27–30.

35. Coss, *All for the King's Shilling*, p. 163; for a detailed examination of tactics, see James R. Arnold, 'A Reappraisal of Column versus Line in the Peninsular War', *The Journal of Military History*, 68.2 (2004), pp. 535–52.

36. *Rules and Regulations for the Formations, Field-Exercise, and Movements, of His Majesty's Forces* (Homer's Head, Charing-Cross: printed and sold by J. Walter, 1792), p. 3.

37. Huf, 'The Junior British Army Officer', pp. 101–04.

38. Richard Glover, *Peninsular Preparation*, p. 194.

39. Huf, 'The Junior British Army Officer', pp. 98–101.

40. Ibid., pp. 95–8.

41. Roderick MacArthur, 'British Army Establishments During the Napoleonic Wars, Part 1: Background and Infantry', *Journal of the Society for Army Historical Research*, 87.350 (2009), pp. 150–72; Roderick MacArthur, 'British Army Establishments During the Napoleonic Wars (Part 2) Cavalry, Artillery, Engineers and Supporting Units', *Journal of the Society for Army Historical Research*, 87.352 (2009), pp. 331–56.

42. Pimlott, 'The Administration of the British Army', pp. 268–73.

43. The best catalogue remains C.T. Atkinson, 'Foreign Regiments in The British Army, 1793-1802', *Journal of the Society for Army Historical Research*, 22.89 (1944), pp. 187–97, 22.90 (1944), pp. 234–50, 22.91 (1944), pp. 265–76, 22.92 (1944), pp. 313–24.

44. Gates, *The British Light Infantry Arm*.

45. Buckley, *Slaves in Red Coats*.

46. Harry Calvert, 'Return of the Number of Men Remaining for Service, Limited in Respect to Place, upon the 1st January and 1st July, in the Years 1805, 1806, & 1807', *Commons Papers*, 1807 vol. 4.

47. Bamford, *Sickness, Suffering, and the Sword*, pp. 88–106.

48. TNA, WO 380/4, Entry for Royal African Corps, York Rangers, and West Indian Rangers.

49. Mann, 'The Corps of Invalids', *Journal of the Society for Army Historical Research*, 66.265 (1988), pp. 5–19.

50. Harry Calvert, 'Returns Presented to the House of Commons, by Mr. Secretary at War, Respecting Recruits Raised for the Army; and the Effective Strength of the Royal Veteran and Garrison Battalions', *Commons Papers*, 1805 vol. 8, pp. 97–100; Harry Calvert, 'Return of the Number of Regiments and Effective Strength of the Royal Veteran Battalions; Specifying Whether Abroad or at Home, and the Length of Time Each Regiment Has Been on Foreign Service', *Commons Papers*, 1813–14 vol. 11, p. 281; White, 'Garrison, Reserve and Veteran Battalions and Companies', *Journal of the Society for Army Historical Research*, 38.156 (1960), pp. 156–67.

51. W.Y. Carman, '7th, 10th & 15th Hussars, 1808-09: Notes on Some Water-Colours By Robert Dighton, Junior', *Journal of the Society for Army Historical Research*, 30.122 (1952), pp. 76–80; T.H. McGuffie, 'The 7th Light Dragoons and Their First Hussar Clothing', *Journal of the Society for Army Historical Research*, 35.142 (1957), pp. 48–52.

52. MacArthur, 'British Army Establishments During the Napoleonic Wars (Part 2)', pp. 331–56.

53. C.T. Atkinson, 'Foreign Regiments in The British Army, 1793-1802', *Journal of the Society for Army Historical Research*, 22.89 (1944), pp. 187–97, 22.90 (1944), pp. 234–50, 22.91 (1944), pp. 265–76, 22.92 (1944), pp. 313–24.

54. William Windham, 'Return of His Majesty's Land Forces, Consisting of Regular Cavalry and Infantry, Fencible Cavalry and Infantry, Independent Corps, and Militia; as They Were Effective in November 1794', *Commons Sessional Papers*, vol, 100, pp. 23–4; William Windham, 'Return of His Majesty's Land Forces, Consisting of Regular Cavalry and Infantry, Fencible Cavalry and Infantry, Independent Corps, Militia, Volunteers and Yeomanry Cavalry and Infantry; as They Were Effective 1st August 1795', *Commons Sessional Papers*, vol. 100, pp. 25–6.

55. Western, 'The Recruitment of the Land Forces', pp. 209–19.

56. Ibid., pp. 12, 214–15, 291–7.

57. Details of establishments taken from WO 380/1, /2, /3, /4.

58. Thomas, *No Want of Courage*, pp. 184, 270

59. For the units sent to Spain and Portugal, see Oman, *Wellington's Army*, pp. 343–73; for the work to support units there, see Bamford, *Sickness, Suffering, and the Sword*, pp. 106–12.

60. Linch, *Britain and Wellington's Army*, p. 100.

61. MacArthur, 'British Army Establishments During the Napoleonic Wars (Part 2) Cavalry, Artillery, Engineers and Supporting Units', pp. 331–56.

62. M.E.S. Laws, 'Foreign Artillery Corps in the British Service, 1: The French Emigrant Artillery', *Journal of the Royal Artillery*, 65.3 (1938), pp. 356–67; M.E.S. Laws, 'Foreign Artillery Corps in the British Service. No. 2, the Dutch Emigrant Artillery. No. 3, the Royal Foreign Artillery', *Journal of the Royal Artillery*, 73 (1946), pp. 250–60.

63. Francis Duncan, *History of the Royal Regiment of Artillery*, 2 vols (London, 1872), vol. 2, p. 30.

64. Something of the varying roles and equipment the artillery used can be traced through its operations in Nick Lipscombe, *Wellington's Guns: The Untold Story of Wellington and His Artillery in the Peninsula and at Waterloo* (Botley, Oxford: Osprey Publishing, 2013).

65. T.W.J. Connolly, *History of the Royal Sappers and Miners, from the Formation of the Corps in March, 1772, to the Date When Its Designation Was Changed to That of Royal Engineers, in October 1856 …*, 2 vols (London: Longman, Brown, Green, Longmans and Roberts, 1857), vol. 1, pp. 2, 58, 197.

66. Gother Mann, 'Return of the Effective Strength of the Corps of Royal Military Artificers, or, Sappers and Miners; on 25th June and 25th December 1814:--Distinguishing, Those Enlisted for Life, or for a Term of Years; and, Specifying the Numbers Serving at Home and Abroad', *Commons Papers*, 1815 vol. 9, p. 303.

67. TNA, WO 25/3224, 'Return of the British Army Serving in Foreign Stations by the Latest Returns' (Horse Guards, 1811); TNA, WO 25/3224 'Return of the British Army Serving in Great Britain, Ireland, and the Islands in the Channel' (Horse Guards, 1811). For the early history of the transport service, see R.N.W. Thomas, 'The Corps of Royal Waggoners and Army Transport during the Campaign in the Low Countries, 1794-1795', *Journal of the Society for Army Historical Research*, 76 (1998), pp. 157–62.

68. Richard Glover, *Peninsular Preparation*, pp. 104–05. See also Mark S. Thompson, *Wellington's Engineers* (Barnsley: Pen and Sword, 2022).

69. TNA, WO 380/2, fols. 196-197, Royal Waggon Train.

70. See for example: TNA, WO 17/2487, Monthly Return … June 1st, 1796, which records 134 enlisted men in the 'Royal Hospital Corps'; and index entries for correspondence about it in WO 2/37, fol. 372, Hospital Corps.

71. Weller, *Wellington in India*; Fortescue, *A History of the British Army*, vol 5.

72. Bamford, *A Bold and Ambitious Enterprise*.

73. Duffy, *Soldiers, Sugar, and Seapower*.

74. See for example, John Moore, *The Diary of Sir John Moore*, 2 vols (E. Arnold, 1904), vol. 1; for the France Empire, see Michael Broers, *Napoleon's Other War: Bandits, Rebels and Their Pursuers in the Age of Revolutions* (Oxford: Peter Lang, 2010).

75. Hall, *British Strategy*, pp. 74–5.

76. Grainger, *British Campaigns in the South Atlantic 1805-1807*.

77. Collins, 'Effectiveness and the British Officer Corps, 1793-1815', *Britain's Soldiers*, pp. 58–64.

78. See for 1793-4: Thomas, *No Want of Courage*.

79. See Claus Telp, *The Evolution of Operational Art, 1740-1813: From Frederick the Great to Napoleon* (London: Frank Cass, 2005) for the European context.

80. Bamford, *Sickness, Suffering, and the Sword*, pp. 179–87.

81. Ibid., pp. 60–85.

82. Coss, *All for the King's Shilling*.

83. Muir, *Tactics and the Experience of Battle*.

84. Collins, 'Effectiveness and the British Officer Corps, 1793-1815', *Britain's Soldiers*, p. 52.

Chapter 9: Army, Society and Culture

1. *With Wellington in the Peninsula: The Adventures of a Highland Soldier, 1808-1814*, ed. by Paul Cowan (London: Frontline Books, 2015), p. 74.

2. Theodore M. Porter, *The Rise of Statistical Thinking: 1820-1900* (Princeton: Princeton University Press, 1986), pp. 17–24; Cookson, *The British Armed Nation*, pp. 96–100; John Cookson, 'Political Arithmetic and War in Britain, 1793-1815', *War & Society*, 1.2 (1983), pp. 37–60.

3. For population figures, see Brian R. Mitchell and Phyllis Deane, *Abstract of British Historical Statistics* (Cambridge: Cambridge University Press, 1962), pp. 8–11.

4. TNA, WO 17/2813, 'Scale of the Age and Standard for Recruits', 1802; TNA, WO 3/585, Harry Calvert, 'Circular on Recruiting', 14 February 1812.

5. Stephen Nicholas and Richard H. Steckel, 'Heights and Living Standards of English Workers During the Early Years of Industrialization, 1770-1815', *The Journal of Economic History*, 51.4 (1991), pp. 937–57; John Komlos and Helmut Küchenhoff, 'The Diminution of the Physical Stature of the English Male Population in the Eighteenth Century', *Cliometrica*, 6.1 (2012), pp. 45–62.

6. Charles James, *The Regimental Companion* (London: printed for T. Egerton [by C. Roworth], 1800), vol. 2, p. 413; Charles James, *The Regimental Companion* (London: Printed for T. Egerton … by C. Roworth …, 1811), vol. 1, p. 462 and vol. 3, p. 487.

7. E.A. Wrigley and Roger Schofield, *The Population History of England, 1541-1871: A Reconstruction* (Cambridge: University Press, 1989); Peter Razzell, 'The Growth of Population in Eighteenth-Century England: A Critical Reappraisal', *The Journal of Economic History*, 53.4 (1993), pp. 743–71.

8. '43 Geo. 3 c. 96, An Act to Amend and Render More Effectual, an Act Passed in the Present Session of Parliament, Intituled, *An Act to Enable His Majesty to Provide for the Defence and Security of the Realm during the Present War, and for Indemnifying Persons Who May Suffer in Their Property by Such Measures as May Be Necessary for That Purpose*; and to Enable His Majesty Most Effectually and Speedily to Exercise His Ancient and Undoubted Prerogative in Requiring the Military Service of His Liege Subjects in Case of Invasion of the Realm [27th July 1803]', *Statutes of the United Kingdom*, vol. 1, pp. 942–57; Fortescue, *County Lieutenancies*, pp. 30–3; Cookson, *British Armed Nation*, pp. 99–100.

9. T. Bartlett, '"A Weapon of War Yet Untried": Irish Catholics and the Armed Forces of the Crown, 1760-1830', in *Men, Women and War: Papers Read before the XXth Irish Conference of Historians, Held at Magee College, University of Ulster, 6-8 June 1991*, ed. by T.G. Fraser and Keith Jeffery (Dublin: Lilliput Press, 1993), pp. 66–85.

10. '33 Geo. 3 c. 21 (Ireland), An Act for the Relief of His Majesty's Popish, or Roman Catholick Subjects of Ireland [1793]', *Statutes at Large, Ireland*, vol. 16, pp. 685–92.

11. For the larger history of religion in the Army, see M.F. Snape, *The Redcoat and Religion: The Forgotten History of the British Soldier from the Age of Marlborough to the Eve of the First World War* (London; New York: Routledge, 2005).

12. Cookson, *British Armed Nation*, p. 165.

13. Ibid., p. 159.

14. Ciarán McDonnell, 'A "Fair Chance"? The Catholic Irish Brigade in the British Service, 1793-1798', *War in History*, 23.2 (2016), pp. 150–68.

15. Cookson, *British Armed Nation*, p. 159; J.E. Rea, 'McDonell, Alexander', *Dictionary of Canadian Biography*, 1988 <http://www.biographi.ca/en/bio/mcdonell_alexander_7E.html>.

16. TNA, WO 27/77, Brigadier-General Hunter, Inspection Report of His Majesty's 107th Regiment of Foot, Newport, Isle of Wight, 28 February 1795.

17. TNA, WO 27/77, Brigadier-General Hunter, Inspection Report of His Majesty's 126th Regiment of Foot, Newport, Isle of Wight, 24 February 1795.

18. Cookson, *British Armed Nation*, pp. 126–8.

19. Ibid., pp. 128 and 154–8.

20. Linch, *Britain and Wellington's Army*, pp. 60–2.

21. Coss, *All for the King's Shilling*, pp. 244–63. These figures are based on a sample of recruiting returns for the Royal Artillery.

22. Linch, *Britain and Wellington's Army*, pp. 65–72.

23. Ibid., p. 176.

24. Linch, 'The Recruitment of the British Army', pp. 278–81; Cookson, *British Armed Nation*, pp. 146–7 and 177.

25. Linch, 'The Recruitment of the British Army', p. 282.

26. TNA, WO 40/26, General Return of Barracks in Great Britain, Jersey, Guernsey and Alderney, 1 April 1807: Cookson, *British Armed Nation*, pp. 56 and 184.

27. Cookson, *British Armed Nation*, pp. 56–7.

28. Buckley, *British Army in the West Indies*, pp. 327–32.

29. Cozens, 'The Experience of Soldiering', pp. 168–89 and 219–26.

30. Cookson, *British Armed Nation*, pp. 144–5.

31. Cozens, 'The Experience of Soldiering', pp. 123–6.

32. Coss, *All for the King's Shilling*, pp. 55 and 66–72.

33. Muir, *Gentlemen of Uncertain Fortune*, pp. 273–6.

34. Coss, *All for the King's Shilling*, pp. 66–72.

35. Coombs, 'Crime and the Soldier', pp. 107–46.

36. Cozens, 'The Experience of Soldiering', p. 112.

37. Coombs, 'Crime and the Soldier', pp. 218–47; for frauds in the Peninsular War, see Coss, *All for the King's Shilling*, p. 109, and for Vitoria, p. 135.

38. Cozens, 'The Experience of Soldiering', pp. 119–22.

39. Daly, *The British Soldier in the Peninsular War*.

40. Quinn, 'Orientalists in Uniform?'.

41. Quinn, 'British Military Orientalism', *War in History*, 28.2 (2019), pp. 263–82.

42. Alice Parker, 'Incorrigible Rogues: The Brutalisation of British Soldiers in the Peninsular War 1808-1814', *British Journal for Military History*, 1.3 (2015), pp. 25–41.

43. Coss, *All for the King's Shilling*, pp. 211–34.

44. Gavin Daly, 'Anglo-French Sieges, the Laws of War, and the Limits of Enmity in the Peninsular War, 1808–1814', *The English Historical Review*, 135.574 (2020), pp. 572–604.

45. Gavin Daly, 'British Soldiers, Sieges, and the Laws of War: The 1807 Siege of Montevideo', in *Redcoats to Tommies: The Experience of the British Soldier from the Eighteenth Century*, ed. by Kevin Linch and Matthew Lord (Woodbridge: Boydell Press, 2021), pp. 103–19.

46. Kevin Linch, 'Desertion from the British Army during the Napoleonic Wars', *Journal of Social History*, 49.4 (2016), pp. 808–28; Linch, 'The Recruitment of the British Army 1807-1815', pp. 210–42; O'Neil, *The Military Adventures of Charles O'Neil*.

47. Bamford, *Sickness, Suffering, and the Sword*, pp. 117–25; Linch, 'The Recruitment of the British Army 1807-1815', pp. 29–30; A.S. White, 'Garrison, Reserve and Veteran Battalions', *Journal of the Society for Army Historical Research*, 38.156 (1960), pp. 156–67.

48. Caroline Nielsen, 'Disability, Fraud and Medical Experience at the Royal Hospital of Chelsea in the Long Eighteenth Century', in *Britain's Soldiers: Rethinking War and Society, 1715-1815*, ed. by Kevin Linch and Matthew McCormack (Liverpool: Liverpool University Press,

2014), pp. 183–201; Caroline Louise Nielsen, 'The Chelsea Out-Pensioners: Image and Reality in Eighteenth-Century and Early Nineteenth-Century Social Care' (unpublished Ph.D., University of Newcastle Upon Tyne, 2014).

49. Nielsen, 'The Chelsea Out-Pensioners', pp. 260–1.

50. Caroline Nielsen, 'Continuing to Serve: Representations of the Elderly Veteran Soldier in the Late Eighteenth and Early Nineteenth Centuries', in *Men After War*, ed. by Stephen McVeigh and Nicola Cooper (London: Routledge, 2013), pp. 18–35.

51. J.E. Cookson, 'Early Nineteenth-Century Scottish Military Pensioners as Homecoming Soldiers', *Historical Journal*, 52.2 (2009), pp. 319–41.

52. 'Statement of Officers Removed from the Half-Pay into Established Regiments of the Line; and a Calculation of the Value of the Half-Pay Saved by Their Appointment', *Commons Papers*, 1810 vol. 10, p. 187.

53. TNA, WO 65/52, pp. 133–4. *The London Gazette*, 5 December 1801, issue 15433, p. 1452.

54. TNA, WO 65/63, p. 290; TNA, WO 65/58, p. 335; TNA, WO 65/56, p. 324; TNA, WO 65/53, im. 218; TNA, WO 65/53, im. 151; TNA, WO 65/53, im. 151; TNA, WO 65/49, im. 113; TNA, WO 64/44, im. 70; TNA, WO 65/43, im. 73.

55. TNA, WO 65/59, p. 311; *The London Gazette*, 3 May 1808, issue 16142, p. 623; TNA, WO 65/50, im. 285; *The London Gazette*, 8 September 1795, issue 13812, p. 928; *The London Gazette*, 27 June 1795, issue 13791, p. 679; *The Dublin Gazette*, 13 June 1795, issue 6183, p. 634 (im. 626); TNA, WO 64/44, im. 322; TNA, WO 64/44, im. 282.

56. Christine Wright, *Wellington's Men in Australia: Peninsular War Veterans and the Making of Empire c. 1820-40* (Houndmills, Basingstoke, Hampshire; New York: Palgrave Macmillan, 2011).

57. Hannah Barker, 'England, 1760-1815', in *Press, Politics and the Public Sphere in Europe and North America, 1760-1820*, ed. by Hannah Barker and Simon Burrows (Cambridge: Cambridge University Press, 2002), pp. 93–112.

58. Zack White, 'From Cintra to Salamanca: Shifting Popular Perceptions of the War in the Iberian Peninsula, 1808-1812', *British Journal for Military History*, 1.3 (2015), pp. 42–61.

59. Thomas, *No Want of Courage*, pp. 36–9.

60. Frederick James Lyon, 'A Total War?: Media Representations and Public Perceptions of the War against Revolutionary France in Britain, 1793-1795' (unpublished MA by research, University of Leeds, 2015).

61. See for example John Andrews, *Andrews's military map of the seat of war in the Netherlands; part of France, Holland and Germany, in which are delineated all the fortified towns, rivers, roads and villages, to shew the operations of the armies* (1794), University of Leeds Special Collections, Geography C-2/AND.

62. Louise Carter, 'Scarlet Fever: Female Enthusiasm for Men in Uniform, 1780-1815', in *Britain's Soldiers: Rethinking War and Society, 1715-1815*, ed. by Kevin Linch and Matthew McCormack, Eighteenth-Century Worlds (Liverpool: University Press, 2014), pp. 155–80.

63. Susan Valladares, *Staging the Peninsular War: English Theatres 1807-1815* (Farnham, Surrey, UK: Ashgate, 2015), pp. 118–23 and 132–44.

64. Gillian Russell, *The Theatres of War: Performance, Politics, and Society, 1793-1815* (Oxford; New York: Clarendon Press; Oxford University Press, 1995), pp. 33–51.

65. 'Bagshot Camp', *Reading Mercury*, 13 August 1792, p. 3.

66. See for example 'Sham Fight On Portsdown', *Hampshire Chronicle*, 5 October 1801, p. 3, where the entire garrison of Portsmouth was involved.

67. Trevor Herbert and Helen Barlow, *Music & the British Military in the Long Nineteenth Century* (New York: Oxford University Press, 2013), pp. 37–47, 54 and 84–101.

68. 'French Eagles', *Saint James's Chronicle*, 18 May 1811, p. 2; 'French Eagles and Colours', *Pilot* (London, 18 May 1811), p. 3; 'French Eagles and Colours', *Kentish Gazette*, 21 May 1811, p. 4.

69. 'The Royal Hospital: Flags, standards, etc.', in *Survey of London: Volume 11, Chelsea, Part IV: the Royal Hospital*, ed. Walter H, Godfrey (London, 1927), pp. 32–6. *British History Online* <http://www.british-history.ac.uk/survey-london/vol11/pt4/pp.32-36>.

70. Denis Dighton, *The Capture of the Eagle of the 8th French Infantry by the 87th (Prince of Wales's Irish) Regiment at the Battle of Barrosa, 1811*, 1812, National Army Museum, Nam. 1980-09-96-1.

71. Jenny Spencer-Smith, 'Dighton, Denis (1791–1827), Military Painter', in *Oxford Dictionary of National Biography*, 2019 <https://doi.org/10.1093/ref:odnb/7641>.

72. Cicely Robinson, 'Conflicts of Conduct: British Masculinity and Military Painting in the Wake of the Siege of Gibraltar', in *Britain's Soldiers: Rethinking War and Society, 1715-1815*, ed. by Matthew McCormack and Kevin Linch (Liverpool: Liverpool University Press, 2014), pp. 149–54.

73. Samuel Drummond, *Study of a Soldier*, British Museum, 1876,0708.2378.

74. Russell, *Theatres of War*, p. 76.

75. Robert Ker Porter, *The Battle of Alexandria, 21 March 1801*, 1801, National Army Museum, Nam. 1999-10-12-1.

76. Russell, *Theatres of War*, pp. 74–8.

77. Philip Shaw, *Waterloo and the Romantic Imagination* (Houndmills, Basingstoke, Hampshire; New York: Palgrave/Macmillan, 2002).

78. Neil Ramsey, *The Military Memoir and Romantic Literary Culture, 1780-1835* (Farnham: Ashgate, 2011), pp. 26–32.

79. Ibid., pp. 36–54.

80. Matilda Greig, *Dead Men Telling Tales: Napoleonic War Veterans and the Military Memoir Industry, 1808-1914* (Oxford: Oxford University Press, 2021).

81. Linch, *Britain and Wellington's Army*, pp. 136–44.

82. Alexander Rodger, *Battle Honours of the British Empire and Commonwealth Land Forces, 1662-1991* (Ramsbury: Crowood, 2003), pp. 27–41.

83. Ramsey, *The Military Memoir*, pp. 194–5.

Conclusion

1. Fortescue, *History of the British Army*, vol. 10, pp. 419–20.

2. A.N. Newman, 'Marsham, Hon. Charles (1744-1811), of Maidstone, Kent', *History of Parliament Online* <http://www.historyofparliamentonline.org/volume/1754-1790/member/marsham-hon-charles-1744-1811>.

3. *Parliamentary History*, vol. 25, cols 1028–1034, 1244–1248; '26 Geo. 3 c. 107, An Act for Amending, and Reducing into One Act of Parliament, the Laws Relating to the Militia, in That Part of Great Britain Called England [1786]', *Statutes at Large*, vol. 35, pp. 860–917.

4. See, for example, Matthew McCormack, 'Citizenship, Nationhood, and Masculinity in the Affair of the Hanoverian Soldier, 1756', *The Historical Journal*, 49.4 (2006), pp. 971–93; Helene Olsen, 'The Social Construction of Mercenaries: German Soldiers in British Service during the Eighteenth Century', *Small Wars & Insurgencies* (2021), pp. 1–20; Linch, 'The Politics of Foreign Recruitment', *Transnational Soldiers*, pp. 50–66.

5. Nir Arielli and Bruce Collins, 'Introduction: Transnational Military Service since the Eighteenth Century', in *Transnational Soldiers: Foreign Military Enlistment in the Modern Era.*, ed. by Nir Arielli and Bruce Collins (London: Palgrave Macmillan UK, 2013), pp. 1–12.

Bibliography

Primary Sources
British Museum
Drummond, Samuel, *Study of a Soldier*, British Museum 1876,0708.2378.

Bodleian Library
Broadside Ballads Online.

Hampshire Record Office
4M81 Brockenhurst Parish records.

Hertfort Museum
HETFM/Military/6242.4.

The National Archives, London, UK
HO 50 Home Office: Military Correspondence.
WO 1 War Office and predecessors: Secretary-at-War, Secretary of State for War, and Commander-in-Chief, In-letters and Miscellaneous Papers.
WO 2 War Office and predecessors: Indexes to Out-letters.
WO 3 Office of the Commander-in-Chief: Out-letters.
WO 4 War Office: Secretary-at-War; Out-letters.
WO 6 Secretary of State for War and Secretary of State for War and the Colonies: Out-letters.
WO 17 Office of the Commander in Chief: Monthly Returns to the Adjutant General.
WO 25 Secretary-at-War, Secretary of State for War, and Related Bodies: Registers.
WO 26 War Office: Entry Books of Warrants, Regulations and Precedents.
WO 30 War Office, predecessors, and associated departments: Miscellaneous Papers.
WO 40 Secretary-at-War, In-letters and Reports.
WO 123 Army Circulars, Memoranda, Orders and Regulations.
WO 380 Regimental Record Series.

The National Army Museum
1960-05-35.
1971-02-33-501.
1972-09-19.
1976-06-21-1.
1980-09-96-1.
1982-04-88.
1999-10-12-1.

National Records Scotland
GD51 Papers of the Dundas Family of Melville, Viscounts Melville (Melville Castle Papers).

Royal Collections Trust
GEO/MAIN/17513-24917, 38043-41696 George IV Calendar as Prince, Regent and King.

Surrey History Centre
BR/QS Borough of Guildford Quarter Sessions and Other Courts Held in The Borough: Records.

Printed Primary Sources

A Collection of State Papers, Relative to the War against France Now Carrying on by Great-Britain and the Several Other European Powers, Containing Authentic Copies of Treaties (London: J. Debrett, 1794–1802).

A Collection of Orders, Regulations, and Instructions, for the Army; on Matters of Finance and Points of Discipline Immediately Connected Therewith (London: Sold by T. Egerton, 1807).

An Act for Punishing Mutiny and Desertion; and for the Better Payment of the Army and Their Quarters (London: printed by C. Eyre and the executors of W. Strahan, printers to the King's most Excellent Majesty, 1786).

An Act for Punishing Mutiny and Desertion and for the Better Payment of the Army and Their Quarters. With an Index. Also, Rules and Articles for the Better Government of All His Majesty's Forces, Rules and Articles for the Better Government of All His Majesty's Forces, from the 24th Day of March, 1809 (London: Printed by G. Eyre and A. Strahan, printers to the King's most Excellent Majesty, 1809).

An Act for Punishing Mutiny and Desertion: And for the Better Payment of the Army and Their Quarters, with an Index: Also, Rules and Articles for the Better Government of All His Majesty's Forces (London: G. Eyre and A. Straham, 1813).

Adjutant-General's Office, *General Regulations and Orders* (London; Quebec: G. Roworth, Printer …; Reprinted by John Neilson, 1804).

Adye, Ralph Willett, *The Little Bombardier, and Pocket Gunner* (T. Egerton, Military Library, Whitehall, 1801).

d'Antoni, Alessandro Vittorio Papacino, *A Treatise on Gun-Powder: A Treatise on Fire-Arms; and a Treatise on the Service of Artillery in Time of War*, trans. by Captain Henry Thomson (T. and J. Egerton, 1789).

Anderson, Aeneas, *A Narrative of the British Embassy to China in the Years 1792, 1793, and 1794; Containing the Various Circumstances of the Embassy, with Accounts of Customs and Manners of the Chinese and a Description of the Country, Towns, Cities &c. &c* (London: J. Debrett, 1795).

Andrews, John, *Andrews's military map of the seat of war in the Netherlands; part of France, Holland and Germany, in which are delineated all the fortified towns, rivers, roads and villages, to shew the operations of the armies* (1794).

Bridgeman, Orlando, *A Young Gentleman at War: The Letters of Captain Orlando Bridgeman 1st Foot Guards in the Peninsula and at Waterloo 1812-15*, ed. by Gareth Glover (Ken Trotman Publishing, 2008).

Bunbury, Sir Henry, *Narratives of Some Passages in the Great War with France, from 1799 to 1810* (London: R. Bentley, 1854).

By Permission of His Excellency the Lord Lieutenant. A List of the Officers of the Several Regiments of Fencible Cavalry and Infantry, and of the Several Regiments and Battalions of Militia, with the Dates of Their Respective Commissions upon the Establishment of Ireland, (with an Alphabetical Index) (Dublin: Printed by James King and Abraham Bradley King, printers to the Honourable the House of Commons, No. 72, Dame-Street, 1796).

Conventions, Proclamations, Manifestoes, Declarations, Memorials, … (London: J. Debrett, 1795).

Castlereagh, Robert Stewart, *Memoirs and Correspondence of Viscount Castlereagh, Second Marquess of Londonderry*, ed. by Charles William Vane Londonderry (London: H. Colburn, 1850).

Cowan, Paul (ed.), *With Wellington in the Peninsula: The Adventures of a Highland Soldier, 1808-1814* (London: Frontline Books, 2015).

Deacon, Edward Erastus, Edward Chitty and Great Britain Court of Review, *Reports of Cases in Bankruptcy: Argued and Determined in the Court of Review, and on Appeal Before the Lord Chancellor* (Saunders and Benning, 1837).

Dodwell, Edward and James Samuel Miles, *Alphabetical List of the Officers of the Indian Army: With the Dates of Their Respective Promotion, Retirement, Resignation, or Death, Whether in India or in Europe, from the Year 1760 to the Year 1834 Inclusive, Corrected to September 30, 1837* (London: Longman, Orme, Brown, 1838)..

Egerton, Thomas, *Military Books, Printed for T. Egerton, at the Military Library, Whitehall* ([London]: s.n., 1795).

Farquhar, George, *The Recruiting Officer. A Comedy. As It Is Acted at the Theatre Royal in Drury-Lane, by Her Majesty's Servants. Written by Mr. Farquhar* (London, 1706).

Fernyhough, Thomas, Robert Fernyhough and John Fernyhough, *Military Memoirs of Four Brothers, (Natives of Staffordshire). Engaged in the Service of Their Country, as Well in the New World and Africa, as on the Continent of Europe* (London: W. Sams, 1829).

General Regulations and Orders for the Conduct of His Majesty's Forces in Great Britain ([London], 1799).

General Regulations and Orders for the Army: Adjutant General's Office, Horse-Guards, 12th August, 1811 (London: W. Clowes, 1811).

General Orders: Spain and Portugal, January 2nd to December 29th 1810 (Whitehall: T. Egerton, 1811).

The Gentleman's Magazine.

Gurwood, John (ed.), *The Dispatches of Field Marshal the Duke of Wellington: During His Various Campaigns in India, Denmark, Portugal, Spain, the Low Countries, and France, from 1799 to 1818*, 13 vols (London: J. Murray, 1837).

Hansard: UK Parliament <https://hansard.parliament.uk/>

Hodson, V.C.P., *List of the Officers of the Bengal Army 1758-1834*, 4 vols (Constable, London, 1927).

House of Commons Papers.

House of Commons Sessional Papers of the Eighteenth Century, ed. Sheila Lambert (Wilmington, Del.: Scholarly Resources, 1795).

Instructions for Officers on the Recruiting Service of Regiments on Foreign Stations (London, 1792).

Jackson, Robert, *A Sketch of the History and Cure of Febrile Diseases: More Particularly as They Appear in the West-Indies Among the Soldiers of the British Army* (Stockton: T. and H. Eeles, 1817).

James, Charles, *The Regimental Companion: Containing the Relative Duties of Every Officer in the British Army; ... By Charles James, ... A New and Enlarged Edition. In Two Volumes*, 2 vols (London: printed for T. Egerton [by C. Roworth], 1800).

James, Charles, *A New and Enlarged Military Dictionary, or, Alphabetical Explanation of Technical Terms: Containing, among Other Matter, a Succinct Account of the Different Systems of Fortification, Tactics, &c. Also the Various French Phrases and Words That Have an Immediate, or Relative, Connection with the British Service, or May Tend to Give General Information on Military Subjects in Either Language* (London: T. Egerton, 1805).

James, Charles, *The Regimental Companion: Containing the Pay, Allowances and Relative Duties of Every Officer in the British Service*, 4 vols (London: Printed for T. Egerton ... by C. Roworth ... , 1811).

Journals of the House of Commons.

The Journals of the House of Commons, of the Kingdom of Ireland, from the Eighteenth Day of May, 1613 [-1794], 31 vols (Dublin: printed by J. King, and A.B. King, 1787).

Kane, John, *List of Officers of the Royal Regiment of Artillery, as They Stood in the Year 1763, with a Continuation to the Present Time ... with a List of the Officers of the Corps of Royal Artillery Drivers ... and of the Officers of the Military Medical Department of the Ordnance, since 1763; with a List of the Chief Commissaries ...* (Greenwich: printed by Elizabeth Delahoy, Albion Printing Office, 1815).

A List of All the Officers of the Army and Royal Marines on Full and Half-Pay: With an Index List of the Officers of the Several Regiments and Corps of Fencible Cavalry and Infantry; of the Officers of the Militia; of the Corps and Troops of Gentlemen and Yeomanry : And of the Corps and Companies of Volunteer Infantry (London: War Office, 1795).

List of the Officers of His Majesty's Foreign Corps under the Inspection of Colonel Nesbit, Inspector General of Foreign Troops (Southampton, 1796).

List of the Officers of His Majesty's Foreign Corps, under the Inspection of Colonel Nesbitt, Inspector General of Foreign Troops, Shewing the Dates of Their Commissions and Role in the British Service (Southampton, 1797).

McGrigor, James, *Medical Sketches of the Expedition to Egypt from India* (London: Printed for John Murray, 32, Fleet-Street; Edinburgh: Bell and Bradfute; Dublin: Gilbert and Hodges, 1804).

Moore, John, *The Diary of Sir John Moore*, 2 vols. (E. Arnold, 1904).

Muller, John, *A Treatise of Artillery: Containing I. General Constructions of Brass and Iron Guns Used by Sea and Land, and Their Carriages. II. General Constructions of Mortars and Howitzers, Their Beds and Carriages. III. Dimensions of All Carriages Used in Artillery. IV. Exercise of the Regiment at Home, and Service Abroad in a Siege of Battle. V. Its March and Encampment, Ammunition, Stores, and Horses. VI. Lastly, The Necessary Laboratory Work for Fire-Ships, &c. To Which Is Prefixed, an Introduction, with a Theory of Powder Applied to Fire-Arms. By John Muller, Professor of Artillery and Fortification, And Preceptor of Engineering, &c. to His Royal Highness the Duke of Gloucester, The third edition, with large additions, alterations, and corrections* (London: printed for John Millan, Whitehall, 1780).

O'Neil, Charles, *The Military Adventures of Charles O'Neil … a Soldier in the Army of Lord Wellington during the Memorable Peninsular War and the Continental Campaigns from 1811 to 1815 … Engravings.* (Worcester, U.S.: 1851).

The Parliamentary Debates from the Year 1803 to the Present Time, 41 vols. (London: T.C. Hansard, 1812–1820).

The Parliamentary History of England from the Earliest Period to the Year 1803, 36 vols (London: T.C. Hansard, 1806–1820).

The Parliamentary Register; Or, History of the Proceedings and Debates of the House of Commons [and House of Lords] Containing an Account of the Most Interesting Speeches and Motions: Accurate Copies of the Most Remarkable Letters and Papers; of the Most Material Evidence, Petitions, Etc. Laid Before, and Offered to the House (London, 1775–1813).

Report of the Commissioners of Military Enquiry, 6 vols (1806–1812).

Regulations and Instructions for Carrying on the Recruiting Service for His Majesty's Forces Stationed Abroad (London: War Office printed; and sold by J. Walter, 1796).

Roberts, David and Thomas Rowlandson, *The Military Adventures of Johnny Newcome, with an Account of His Campaign on the Peninsula and in Pall Mall and Notes, by an Officer. With Fifteen Coloured Sketches by T. Rowlandson* (London, Methuen and co., 1904).

Royal Commission on Historical Manuscripts (ed.), *The Manuscripts of J. B. Fortescue, Esq: Preserved at Dropmore* (London: H.M.S.O., 1912).

The Royal Kalendar (Calendar). Or, Complete and Correct Annual Register, for England, Scotland, Ireland, and America, for the Year 1807 (Etc.) (Stockdale, 1807).

Rules and Regulations for the Cavalry (London, 1795).

Rules and Regulations for the Formations, Field-Exercise, and Movements, of His Majesty's Forces (Homer's Head, Charing-Cross: printed and sold by J. Walter, 1792).

Rules and Regulations for the Sword Exercise of the Cavalry (Whitehall: War Office, printed; and sold by T. Egerton, Military Library, 1796).

Standing Orders and Regulations for the Army in Ireland (Dublin, 1794).

The Statutes at Large, from Magna Charta to the End of the Eleventh Parliament of Great Britain

Statutes at Large, Passed in the Parliaments Held in Ireland: From the Third Year of Edward the Second, A.D. 1310, to the Twenty Sixth-[Fortieth] Year of George the Third, A.D. 1786-[A.D.

1800], Inclusive : With Marginal Notes, and a Compleat Index to the Whole ... , 20 vols (Dublin: Printed by George Grierson, 1801).

Statutes of the United Kingdom of Great Britain and Ireland (London : George Eyre and Andrew Strahan, 1803–1816).

Tyndale, William, *A Treatise on Military Equitation. By W. Tyndale, Lieut. Col. And Major Of The First Regiment Of Life Guards* (London: printed for the author, and sold by T. Egerton, Military Library, Near Whitehall, 1797).

War Office, *A Collection of Orders, Regulations, and Instructions, for the Army; on Matters of Finance and Points of Discipline Immediately Connected Therewith* (London: Sold by T. Egerton, 1807).

Wellesley, Arthur, *Supplementary Despatches and Memoranda of Field Marshal Arthur, Duke of Wellington, K. G.* , ed. by Arthur Richard Wellesley, 15 vols (London: J. Murray, 1858–1872).

Williamson, John, *A Treatise on Military Finance; Containing the Pay of the Forces on the British and Irish Establishment; with the Allowances in Camp, Garrison and Quarters, &c.* (London: Printed for T. Egerton, at the Military Library, near Whitehall., 1799).

Windham, William, *The Windham Papers: The Life and Correspondence of the Rt. Hon. William Windham, 1750-1810 ... Including Hitherto Unpublished Letters from George III, the Dukes of York and Gloucester, Pitt, Fox, Burke, Canning ... Etc.; with an Introduction by the Earl of Rosebery,* 2 vols (Boston, 1913).

Newspapers

Aberdeen Press and Journal.
Bristol Times and Mirror.
Bury and Norwich Post.
Caledonian Mercury.
Cambridge Intelligencer.
Chester Chronicle.
Dublin Evening Post.
The Dublin Gazette.
Evening Mail.
Hampshire Chronicle.
Hereford Journal.
The Ipswich Journal.
Kentish Gazette.
Kentish Weekly Post or Canterbury Advertiser.
The London Gazette.
Manchester Courier.
Manchester Mercury
Morning Post.
Pilot.
Public Ledger and Daily Advertiser.
Reading Mercury.
Saunders's News-Letter.
The Scots Magazine.
Stamford Mercury.
Sainte James's Chronicle.

Secondary Sources

Ackroyd, Marcus, Laurence Brockliss, Michael Moss, Kate Retford and John Stevenson, *Advancing with the Army: Medicine, the Professions and Social Mobility in the British Isles 1790-1850* (OUP Oxford, 2007).

Agostini, Thomas, '"The Provincials Will Work like Giants": British Imperialism, American Colonial Troops, and Trans-Atlantic Labor Economics during the Seven Years' War', *Early American Studies: An Interdisciplinary Journal*, 15.1 (2017), pp. 64–98 <https://doi.org/10.1353/eam.2017.0002>

Alan Eyre, L., 'The Maroon Wars in Jamaica – a Geographical Appraisal', *Jamaican Historical Review; Kingston*, 12 (1980), pp. 5–19.

Allen, Robert S., *His Majesty's Indian Allies: British Indian Policy in the Defence of Canada, 1774–1815* (Toronto [Ont.]: Dundurn Press, 1992).

Anderson, Olive, 'The Constitutional Position of the Secretary at War, 1642-1855', *Journal of the Society for Army Historical Research*, 36.148 (1958), pp. 165–9.

Arielli, Nir, and Bruce Collins, 'Introduction: Transnational Military Service since the Eighteenth Century', in *Transnational Soldiers: Foreign Military Enlistment in the Modern Era*, ed. by Nir Arielli and Bruce Collins (London: Palgrave Macmillan UK, 2013), pp. 1–12.

Arnold, James R., 'A Reappraisal of Column versus Line in the Peninsular War', *The Journal of Military History*, 68.2 (2004), pp. 535–52

Arthur, George, *The Story of the Household Cavalry*, 2 vols (London: A. Constable, 1909).

Aspanall, Arthur, 'The Cabinet Council, 1783-1835', *Proceedings of the British Academy*, 38 (1954), pp. 145–252 and appendix.

Atkinson, C.T., 'Foreign Regiments in The British Army, 1793-1802: Part I—General', *Journal of the Society for Army Historical Research*, 21.84 (1942), pp. 175–81.

———, 'Foreign Regiments in The British Army, 1793-1802: Part III—Quiberon', *Journal of the Society for Army Historical Research*, 22.86 (1943), pp. 45–52.

———, 'Foreign Regiments in The British Army, 1793-1802: Part II—The Continent, 1793-1802', *Journal of the Society for Army Historical Research*, 22.85 (1943), pp. 2–14.

———, 'Foreign Regiments in The British Army, 1793-1802: Part IV—The West Indies', *Journal of the Society for Army Historical Research*, 22.87 (1943), pp. 107–15.

———, 'Foreign Regiments in The British Army, 1793-1802: Part VI—Notes on Each Corps or Regiment, Section I—Albanian Regiment to Dillon's', *Journal of the Society for Army Historical Research*, 22.89 (1944), pp. 187–97.

———, 'Foreign Regiments in The British Army, 1793-1802: Part VI—Notes on Each Corps or Regiment, Section II—Du Dressnay's to Maclean's Chasseurs', *Journal of the Society for Army Historical Research*, 22.90 (1944), pp. 234–50.

———, 'Foreign Regiments in The British Army, 1793-1802: Part VI—Notes on Each Corps or Regiment, Section III—Maltese Corps to Roll's', *Journal of the Society for Army Historical Research*, 22.91 (1944), pp. 265–76.

———, 'Foreign Regiments in The British Army, 1793-1802: Part VI—Notes on Each Corps or Regiment, Section IV—Royal Louis to York Rangers', *Journal of the Society for Army Historical Research*, 22.92 (1944), pp. 313–24.

———, 'Foreign Regiments in The British Army, 1793-1802: Part V–The Mediterranean and Southern Europe', *Journal of the Society for Army Historical Research*, 22.88 (1943), pp. 132–42.

Austen, Jane, and Pat Rogers (eds), 'Thomas Egerton and the Publication History', in *Pride and Prejudice*, The Cambridge Edition of the Works of Jane Austen (Cambridge: Cambridge University Press, 2006), pp. 437–40 <https://doi.org/10.1017/9781108991308.066>

Baldry, W.Y., and A.S. White, 'Disbanded Regiments. The New Brunswick Fencibles—Afterwards The 104th Foot', *Journal of the Society for Army Historical Research*, 1.3 (1922), pp. 90–2.

Bamford, Andrew, *A Bold and Ambitious Enterprise: The British Army in the Low Countries, 1813–1814* (Barnsley: Frontline Books, 2013).

———, *Sickness, Suffering, and the Sword: The British Regiment on Campaign, 1808-1815* (Norman, OK: University of Oklahoma Press, 2013).

———, '"Infamous", or Incomplete? The Origins and Structure of Wellington's 1815 Field Army', *Journal of the Society for Army Historical Research*, 93.374 (2015), pp. 102–19.

Bandyopadhyay, Premansukumar, *Sepoys in the British Overseas Expeditions* (Kolkata: K P Bagchi & Co., 2011).

Blaufarb, Rafe, 'Noble Privilege and Absolutist State Building: French Military Administration after the Seven Years' War', *French Historical Studies*, 24.2 (2001), pp. 223–46 <https://doi.org/10.1215/00161071-24-2-223>

Barker, Hannah, 'England, 1760-1815', in *Press, Politics and the Public Sphere in Europe and North America, 1760-1820*, ed. by Hannah Barker and Simon Burrows (Cambridge: Cambridge University Press, 2002), pp. 93–112.

Bartlett, Thomas, 'Defence, Counter-Insurgency and Rebellion: Ireland, 1793-1803', in *A Military History of Ireland*, ed. by Thomas Bartlett and Jeffery Keith (Cambridge: Cambridge University Press, 1996), pp. 247–93.

———, '"A Weapon of War Yet Untried": Irish Catholics and the Armed Forces of the Crown, 1760-1830', in *Men, Women and War: Papers Read before the XXth Irish Conference of Historians, Held at Magee College, University of Ulster, 6-8 June 1991*, ed. by T.G. Fraser and Keith Jeffery, Historical Studies, 18 (Dublin: Lilliput Press, 1993), pp. 66–85.

Bayly, Christopher Alan, *Imperial Meridian : The British Empire and the World 1780-1830* (London: Longman, 1989).

Bayley, Chris, 'The British Military-Fiscal State and Indigenous Resistance. India 1750-1820', in *An Imperial State at War: Britain from 1689 to 1815*, ed. by Lawrence Stone (London: Routledge, 1994), pp. 322–54.

Bazouges, Hughes de, and Alistair Nichols, *For God and King: A History of the Damas Legion* (Helion and Company, 2021).

Beattie, J.M., *Crime and the Courts in England, 1660-1800* (Clarendon Press, 1986).

Berkovich, Ilya, *Motivation in War: The Experience of Common Soldiers in Old-Regime Europe* (Cambridge: Cambridge University Press, 2017).

Biddulph, John, *The Nineteenth and Their Times : Being an Account of the Four Cavalry Regiments in the British Army That Have Borne the Number Nineteen and of the Campaigns in Which They Served* (London: Murray, 1899).

Blackstock, Allan, *An Ascendancy Army : The Irish Yeomanry, 1796-1834* (Dublin: Four Courts Press, 1998).

———, 'The Union and the Military, 1801-c.1830', *Transactions of the Royal Historical Society*, 10 (2000), pp. 329–51.

Blanco, Richard L., *Wellington's Surgeon General : Sir James McGrigor* (Durham (NC), 1974).

Blanning, T.C.W., *The Origins of the French Revolutionary Wars*, Origins of Modern Wars (London: Longman, 1986).

Bohstedt, John, *Riots and Community Politics in England and Wales, 1790-1810* (Cambridge, Mass.: Harvard University Press, 1983).

Bollettino, Maria Alessandra, '"Of Equal or of More Service": Black Soldiers and the British Empire in the Mid-Eighteenth-Century Caribbean', *Slavery & Abolition*, 38.3 (2017), pp. 510–33 <https://doi.org/10.1080/0144039X.2016.1251057>

Bond, Gordon C., *The Grand Expedition: The British Invasion of Holland in 1809* (Athens: University of Georgia Press, 1979).

Bourne, Kenneth, *Palmerston: The Early Years 1784-1841* (London: Allen Lane, 1982).

Bowyer-Bower, T.A., 'A Pioneer of Army Education: The Royal Military Asylum, Chelsea, 1801-1821', *British Journal of Educational Studies*, 2.2 (1954), pp. 122–32 <https://doi.org/10.2307/3118309>

Boyden, Peter B., *Tommy Atkins' Letters : The History of the British Army Postal Service from 1795* (National Army Museum, 1990).

Breihan, John R., 'Army Barracks in the North East in the Era of the French Revolution', *Archaeologia Aeliana*, 5th Series, 18 (1990), pp. 165–76 <https://doi.org/10.5284/1060867>

Broers, Michael, *Napoleon's Other War: Bandits, Rebels and Their Pursuers in the Age of Revolutions* (Oxford: Peter Lang, 2010).

Brown, Michael and Joanne Begiato, 'Visualising the Aged Veteran in Nineteenth-Century Britain: Memory, Masculinity and Nation', in *Martial Masculinities : Experiencing and Imagining the Military in the Long Nineteenth Century*, ed. by Michael Brown, Anna Maria Barry, and Joanne Begiato, Cultural History of Modern War (Manchester: Manchester University Press, 2019), pp. 102–36.

Brown, Steve, *By Fire and Bayonet: Grey's West Indies Campaign of 1794* (Warwick: Helion, 2018).

Bruce, A.P.C., *The Purchase System in the British Army, 1660-1871* (London: Royal Historical Society, 1980).

Brumwell, Stephen, *Redcoats: The British Soldier and War in the Americas, 1755-1763* (Cambridge: Cambridge University Press, 2002).

Buckley, Roger Norman, *The British Army in the West Indies: Society and the Military in the Revolutionary Age* (Gainesville, Fla: University Press of Florida, 1998).

——, *Slaves in Red Coats: The British West India Regiments, 1795-1815* (New Haven; London: Yale University Press, 1979).

——, 'The Destruction of the British Army in the West Indies 1793-1815: A Medical History', *Journal of the Society for Army Historical Research*, 56.226 (1978), pp. 79–92.

Burne, Alfred Higgins, *The Noble Duke of York: The Military Life of Frederick, Duke of York and Albany* (London: Staples Press, 1949).

Butcher, Rory, '"By Beat of Drum or Otherwise": Assessing Recruitment to the Fencible Regiments, 1793-1802', in *One Hundred Years of Army Historical Research: Proceedings of the SAHR Centenary Conference*, ed. by Andrew Bamford (Warwick: Helion, 2022), pp. 103–28.

Campbell, Alexander V., *The Royal American Regiment : An Atlantic Microcosm, 1755-1772* (Norman: University of Oklahoma Press, 2010).

Candlin, Kit, 'The Role of the Enslaved in the "Fedon Rebellion" of 1795', *Slavery & Abolition*, 39.4 (2018), pp. 685–707 <https://doi.org/10.1080/0144039X.2018.1464623>

Cannon, Richard, *Historical Record of the Fifty-Sixth, or the West Essex Regiment of Foot: Containing an Account of the Formation of the Regiment in 1755, and of Its Subsequent Services to 1844*, Historical Records of the British Army (London: Parker, Furnivall, and Parker, 1844).

——, *Historical Record of the First, or King's Regiment of Dragoon Guards: Containing an Account of the Formation of the Regiment in the Year 1685 and of Its Subsequent Services to 1836*, Historical Records of the British Army (London: William Clowes and Sons, 1837).

——, *Historical Record of the Fourteenth, or the Buckinghamshire Regiment of Foot: Containing an Account of the Formation of the Regiment in 1685, and of Its Subsequent Services to 1845*, Historical Records of the British Army (London: Parker, Furnivall, and Parker, 1845).

——, *Historical Record of the Seventy-Third Regiment: Containing an Account of the Formation of the Regiment from the Period of Its Being Raised as the Second Battalion of the Forty-Second Royal Highlanders in 1870 and of Its Subsequent Services to 1851*, Historical Records of the British Army, 41 (London: Parker, Furnivall, and Parker, 1850).

——, *Historical Record of the Sixth Regiment of Dragoon Guards, or the Carabineers : Containing an Account of the Formation of the Regiment in 1685, and of Its Subsequent Services to 1839*, Historical Records of the British Army (London: Longman, Orme; Clowes, 1839).

——, *Historical Record of the Thirty-First, or, the Huntingdonshire Regiment of Foot*, Historical Records of the British Army (London, England: Parker, Furnivall and Parker, 1850).

——, *Historical Record of the Twelfth, or the East Suffolk, Regiment of Foot: Containing an Account of the Formation of the Regiment in 1685, and of Its Subsequent Services to 1847*, Historical Records of the British Army (London: Parker, Furnivall, and Parker, 1848).

——, *Historical Record of the Fourth or Royal Irish Regiment of Dragoon Guards*, Historical Records of the British Army (London: William Clowes and Sons, 1839).

————, *Historical Record of the Life Guards: Containing an Account of the Formation of the Corps in the Year 1660 and of Its Subsequent Services to 1835*, Historical Records of the British Army(London: Adjutant General's Office, Horse Guards, 1837).

Cantlie, Neil, *A History of the Army Medical Department*, 2 vols (Edinburgh: Churchill Livingstone, 1974).

Carman, W.Y., '7th, 10th & 15th Hussars, 1808-09: Notes on Some Water-Colours By Robert Dighton, Junior', *Journal of the Society for Army Historical Research*, 30.122 (1952), pp. 76–80.

————, 'The Cavalry Staff Corps', *Journal of the Society for Army Historical Research*, 47.189 (1969), pp. 33–4.

Carter, Louise, 'Brothers in Arms? Martial Masculinities and Family Feeling in Old Soldiers' Memoirs, 1793–1815', in *Martial Masculinities: Experiencing and Imagining the Military in the Long Nineteenth Century*, ed. by Michael Brown, Anna Maria Barry and Joanne Begiato, Cultural History of Modern War (Manchester: Manchester University Press, 2019), pp. 35–57.

————, 'Scarlet Fever: Female Enthusiasm for Men in Uniform, 1780-1815', in *Britain's Soldiers: Rethinking War and Society, 1715-1815*, ed. by Kevin Linch and Matthew McCormack, Eighteenth-Century Worlds (Liverpool: University Press, 2014), pp. 155–80.

Cathcart, Brian, *The News from Waterloo: The Race to Tell Britain of Wellington's Victory* (London: Faber & Faber, 2015).

Chandler, David G., *The Campaigns of Napoleon* (London: Weidenfeld and Nicolson, 1967).

Chartrand, René, '1623. The York Rangers', *Journal of the Society for Army Historical Research*, 80.322 (2002), pp. 162–3.

————, 'Black Corps in the British West Indies, 1793-1815', *Journal of the Society for Army Historical Research*, 76.308 (1998), pp. 248–54.

————, 'The British Army's Unknown, Regular, African-West Indian Engineer and Service Corps, 1783 To The 1840s', *Journal of the Society for Army Historical Research*, 89.358 (2011), pp. 117–38.

Chaudhuri, Sashi Bhusan, *Civil Disturbances During The British Rule In India (1765-1857)* (Calcutta: The World Press, 1955).

Cherian, Neema, 'Spaces for Races : Ordering of Camp Followers in the Military Cantonments, Madras Presidency, c. 1800-64', *Social Scientist*, 32.5–6 (2004), pp. 32–50.

Childs, John, *The British Army of William III, 1689-1702* (Manchester: Manchester University Press, 1987).

Clammer, David, 'Soldiers and Civilians: Troops in Dorset, 1793 – 1805', *Journal of the Society for Army Historical Research*, 93.375 (2015), pp. 214–30.

Clode, Charles Mathew, *The Military Forces of the Crown: Their Administration and Government*, 2 vols (London: J. Murray, 1869).

Cockerill, A.W., *Sons of the Brave: The Story of Boy Soldiers* (London: Cooper in association with Secker & Warburg, 1984).

————, 'The Royal Military Asylum (1803-15).', *Journal of the Society for Army Historical Research*, 79.317 (2001), pp. 25–44.

Cole, Gareth, *Arming the Royal Navy, 1793-1815 : The Office of Ordnance and the State* (London: Pickering and Chatto, 2012).

Colley, Linda, *Britons: Forging the Nation 1707-1837* (London: Pimlico, 2003).

Collins, Bruce, *War and Empire : The Expansion of Britain, 1790-1830* (London: Routledge, 2014).

————, 'Effectiveness and the British Officer Corps, 1793-1815', in *Britain's Soldiers : Rethinking War and Society, 1715-1815*, ed. by Kevin Linch and Matthew McCormack (Liverpool: Liverpool University Press, 2014), pp. 57–76.

Connolly, T.W.J., *History of the Royal Sappers and Miners, from the Formation of the Corps in March, 1772, to the Date When Its Designation Was Changed to That of Royal Engineers, in October 1856 …*, 2 vols (London: Longman, Brown, Green, Longmans and Roberts, 1857).

Connor, J., 'Climate, Environment, and Australian Frontier Wars: New South Wales, 1788-1841', *Society for Military History* (Society for Military History, 2017), pp. 985–1003

Connor, John, *The Australian Frontier Wars, 1788-1838* (UNSW Press, 2002).

Conway, Stephen, *The British Army, 1714–1783: An Institutional History* (Barnsley: Pen & Sword Military, 2021).

———, *War, State, and Society in Mid-Eighteenth-Century Britain and Ireland* (Oxford: Oxford University Press, 2006).

———, *The British Isles and the War of American Independence* (Oxford: Oxford University Press, 2000).

Cook, Chris, *British Historical Facts, 1760-1830* (London : Macmillan, 1980).

Cookson, J.E., 'Early Nineteenth-Century Scottish Military Pensioners as Homecoming Soldiers', *Historical Journal*, 52.2 (2009), pp. 319–41 <https://doi.org/10.1017/s0018246x09007481>

———, 'Service without Politics? Army, Militia and Volunteers in Britain during the American and French Revolutionary Wars', *War in History*, 10.4 (2003), pp. 381–97 <https://doi.org/10.1191/0968344503wh288oa>

———, *The British Armed Nation, 1793-1815* (Oxford: Clarendon, 1997).

———, 'Political Arithmetic and War in Britain, 1793-1815', *War & Society*, 1.2 (1983), pp. 37–60.

———, 'Regimental Worlds : Interpreting the Experience of British Soldiers during the Napoleonic Wars', in *Soldiers, Citizens and Civilians: Experiences and Perceptions of the French Wars, 1790-1820*, ed. by Alan Forrest, Karen Hagemann, and Jane Rendall (Basingstoke: Palgrave Macmillan, 2009), pp. 23–42.

Cooper, Randolf G.S., 'Culture, Combat, and Colonialism in Eighteenth- and Nineteenth-Century India', *International History Review*, 27.3 (2005), pp. 534–49.

———, *The Anglo-Maratha Campaigns and the Contest for India: The Struggle for Control of the South Asian Military Economy* (Cambridge: University Press, 2007).

Coss, Edward J., *All for the King's Shilling : The British Soldier under Wellington, 1808-1814* (Norman: University of Oklahoma Press, 2010).

Cozens, Joseph, '"The Blackest Perjury": Desertion, Military Justice, and Popular Politics in England, 1803-1805', *Labour History Review*, 79.3 (2014), pp. 255–80 <https://doi.org/10.3828/lhr.2014.14>

Craton, Michael, *Testing the Chains: Resistance to Slavery in the British West Indies* (Ithaca N.Y.: Cornell University Press, 1982).

Crooks, J.J., *Historical Records of the Royal African Corps* (Dublin, etc., 1925).

———, *History of the Royal Irish Regiment of Artillery* (Dublin: Browne and Nolan, 1914).

Crowhurst, Patrick, *The Defence of British Trade, 1689-1815* (Folkestone: Dawson, 1977).

Dalton, Charles, *The Waterloo Roll Call. With Biographical Notes and Anecdotes*, 2nd edn (London: Eyre and Spottiswoode, 1904).

Daly, Gavin, 'British Soldiers, Sieges, and the Laws of War: The 1807 Siege of Montevideo', in *Redcoats to Tommies: The Experience of the British Soldier from the Eighteenth Century*, ed. by Kevin Linch and Matthew Lord (Woodbridge: Boydell Press, 2021), pp. 103–19.

———, 'Liberators and Tourists: British Soldiers in Madrid during the Peninsular War', in *Soldiering in Britain and Ireland, 1750-1850: Men of Arms*, ed. by Catriona Kennedy and Matthew McCormack (Palgrave Macmillan, 2013), pp. 117–35.

———, *The British Soldier in the Peninsular War: Encounters with Spain and Portugal, 1808-1814* (Houndmills, Basingstoke; New York: Palgrave Macmillan, 2013).

———, 'Anglo-French Sieges, the Laws of War, and the Limits of Enmity in the Peninsular War, 1808–1814', *The English Historical Review*, 135.574 (2020), pp. 572–604 <https://doi.org/10.1093/ehr/ceaa190>

Das, Amita, *Defending British India against Napoleon: The Foreign Policy of Governor-General Lord Minto, 1807-13*, ed. by Aditya Das (Woodbridge: The Boydell Press, 2016).

Davies, Huw J., *Spying for Wellington: British Military Intelligence in the Peninsular War* (Norman (OK): University of Oklahoma Press, 2018).

Dawnay, Nicolas Payan, *The Distinction of Rank of Regimental Officers, 1684 to 1855* (London: Printed for the Society for Army Historical Research by Gale & Polden, 1960).

Dawson, Paul L., *Boots and Saddles!: Horses and Riders of Wellington's Army* (Stockton-on-Tees: Black Tent Publications, 2014).

———, *Waterloo: The Truth at Last : Why Napoleon Lost the Great Battle* (Barnsley: Frontline Books, 2018).

Demet, Paul, *'We Are Accustomed to Do Our Duty': German Auxiliaries with the British Army 1793-95* (Warwick, England: Helion & Company, 2018).

Dempsey, Guy C., *Albuera, 1811: The Bloodiest Battle of the Peninsular War* (Barnsley: Frontline Books, 2011).

Dewar, David, and Warwick Funnell, *A History of British National Audit: The Pursuit of Accountability* (Oxford University Press, 2017).

Douet, James, *British Barracks 1600-1914: Their Architecture and Role in Society* (London: Stationery Office, 1998).

Douglas, Mary (ed.), *Constructive Drinking: Perspectives on Drink from Anthropology* (Abingdon, Oxon: Routledge, 2003).

Dubois, Laurent, *Avengers of the New World: the Story of the Haitian Revolution* (Cambridge, Mass.: Belknap, 2005).

Duffy, Michael, "A Particular Service': The British Government and the Dunkirk Expedition of 1793', *The English Historical Review*, XCI.CCCLX (1976), pp. 529–54 <https://doi.org/10.1093/ehr/XCI.CCCLX.529>

———, *Soldiers, Sugar, and Seapower : The British Expeditions to the West Indies and the War against Revolutionary France* (Oxford [Oxfordshire]; New York: Clarendon Press ; Oxford University Press, 1987).

———, 'The British Army and the Caribbean Expeditions of the War Against Revolutionary France 1793-1801', *Journal of the Society for Army Historical Research*, 62.250 (1984), pp. 65–73.

Duncan, Francis, *History of the Royal Regiment of Artillery*, 2 vols (London, 1872).

Durey, Michael, *William Wickham, Master Spy : The Secret War against the French Revolution* (London: Pickering & Chatto, 2009).

———, 'White Slaves: Irish Rebel Prisoners and The British Army in The West Indies 1799-1804', *Journal of the Society for Army Historical Research*, 80.324 (2002), pp. 296–312

———, "Black Bob' Craufurd and Ireland, 1798-1804', *War in History*, 16.2 (2009), pp. 133–56 <https://doi.org/10.1177/0968344508100987>

Dziennik, Matthew P., *The Fatal Land: War, Empire, and the Highland Soldier in British America* (New Haven: Yale University Press, 2015).

Ehrman, John, *The Younger Pitt*, 3 vols (London: Constable, 1996).

Elting, John Robert, *Amateurs, to Arms!: A Military History of the War of 1812* (Chapel Hill, N.C.: Algonquin Books of Chapel Hill, 1991).

Emsley, Clive, 'Political Disaffection and the British Army in 1792', *Historical Research*, 48.118 (1975), pp. 230–45 <https://doi.org/10.1111/j.1468-2281.1975.tb00751.x>

———, 'The Military and Popular Disorder in England 1790-1801 (Continued).', *Journal of the Society for Army Historical Research*, 61.246 (1983), pp. 96–112.

Esdaile, Charles J., *The Wars of the French Revolution: 1792-1801* (London ; New York, NY: Routledge, 2018).

———, *Women in the Peninsular War* (Norman: University of Oklahoma Press, 2014).

Flayhart, William Henry, *Counterpoint to Trafalgar: the Anglo-Russian Invasion of Naples, 1805-1806* (Gainesville: University Press of Florida, 2004).

Fletcher, Ian, *Galloping at Everything: The British Cavalry in the Peninsular War and Waterloo Campaign 1808-15* (Staplehurst: Spellmount, 1999).

Floud, Roderick, *Height, Health and History: Nutritional Status in the United Kingdom, 1750-1980* (Cambridge: University Press, 1990).

——, 'The Dimensions of Inequality: Height and Weight Variation in Britain, 1700-2000', *Contemporary British History,* 16.3 (2002), pp. 13–26 <https://doi.org/10.1080/713999458>

Forbes, A., *A History of the Army Ordnance Services,* 3 vols (London: Medici Society, 1929).

——, *The 'Black Watch': The Record of an Historic Regiment* (London: Cassell and Company, 1896).

Forrest, Alan, *Waterloo* (Oxford: Oxford University Press, 2015).

Fortescue, J.W., *A History of the British Army,* 13 vols (London; New York: Macmillan and Co.; Macmillan Co., 1899–1920).

——, *The County Lieutenancies and the Army, 1803-1814* (London: Macmillan and Co., limited, 1909).

Frenz, Margret, *From Contact to Conquest: transition to British rule in Malabar, 1790-1805* (New Delhi: Oxford University Press, 2003).

Frontier and Overseas Expeditions from India, 6 vols (Calcutta: Superintendent Government Printing India, 1911).

Funnell, Warwick, 'The "Proper Trust of Liberty": Economical Reform, the English Constitution and the Protections of Accounting during the American War of Independence', *Accounting History,* 13.1 (2008), pp. 7–32 <https://doi.org/10.1177/1032373207083925>

Gaffield, Julia, *Haitian Connections in the Atlantic World: Recognition after Revolution* (Chapel Hill: University of North Carolina Press, 2015).

Gapps, Stephen, *The Sydney Wars: Conflict in the Early Colony, 1788-1817* (Sydney, NSW: University of New South Wales Press, 2018).

Gash, Norman, 'After Waterloo : British Society and the Legacy of the Napoleonic Wars', *Transactions of the Royal Historical Society,* 5th ser., 28 (1978), pp. 145–57 <https://doi.org/10.2307/3679205>

Gates, David, *The British Light Infantry Arm c. 1790-1815: Its Creation, Training and Operational Role* (London: Batsford, 1987).

Gee, Austin, *The British Volunteer Movement, 1794-1814* (Oxford; New York: Clarendon Press ; Oxford University Press, 2003).

Geggus, David, *Slavery, War, and Revolution: The British Occupation of Saint Domingue, 1793-1798* (New York and Oxford, 1982).

——, 'The British Government and the Saint Domingue Slave Revolt, 1791-1793', *The English Historical Review,* 96.379 (1981), pp. 285–305

——, 'The Enigma of Jamaica in the 1790s: New Light on the Causes of Slave Rebellions', *The William and Mary Quarterly,* 44.2 (1987), pp. 274–99 <https://doi.org/10.2307/1939665>

——, 'Yellow Fever in the 1790s : The British Army in Occupied Saint Domingue', *Medical History,* 23 (1979), pp. 38–58.

Gilbert, Alan, *Black Patriots and Loyalists : Fighting for Emancipation in the War for Independence* (Chicago (IL).: Chicago University Press, 2012).

——, 'A Tale of Two Regiments: Manpower and Effectiveness in British Military Units During the Napoleonic Wars', *Armed Forces & Society,* 9.2 (1983), pp. 275–92 <https://doi.org/10.1177/0095327X8300900205>

——, 'An Analysis of Some Eighteenth Century Army Recruiting Records', *Journal of the Society for Army Historical Research,* 54.217 (1976), pp. 38–47.

Gleadle, Kathryn, 'The Juvenile Enlightenment: British Children and Youth During the French Revolution', *Past & Present,* 233.1 (2016), pp. 143–84 <https://doi.org/10.1093/pastj/gtw043>

Glover, Gareth, *Waterloo: The Defeat of Napoleon's Imperial Guard; Henry Clinton, the 2nd Division and the End of a 200-Year-Old Controversy* (Barnsley: Frontline Books, 2015).

Glover, Michael, 'The Purchase of Commissions: A Reappraisal', *Journal of the Society for Army Historical Research,* 58.236 (1980), pp. 223–35.

———, *Wellington's Army: In the Peninsula, 1808-1814* (Newton Abbot: David & Charles, 1977).

Glover, Richard, *Britain at Bay: Defence against Bonaparte, 1803-14* (London: Allen & Unwin, 1973).

———, *Peninsular Preparation: The Reform of the British Army, 1795-1809* (Cambridge: University Press, 1963).

———, 'The French Fleet, 1807-1814; Britain's Problem; and Madison's Opportunity', *The Journal of Modern History*, 39.3 (1967), pp. 233–52.

Godfrey, Walter H. (ed.), *Survey of London: Volume 11, Chelsea, Part IV: the Royal Hospital* (London, 1927).

Gopalakrishnan, S., Session, S. Gopalakrishnan and South Indian History Congress, *The South Indian Rebellions: Before and after 1800* (Chennai: Palaniappa Bros., 2007).

Gould. Robert W., *Mercenaries of the Napoleonic Wars* (Brighton: Tom Donovan, 1995).

Grainger, John D., *British Campaigns in the South Atlantic 1805-1807: Operations in the Cape and the River Plate and Their Consequences* (Barnsley: Pen & Sword Military, 2014).

Graves, Donald E., *Where Right and Glory Lead!: The Battle of Lundy's Lane, 1814* (Toronto: Robin Brass Studio, 2000).

Greenleaf, W.H., 'The Commission of Military Enquiry, 1805-12', *Journal of the Society for Army Historical Research*, 41.168 (1963), pp. 171–81.

Gregory, Desmond, *The Beneficent Usurpers: A History of the British in Madeira* (Rutherford, N.J: Fairleigh Dickinson University Press, 1988).

———, *Sicily: The Insecure Base: A History of the British Occupation of Sicily, 1806-1815* (London: Associated University Press, 1988).

Greig, Matilda, 'Accidental Authors? Soldiers' Tales of the Peninsular War and the Secrets of the Publishing Process', *History Workshop Journal*, 86 (2018), pp. 224–44 <https://doi.org/10.1093/hwj/dby025>

———, *Dead Men Telling Tales: Napoleonic War Veterans and the Military Memoir Industry, 1808-1914* (Oxford: Oxford University Press, 2021).

Gretton, Tom, 'Waterloo in Richard Caton Woodville's "Battles of the British Army": Series for the Illustrated London News, 1893–99', *Victorian Periodicals Review*, 48.4 (2015), pp. 531–56 <https://doi.org/10.1353/vpr.2015.0050>

Gray, D.S., '"Prisoners, Wanderers and Deserters": Recruiting for the King's German Legion, 1803-1815', *Journal of the Society for Army Historical Research*, 53 (1975), pp. 148–58.

Griffith, Robert, *Riflemen: The History of the 5th Battalion, 60th (Royal American). Regiment – 1797-1818* (Warwick: Helion & Company, 2021).

Grundy, Kenneth William, *Soldiers without Politics: Blacks in the South African Armed Forces* (Berkeley: University of California Press, 1983).

Guggisberg, Frederick Gordon, *'The Shop'; the Story of the Royal Military Academy* (London, New York: Cassell, 1902).

Hall, Christopher D., *British Strategy in the Napoleonic War, 1803-15* (Manchester: Manchester University Press, 1992).

Hariharan, Shantha, and P.S. Hariharan, 'The Expedition to Garrison Portuguese Macao with British Troops: Temporary Occupation and Re-Embarkation, 1808', *International Journal of Maritime History*, 25.2 (2013), pp. 85–116 <https://doi.org/10.1177/084387141302500209>

Harling, Philip, 'The Duke of York Affair (1809) and the Complexities of Wartime Patriotism', *Historical Journal*, 39 (1996), pp. 963–84 <https://doi.org/10.1017/S0018246X00024729>

———, *The Waning of 'Old Corruption': The Politics of Economical Reform in Britain, 1779-1846* (Oxford: Clarendon Press, 1996).

Harrison, Mark, 'Disease and Medicine in the Armies of British India, 1750-1830: The Treatment of Fevers and the Emergence of Tropical Therapeutics', in *British Military and Naval Medicine, 1600-1830* (Amsterdam; New York: Rodopi, 2007), pp. 87–119.

Harvey, A.D., 'The Ministry of All the Talents: The Whigs in Office, February 1806 to March 1807', *The Historical Journal*, 15.4 (1972), pp. 619–48.

Haythornthwaite, Philip, '1353 Inspectors of Yeomanry and Volunteers', *Journal of the Society for Army Historical Research*, 70.284 (1992), pp. 270–1.

Herbert, Trevor, and Helen Barlow, *Music & the British Military in the Long Nineteenth Century* (New York: Oxford University Press, 2013).

Hickey, Donald R., *The War of 1812: A Forgotten Conflict* (Urbana: University of Illinois Press, 1989).

Hill, R. Maurice, 'A Short History of The New South Wales Corps 1789-1818', *Journal of the Society for Army Historical Research*, 13.51 (1934), pp. 135–40.

Historical Records of the XXX. Regiment (London, 1887).

Hodge, William Barwick, 'On the Mortality Arising from Military Operations', *Journal of the Statistical Society of London*, 19.3 (1856), 219–71 <https://doi.org/10.2307/2338189>

Hodson, V., 'The Royal Military Academy, Woolwich, in 1809', *Journal of the Society for Army Historical Research*, 1.4 (1922), pp. 146–53.

Hofschröer, Peter, *1815: The Waterloo Campaign: The German Victory* (London: Greenhill, 1999).

———, *1815, the Waterloo Campaign: Wellington, His German Allies and the Battles of Ligny and Quatre Bras* (London: Greenhill, 1998).

Hogarth, Rana A., 'An African Corps in a Most Distressed and Sickly Condition: Yellow Fever in the West Indies', in *Medicalizing Blackness, Making Racial Difference in the Atlantic World, 1780-1840* (University of North Carolina Press, 2017), pp. 48–78 <https://www.jstor.org/stable/10.5149/9781469632889_hogarth.7>

———, 'Black Immunity and Yellow Fever in the American Atlantic', in *Medicalizing Blackness, Making Racial Difference in the Atlantic World, 1780-1840* (University of North Carolina Press, 2017), pp. 17–47 <https://www.jstor.org/stable/10.5149/9781469632889_hogarth.6> [accessed 23 July 2020].

Honeyman, Katrina, *Child Workers in England, 1780-1820: Parish Apprentices and the Making of the Early Industrial Labour Force*, Studies in Labour History (Aldershot: Ashgate, 2007).

Hoock, Holger, *Empires of the Imagination: Politics, War and the Arts in the British World, 1750-1850* (London: Profile Books, 2010).

Horne, Gerald, *Negro Comrades of the Crown African Americans and the British Empire Fight the U.S. Before Emancipation* (New York: University Press, 2012).

Houlding, J.A., *Fit for Service: The Training of the British Army, 1715-1795* (Oxford: Clarendon, 1981).

———, 'The Number of Commissioned British Military Officers, 1725-1792', *Journal of the Society for Army Historical Research*, 91.366 (2013), pp. 92–7.

Howard, Martin, *Wellington's Doctors: The British Army Medical Services in the Napoleonic Wars* (Staplehurst: Spellmount, 2002).

———, 'Walcheren 1809: A Medical Catastrophe', *British Medical Journal*, 319.7225 (1999), pp. 1642–5 <https://doi.org/10.1136/bmj.319.7225.1642>

Hudson, Robert P., *Disease and Its Control: The Shaping of Modern Thought* (New York: Praeger, 1983).

Huf, David, 'British National and Patriotic Identities in the Army Officer Corps, 1793–1815', *Historical Research*, 92.256 (2019), pp. 340–61 <https://doi.org/10.1111/1468-2281.12266>

Hughes, Ben, *Conquer or Die!: Wellington's Veterans and the Liberation of the New World* (Oxford: Osprey, 2010).

Hurl-Eamon, Jennine, *Marriage and the British Army in the Long Eighteenth Century: 'The Girl I Left behind Me'* (Oxford: Oxford University Press, 2014).

Huttenback, R. A., 'The French Threat to India and British Relations with Sind, 1799-1809', *The English Historical Review*, 76.301 (1961), pp. 590–9 <https://doi.org/10.1093/ehr/LXXVI.CCCI.590>

Iglesias Rogers, Graciela, *British Liberators in the Age of Napoleon: Volunteering under the Spanish Flag in the Peninsular War* (London; New York: Bloomsbury, 2013).

Innes, Joanna, 'Forms of "Government Growth", 1780-1830', in *Structures and Transformations in Modern British History*, ed. by David Feldman and Jon Lawrence (Cambridge: Cambridge University Press, 2011), pp. 74–99.

Irving, L. Homfray, *Officers of the British Forces in Canada during the War of 1812-15* ([Welland], 1908).

Jameson, Robert, *Historical Record of the Seventy-Ninth Regiment of Foot: Or Cameron Highlanders* (Edinburgh; London: William Blackwood, 1863).

Jennings, Paul, *A History of Drink and the English, 1500-2000*, Perspectives in Economic and Social History, 44 (London: Routledge, 2016).

Jones, K.R., 'Cox and Co.: Army Agents Craig's Court: The Nineteenth Century', *Journal of the Society for Army Historical Research*, 40.164 (1962), pp. 178–86.

——, 'Richard Cox, Army Agent and Banker', *Journal of the Society for Army Historical Research*, 34.140 (1956), pp. 178–81.

Jones, Randolph, 'The Bourbon Regiment and the Barbados Slave Revolt of 1816', *Journal of the Society for Army Historical Research*, 78.313 (2000), pp. 3–10.

——, 'The Ceylon Light Dragoons, 1803-32', *Journal of the Society for Army Historical Research*, 80.324 (2002), pp. 313–25.

——, 'The Lascorins of Ceylon in British Service', *Journal of the Society for Army Historical Research*, 80.321 (2002), pp. 1–15.

Jones, Randolph T., 'The Trinidad Militia, 1801-38', *Journal of the Society for Army Historical Research*, 82.330 (2004), pp. 132–54.

Jones, William Daniel, *Records of the Royal Military Academy (1741-1840)* (Woolwich, 1851).

Joseph, Michael, 'Military Officers, Tropical Medicine, and Racial Thought in the Formation of the West India Regiments, 1793–1802', *Journal of the History of Medicine and Allied Sciences*, 72.2 (2017), pp. 142–65 <https://doi.org/10.1093/jhmas/jrw037>

Jupp, Peter, 'The British State and the Napoleonic Wars, 1799-1815', in *Collaboration and Resistance in Napoleonic Europe: State Formation in an Age of Upheaval, c. 1800-1815*, ed. by Michael Rowe (Basingstoke; New York: Palgrave Macmillan, 2003), pp. 213–37.

Katcher, Philip R.N., *Encyclopedia of British, Provincial, and German Army Units 1775-1783* (Harrisburg: Stackpole, 1973).

Kelly, Catherine, *War and the Militarization of British Army Medicine, 1793-1830* (London: Pickering & Chatto, 2011).

Kelly, Paul, 'British Politics 1783-4 : The Emergence and Triumph of the Younger Pitt's Administration', *Bulletin of the Institute of Historical Research*, 54.129 (1981), pp. 62–78.

Kennaway, James, 'Military Surgery as National Romance: The Memory of British Heroic Fortitude at Waterloo', *War & Society*, 39.2 (2020), pp. 77–92.

Kennedy, Catriona, *Narratives of the Revolutionary and Napoleonic Wars: Military and Civilian Experience in Britain and Ireland* (Basingstoke: Palgrave Macmillan, 2013).

Klein, Lawrence E., 'Politeness and the Interpretation of the British Eighteenth Century', *The Historical Journal*, 45.4 (2002), pp. 869–98.

Klooster, Wim, 'Slave Revolts, Royal Justice, and a Ubiquitous Rumor in the Age of Revolutions', *The William and Mary Quarterly*, 71.3 (2014), pp. 401–24 <https://doi.org/10.5309/willmaryquar.71.3.0401>

Knežević, Saša, and Boris Vukićević, 'Montenegrin-British Military Cooperation against the French in the Bay of Kotor (1813-1814).', *War in History*, 28.4 (2020), pp. 781–96 <https://doi.org/10.1177/0968344520904065>

Knight, Roger, *Britain against Napoleon : The Organization of Victory, 1793-1815* (London: Allen Lane, an imprint of Penguin Books, 2013).

Komlos, John, and Helmut Küchenhoff, 'The Diminution of the Physical Stature of the English Male Population in the Eighteenth Century', *Cliometrica*, 6.1 (2012), pp. 45–62

Kopperman, Paul E., "The Cheapest Pay': Alcohol Abuse in the Eighteenth-Century British Army', *Journal of Military History*, 60.3 (1996), pp. 445–70 <https://doi.org/10.2307/2944520>

Lambert, David, "[A] Mere Cloak for Their Proud Contempt and Antipathy towards the African Race": Imagining Britain's West India Regiments in the Caribbean, 1795–1838', *Journal of Imperial and Commonwealth History*, 46.4 (2018), pp. 627–50 <https://doi.org/10.1080/030 86534.2018.1463612>

Latimer, Jon, *1812 : War with America* (Cambridge, Mass.; London: Belknap Press of Harvard University Press, 2007).

Laws, M.E.S, *Battery Records of the Royal Artillery, 1716-1859* (Woolwich, Eng.: Royal Artillery Institute, 1952).

———, 'Foreign Artillery Corps in the British Service, 1 : The French Emigrant Artillery', *Journal of the Royal Artillery*, 65.3 (1938), pp. 356–67.

———, 'Foreign Artillery Corps in the British Service. No. 2, the Dutch Emigrant Artillery. No. 3, the Royal Foreign Artillery', *Journal of the Royal Artillery*, 73 (1946), pp. 250–60.

Limm, Andrew, 'The British Army, 1795-1815 : An Army Transformed?', in *A Military Transformed? : Adaption and Innovation in the British Military, 1792-1945,* ed. by Locicero, Michael, Mitchell, Stuart, and Mahoney, Ross, (Solihull: Helion, 2014), pp. 21–35.

Lin, Patricia Y.C.E., 'Caring for the Nation's Families : British Soldiers' and Sailors' Families and the State, 1793-1815', in *Soldiers, Citizens and Civilians: Experiences and Perceptions of the Revolutionary and Napoleonic Wars, 1790-1820* (Basingstoke: Palgrave Macmillan, 2009), pp. 99–117.

Linch, Kevin, *Britain and Wellington's Army: Recruitment, Society and Tradition, 1807-15,* (Houndmills, Basingstoke, Hampshire; New York: Palgrave Macmillan, 2011).

———, 'Desertion from the British Army during the Napoleonic Wars', *Journal of Social History*, 49.4 (2016), pp. 808–28 <https://doi.org/10.1093/jsh/shw007>

———, 'Making New Soldiers', in *Britain's Soldiers: Rethinking War and Society, 1715-1815*, ed. by Kevin Linch and Matthew McCormack (Liverpool: Liverpool University Press, 2014), pp. 202–19

———, 'The Politics of Foreign Recruitment in Britain during the French Revolutionary and Napoleonic Wars', in *Transnational Soldiers: Foreign Military Enlistment in the Modern Era*, ed. by Nir Arielli and Bruce Collins (Basingstoke: Palgrave Macmillan, 2012), pp. 50–66

Lipscombe, Nick, *Wellington's Guns: The Untold Story of Wellington and His Artillery in the Peninsula and at Waterloo* (Botley, Oxford: Osprey Publishing, 2013).

Lord, Walter Frewen, 'Goree: A Lost Possession of England', *Transactions of the Royal Historical Society*, 11 (1897), pp. 139–52 <https://doi.org/10.2307/3678219>

Lynn, John A., 'Essential Women, Necessary Wives, and Exemplary Soldiers: The Military Reality and Cultural Representation of Women's Military Participation (1600–1815).', in *A Companion to Women's Military History*, ed. by Barton Hacker and Margaret Vining (Brill, 2012), pp. 93–136 <https://doi.org/10.1163/9789004206823_005>

MacArthur, Roderick, 'British Army Establishments During the Napoleonic Wars, Part 1: Background and Infantry', *Journal of the Society for Army Historical Research*, 87.350 (2009), pp. 150–72.

———, 'British Army Establishments During the Napoleonic Wars (Part 2). Cavalry, Artillery, Engineers and Supporting Units', *Journal of the Society for Army Historical Research*, 87.352 (2009), pp. 331–56.

Mackesy, Piers, *The War For America 1775-1783* (London: Longman, 1964).

———, *The War in the Mediterranean, 1803-1810* (London: Longmans, 1957).

———, *Statesmen at War: The Strategy of Overthrow, 1798-1799* (London; New York: Longman, 1974).

MacKillop, Andrew, 'For King, Country and Regiment? Motive and Identity in Highland Soldiering 1746-1815', in *Fighting for Identity: Scottish Military Experience c. 1550-1900*, ed. by Steve Murdoch and Andrew MacKillop (Leiden: Brill Academic, 2002), pp. 185–212.

——, 'Continuity, Coercion and Myth: The Recruitment of Highland Regiments in the Later Eighteenth Century', *International Review of Scottish Studies*, 26 (2001), pp. 30–55 <https://doi.org/10.21083/irss.v26i0.210>

——, *More Fruitful than the Soil : Army, Empire, and the Scottish Highlands, 1715-1815* (East Linton: Tuckwell, 2000).

Mann, Michael, 'The Corps of Invalids', *Journal of the Society for Army Historical Research*, 66.265 (1988), pp. 5–19.

Mathews, Joseph James, *Reporting the Wars* (Minneapolis: University of Minnesota Press, 1957).

McAleer, John, "The Key to India': Troop Movements, Southern Africa, and Britain's Indian Ocean World, 1795–1820', *The International History Review*, 35.2 (2013), pp. 294–316 <https://doi.org/10.1080/07075332.2012.761147>

McCormack, Matthew, *Embodying the Militia in Georgian England* (Oxford: Oxford University Press, 2015).

——, *The Independent Man: Citizenship and Gender Politics in Georgian England* (Manchester, U.K.; New York: Manchester University Press, 2011).

——, 'Citizenship, Nationhood, and Masculinity in the Affair of the Hanoverian Soldier, 1756', *The Historical Journal*, 49.4 (2006), pp. 971–93 <https://doi.org/10.1017/S0018246X0600570X>

McDonald, Terry, "'It Is Impossible for His Majesty's Government to Withdraw from These Dominions": Britain and the Defence of Canada, 1813 to 1834', *Journal of Canadian Studies*, 39.3 (2005), pp. 40–59.

McDonnell, Ciarán, 'A Fair Chance? The Catholic Irish Brigade in the British Service, 1793-1798', *War in History*, 23.2 (2016), pp. 150–68 <https://doi.org/10.1177/0968344514559872>

——, 'Loyalty and Rebellion: Irish Soldiers in the British Military during the French Revolutionary and Napoleonic Wars', *British Journal for Military History*, 8.3 (2022), pp. 57–78 <https://doi.org/10.25602/GOLD.bjmh.v8i3.1644>

McGuffie, T.H., 'The 7th Light Dragoons and Their First Hussar Clothing', *Journal of the Society for Army Historical Research*, 35.142 (1957), pp. 48–52.

——, 'The Short Life and Sudden Death of an English Regiment of Foot: An Account of the Raising, Recruiting, Mutiny and Disbandment of the 113th Regiment Of Foot, or 'Royal Birmingham Volunteers' (April, 1794, to September, 1795).', *Journal of the Society for Army Historical Research*, 33.133 (1955), pp. 16–25.

——, 'The Significance of Military Rank in the British Army between 1790 and 1820', *Bulletin of the Institute of Historical Research*, 30 (1957), pp. 207–24.

McLynn, F.J., *Invasion: From the Armada to Hitler, 1588-1945* (London: Routledge & Kegan Paul, 1987).

Mendis, Vernon L.B., *The Advent of the British to Ceylon, 1762-1803* (Dehiwala: Tisara Prakasakayo, 2012).

Meuron, Guy de, *Le régiment Meuron, 1781-1816* (Lausanne: Le Forum historique, 1982).

Michell, John Edward, *Records of the Horse Brigade, from Its Formation to the Present Time* (Woolwich, 1874).

Miles, William R., 'Irish Soldiers, Pensions and Imperial Migration during the Early Nineteenth Century', *Britain and the World*, 6.2 (2013), pp. 243–57 <https://doi.org/10.3366/brw.2013.0098>

Mills, R.J.W., "L'Île Des Bannis': Jersey, Britain and the French Emigration 1789–1815', *European Review of History: Revue Européenne d'histoire*, 28.1 (2021), pp. 99–123 <https://doi.org/10.1080/13507486.2020.1823324>

Mitchell, Brian R., and Phyllis Deane, *Abstract of British Historical Statistics* (Cambridge: Cambridge University Press, 1962).

Moodley, Devedas, 'Vellore 1806: The Meanings of Mutiny', in *Rebellion, Repression, Reinvention: Mutiny in Comparative Perspective*, ed. by Jane Hathaway (Westport, Conn: Praeger, 2001), pp. 87–102.

Moon, Joshua Lee, *Wellington's Two-Front War: The Peninsular Campaigns, at Home and Abroad, 1808-1814* (Norman: University of Oklahoma Press, 2011).

Moore-Colyer, R.J., 'Horse Supply and the British Cavalry: A Review, 1066-1900', *Journal of the Society for Army Historical Research*, 70.284 (1992), pp. 245–60.

Morton, Desmond, 'How Lower Canada Won the War of 1812', *American Review of Canadian Studies*, 42.3 (2012), pp. 321–8 <https://doi.org/10.1080/02722011.2012.707050>

Mostert, Noël, *Frontiers: The Epic of South Africa's Creation and the Tragedy of the Xhosa People* (London: Cape, 1992).

Mouser, Bruce, 'Rebellion, Marronage and *Jihad*: Strategies of Resistance to Slavery on the Sierra Leone Coast, c. 1783-1796', *The Journal of African History*, 48.1 (2007), pp. 27–44 <https://doi.org/10.1017/S0021853706002490>

Muir, Rory, *Gentlemen of Uncertain Fortune: How Younger Sons Made Their Way in Jane Austen's England* (New Haven: Yale University Press, 2019).

——, *Tactics and the Experience of Battle in the Age of Napoleon* (New Haven, Conn.: Yale University Press, 1998).

——, *Wellington: the Path to Victory, 1769-1814* (New Haven: Yale University Press, 2013).

——, *Britain and the Defeat of Napoleon, 1807-1815* (New Haven (CT). and London: Yale University Press, 1996).

Munch-Petersen, Thomas, *Defying Napoleon : How Britain Bombarded Copenhagen and Seized the Danish Fleet in 1807* (Stroud: Sutton, 2007).

Murphy, John A., *The French Are in the Bay: The Expedition to Bantry Bay, 1796* (Cork and Dublin: Mercier Press, 1997).

Myerly, Scott Hughes, *British Military Spectacle: From the Napoleonic Wars through the Crimea* (Cambridge, Mass.: Harvard University Press, 1996).

Nafziger, George, *Imperial Bayonets: Tactics of the Napoleonic Battery, Battalion and Brigade as Found in … Contemporary Regulations* (Warwick: Helion and Company, 2021).

Napier, William Francis Patrick, *History of the War in the Peninsula and in the South of France from the Year 1807 to the Year 1814*, 6 vols (London: John William, 1828–40).

Neale, Matt, 'Making Crime Pay in Late Eighteenth-Century Bristol: Stolen Goods, the Informal Economy and the Negotiation of Risk', *Continuity and Change*, 26.3 (2011), pp. 439–59 <https://doi.org/10.1017/S026841601100021X>

Nelson, Ivan V., *The Irish Militia, 1793-1802: Ireland's Forgotten Army* (Dublin: Four Courts Press Ltd, 2007).

Nicholas, Stephen, and Richard H. Steckel, 'Heights and Living Standards of English Workers During the Early Years of Industrialisation, 1770-1815', *The Journal of Economic History*, 51.4 (1991), pp. 937–57.

Nichols, Alistair, *Wellington's Mongrel Regiment: A History of the Chasseurs Britanniques Regiment 1801-1814* (Staplehurst: Spellmount, 2005).

Niebyl, Peter H., 'The English Bloodletting Revolution, or Modern Medicine before 1850', *Bulletin of the History of Medicine; Baltimore, Md.* , 51.3 (1977), pp. 464–83.

Nielsen, Caroline, 'Disability, Fraud and Medical Experience at the Royal Hospital of Chelsea in the Long Eighteenth Century', in *Britain's Soldiers : Rethinking War and Society, 1715-1815*, ed. by Kevin Linch and Matthew McCormack (Liverpool: Liverpool University Press, 2014), pp. 183–201.

——, 'Continuing to Serve: Representations of the Elderly Veteran Soldier in the Late Eighteenth and Early Nineteenth Centuries', in *Men After War*, ed. by Stephen McVeigh and Nicola Cooper (London: Routledge, 2013), pp. 18–35.

Nosworthy, Brent, *Battle Tactics of Napoleon and His Enemies* (London: Constable, 1995).

Ó Grada, Cormac, 'The Population of Ireland 1700-1900: A Survey', *Annales de Démographie Historique*, 1979.1 (1979), pp. 281–99 <https://doi.org/10.3406/adh.1979.1425>

O'Donnell, Ruan, *Aftermath: Post-Rebellion Insurgency in Wicklow, 1799-1803* (Dublin ; Portland, OR: Irish Academic Press Ltd, 1999).

Olsen, Helene, 'The Social Construction of Mercenaries: German Soldiers in British Service during the Eighteenth Century', *Small Wars & Insurgencies* (2021), pp. 1–20 <https://doi.org/10.1080/09592318.2021.1978751>

Oman, Charles, *A History of the Peninsular War*, 7 vols (Oxford: Clarendon Press, 1902).

———, *Wellington's Army, 1809-1814* (London: E. Arnold, 1912).

Otley, C.B., 'The Social Origins of British Army Officers', *Sociological Review*, 18 (1970), pp. 213–39 <https://doi.org/10.1111/j.1467-954X.1970.tb00191.x>

Page, F.C.G., *Following the Drum: Women in Wellington's Wars* (London: Andre Deutsch, 1986).

Parker, Alice, 'Incorrigible Rogues: The Brutalisation of British Soldiers in the Peninsular War 1808-1814', *British Journal for Military History*, 1.3 (2015), pp. 25–41.

Parkes, Simon, 'Wooden Legs and Tales of Sorrow Done: The Literary Broken Soldier of the Late Eighteenth Century', *Journal for Eighteenth-Century Studies*, 36.2 (2013), pp. 191–207 <https://doi.org/10.1111/j.1754-0208.2012.00501.x>

Parks, Edwin, *The Royal Guernsey Militia: A Short History and List of Officers* (St. Peter Port: La Societé guernesiaise, 1992).

Partridge, Michael Stephen, 'Palmerston and the War Office, 1809-1828', in *Palmerston Studies II*, ed. by Miles Taylor and David Brown ([Southampton]: Hartley Institute, University of Southampton, 2007), pp. 1–23.

Peck, Louis F., *A Life of Matthew G. Lewis* (Cambridge, 1961).

Peers, Douglas M., 'Army Discipline, Military Cultures, and State-Formation in Colonial India, c.1780–1860', in *Britain's Oceanic Empire : Atlantic and Indian Ocean Worlds, c.1550-1850* (Cambridge: Cambridge University Press, 2012), pp. 282–308.

———, 'Imperial Vice: Sex, Drink and the Health of British Troops in North Indian Cantonments, 1800-1858', in *Guardians of Empire : The Armed Forces of the Colonial Powers c.1700–1964* (Manchester: Manchester University Press, 1999), pp. 25–52.

———, 'Soldiers, Surgeons and the Campaigns to Combat Sexually Transmitted Diseases in Colonial India, 1805-1860', *Medical History*, 42 (1998), pp. 137–60 <https://doi.org/10.1017/s0025727300063651>

Phillips, Emir, 'The Bank of England and Parliament Were Monetarily Adroit during the Napoleonic Wars', *Journal of Post Keynesian Economics*, 41.4 (2018), pp. 620–47 <https://doi.org/10.1080/01603477.2018.1455516>

Phillipson, Andy, 'The Raid on Ostend 1798 : Combined Operations against Revolutionary France', *Journal of the Society for Army Historical Research*, 81.325 (2003), pp. 31–46.

Pimlott, J. L., 'The Raising of Four Regiments for India, 1787-8', *Journal of the Society for Army Historical Research*, 52.210 (1974), pp. 68–88.

———, 'The Reformation of The Life Guards, 1788', *Journal of the Society for Army Historical Research*, 53.216 (1975), pp. 194–209.

Porter, Theodore M., *The Rise of Statistical Thinking: 1820-1900* (Princeton ; Princeton University Press, 1986).

Powell, Geoffrey, *The Kandyan Wars: The British Army in Ceylon, 1803-1818* (New Delhi: Navrang, 1984).

Prebble, John, *Mutiny : Highland Regiments in Revolt, 1743-1804* (London: Secker & Warburg, 1975).

Quinn, Simon, 'British Military Orientalism: Cross-Cultural Contact with the Mamluks during the Egyptian Campaign, 1801', *War in History*, 28.2 (2019), pp. 263–82 <https://doi.org/10.1177/0968344519837303>

Ramsey, Neil, *The Military Memoir and Romantic Literary Culture, 1780-1835* (Farnham: Ashgate, 2011).

Razzell, P. E., 'Social Origins of Officers in the Indian and British Home Army: 1758-1962', *The British Journal of Sociology*, 14.3 (1963), pp. 248–60 <https://doi.org/10.2307/587735>

——, 'The Growth of Population in Eighteenth-Century England: A Critical Reappraisal', *The Journal of Economic History*, 53.4 (1993), pp. 743–71.

Reboul, Juliette, *French Emigration to Great Britain in Response to the French Revolution*, War, Culture and Society, 1750-1850 (Basingstoke: Palgrave Macmillan, 2017).

Reinarz, Jonathan, and Rebecca Wynter, 'The Spirit of Medicine: The Use of Alcohol in Nineteenth-Century Medical Practice', in *Drink in the Eighteenth and Nineteenth Centuries*, ed. by Barbara Schmidt-Haberkamp and Susanne Schmid (Pickering & Chatto, 2016), pp. 127–40.

Reitan, E.A., *Politics, Finance, and the People: Economical Reform in England in the Age of the American Revolution, 1770-92* (Basingstoke: Palgrave Macmillan, 2007).

Reiter, Jacqueline, 'Citizen Soldiers: "Military Spirit" and Recruitment in Britain during the Wars against France, 1793–1815', in *Redcoats to Tommies: The Experience of the British Soldier from the Eighteenth Century*, ed. by Kevin Linch and Matthew Lord (Woodbridge: Boydell Press, 2021), pp. 19–39.

Robinson, Cicely, 'Conflicts of Conduct: British Masculinity and Military Painting in the Wake of the Siege of Gibraltar', in *Britain's Soldiers : Rethinking War and Society, 1715-1815*, ed. by Matthew McCormack and Kevin Linch (Liverpool: Liverpool University Press, 2014), pp. 133–54.

Rodger, Alexander, *Battle Honours of the British Empire and Commonwealth Land Forces, 1662-1991* (Ramsbury: Crowood, 2003).

Rodger, N.A.M., *The Command of the Ocean*, A Naval History of Britain (London: HarperCollins, 1997).

Rogers, S., *Historical Record of the Eighty-First Regiment, or Loyal Lincoln Volunteers; Containing an Account of the Formation of the Regiment in 1793, and of Its Subsequent Services to 1872* (Gibraltar: Printed by the Twenty-Eighth Regimental Press, 1872).

Roper, Michael, *The Records of the War Office and Related Departments, 1660-1964* (Kew: Public Record Office, 1998).

Rowbotham, W.B., 'Soldiers in Lieu of Marines', *Journal of the Society for Army Historical Research*, 33.133 (1955), pp. 26–34.

Roy, Kaushik, and Sabyasachi Dasgupta, 'Discipline and Disobedience in the Bengal and Madras Armies, 1807-56', in *War and Society in Colonial India, 1807-1945*, Oxford in India Readings. Themes in Indian History (New Delhi ; Oxford: Oxford University Press, 2006), pp. 55–81.

Roy, Kaushik, 'The Armed Expansion of the English East India Company : 1740s-1849', in *A Military History of India and South Asia : From the East India Company to the Nuclear Era*, ed. by Daniel Marston, Chandar S. Sundaram, and Stephen Philip Cohen (Westport (CT); Oxford: Praeger, 2006), pp. 1–15, 198–200.

——, 'The Hybrid Military Establishment of the East India Company in South Asia: 1750–1849', *Journal of Global History*, 6.2 (2011), pp. 195–218 <https://doi.org/10.1017/S1740022811000222>

Russell, Gillian, *The Theatres of War: Performance, Politics, and Society, 1793-1815* (Oxford; New York: Clarendon Press ; Oxford University Press, 1995).

Russell, Gillian and Neil Ramsey (eds), *Tracing War in British Enlightenment and Romantic Culture*, Palgrave Studies in the Enlightenment, Romanticism and the Cultures of Print (Basingstoke: Palgrave Macmillan, 2015).

Sargeaunt, Bertram Edward, *The Royal Manx Fencibles* (Aldershot: Gale & Polden, 1947).

Scouller, R.E., 'Purchase of Commissions and Promotions', *Journal of the Society for Army Historical Research*, 62.252 (1984), pp. 217–26.

Seaward, Paul, 'Parliament and the Idea of Political Accountability in Early Modern Britain', in *Realities of Representation: State Building in Early Modern Europe and European America*, ed. by Maija Jansson (New York: Palgrave Macmillan US, 2007), pp. 45–62.

Shaw, Philip, 'Dead Soldiers: Suffering in British Military Art, 1783–1789', *Romanticism*, 11.1 (2005), pp. 55–69 <https://doi.org/10.3366/rom.2005.11.1.55>

———, *Waterloo and the Romantic Imagination* (Houndmills, Basingstoke, Hampshire; New York: Palgrave/Macmillan, 2002).

Sheller, Mimi, 'Jamaican-Haitian Relations in the Nineteenth Century : The Origins of Trans-Caribbean Black Radicalism', *Jamaican Historical Review*, 23 (2007), pp. 37–49.

Siborne, William, *History of the War in France and Belgium, in 1815*, 2 vols (London: T. and W. Boone, 1844).

Sichart, L. von, *Geschichte Der Könglich-Hannoverschen Armee*, 4 vols (Hanover: Hahn'sche Hofbuchhandel, 1871).

Sivasundaram, Sujit, 'Tales of the Land : British Geography and Kandyan Resistance in Sri Lanka, c. 1803-1850', *Modern Asian Studies*, 41.5 (2007), pp. 925–65.

Smith, Paul H., 'The American Loyalists: Notes on Their Organization and Numerical Strength', *The William and Mary Quarterly*, 25.2 (1968), pp. 259–77 <https://doi.org/10.2307/1919095>

Snape, M.F., *The Redcoat and Religion: The Forgotten History of the British Soldier from the Age of Marlborough to the Eve of the First World War* (London; New York: Routledge, 2005).

Sperling, J., 'The International Payments Mechanism in the Seventeenth and Eighteenth Centuries', *The Economic History Review*, 14.3 (1962), pp. 446–68 <https://doi.org/10.2307/2591887>

Stanley, George F.G., 'The Canadian Militia during the Colonial Period', *Journal of the Society for Army Historical Research*, 24.97 (1946), pp. 30–41.

———, 'The Royal Nova Scotia Regiment, 1793-1802', *Journal of the Society for Army Historical Research*, 21.84 (1942), pp. 157–70.

Stanley, Peter, 'British Soldiers in Colonial Australia', in *Before the Anzac Dawn: A Military History of Australia to 1915*, ed. by Stockings, Craig A. J. and Connor, John (Sydney: NewSouth Publishing, 2013), pp. 39–61.

Stephens, H.M., and John Van der Kiste, 'Frederick, Prince, Duke of York and Albany (1763–1827), Army Officer and Bishop of Osnabrück', *Oxford Dictionary of National Biography*, 2007 <https://doi.org/10.1093/ref:odnb/10139> [accessed 25 March 2020]

Steppler, G.A., 'British Military Law, Discipline, and the Conduct of Regimental Courts Martial in the Later Eighteenth Century', *The English Historical Review*, CII.405 (1987), pp. 859–86 <https://doi.org/10.1093/ehr/CII.405.859>

Stevenson, John, *Popular Disturbances in England, 1700-1832*, 2nd edn (London, New York: Longman, 1992).

———, 'The London 'Crimp' Riots of 1794', *International Review of Social History*, 16 (1971), pp. 40–58 <https://doi.org/10.1017/S0020859000004004>

Stevenson, Lloyd G., 'John Hunter, Surgeon-General 1790-1793', *Journal of the History of Medicine and Allied Sciences*, 19.3 (1964), pp. 239–66.

Sutclife, Robert K., *British Expeditionary Warfare and the Defeat of Napoleon 1793-1815* (Woodbridge: Boydell & Brewer Ltd., 2014).

Sunter, Ronald M., 'Raising the 97th (Inverness-Shire). Highland Regiment of Foot', *Journal of the Society for Army Historical Research*, 76.306 (1998), pp. 93–110.

Telp, Claus, *The Evolution of Operational Art, 1740-1813: From Frederick the Great to Napoleon* (London: Frank Cass, 2005).

Thomas, R.N.W., *No Want of Courage: The British Army in Flanders, 1793-1795* (Warwick, England: Helion & Company Limited, 2022).

———, 'The Corps of Royal Waggoners and Army Transport during the Campaign in the Low Countries, 1794-1795', *Journal of the Society for Army Historical Research*, 76 (1998), pp. 157–62.

———, 'The Treasury, the Commissariat, and the Supply of the Duke of York's Army during the Flanders Campaign of 1793', *Proceedings of the Consortium on Revolutionary Europe, 1750 to 1850*, 22 (1992), pp. 567–75.

———, 'Wellington in the Low Countries, 1794-1795', *The International History Review*, 11.1 (1989), pp. 14–30.

Thompson, E.P., *The Making of the English Working Class* (London: Penguin Books, 2013).

Thompson, Mark S., *Wellington's Engineers* (Barnsley: Pen and Sword, 2022).

Thoumine, R.H., *Scientific Soldier: A Life of General Le Marchant 1766-1812* (London: Oxford University Press, 1968).

Torrance, John, 'Social Class and Bureaucratic Innovation: The Commissioners For Examining The Public Accounts 1780–1787', *Past & Present*, 78.1 (1978), pp. 56–81 <https://doi.org/10.1093/past/78.1.56>

Tullett, William, 'Political Engines: The Emotional Politics of Bells in Eighteenth-Century England', *Journal of British Studies*, 59.3 (2020), pp. 555–81 <https://doi.org/10.1017/jbr.2020.41>

Turner, Edward Raymond, and Gaudens Megaro, 'The King's Closet in the Eighteenth Century', *The American Historical Review*, 45.4 (1940), pp. 761–76 <https://doi.org/10.2307/1854450>

Turner, J.D., 'Army Agency', *Journal of the Society for Army Historical Research*, 13.49 (1934), pp. 27–37.

Tylden, G., 'The Ceylon Regiments, 1796 to 1874', *Journal of the Society for Army Historical Research*, 30.123 (1952), pp. 124–8.

———, 'The Third Kaffir War, 1799-1802', *Journal of the Society for Army Historical Research*, 37.150 (1959), pp. 72–82.

Ulrich, Nicole, 'Abolition from below: The 1808 Revolt in the Cape Colony', in *Humanitarian Intervention and Changing Labor Relations: The Long-Term Consequences of the Abolition of the Slave Trade* (Leiden: Brill, 2011), pp. 193–222.

Uythoven, Geert van, *The Secret Expedition: The Anglo-Russian Invasion of Holland 1799* (Warwick: Helion, 2018).

Valladares, Susan, *Staging the Peninsular War: English Theatres 1807-1815* (Farnham, Surrey, UK: Ashgate, 2015).

Vartavarian, Mesrob, 'An Open Military Economy: The British Conquest of South India Reconsidered, 1780-1799', *Journal of the Economic and Social History of the Orient*, 57.4 (2014), pp. 486–510.

———, 'Pacification and Patronage in the Maratha Deccan, 1803–1818', *Modern Asian Studies*, 50.6 (2016), pp. 1749–91 <https://doi.org/10.1017/S0026749X16000044>

———, 'Warriors and States: Military Labour in Southern India, circa 1750–1800', *Modern Asian Studies*, 53.2 (2019), pp. 313–38 <https://doi.org/10.1017/S0026749X17000038>

———, 'Warriors and the Company State in South India, 1799–1801', *South Asia: Journal of South Asian Studies*, 37.2 (2014), pp. 212–24 <https://doi.org/10.1080/00856401.2014.904764>

Wald, Erica, *Vice in the Barracks: Medicine, the Military and the Making of Colonial India, 1780-1868*, Cambridge Imperial and Post-Colonial Studies (Basingstoke, Hampshire: Palgrave Macmillan, 2014).

Wallace, Nesbit Willoughby, *A Regimental Chronicle and List of Officers of the 60th, or the King's Royal Rifle Corps, Formerly the 62nd, or the Royal American Regiment of Foot* (London : Harrison, 1879).

Watts, Sheldon, 'Yellow Fever Immunities in West Africa and the Americas in the Age of Slavery and beyond: A Reappraisal', *Journal of Social History*, 34.4 (2001), pp. 955–67.

Webb, Denver A., 'War, Racism, and the Taking of Heads: Revisiting Military Conflict in the Cape Colony and Western Xhosaland in the Nineteenth Century', *Journal of African History*, 56.1 (2015), pp. 37–55 <https://doi.org/10.1017/S0021853714000693>

Wells, Roger, *Insurrection: The British Experience 1795-1803* (Gloucester: Alan Sutton, 1983).

———, *Wretched Faces: Famine in Wartime England, 1793-1801* (Gloucester: Sutton, 1988).

Weller, Jac, *Wellington in India* (London: Greenhill Books, 1993).

Western, John Randle, 'The County Fencibles and Militia Augmentation of 1794', *Journal of the Society for Army Historical Research*, 34.137 (1956), pp. 3–11.

———, *The English Militia in the Eighteenth Century : The Story of a Political Issue 1660-1802* (London: Routledge & Kegan Paul, 1965).

White, A.S., 'Garrison, Reserve and Veteran Battalions and Companies', *Journal of the Society for Army Historical Research*, 38.156 (1960), pp. 156–67.

———, 'The Army List', *Journal of the Society for Army Historical Research*, 25.103 (1947), pp. 118–27.

White, Zach, 'From Cintra to Salamanca : Shifting Popular Perceptions of the War in the Iberian Peninsula, 1808-1812', *British Journal for Military History*, 1.3 (2015), pp. 42–61.

Willcox, Walter Temple, *The Historical Records of the Fifth (Royal Irish) Lancers from Their Foundation as Wynne's Dragoons (in 1689). to the Present Day* (London: A. Doubleday & Co., 1908).

Willis, James J., 'Transportation versus Imprisonment in Eighteenth- and Nineteenth-Century Britain: Penal Power, Liberty, and the State', *Law & Society Review*, 39.1 (2005), pp. 171–210.

Willis, Richard E., 'Cabinet Politics and Executive Policy-Making Procedures, 1794-1801', *Albion: A Quarterly Journal Concerned with British Studies*, 7.1 (1975), pp. 1–23 <https://doi.org/10.2307/4048395>

Wilson, Evan, *A Social History of British Naval Officers, 1775-1815* (Woodbridge, Suffolk: The Boydell Press, 2017).

Wilson, Jon E., *India Conquered: Britain's Raj and the Chaos of Empire* (London: Simon & Schuster, 2016).

Wilson, Peter H., 'The German "Soldier Trade" of the Seventeenth and Eighteenth Centuries: A Reassessment', *The International History Review*, 18.4 (1996), pp. 757–92.

Wishon, Mark, *German Forces and the British Army: Interactions and Perceptions, 1742-1815* (Basingstoke (GB).; New York: Palgrave Macmillan, 2013).

Wood, Herbert J., 'England, China, and the Napoleonic Wars', *Pacific Historical Review*, 9.2 (1940), pp. 139–56 <https://doi.org/10.2307/3633081>

Worden, Nigel, 'Armed with Swords and Ostrich Feathers: Militarism and Cultural Revolution in the Cape Slave Uprising of 1808', in *War, Empire and Slavery, 1770–1830*, ed. by Richard Bessel, Nicholas Guyatt, and Jane Rendall, War, Culture and Society, 1750–1850 (London: Palgrave Macmillan UK, 2010), pp. 121–38.

Wright, Christine, *Wellington's Men in Australia: Peninsular War Veterans and the Making of Empire c. 1820-40* (Houndmills, Basingstoke, Hampshire; New York: Palgrave Macmillan, 2011).

Wrigley, E. A., and Roger Schofield, *The Population History of England, 1541-1871: A Reconstruction*, paperback edition with new introduction (Cambridge: University Press, 1989).

Yaple, R. L., 'The Auxiliaries; Foreign and Miscellaneous Regiments in The British Army 1802 – 1817', *Journal of the Society for Army Historical Research*, 50.201 (1972), pp. 10–28.

Unpublished Theses

Bartlett, Keith John, 'The Development of the British Army during the Wars with France, 1793-1815' (unpublished Ph.D., Durham University, 1998) <http://etheses.dur.ac.uk/699/>

Burley, Roy David, 'An Age of Negligence? British Army Chaplaincy, 1796–1844' (unpublished MPhil, University of Birmingham, 2013) <https://etheses.bham.ac.uk/id/eprint/4329/1/Burley13MPhil.pdf>

Coombs, Danielle S. E., 'Crime and the Soldier : Identifying a Soldier-Specific Experience of Crime in the British Army, 1740-1830' (unpublished Ph.D., University of Leeds, 2015) <http://etheses.whiterose.ac.uk/9203/>

Cozens, Joseph Thomas, 'The Experience of Soldiering : Civil-Military Relations and Popular Protest in England, 1790-1805' (unpublished Ph.D., University of Essex, 2016) <http://repository.essex.ac.uk/16495/>

Faulkner, Jacqueline Suzanne Marie Jeanne, 'The Role of National Defence in British Political Debate, 1794-1812' (unpublished PhD, University of Cambridge, 2006) <https://www.repository.cam.ac.uk/handle/1810/271636>

Ferguson, Kenneth Patrick, 'The Army in Ireland from the Restoration to the Act of Union' (unpublished PhD, Trinity College, 1981) <http://hdl.handle.net/2262/77144>

Fletcher, William, '"Scientifics" and "Wycombites": A Study of the Quartermaster General's Department of the British Army, 1799-1814' (unpublished PhD, King's College London, 2019) <https://ethos.bl.uk/OrderDetails.do?uin=uk.bl.ethos.803265>

Gerges, Mark T., 'Command and Control in the Peninsula: The Role of the British Cavalry 1808-1814' (unpublished PhD, Florida State University, 2005) <https://diginole.lib.fsu.edu/islandora/object/fsu%3A182486/> [accessed 2 August 2020].

Gray, Daniel Savage, 'The Services of the King's German Legion in the Army of the Duke of Wellington, 1809-1815' (unpublished PhD, Florida State University, 1969).

Huf, David, 'The Junior British Army Officer: Experience and Identity, 1793-1815' (unpublished PhD, University of Tasmania, 2017) <https://eprints.utas.edu.au/23780/1/Huf_whole_thesis.pdf>

Limm, Andrew Robert, '"Fairly out-Generalled and Disgracefully Beaten' : The British Army in the Low Countries, 1793-1814' (unpublished Ph.D., University of Birmingham, 2015) <http://etheses.bham.ac.uk//id/eprint/5792/> [accessed 28 May 2019].

Linch, Kevin Barry, 'The Recruitment of the British Army 1807-1815' (unpublished PhD, University of Leeds, 2001) <https://ethos.bl.uk/OrderDetails.do?uin=uk.bl.ethos.409358>

Lyon, Frederick James, 'A Total War?: Media Representations and Public Perceptions of the War against Revolutionary France in Britain, 1793-1795' (unpublished MA by research, University of Leeds, 2015).

Michael Siva, 'After the Treaties: A Social, Economic and Demographic History of Maroon Society in Jamaica, 1739-1842' (unpublished PhD, University of Southampton, 2018).

Moore, Zeta Mary, 'Army Recruitment and the Uncertainties of the 'fiscal-Military' State in Britain, 1793-1815' (unpublished Ph.D., Royal Holloway, University of London, 2006) <https://ethos.bl.uk/OrderDetails.do?did=1&uin=uk.bl.ethos.428326>

Nielsen, Caroline Louise, 'The Chelsea Out-Pensioners : Image and Reality in Eighteenth-Century and Early Nineteenth-Century Social Care' (unpublished Ph.D., University of Newcastle Upon Tyne, 2014). <http://theses.ncl.ac.uk/jspui/handle/10443/2702>

Reynolds, Luke, 'Who Owned Waterloo? Wellington's Veterans and the Battle for Relevance' (unpublished Ph.D., City University of New York, 2019) <https://academicworks.cuny.edu/cgi/viewcontent.cgi?article=4392&context=gc_etds>

Phillipson, A., '"The Business of Engineers": The Organization and Education of Military Engineers during the Eighteenth Century' (unpublished Ph.D., University of Portsmouth, 2007). <https://ethos.bl.uk/OrderDetails.do?did=211&uin=uk.bl.ethos.496672> [accessed 28 May 2019]

Pimlott, J.L., 'The Administration of the British Army, 1783-1793' (unpublished Ph.D., University of Leicester, 1975), ethos.bl.uk, uk.bl.ethos.469017 <https://ethos.bl.uk/OrderDetails.do?did=1&uin=uk.bl.ethos.469017>

Quinn, Simon, 'Orientalists in Uniform?: British Military Encounters and Experiences in Egypt, C1798-1801' (unpublished Ph.D., University of York, 2017). <http://etheses.whiterose.ac.uk/19875/>

Roeder, Tobias Uwe, 'Professional Identity of Army Officers in Britain and the Habsburg Monarchy, 1740-1790' (unpublished Ph.D., University of Cambridge, 2018). <https://doi.org/10.17863/Cam.25165>

Salmon, Stuart, 'The Loyalist Regiments of the American Revolutionary War 1775-1783' (unpublished Ph.D., University of Stirling, 2009) <http://hdl.handle.net/1893/2514>

Smith, Shane, 'Forgotten Settlers : The Migration, Society and Legacies of British Military Veterans to Upper Canada (Ontario), from 1815-1855' (unpublished Ph.D., Northumbria University, 2018) <http://nrl.northumbria.ac.uk/id/eprint/39625/> [accessed 15 June 2022].

Soulsby, Ian, 'The Irish Military Establishment 1796-1798. A Study in the Evolution of Military Effectiveness' (unpublished MA, National University of Ireland, 2018) <https://www.researchgate.net/publication/338454747_The_Irish_Military_Establishment_1796-1798_A_Study_in_the_evolution_of_military_effectiveness_MA_Dissertation_September_2018>

Villalard, James Michael, 'A Re-Assessment of the Strategic Role of the Channel Islands during the Great French War (1792-1815)' (unpublished Ph.D., University of Exeter, 2017) <http://hdl.handle.net/10871/32459>

Western, J. R., 'The Recruitment of the Land Forces in Great Britain, 1793-99' (unpublished PhD, University of Edinburgh, 1953), British Library EThOS, uk.bl.ethos.663667 <http://hdl.handle.net/1842/17729>

White, Zack, 'Pragmatism & Discretion: Discipline in the British Army, 1808-1818' (unpublished PhD, University of Southampton, 2022) <https://eprints.soton.ac.uk/467445/>

Wood, Andrew B., 'The Limits of Social Mobility : Social Origins and Career Patterns of British Generals, 1688-1815' (unpublished Ph.D., London School of Economics and Political Science (LSE), 2011). <http://etheses.lse.ac.uk/223/> [accessed 28 May 2019].

Websites

'Army Estimates, 21 January 1807', *Hansard: UK Parliament*, 1807 <https://bit.ly/3b4bBqa> [accessed 4 May 2020].

Baigent, Elizabeth, 'Brereton, Thomas (1782–1832), Army Officer', *Oxford Dictionary of National Biography*, 2006 <https://doi.org/10.1093/ref:odnb/3331>

Bamford, Andrew, 'British Army Unit Strengths: 1808-1815', *The Napoleon Series* <https://www.napoleonseries.org/military/organization/Britain/Strength/Bamford/c_BritishArmyStrengthStudyIndividualUnitsCavalry.html>

Bayne, Ronald, and Elizabeth Baigent, 'Barker, Collet (1784–1831), Army Officer and Explorer', *Oxford Dictionary of National Biography*, 2004 <https://doi.org/10.1093/ref:odnb/1391>

Booker, John, 'Cox, Richard (1718–1803), Army Agent', *Oxford Dictionary of National Biography*, 2008 <https://www.oxforddnb.com/view/10.1093/ref:odnb/9780198614128.001.0001/odnb-9780198614128-e-45706> [accessed 15 August 2019].

Brooke, John, 'The House of Commons', *History of Parliament Online* <http://www.historyofparliamentonline.org/volume/1754-1790/survey/iv-house-commons>

Brown, Andrew, 'Lytton, Edward George Earle Lytton Bulwer [Formerly Edward George Earle Lytton Bulwer], First Baron Lytton (1803–1873), Writer and Politician', *Oxford Dictionary of National Biography*, 2004 <https://doi.org/10.1093/ref:odnb/17314>

Brown, Steve, 'British Artillery Regiments and the Men Who Led Them 1793-1815', *The Napoleon Series*, 2015 <https://www.napoleon-series.org/military-info/organization/Britain/Artillery/c_ArtilleryRegimentsIntro.html>

———, 'The Expansion of the British Army 1793-1800: Second Battalions', *The Napoleon Series* <https://www.napoleon-series.org/military/organization/Britain/Strength/c_Expansion.html>

———, 'Wellington's Sharpes: British Army Ranker Officers 1793-1815', *The Napoleon Series* <https://www.napoleon-series.org/research/biographies/GreatBritain/c_Wellington'sSharpes.html>

Chichester, H.M., and David Gates, 'Bingham, Sir George Ridout (1777–1833), Army Officer', *Oxford Dictionary of National Biography*, 2011 <https://doi.org/10.1093/ref:odnb/2408>

Chichester, H. M. and S. Kinross, 'Hope, Sir Alexander (1769–1837), Army Officer', *Oxford Dictionary of National Biography*, 2008 <https://0-doi-org.wam.leeds.ac.uk/10.1093/ref:odnb/13712> [accessed 1 July 2019].

Christine Lodge, 'Gordon [Née Maxwell], Jane, Duchess of Gordon (1748/9–1812).', *Oxford Dictionary of National Biography*, 2007 <https://doi.org/10.1093/ref:odnb/11059>

'Christopher Teesdale', *Westminster Abbey* <https://www.westminster-abbey.org/abbey-commemorations/commemorations/christopher-teesdale>

'Cox's & King's Records', *Archives Hub* <https://archiveshub.jisc.ac.uk/data/gb386-a/56> [accessed 15 August 2019]

David R. Fisher, 'Burland, John Berkeley (1754–1804), of Steyning, Stogursey, Som. and Stock House, Stock Gaylard, Dorset', *History of Parliament Online* <http://www.historyofparliamentonline.org/volume/1790-1820/member/burland-john-berkeley-1754-1804>

Farrell, S. M., 'Pratt, John Jeffreys, First Marquess Camden (1759–1840), Politician', *Oxford Dictionary of National Biography*, 2008 <https://doi.org/10.1093/ref:odnb/22705>

Fisher, David R., 'Wardle, Gwyllym Lloyd (?1761–1833), of Hartsheath, Nr. Mold, Flints.', History of Parliament Online <https://www.historyofparliamentonline.org/volume/1790-1820/member/wardle-gwyllym-lloyd-1761-1833>

———, 'Fitzpatrick, Richard (1748–1813)', *Oxford Dictionary of National Biography*, 2008 <https://doi.org/10.1093/ref:odnb/9624> [accessed 17 February 2020].

'Gunning, John (1773 – 1863)', *Plarr's Lives of the Fellows* <https://livesonline.rcseng.ac.uk/client/en_GB/lives/search/results?qu=%22RCS: E000405%22&rt=false |||IDENTIFIER|||Resource+Identifier>

Harris, C. A., and James Falkner, 'Nickle, Sir Robert (1786–1855), Army Officer', *Oxford Dictionary of National Biography*, 2004 <https://doi.org/10.1093/ref:odnb/20158>

Kenny, Shirley Strum, 'Farquhar, George (1676/7–1707)', *Oxford Dictionary of National Biography*, 2004 <https://doi.org/10.1093/ref:odnb/9178>

Longford, Elizabeth, 'Edward, Prince, Duke of Kent and Strathearn (1767–1820)', *Oxford Dictionary of National Biography*, 2009 <https://doi.org/10.1093/ref:odnb/8526>

Lowe, William C., 'Lennox, Charles, Third Duke of Richmond, Third Duke of Lennox, and Duke of Aubigny in the French Nobility (1735–1806)', *Oxford Dictionary of National Biography*, 2013 <https://doi.org/10.1093/ref:odnb/16451>

Lunt, James, 'Cannon, Richard (1779–1865)', *Oxford Dictionary of National Biography*, 2008 <https://doi.org/10.1093/ref:odnb/4559> [accessed 16 August 2019].

Mandler, Peter, 'Hall, Samuel Carter (1800–1889), Journal Editor and Writer', *Oxford Dictionary of National Biography*, 2008 <https://doi.org/10.1093/ref:odnb/11987>

McGuigan, Ron, 'The Forgotten Army: Fencible Regiments of Great Britain 1793-1816', *The Napoleon Series*, 2003 <https://www.napoleon-series.org/military/organization/fencibles/c_fencibles.html> [accessed 17 March 2020].

Newman, A N., 'Marsham, Hon. Charles (1744–1811), of Maidstone, Kent', *History of Parliament Online* <http://www.historyofparliamentonline.org/volume/1754-1790/member/marsham-hon-charles-1744-1811>

Nichols, Alistair, 'Officers and Organization of the Dutch Brigade 1802', *The Napoleon Series*, 2019 <https://www.napoleon-series.org/military-info/organization/Britain/Foreign/BritishDutchBrigade1802.pdf> [accessed 14 January 2022].

Peers, Douglas M., 'Bentinck, Lord William Henry Cavendish [Known as Lord William Bentinck] (1774–1839), Army Officer, Diplomatist, and Governor-General of India', *Oxford Dictionary of National Biography* <https://doi.org/10.1093/ref:odnb/2161>

Port, M.H., 'Thomas, Sir George, 3rd Bt. (c.1748–1815), of Dale Park, Nr. Arundel, Suss.', *History of Parliament Online* <http://www.historyofparliamentonline.org/volume/1790-1820/member/thomas-sir-george-1748-1815>

Rea, J.E., 'McDonell, Alexander', *Dictionary of Canadian Biography*, 1988 <http://www.biographi.ca/en/bio/mcdonell_alexander_7E.html>

Spain, Jonathan, 'Beckwith, Sir George (1752/3–1823), Army Officer and Colonial Governor', *Oxford Dictionary of National Biography*, 2008 <https://doi.org/10.1093/ref:odnb/1911>

Spencer-Smith, Jenny, 'Dighton, Denis (1791–1827), Military Painter', in *Oxford Dictionary of National Biography*, 2019 <https://doi.org/10.1093/ref:odnb/7641>

Stephens, H. M. and S. Kinross, 'Anstruther, Robert (1768–1809)', *Oxford Dictionary of National Biography*, 2006 <https://doi.org/10.1093/ref:odnb/588> [accessed 20 April 2020]

Stephens, H.M. and James Lunt, 'Beckwith, John Charles (1789–1862), Army Officer and Missionary', *Oxford Dictionary of National Biography*, 2008 <https://doi.org/10.1093/ref:odnb/1912>

Stephens, H.M. and Roger T. Stearn, 'Beckwith, Sir Thomas Sydney (1772–1831), Army Officer', *Oxford Dictionary of National Biography*, 2004 <https://doi.org/10.1093/ref:odnb/1915

Thomas, Peter D. G., 'Vaughan, Sir John (c. 1731–95).', *Oxford Dictionary of National Biography*, 2008 <https://doi.org/10.1093/ref:odnb/28136>

Thorne, R.G., 'Feilding, William Robert, Visct. Feilding (1760–99), of Chesterfield Street, Mdx', *The History of Parliament* <http://www.historyofparliamentonline.org/volume/1790-1820/member/feilding-william-robert-1760-99> [accessed 20 April 2020].

Thorne, R. G., 'Loft, John Henry (?1769–1849), of Camby House, Louth and Healing House, Nr. Grimsby, Lincs.', History of Parliament Online <http://www.historyofparliamentonline.org/volume/1790-1820/member/loft-john-henry-1769-1849>

Ward, S.G.P., 'Murray, Sir George (1772–1846).', *Oxford Dictionary of National Biography*, 2008 <https://doi.org/10.1093/ref:odnb/19608>

Wilkinson, David, 'Windham, William (1750–1810).', *Oxford Dictionary of National Biography*, 2008 <https://doi.org/10.1093/ref:odnb/29725>

Index